The Language Arts in Childhood Education ❧ Fifth Edition

PAUL C. BURNS
BETTY L. BROMAN

University of Tennessee

HOUGHTON MIFFLIN COMPANY   BOSTON

*Dallas   Geneva, Ill.   Hopewell, N.J.
Palo Alto   London*

Printed in the U.S.A.

Library of Congress Catalog Card Number: 82-83367

ISBN: 0-395-32756-3

CONTENTS

iii

*P*ART *IV: WRITTEN COMMUNICATION*   182

7: *Written Composition*   185

PART V: VOCABULARY, READING, AND LITERATURE   310

11: Reading   353

12: *Literature*   381

PREFACE

The Language Arts in Childhood Education, fifth edition, has been prepared for prospective teachers in elementary language arts programs; it will also be helpful to practicing teachers in introductory graduate programs.

ORGANIZATION

This edition is organized in six parts. "Part 1: Foundation" provides an introductory overview of the language arts. "Part 2: Language and Grammar" presents information about language development and children's study of language and grammar. "Part 3: The Young Child, Listening, and Speaking" surveys programs in early childhood classrooms and explores the listening and oral language curriculums. "Part 4: Written Communication" discusses written composition and the mechanics of spelling and handwriting. "Part 5: Vocabulary, Reading, and Literature" provides programs for vocabulary development and the enhancement of research skills; also discussed are the interrelation of reading and the other language arts and the role of literature in a vital elementary school program. "Part 6: Issues and Teaching" considers the exceptional child and outlines patterns of effective classroom organization and management.

FEATURES

Each chapter begins with an overview—which sets the stage for the discussion to follow—and a vocabulary list—which provides the key concepts and terms in the chapter. Towards the end of each chapter appear a set of thought questions about the issues raised therein and a set of learner response options. These features are designed to promote the reader's understanding of the language arts through both further consideration of the ideas and actual work with children and other teachers. At the very end of each chapter, references and additional readings are cited.

Within the chapters numerous classroom examples, activities, and teaching suggestions provide the reader with a practical understanding of each of the key components of the language arts. Many chapters, as well, relate the use of the computer to specific topics, and most chapters contain a section on "Some Instructional Concerns"—crucial areas in the teaching of the language arts that all future and in-service teachers will encounter.

At the end of the text two appendixes provide a glossary of key terms and a checklist of the skills necessary for successful teaching in the language arts.

THE FIFTH EDITION

We have explored recent developments in the language arts in all chapters, and recent research evidence is cited throughout the text. Significant revisions in this new edition include:

1. Expansion of the chapter on grammar to provide more coverage of the various types of grammar.
2. Increased coverage of oral communication, written expression, and exceptional children.
3. Addition of a section on research and study skills in Chapter 10.
4. Rewriting of the chapter on reading in its entirety so as to emphasize the interrelation of reading and the other language arts.

ACKNOWLEDGMENTS

The authors wish to express their appreciation to the following reviewers who helped in the preparation of this new edition: Steven DeLapp of the University of Northern Colorado, Sheila Fitzgerald of Michigan State University, Richard Hodges of the University of Puget Sound, David Yellin of Oklahoma University.

PAUL C. BURNS
BETTY L. BROMAN
University of Tennessee
Knoxville, Tennessee

PART I: FOUNDATION

CHAPTER 1: An Introduction to the Language Arts Program

OVERVIEW

This chapter is an introduction to the field of elementary school language arts. It begins with a brief look at the language arts at the primary and intermediate levels, and defines and relates the experiences and skills that are major components of the program. The discussion continues with an analysis of basic instructional materials and ways to use them, and a comparison of the exploratory and systematic approaches to instruction. Finally, the chapter closes with an examination of the lesson-planning process and guidelines that make that process effective.

KEY VOCABULARY

primary years

intermediate years

listening experiences, abilities, and skills

speaking experiences, abilities, and skills

reading experiences, abilities, and skills

writing experiences, abilities, and skills

interrelationship

picture file

poetry file

skill file

story file

word file

learning center

contract

activities and games

trade books

exploratory approach

systematic approach

lesson plan

THE PROGRAM IN THE ELEMENTARY SCHOOL

The language arts are a vital force in early learning. They are the core of the elementary school program—the foundation of almost all classroom activities and the bond that links the many areas of curriculum. How well we teach them, then, is as essential to the entire program of the school as it is to each child's learning.

Primary Years

The program in the primary grades (Grades K–3) is an interrelated one. The strands of language study are so interwoven that speaking, listening, reading, and writing are almost indistinguishable.

Literature is a core component of the primary program. Teachers and children tell or read aloud stories and poems that develop the child's vocabulary and feeling for language—its rhythms, patterns, intonations, and meanings. Stories and poems in turn furnish material for oral expression, in conversation, discussion, or creative drama. Naturally, listening is an integral part of speaking experiences.

From oral activities the act of composing begins to develop. In giving form to composition, children draw mainly on direct experiences; to a lesser extent on the ideas gleaned from sharing and planning activities with other children. Short compositions result—first oral, then dictated to the teacher, and finally written. In this way the need for spelling and handwriting arises, as do choice of words (vocabulary) and usage patterns.

Intermediate (Middle) Years

Although individual elements of the language arts are more clearly delineated at the intermediate level (Grades 4–6), an interrelated program is still important. For example, oral reading of prose and poetry to and by children continues to relate language to composition. The author's craft begins to have meaning as learners recount their own real or imaginary experiences.

Dramatization continues here, helping to establish a sounder basis for judgments about people and ideas. Dialectal differences appear in historical or regional fiction; and, using those differences in vocabulary and syntax, the teacher can promote principles of usage more effectively than from weeks spent on isolated workbook drills. Dialogue, discussion, and "group talk" are material for more sophisticated statements—ways of manipulating sentences by adding, deleting, and changing elements. Acts of speech create a functional need to listen. In studying written composi-

tion, children (and teacher) sense that, although the first concern should be with substantive matters, effective communication demands proofreading for spelling, capitalization, punctuation, and handwriting. These practical applications of convention give meaning to instruction.

SPECIAL EXPERIENCES AND ABILITIES IN LANGUAGE

Listening, speaking, reading, and writing are the bases of the language arts curriculum at the elementary school level. These experiences occur at all grade levels, but some are emphasized more at one level than another.

Listening

Just as children must develop competence in a variety of reading skills, they must also develop competence in specific listening skills. Although listening is best developed indirectly in an oral language program, there are times when efficient teaching and learning demand concentration on listening skills: listening attitudes toward individuals and in group situations of all types; listening for directions and instructions; listening for explanations; listening for information; listening for appreciation; and listening for analysis.

Speaking

Storytelling, planning class activities, and other functional experiences cause teacher and learner to focus on such related abilities and skills as voice and diction; vocabulary and language patterns; courtesies; ideas for stories, reports, or discussions; logical sequence; or simple parliamentary procedures.

Reading

Major reading skills are discussed in later chapters, particularly Chapter 11 and Chapter 12: Chapter 11 treats the relationship of reading and the other language arts; and Chapter 12 presents a planned literature program.

Writing

Many abilities and skills are a part of writing experiences: sentence and paragraph construction, letter structure, word choice, bibliography development, dictionary study, proofreading, handwriting, spelling, and neatness.

The Interrelationship of Experiences and Abilities

The language arts program has a major objective: to help children use language more effectively. To meet that objective, we have to provide activities that integrate and develop listening, speaking, reading, and writing skills. Look, for example, at the accompanying checklist for a trip to the zoo. In each phase of the activity—introduction, development, and follow-up—we integrate all four basic skills. The trip to the zoo is an integrating activity that encourages children to develop and use those skills.

CLASSROOM MATERIALS

Basic materials for a language arts program include textbooks, workbooks, files, learning centers, contracts, activities and games, and trade books.

CHECKLIST: *Integrating Activities*

A Trip to the Zoo Introduction	Listening	Speaking	Reading	Writing
Discuss the zoo—who has been there, what can be seen there, and so on.	✓	✓		
Show the film *Forgotten Wilderness*.	✓	✓		
Read material and pamphlets about the zoo.			✓	
Discuss the setting; what to bring and wear; and conduct, courtesy, and safety on the trip.	✓	✓		
Organize small groups and define objectives—questions to ask, things to note, and so on.	✓	✓		
List arrangements to be made by teacher and students.	✓	✓		✓
Development				
Write a letter requesting a visit date and time.		✓		✓
Write a permission letter to parents.		✓		✓
Ask for parent helpers.	✓	✓		
Introduce guides to the groups.	✓	✓		
Record information (small-group leaders).	✓			✓
Listen and observe (individually).	✓			✓
Tape-record animal sounds.	✓			
Follow-up				
Summarize collected information.		✓		✓
Write a record, diary, or log about the trip.				✓
Describe the animals, feelings about them, and so on.		✓		✓
List descriptive words about the animals.	✓	✓		✓
Write a report, using the data above, for other classes, parents, and so on.		✓		✓
Interview a resource person (follow-up, questions).	✓	✓		
Write thank-you letters.				✓
Write an article on an endangered animal.		✓		✓
Read poems and stories about wild animals.			✓	

Textbooks

In many schools no other single source of language knowledge is more available to all students than the textbook. Although it is unthinkable that a language program would be limited to a series of page assignments in a single text, it is well to keep in mind that the textbook is a very important teaching aid.

Obviously a good textbook has a number of strengths:

Organized and carefully structured material.

Ideas for expressional skills that can be applied to any subject in the curriculum.

Models (letters, book reports, and so on) that can be used in discussions of content and organization.

Supplementary and practice exercises for pupils needing reinforcement materials.

In text and teacher's edition, a ready source of evaluation materials (diagnostic pretests, inventory tests, self-checking devices, spot reviews, chapter reviews and tests, cumulative reviews, and other elements that can help the pupil develop self-direction and independence, and help the teacher individualize instruction).

Many texts carry enrichment and remedial suggestions. However, a single text or manual simply cannot provide materials for every pupil from every cultural or socioeconomic background. Even two or three textbooks in a class can scarcely meet this need. But texts can give the teacher ideas. And the teacher's edition serves as a reservoir of instructional suggestions. Teachers who do not use manuals are neglecting a helpful resource.

How do we make the most effective use of language textbooks and related materials? By building classroom interest, by using them as a reference source, and by modifying our use of them in light of classroom abilities. In introducing a lesson or topic, the teacher can build interest and motivation by first asking pupils to reveal what they already know about the topic—not by beginning with "Open your textbooks to page sixty-three for the lesson on paragraph writing."

Most language concepts are best taught and learned when students use a textbook as a reference source—to write a business letter, to research an oral or written report, or to check a grammar point—instead of going through it page by page.

In every case, modification is needed for variations in ability and achievement within the class (without overlooking the importance of a year-by-year developmental program). Textbooks for various age levels—and from various publishers—offer valuable corrective and remedial materials as well as enrichment ideas. Of course, modification demands that the teacher have a total picture of the developmental sequences of language arts skills and the instructional approaches for attaining them. A teacher who knows what is involved in sentence making, paragraph composing, story writing, reporting, and the like, and who can diagnose what students have learned and what still needs attention, is better able to provide the level and amount of instruction needed to compensate for varied ability and achievement.

Workbooks

There are arguments for and against workbooks and other supplementary materials. These sources do provide a ready supply of additional instructional materials, drills, and practice materials similar to those found in the textbook. The best ones have inventory tests, self-checking devices, and other features that, if properly used, can help the teacher individualize language instruction. On the other hand, research dating back many years has consistently shown little or no carryover from the kinds of skills developed by supplementary materials to the practical application of those skills in related writing.

The "good" or "bad" of a workbook probably lies in its use, not in the material itself. Below are some guidelines to make that use more effective:

1. Know what you want to accomplish through the use of the material. (This means an analysis, not only of students' abilities, but also of the material's emphasis.)
2. Use inventory tests to identify for individual pupils the skill areas in which they need practice.
3. Keep a record of each pupil's progress. (Students can do this themselves.)
4. Do not assign the same practice or workbook lesson to the entire class unless everyone actually needs it.

Workbooks, like textbooks, can be either a valuable resource for learning or a substitute for good teaching. Don't use them simply to keep a child busy. Use them, instead, to individualize instruction, to provide practice in needed skills, and to help pupils develop self-direction and independence.

Files

Picture Pictures can be obtained from magazines, old books, calendars, book jackets, posters, travel pamphlets, picture maps, and other sources. Pictures help initiate new topics and revitalize old ones, catching the interest of children as they look at and talk about them. Or, they can be used to illustrate a child's favorite poem or story. Use questions (write them on the back of the picture) to guide discussion:

Is this picture about something you have seen or done?
Who do you see in the picture?
How does the person feel?
Where is the person?
Where is he or she going?
What has the person been doing?
Do you like this person or not? Why?
What time is it?

Poetry To be ready with the right poem at the right moment often means having your own poetry collection. Large index cards or looseleaf notebooks are handy. File the poems under different categories and by suitability for dramatization, choric reading, memorization, or reading for enjoyment.

FILE CARD: *Poetry*

"Husky Hi" (Norwegian)
Ages 9–12

> Husky hi, husky hi,
> Here comes Keery galloping by.
> She carries her husband tied in a sack,
> She carries him home on her horse's back.
> Husky hi, husky hi,
> Here comes Keery galloping by![1]

Suitability

Choric reading (unison)

Type

Humorous

Skill A skill file may be nothing more than pages cut from various grade level workbooks, grouped according to skill, and then filed by levels in a cabinet or box. (Handwriting, spelling, grammar, and usage lend themselves particularly well to this type of organization, as do punctuation, capitalization, sentence construction, outlining, use of the dictionary and other references, proofreading, and even functional and creative writing.) Then, when you discover that a child needs additional practice with commas (or with run-on sentences, the cursive letters *d* and *r*, synonyms for *said,* or whatever), you have one or more worksheets at the correct level of difficulty to use.

Commercial and teacher-made worksheets can be reused if they are mounted on oaktag, and covered with clear contact paper or laminated.

---

1. From *Picture Rhymes from Foreign Lands* by Rose Fyleman. Copyright 1935. © renewed 1963 by Rose Fyleman. Reprinted by permission of J. B. Lippincott Company.

Pupils can write on them with grease pencils or water-soluble markers. Each sheet should be labeled or color coded with level of difficulty, skill, and worksheet number. Sheets can be self-checked if answers are pasted on the back or kept in an accessible file.

Other learning materials can be part of a skill file too. Games, transparencies, filmstrips, and audio tapes can be prescribed and used individually or in small groups without direct teacher supervision.

Story A story file (on index cards or in a notebook) lists the name, author, publisher, and age level of each story, and a brief summary of plot and characters. The stories may be categorized as suitable for telling, dramatizing, puppetry, making up other endings, or reading for enjoyment.

FILE CARD: *Story*

Peter's Chair, Ezra Jack Keats   Illustrated by author
Harper & Row, 1967   (collage illustrations
Ages 5–8   are excellent)

Summary

Peter's old cradle, high chair, and crib are all painted pink for his new baby sister. He is so unhappy that he decides to take his little blue chair and run away from home. Finally, he discovers his chair is too small for him and he gives it to Susie, his baby sister.

Suitability/Topics

Read for enjoyment; multiethnic; family-life story about a new baby; discover Peter's feelings with children.

Word One idea for a word file would be to choose a topic (say, "fabrics"), list twelve to fifteen words related to the topic (cotton, silk, wool, and so on), and then paste an example of each word (patches of each fabric) on a piece of oaktag. Of value to intermediate-level pupils would be a word-origin file.

Learning Centers

A learning center is an area in the classroom set aside for activities related to particular skills or knowledge. It should have four basic elements:

A stated objective
Materials
Task cards
Evaluation

Pretests and posttests help with the objective and evaluation elements.

Below is an alphabetization activity, something to help students who are having difficulty using a telephone book, a card catalog, an index, an encyclopedia, or a dictionary.

LEARNING CENTER ACTIVITY: *Alphabetization*

Objective:
To increase abilities with alphabetical order.

Materials:
3 separate sets of lists of words, color coded and covered with contact paper
Grease pencil
Answer key

Task Card:
Choose the color card you like. Put the words in alphabetical order.

Set 1 (Red)	*Set 2 (Green)*	*Set 3 (Blue)*
fountain	broke	slip
basket	baby	slope
rabbit	bit	slap
ghost	blame	sleep
turkey	better	slum

Evaluation:
(Check your work with the answer key.)

Contracts

A contract can be used for a number of language arts assignments and tasks. A contract states what the pupil will do and when the task will be completed. The sample here could be used to help students become more sensitive to words.

CONTRACT: *Language Arts*

A. Read one of the following books by Joan Hanson:
   1. *Homographs*
   2. *Homographic Homophones*
   3. *Homonyms*
   4. *Similes*
   5. *Synonyms*
B. Share your findings in one of these ways:
   1. Draw three pictures to illustrate three of the special words in your book.
   2. Take turns with a partner telling each other about one special word in the book.
   3. Take turns with a partner reading to each other about one special word in the book.
   4. Write a paragraph trying to use as many of the special words in the book as you can.
   5. With another person who has read the book, write a paragraph telling two things you learned from the book.

Choose one book from A and one method from B for your contract.
I plan to do A _____ and B _____ . I will have this contract completed by _____ .

Student's signature _____

Teacher's signature _____

Activities and Games

Activities and games are valuable teaching tools. There are a number of activity resource materials, among them *Language Arts Activities for Elementary Schools*.[2] On page 17 is a typical activity from that text.

Trade Books

Most of the chapters here contain a list of trade (library) books that are useful for various components of the language arts. For example, see page 41.

2. Paul C. Burns and Randall K. Bassett (Boston: Houghton Mifflin, 1982).

7.2 Picture Writing (Primary)

Objective: To utilize visual senses to develop writing skills.

Materials: Writing materials, scissors, poster board, and crayons or felt-tip markers.

Directions: Several shapes are presented to the students. After selecting one, each student constructs that shape out of poster board. On that particular shape, the student writes about the concept or topic which the shape represents, staying within the limits of the shape itself.

APPROACHES TO TEACHING

With such a wide variety of materials available, teachers can choose the instructional strategies that best fit their needs, the needs of their students, and the topic under consideration. The two major approaches to language arts instruction are *exploratory* and *systematic*.

Exploratory

The guided-discovery pattern is a basic instructional procedure. It creates a problem situation and leads pupils to resolve that situation, in the process mastering skills. This "find-out-for-yourself" approach allows teachers to use the tremendous background in language that children bring with them to school. It does not assume that children are learning everything about language for the first time. Instead it challenges them to think for themselves to learn the skills of language by observing how they and the people around them use it.

LESSON PLAN: *Improving Opening Sentences*

Problem

On the board the teacher writes a set of four sentences and asks which one is the best.

1. On our vacation, we went to Yellowstone.
2. Slowly the door inched open.
3. Bob could never seem to avoid getting into trouble.
4. There was a fire at our neighbor's house last week.

Speculation

Pupils respond with choices and provide reasons for their selection. From this discussion, they suggest some "dos" and "don'ts" for opening sentences.

Verification

To check their suggestions and to find more, the children examine several language textbooks.

Expansion

After studying the text material, the class draws up a summary of ideas for a good opening sentence.

A Good Opening Sentence

1. is an important part of the story.
2. makes you want to know more.
3. does *not* let the reader know what happened.

Practice

A worksheet with sets of opening sentences on it is provided for pupils to choose the best one from each set and give an explanation for their choices. Then a story recently written by each child is examined with the direction, "Write the best possible opening sentence for your story."

The lesson plan above illustrates several characteristics of the exploratory approach. It would be used after the children have written several stories during the school year, if the teacher detects a common need for improving opening sentences.

Here is another example of the approach:

Here are three sets of sentences. Notice that each set uses a different
spelling—*to, two, too*. You are to figure out what differences among the three
sets account for the differences in the spelling of these words. You can ask me
questions to help you gather the facts you need to construct your ideas or
reasons.

Set A: *to*	Set B: *two*	Set C: *too*
1. Jill went *to* school.	1. Alice ate *two* pies.	1. Bill ate *too* much.
2.	2.	2. . . . .
3.	3.	3. . . . .

You have presented a problem situation, and have encouraged the children
to see a pattern for themselves and to come to an acceptable conclusion
about the three different spellings. You could then test that conclusion by
referring to printed material, including the language textbook. Later, practice would be individualized according to need.

The advantages of the exploratory approach are obvious. The importance of clear-cut learning objectives cannot be overemphasized. They
provide direction for individual efforts and are also a powerful motivating
factor. The emphasis on activity—rather than passive listening—leading
to the development of new facts, concepts, or generalizations agrees with
the soundest principles of learning. The approach fosters curiosity and
enthusiasm. It helps pupils develop and exercise initiative. And, perhaps
most important, it facilitates the rediscovery of forgotten language patterns.

Systematic

For follow-up work with an individual or a small group of children who
reveal a common weakness in a language ability or skill, a systematic
approach is effective. (The approach assumes that the teacher has defined
the instructional program in terms of specific skills and has determined
the child's level of performance in the skill and subskills.)

The following lesson plan shows how the systematic approach works.
First, a specific skill must be identified and stated in a *performance objective*—a definition of what learners can do when they possess the skill.
Next, a *pretest* helps determine whether the learner needs practice in the
skill. Then direct instruction is designed to develop the skill; and a *posttest*
is used to determine whether that instruction has been successful. Finally,
reteaching suggestions are provided for children who need further practice
to reach the mastery criterion.

LESSON PLAN: *Oral Announcement (School Program)*

Performance Objective

Given a set of data, the learner makes an oral announcement about a school program, including five basic facts of information.

Pretest

Select an announcement appropriate to the learner and the situation and read it to the class. For example: "Miss Brown's class invites you to our program about tools on Wednesday, November 23, at 2:00 P.M., in our classroom, room 112. We hope you will be able to come." Then ask the learner for the number of basic facts supplied. These facts should be of the *who, what, when, where,* and *why* nature. Included would be a description of the event, who is invited, the date, the time, the place, and the price of admission if required. Criterion for mastery is 80 percent of the five or six items. The purpose of this exercise is to be certain that the learner attends to the basic facts needed in an oral announcement about a school program.

Teaching Suggestions

1. Before reading another announcement, write the following purpose-setting formula on the chalkboard: Who? What? When? Where? Why?
2. Ask the learner to write an announcement about a pet show to be held by the class, using this formula as a guide.

Mastery or Posttest Suggestions

1. Assign a coming event as a topic for an oral announcement. Direct the learner to list the five facts contained in the statement before making the announcement.
2. The pretest suggestions can be adopted and used in the posttest.

Reteaching Suggestions

1. Select a well-written announcement to read aloud to the learner. Direct the child to find the five Ws.
2. Ask the learner to list the key words that answer the five formula questions in his or her announcement.

Whatever decisions are made by the teacher about the basic or supplementary instructional strategy, the teacher must (1) be aware of specific experiences and skills of the language arts; (2) know and be able to use specific procedures to effectively teach those experiences and skills; and (3) be able to blend a number of situations that provide each child with optimal language learnings.

TEACHING PLANS

In every classroom activity—planning for a science field trip, or writing letters requesting materials for a social studies project, or telling a story—there's an opportunity for a language lesson. These lessons should include the following:

1. Objectives of the lesson
   This part is primarily for the teacher. The more precise teachers are in stating objectives, the better they will be able to plan and execute a successful lesson.
2. Preliminary preparation
   This involves any special arrangements, equipment, and materials needed for the execution of the lesson plan.
3. Introduction
   The introduction may include these points:
   a. Relating the lesson to the children's experiences
   b. Using motivating techniques to involve the . . . children
   c. Discussing with pupils the purpose for the lesson
4. Development
   The activities (questions, examples, materials) needed to help the pupils attain the objectives are stated. Each step in the sequence is listed. (Several alternate suggestions are provided for varied teaching and reteaching.)
5. Summary and evaluation
   This part may include these points:
   a. Summary ties together the learnings and makes sure understanding is complete.
   b. Evaluation consists of evidence that the desired outcomes have been achieved. (Progress and interest of each child may be noted)
   c. Steps and assignments may be defined, including individual enrichment ideas.[3]

On the basis of the results of the instruction, the teacher may need to follow up with small groups (the same specific learning is needed or additional practice is needed for retention and transfer) or individuals (difficulties of an individual nature that can be corrected individually). There may be combinations of small-group and individual activities with

3. *Teaching Elementary Language Arts* by Dorothy Rubin. Copyright © 1975, 1980 by Holt, Rinehart and Winston. Reprinted by permission of Holt, Rinehart and Winston, CBS College Publishing.

the teacher working first with one and then the other. Children who have mastered the concept can be channeled into enrichment activities. Children who have not learned from the instructional sequence should be rechanneled through a different set of experiences.

This flexible classroom structure relies on a record of each individual. (There are many ways to maintain such records. One possibility is to use a looseleaf notebook or ring binder with a tabbed section for each child.) The primary purpose of the record is to note learnings the child has achieved and those yet to be acquired. It provides the basis for teaching, either in groups or with individuals, to meet an immediate need, and it helps organize learners into useful and defensible teaching groups.

These suggestions attempt to meet many learning needs. The use of clear-cut objectives helps in defining goals and evaluating pupil progress. The whole-class activities help each child identify with the total peer group, providing interaction and interchange with the entire spectrum of children. At the same time, small-group or individual instruction answers each child's demonstrated needs. Intergroup mobility is made easy. The unpleasant results of labeling, characteristic of many plans that use some type of homogeneous grouping, are prevented. Finally, the children have continuous feedback from peers and teachers, with evaluations of their relative success.

TEACHER QUALIFICATIONS

Refer to Appendix A to see your present level of development. Return to the checklist near the middle of the term and again at the end of the term to check your progress. You may not understand all of the terms used in the checklist, but you'll come to know them as you study the text.

Notice that the checklist includes *knowledge* needed by teachers of English, *abilities* to perform within the classroom, and *attitudes* about teaching. You can acquire or supplement your knowledge through broad reading and additional course work (a study of the language development of children through adolescence, an introductory study of the English language, a study of modern English grammars, linguistics for teachers, reading-education courses, children's and adolescents' literature, educational media, tests and measurements). To further develop your abilities, take advantage of directed field experiences to observe and participate in a variety of teaching-learning situations. Attitudes emphasize the need to respect students and to adjust instruction to meet their needs.

Try to improve in each of these areas, but don't expect high development in each and every aspect of them by the end of this course. Remember, initial preparation is only a beginning: To become a superior teacher demands a lifelong commitment to continued professional growth and development.

THOUGHT QUESTIONS

1. What differences do you perceive in the language arts program at the primary and intermediate levels?
2. How are the basic language arts skills interrelated? Illustrate.
3. Why are materials (beyond textbooks) needed for an effective language arts program?
4. Compare the exploratory and systematic approaches.
5. How can using a daily lesson plan promote more effective learning?
6. List the items on the qualifications checklist (Appendix A) that represent your strengths and your weaknesses (areas where you feel you need the most development) at this time.

LEARNER RESPONSE OPTIONS

1. Choose a language arts experience (listening, speaking, reading, or writing), and list a number of specific abilities and skills related to it.
2. Choose an experience appropriate for a grade level of your interest. Prepare a chart like the one on page 9 to show how you would integrate language arts skills in the activity.
3. Examine a recent language arts textbook series for children. Describe its program for
   a. listening instruction.
   b. speaking instruction.
   c. writing instruction.
4. Begin a picture, poetry, skill, story, or word file.
5. Using the lesson plan on page 18 as a model, develop an exploratory lesson for a specific language arts ability or skill.
6. Using the lesson plan on page 20 as a model, develop a systematic lesson for a specific language arts ability or skill.
7. Use the outline on page 21 to prepare a lesson plan for a specific language arts ability or skill.

REFERENCES AND ADDITIONAL READINGS

A good way to broaden your study of elementary school language arts is to join the National Council of Teachers of English. The meetings, publications (particularly *Language Arts*), and the projects sponsored by the organization are some of the best ways to keep informed about new ideas for teaching the subject.

Other periodicals in the field include the following:

Elementary School Journal, University of Chicago Press, 5835 Kimbark Avenue, Chicago, IL 60637

Exceptional Children, Council for Exceptional Children, 1920 Association Drive, Reston, VA 22091

Horn Book Magazine, Horn Book, 585 Boylston Street, Boston, MA 02116

Instructor, Instructor Publications, Box 6099, Duluth, MN 55806

Learning, Education Today, 530 University Avenue, Palo Alto, CA 94301

National Elementary Principal, Department of Elementary School Principals, NEA, 201 Sixteenth Street NW, Washington, DC 20036

Reading Teacher, International Reading Association, 800 Barksdale Road, Newark, DE 19711

PART II: LANGUAGE

tal is big.

s are people

help doctor

g to the

CHAPTER 2: Children's Language and Language Study

OVERVIEW

This chapter presents the development of children's language, several features of language, and ideas for children's study of the English language. The text traces the acquisition and development of language in terms of four important features: phonology, morphology, semantics, and syntax. The chapter also describes four major characteristics of language that enable teachers to help children achieve maximum performance. The discussion ends with specific examples of language areas that can be incorporated successfully in the overall instructional program.

KEY VOCABULARY

language functions

phoneme

intonation

stress

pitch

juncture

morpheme

syntax

semantics

holophrases

analogical substitutions

telegraphic speech

pivot–open class construction

transformation

S-V-O sentence

reduction

expansion

double-function words

homographs

euphemism

dialect

idiolect

nonverbal language

FUNCTIONS OF LANGUAGE

Language acquisition is a marvelous, yet natural, occurrence. Children acquire language largely on their own, but family, teachers, and friends have enormous impact on the development and shape of that acquisition.

To children, the most obvious characteristic of language is that it communicates their needs. Their first words, then, are the names of things in their immediate environment (mama, dada, milk). As they grow (and as their environment widens), they learn to express feelings and ideas. Eventually, when they become interacting members of society, language takes on a social function.

There are seven basic functions of language:[1]

Instrumental: To get things ("I want . . . " or "May I . . . ?").
Regulatory: To control others ("Don't do that" or "Let's do this").
Interpersonal: To maintain personal relationships (using names or greetings).
Personal: To express personality or individuality ("I'm going to become a dentist" or "I like playing softball better than swimming").
Imaginative: To create one's own worlds, to pretend ("Once upon a time . . .").
Informative: To convey information.
Heuristic: To discover ("Why . . . ?" or "What for?" or "I wonder if . . . ?").

To use language effectively, children must be aware of its functions and must develop the skill to use it for those functions. A balanced language arts program, then, must extend to the full range of language functions. Language cannot be learned independently of functions, nor can functions be separated from the study of language.

THEORIES OF LANGUAGE ACQUISITION AND DEVELOPMENT

Before we can begin to examine the two major theories of language acquisition and trace its development, we should define several important terms.

1. M. A. K. Halliday, *Learning How to Mean: Explorations in Development of Language* (London: Arnold, 1975), pp. 19–21.

A *phoneme* is the smallest distinctive unit of sound in a language. For example, the word *fat* is composed of three phonemes. There are about forty significant units of speech sounds, or phonemes, in the English language. (*Intonation*—the manipulation of phonemes through stress, pitch, and juncture—is a part of phonology.)

A *morpheme* is the smallest unit of meaning in a language. For example, *sing* is one word and one morpheme, but *singer* is one word and two morphemes—*sing* and *er*. *Sing,* which can stand by itself, is called a *free-form morpheme.* A *bound morpheme,* such as *er,* must always be joined to another morpheme.

Morphemes are put together in larger patterns that transmit ideas; this structure is called *syntax.* Syntax involves word order, parts of speech, and function words. *Semantics* is the study of meaning in language structures.

What follows is an overview of the major theories of language development.[2] The most widely argued theories of language acquisition focus on environmental factors and innate factors.[3]

Environmental Theory

Some linguists believe that imitation and reinforcement account for language acquisition. Generally, evidence in support of this view shows that children learn the language of their environment, that they use the words and expressions of those around them. Those around a child, then, provide a model and the rewards that motivate the child to learn.

But the theory raises three issues. First, it ignores physiological limitations that make it impossible to memorize every conceivable language structure. Second, it does not explain the unusual structures produced by children ("I comed"), structures unlikely to be heard in any environment. Finally, it fails to respond to the supported fact that children's language is highly resistant to alteration by adult intervention.

Innate Theory

The innate theory of language acquisition seems to account for more of the observable data in research and to offer a more nearly complete

2. For a summary of the nature of language, its functions, language development, and theories of learning, see Walter M. McGinitie, "Language Development," *Encyclopedia of Educational Research,* 4th ed. (New York: Macmillan, 1969), pp. 686–699.
3. Lester G. Butler, "Language Acquisition of Young Children: Major Theories and Sequences," *Elementary English* 51 (November-December 1974): 1120–1123, 1137.

explanation of the process. Proponents of the theory argue that language arises from within, not from external factors (imitation, rewards). They propose that we are born with a predisposition to use language. They support their theory by noting (1) the species-specific nature of language, and the human anatomic and psychological features that enable language; (2) real language cannot be taught to nonhuman forms of life; (3) it is very difficult to suppress language acquisition among all humans; and (4) the uniform sequence of development in all people (though there may be variations in the pace of acquisition).

Lenneberg has expanded the theory to include the impact of environment and the exposure to language as secondary influences on the shape of language acquisition.[4] Chomsky proposes that a child "discovers" the theory of language, and then uses innate, intuitive knowledge of language universals to construct hypotheses and test features of the language. In this way, the child develops the syntactic process of the language that is acquired from the environment.[5] Piaget also emphasizes the innateness of language acquisition. He postulated that cognitive development is continuous, successively staged, and dependent on maturation.[6] Language, in this view, is a part of the total cognitive activity and is learned in the same way as other cognitive activities. More than this, the complexity of language structures increases as cognitive abilities increase. Language learning, then, is a part of the child's broader developmental process.

ACQUISITION BEFORE AGE FIVE

Phonology

The onset of speech is regular; it follows a fixed sequence of events. Speech sounds begin in the early months of life. Vowel phonemes are first; then, around the age of five months, consonant phonemes appear. These sounds become distinguishable words at about nine to twelve months. Not all children reach the same developmental level at the same time, but there is a general order (subject to dialectal variations and acculturation) to the facile use of sounds:

---

4. E. H. Lenneberg, *Biological Foundations of Language* (New York: Wiley, 1967).
5. Noam Chomsky, *Current Issues in Linguistic Theory* (The Hague: Mouton, 1964).
6. Jean Piaget, *The Language and Thought of the Child*, 3d ed. (New York: Humanities Press, 1962). For a different emphasis, see Lev Vygotsky, *Thought and Language*, trans. Eugenia Hanfmann and Gertrude Vakar (Cambridge, MA: MIT Press, 1962).

3 years: *m, n, ng, p, f, h, w*
3½ years: *y*
4 years: *k, b, d, g, r*
4½ years: *s, sh, ch*
6 years: *t, th, v, l*
7 years: *th* (voiced), *z, zh, j*[7]

Morphology

The one-word utterances at nine to twelve months or later are usually nouns—names of common objects. Verbs follow shortly. Single-word utterances expressing a complex of ideas (*holophrases*) are prevalent from twelve months to eighteen months. "Milk," for example, may convey "I want some milk."

Once the child has developed some capacity with morphemes, language growth is rapid from eighteen to thirty-six months. In this period, the child makes every effort to assimilate the basic elements of the linguistic culture. In these efforts, the child often overgeneralizes—using such terms as *foots* or *digged*—before recognizing the exceptions. These "errors" (*analogical substitutions*) suggest that children innately understand construction rules and do not just imitate language patterns.

Syntax

The child begins combining words between eighteen and twenty-four months. These first sentences are often *telegraphic*. The structure of these two-word sentences is called *pivot–open class construction*:

Front position pivot: *More* cake, *more* milk, *more* soup.
Second-position pivot: Shoe *off*, light *off*, dress *off*.

Negative and question *transformations* appear:

Negative: *I can go.*   *I cannot go.*
Question: *Bill is playing.*   *Is Bill playing?*

7. Mildred A. Templin, *Certain Language Skills in Children: Their Development and Interrelationships* (Minneapolis: University of Minnesota Press, 1957), p. 53.

By five years of age, the S-V-O (subject-verb-object) sentence order is strongly grounded, although the child may have produced every conceivable sentence type. By this age the child speaks 5.5 words per utterance. Judged on the basis of sentence structure, the child's spoken language has reached 90 percent of its mature level.[8] It is in this period that two processes—reduction and expansion—are operating.

Reduction In early speech, the child often imitates adult speech (for example, "Little baby will go to sleep") but omits the function words—articles, prepositions, auxiliary verbs ("Baby sleep"). This is called *telegraphic speech.*

Expansion Parents and others often imitate the child's speech with expansion ("Yes, baby will go to sleep now"). These expansions on the child's telegraphic speech into more complex sentence structures probably do have an effect on the child's language performance.[9]

Semantics

The age at which the child becomes aware of semantics is difficult to pinpoint. We do know, though, that semantic development takes place over a much longer period of time than any of the other language factors; the child's grasp of phonology, morphology, and syntax are quite well along by age five. Children begin to differentiate among antonyms—making more discriminating responses as they grow older. They overgeneralize in semantics as they do in morphology. For example, once a child has learned the word *car,* he or she may apply it to any motor vehicle, making no differentiation for trucks or motorcycles or buses.

DEVELOPMENT BEYOND AGE FIVE

By the time a child reaches school age, phonological and morphological development is well along. Real advancement now is in syntactic and semantic development.

8. Susan M. Ervin and Wick R. Miller, *Language Development, 62d Yearbook of the National Society for the Study of Education,* vol. 62, pt. 1 (Chicago: University of Chicago Press, 1963), pp. 108–143.
9. C. B. Cazden, *Child Language and Education* (New York: Holt, Rinehart and Winston, 1972).

Phonology

The list on page 33 shows the usual phonological development at ages six and seven. Changes here are most dramatic in the middle- and final-position speech sounds.

Morphology

Four features usually appear beyond age five:

Plurals for /s/, /z/, /əz/ (*bets, beds, matches*).
Possessives (Mary*'s* hat).
Third-person singular of the verb (*wishes*).
Inflections for the past tense of regular verbs /t/, /d/, /ed/ (as in *asked, begged,* and *dusted*).

Syntax

There's considerable growth in syntactic structure from age five up. At ages six and seven, complex sentences, especially those with adjectival clauses, occur more frequently. *Because* begins to be used as a coordinating conjunction, moving beyond the cause-effect use by younger children; and conditional dependent clauses, starting with *if,* for example, begin to appear. The mean number of words per utterance ranges from 6.6 to 8.1.

At ages seven and eight, subordinate clauses beginning with *when, if,* and *because* appear more frequently. The average number of words per oral sentence is now about 7.6.

About half of the children begin to use the connector *although* properly between ages eight and ten. The present participle, the perfect participle, and the gerund as the object of a preposition ("Sitting on the floor, I jumped up" or "Having done the dishes, I watched television") appear. The average number of words in an oral sentence is 9.0.

At ten through twelve, students increase the length of communication units (9.5 words in an oral sentence, 9 words in a written unit). Complex sentences with subordinates like *nevertheless* and *in spite of* appear more frequently. And *if-then* conditional expressions begin to emerge.

Two other syntactic developments appear during the elementary school years: ask-tell relationships ("Ask John that girl's name" or "Tell John your name"; and passive sentences ("The boy was hit by the truck"). Throughout these years, as the occurrence of incomplete grammatical structures decreases, a greater variety of sentence patterns appears, and

the structures within sentences become more varied.[10] Syntactic maturity, then, is not only a function of sentence *length* but also of sentence *complexity*.

Semantics

Children increase their vocabulary at a rapid rate during the elementary school years. It has been estimated that the typical child learns at a rate of about 1,000 words a year in the primary grades, 2,000 words a year in the intermediate grades. Others suggest that a child can add even more words each year during the elementary school period. Although the estimates vary, they do reflect the general trend in vocabulary growth with age. This growth is not limited to new words. It extends to increased comprehension and usage of several special kinds of words:

10. These data were selected from Walter D. Loban, *Language Development: Kindergarten Through Grade Twelve* (Urbana, IL: National Council of Teachers of English, 1976); and Carol Chomsky, *The Acquisition of Syntax in Children from Five to Ten* (Cambridge, MA: MIT Press, 1969).

Double-function words (*sweet*—the psychological characteristic of a person *and* the physical characteristic (ie., taste) of an object).

Abstract definitions (from descriptive definitions—"A hole is to dig"—to conceptual ones—"A hole is an opening in the ground.").

Homonyms ("He will take the *plane* to Lexington," "She has on a *plain* dress").

Homographs ("I will *read* the newspaper," "I have *read* the newspaper").

Synonyms ("Marty was *sad* about leaving," "Marty was *unhappy* about leaving").

Antonyms ("Bill is a *slow* runner, but Mary is a *fast* runner").

Relational terms (*small, smaller, smallest; large, larger, largest*).

And throughout this period, students continue to consolidate language structures (expansion and restructuring).

General Language Growth

In the elementary school years students (1) learn to use language to serve a variety of functions in different communication situations; (2) begin to talk about language in a conscious way (*metalanguage*); and (3) produce language that is less tied to immediate context. As youngsters mature, they interact with an expanded social world in a widening range of settings and for an increasing number of purposes. As functions and purposes grow wider, students' communication range expands to include reading and writing. During this time, the focus on language structure increases metalinguistic awareness. In school there is often more "talking about" language than there is "using" language. And finally, as children mature cognitively, they are better able to manipulate all kinds of symbols, including language. Children move from concrete uses of language (describing a picture they are looking at) toward more abstract uses (describing a hypothetical situation: "What advice would you have offered to the framers of the Constitution?").

LANGUAGE FAMILIES

The language arts is such an integral part of everyday life that often we forget what a miracle language really is. Some 5,000 different languages in 200 language families have developed since humanity first began to speak.

Indo-European is the most familiar language family to us. It is spoken principally by people living in the area from northern India and other parts of Asia across the continents of Europe and North and South America. There are ten branches of this family; English is part of the Germanic branch, as shown in Figure 2.1.

LANGUAGE CHARACTERISTICS

We will examine here four major characteristics of language: the arbitrary relation between words and the objects and ideas they represent; the systematic nature of language; historical changes in language; and the social varieties of language.

Figure 2.1: *Major Branches of the Indo-European Language Family*

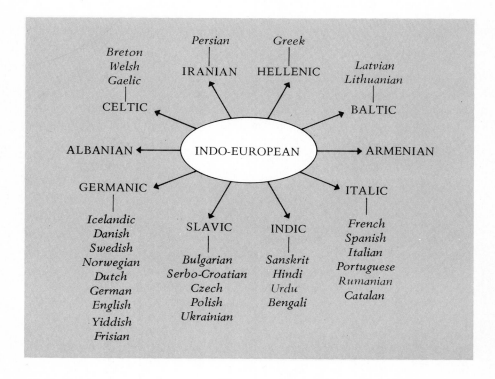

Arbitrariness

The elementary school child must understand that the connection between the sounds (words) and the objects and ideas they represent is purely arbitrary. You can show this by counting to ten in several languages or by pointing out that certain sounds in other languages (the German *ü*, for example) do not exist in English. A corollary, then, is that patterns of sound convey meaning only to those who know a language. Children learning a foreign language will understand this; other children can be exposed to the concept by building a glossary of words as they study various countries or even by learning songs of different countries.

System

Children also need to learn that language is systematic: Sounds are put together in recurring designs. Children learning to speak and to be understood have had to detect and use language structure. They have had to recognize that sounds convey meaning only when put together in patterns of words and sentences.

Studies by Loban, Noell, Strickland, and others have shown that children's language patterns are largely set by the time they reach school age and that they have already learned to use whatever sound system, grammar, and vocabulary are characteristic of their home and neighborhood.[11] These reports indicate that children employ all the common sentence patterns basic to the English language. Although Loban's study showed that elementary school boys of low socioeconomic status are typically less proficient in oral language than girls in the same group, the implication of his work is that most preschool children are linguistically sophisticated.[12] Furthermore, this same research indicates that those children with the greatest proficiency use the same basic sentence patterns as those with less proficiency. The difference lies more in the precision and complexity of thinking.

11. Loban, *Language of Elementary School Children* (NCTE, 1963); Doris L. Noell, "A Comparative Study of the Relationship Between the Quality of the Child's Language Usage and the Quality and Types of Language Used in the Home," *Journal of Educational Research* 47 (November 1953): 161–167; and Ruth Strickland, "Language of Elementary School Children," Indiana University Bulletin of School Education 38 (July 1962): 1–131.
12. Loban, *Language of Elementary School Children*, pp. 84, 86.

Change

The English language we speak today is not the same English language spoken at its origin. Language is constantly changing. Successive translations of the Bible offer wonderful examples of language change over time. (See Figure 2.2.)

Children should understand that language changes—that old words are given new meanings or new uses, and that new words (*television, supersonic*) are coined from parts or modifications of old ones. Very early in the language arts program, in Mother Goose rhymes, pupils come across *fetch* and *tuffet* and other words, that are rarely if ever used today. Folk stories, too are filled with old words.

It has been said, "Change is an aspect of human language as regular and relentless as the birth and death of man. It asks no man's permission and waits on no man's approval."[13] Words change in several ways:

Amelioration: The meaning changes to something better than it was. For example, at one time a person who was *enthusiastic* was considered a fanatic; today an *enthusiastic* person is admired.

Pejoration: The meaning changes to something less desirable than it was. For example, a *villain* once was a feudal serf or a servant of a villa; in current usage, a *villain* is a scoundrel.

Generalization: Meaning becomes broader than it was. Once upon a time, only a painting was a *picture*; now a *picture* can be a print, a photograph, or a drawing as well.

Specialization: Meaning becomes more specific than it was. At one time *meat* was any food, not just mutton, pork, or beef.

Euphemism: This is a neutral term in place of a word or phrase that some find offensive. For example, a *janitor* becomes a *custodian* or *maintenance engineer*, or *dying* becomes *passing away*.

Hyperbole: This is an extreme exaggeration. No one could really "sleep for a year," but the exaggeration is a way to emphasize fatigue. Many people use *fantastic* to describe everything as exciting, although *fantastic* literally means "strange, wonderful, unreal, and illusory."

The more we know about the historical development of the English language—changes in sounds, spelling, vocabulary, and syntax—the better able we are to help children recognize linguistic devices.

13. Donald Lloyd and Henry Warfel, *American English in Its Cultural Setting* (New York: Knopf, 1956), p. 7.

FIGURE 2.2: *Historical Translations (Matthew 8:27)*

Before the year 1000 (Old English):

Ɖeƿisslice ꝺā men þunꝺroꝺen and ꝺus cƿæꝺon·Ƕƿæt is ꝺēs · ꝺæꞇ ƿinꝺas and sǣ him hyrsumiaþ꞉

About 1385 (Middle English):

Forsothe the men wondreden, sayinge, What manere man is he, for the wydis and the see obeishen to hym?

About 1525 (Modern English):

And men amarveyled, and said, What man is this, that bothe wydes and see obey him?

In 1611 (The King James Version):

But the men marveiled, saying, What manner of man is this, that even the winds and sea obey him?

In 1946 (The Revised Standard Version):

And the men marvelled, saying, What sort of man is this, that even winds and sea obey him?

In 1976 (Good News Bible):

Everyone was amazed. "What kind of man is this?" they said. "Even the winds and waves obey him."

There are several good sources for students on the subject of language change:

Leone Adelson, *Dandelions Don't Bite: The Story of Words* (New York: Pantheon, 1972).
Palley Balian, *Symbols: The Language of Communication* (Philadelphia: Franklin Watts, 1975).
Jessica Davidson, *Is That Mother in the Bottle? Where Language Comes From and Where It's Going* (Philadelphia: Franklin Watts, 1972).

Variety

The term most often applied to linguistic variety is *dialect*. Dialect is a linguistic variation sufficiently different to be considered a separate entity but not different enough to be classified a separate language. Dialectal differences occur in pronunciation, vocabulary, and, to a limited extent, syntax.

On all social levels in most of the South, the diphthongal vowel in *down, cow,* and *crowd* begins like the vowel sound in *man*; in New England and elsewhere, this pronunciation is confined to folk speech. Eastern New England and western Pennsylvania use the same vowel sound in *law, caught,* and *salt* as in *lot, cot,* and *rod*; all other sections of the eastern states use contrasting vowels in the two sets. In eastern New England, the /r/ in *park* or *father* is lost, and the linking or intrusive /r/ is common, as in *idea(r)*. In the Midwest, /r/ frequently intrudes, as in *wa(r)sh*. On the Atlantic Seaboard, the vowel sound in *care, chair,* and *stair* ranges all the way from the /æ/ of *cat* to the /ɛ/ of *get* and the /e/ of *gate*. *Hoarse* and *horse* and *mourning* and *morning* are homophonous in some, but not all, parts of the eastern states. In eastern New England, middle New York, Virginia, and South Carolina, the postvocalic /r/ as in *ear, care, four,* and *poor* is not pronounced by a considerable majority; this /r/ is kept in the Midwest though. In eastern Virginia, South Carolina, and the Georgia low country, the words *log, hog, frog,* and *fog* rhyme, but *dog* doesn't. Many southerners do not distinguish /I/ and /ɛ/ before nasals, so that *pin* and *pen* sound alike.

Dialects affect vocabulary too. In the North (eastern New England, Inland North, and New York City) the *earthworm* is an *angleworm*; in other areas, it is a *fishworm* or *mudworm*. *Cottage cheese* is *dutch cheese* in the Inland North, *pot cheese* in the Hudson Valley, *smearcase* in Pennsylvania, and *clabber cheese* in the South. And there are other terms that have regional associations: *bucket/pail, clapboard, cherry pit, blinds/window shades, pavement, skillet/frying pan, clabber milk, snap beans/string beans, mouthharp, fritters, batter bread/light bread,* and *pully bone.*

Syntactic variations show up in "He dove in," "quarter till eleven," "hadn't ought," and "I might could."[14]

We all speak a regional dialect of some sort, tempered, even within a region, by class patterns. In fact, we all have our own unique dialect, or *idiolect*, that reflects our individual style of speech. There is no such thing, then, as a "standard" or "substandard" dialect. Differences and deficien-

---

14. Examples drawn in large part from Hans Kurath, "Area Linguistics and the Teacher of English," *Language Learning* 2 (March 1961): 9–14.

cies are not the same. This makes the teacher's job more difficult. We cannot say that this is the *only* way to pronounce *dog* or the *only* word that means cottage cheese, or the *only* way to say it's quarter to ten. We have a responsibility to respect dialectal differences.

The first step in carrying out that responsibility is to fully understand the range of dialectal variations. Obviously, books and journals are two sources of information.[15] Two others are the American Dialect Society and the Center for Applied Linguistics.[16]

Remember the objective here is not simply to increase your knowledge. It is as much to broaden your attitudes toward language. The concept of individual differences is easier to accept when we expect them, and when we realize that our function is not to tell children their idiolect is wrong, but to add to it in order to increase their social and intellectual development.

CHILDREN'S STUDY OF LANGUAGE

How can the teacher use the material we have been talking about? Obviously the formal study of language does not belong in a beginning language arts program. But there are elements of that study that can enrich the language arts program:

Primary Level

Language as symbols
Word order in sentences
Pitch, stress, and juncture in speech
Word changes in meaning and spelling
Development of the alphabet
Origins of words

Intermediate Level

Celtic, Latin, and Anglo-Saxon words in English
Dictionary as a source of language history

15. Hans Kurath et al., eds., *Linguistic Atlas of New England* (1939; ed. New York: AMS Press); and Harold B. Allen, *Linguistic Atlas of the Upper Middle West,* vol. 1 (Minneapolis: University of Minnesota Press, 1973).
16. American Dialect Society, Department of English, MacMurray College, Jacksonville, IL 62650; Center for Applied Linguistics, 1611 N. Kent, Arlington, VA 22209.

Euphemisms
Comparison of British and American English
English loanwords
Development of a written language
Changes in language
Idioms
Dialectal differences
The development of American dictionaries

These topics can be introduced throughout the program, in response to students' questions and where they pertain to a specific learning objective. We use them, then, to give students a better understanding of the language system and the way it operates.

Nonverbal Language

There are many different ways to teach the concept of nonverbal language. Pictures and photographs show facial (nonverbal) expressions of emotion. Objects convey information: A fence with barbed wire says, "Stay out"; a rural mailbox with the flag up says, "Collect the mail." Pantomime shows how a message can be sent without language. For example, you could have an individual or small group mime an incident described on a task card. All these activities are effective ways to point out how we communicate and what role language plays in effective communication.

TASK CARD: *Mime*

Our scout cabin is on fire. It started in the kitchen. Some people may be trapped in the flames and cannot escape. There is no water nearby to put out the fire. The cabin is just a short distance from here. We must hurry. Get everyone together, and let's go at once.

Language Characteristics

A bulletin board (Title: "What Are the Names of These Objects?") can highlight the arbitrary relation of sounds to objects. That is, an object is

usually named by a different pattern of sounds (word) in different parts of the world:

truck   *camion* (French)   *Lastwagen* (German)
cat   *chat* (French)   *Katze* (German)

   To give students a sense of the system of language, make up a sentence, write each word of the sentence on a separate card, and then distribute the cards to members of the class.

| his | he | a | yesterday | bought | tie | father |

Instruct the students to make a sentence out of the words by lining up in the right order. The sentence could read, "He bought his father a tie yesterday," or "Yesterday he bought his father a tie." This activity not only helps students recognize ungrammatical sentence patterns; it is a good way, too, to introduce "movables" (*yesterday*) to the class.

Another language characteristic is change. You can often find "old" words in rhymes or stories, particularly those that tell of older days. For example, you might compare the knight's question ("Prithee, sir, whither goest thou?") to a modern rewording ("Hey, you, where're you going?").

WORKSHEET: *Vocabulary Differences*

1. In what way are all the answers alike?
2. Do you know another way to state the same time?
3. Which of these terms do you use? Circle them.

   hot cakes   flapjacks   pancakes   griddlecakes

4. What terms have you heard or read refer to a device over a sink for drawing water? (Example: *spigot*.)
5. Here are some other terms. Circle any used in your area. Add other terms you have heard or read for the same thing.

bedspread	couch	brook
coverlet	davenport	bayou
roasting ears	earthworm	doughnuts
table corn	angleworm	sinkers

6. What other words do you know for *bag, pail, salt pork, snap bean,* and *peanut?*

Distinctions between "American English" and "English English" can be used effectively: *petrol/gasoline, bonnet/hood, roundabout/traffic circle, biscuits/cookies, porridge/oatmeal, sweets/candy, mackintosh/raincoat, flat/apartment, lift/elevator, wireless/radio, chemist's shop/drugstore.*

Show pronunciation differences by playing a record of voices from various parts of the country.[17] Use worksheets (like the ones here) to point out vocabulary and dialectal differences. Reading is a particularly effective avenue for studying the latter.

WORKSHEET: *Dialectal Differences*

Read *Birthday* by John Steptoe.[18] When you're done, make a list of dialect language. Here's a start:

Him and his friends couldn't live there.
That we ain't got.
I didn't have to do nothin' but party.

1. How would the same ideas be stated in standard English?
2. In what situations would each dialect be more likely to occur?

Word Formation

The structure of words can be analyzed through their roots. Roots also give us *families of words*, words related to a single base. *Porter, import, export, deport, report, transport,* and *portable* all relate to a single base—*port.* Systematic instruction about related words could follow the format of the lesson plan on page 49.

Compounding is another way words are formed. Have children pick out the compound words in a set of sentences ("The *hillside* was covered with *sunflowers*," "Billy spent the *weekend* with Sam," "The *classroom* was empty.") and explain what words were joined to form them. Portmanteau words (*smog, motel, brunch*) are variations on compound words.

---

17. A good one is *Americans Speaking,* prepared by Raven McDavid, Jr., et al., and available from the National Council of Teachers of English, 111 Kenyon Road, Urbana, IL 61801.
18. New York: Holt, Rinehart and Winston, 1972.

Language History

To relate the concept of hieroglyphics to the alphabet, have children write a rebus story. Look for stories that tell about place names and other word origins. Then too, stories from the past are another source of information. See Maria Edgeworth's stories, for example.

Here is an activity that focuses on historical changes in words:[19]

Worksheet: Yesterday's and Today's Meaning

YESTERDAY	TODAY
Autopsy: seeing a thing one's self	*Autopsy*:
Catsup: a kind of Indian pickle, imitated by pickled mushroom.	*Catsup*:
Knave: a boy or servant	*Knave*:
Lunch: as much food as one's hand can hold	*Lunch*:
Minister: a servant	*Minister*:
Pioneer: a foot soldier	*Pioneer*:
Rum: a country parson	*Rum*:
Salvo: an exception or an excuse	*Salvo*:
Villain: a farmer	*Villain*:

Can you write pairs of sentences using each word to show its meaning over 200 years ago and its meaning today?

There are many books that deal with word histories. For example:

Pauline Arnold, *How We Name Our States* (New York: Criterion, 1966).
Elois Lambert, *Our Names: Where They Came From, What They Mean* (New York: Lothrop, 1959).
Peter Limburg, *What's in the Names of Fruit?* (New York: Coward, McCann and Geoghegan, 1972).
————, *What's the Names of Wild Animals?* (New York: Coward, McCann and Geoghegan, 1977).
Flora H. Longhead, *Dictionary of Given Names with Origins and Meanings* (Glendale, CA: Arthur Clark, 1974).
Vernon Pizer, *Ink, Ark., and All That: How American Places Got Their Names* (New York: Putnam, 1976).

---

19. Burns and Bassett, *Language Arts Activities*, p. 15.

LESSON PLAN: *Related Words*

Performance Objective

Given a base for a "word family," the learner writes other related words.

Pretest

Write the word *head* on the board. Then ask, "What six words do you know that are related to this one?" An example is *headache*. (Six is an arbitrary number to emphasize the concept that words exist in families, as the child does.)

Teaching Suggestion

Write another word on the board, such as *heart*. Develop with the learner a list of related words (*heartless, heartful, heartstring, heartland, heartily, heartrending, heartsick, hearty.*)

Mastery or Posttest Suggestions

1. Ask the learner to select a word and write six related words.
2. The suggestion provided in the pretest can be adapted (using a different base word) to the posttest.

Reteaching Suggestions

1. Write other words on the board (*light, love*). Ask, "What are some other related words?" Prepare an appropriate list for each word.
2. Write a paragraph that contains a number of related words. Ask the learner to find the related words.
3. Ask the learner to find related words in a reading selection.

Elsdon Smith, *New Dictionary of American Family Names* (New York: Harper & Row, 1973).

SOME INSTRUCTIONAL CONCERNS

There are at least three potential problems associated with language study. The first is in the teacher's approach. It cannot be formal. Although there is a place for analysis of certain aspects of language at the elementary school level, the emphasis here should be on the *uses* of language and the ability of students to apply those uses. How do we avoid a too-formal approach? By focusing on children's everyday experiences in oral and written expression (the kinds of experiences discussed in Chapter 1) and by teaching only those concepts that can help them express themselves.

The second problem relates to student maturity and is in many ways closely tied to the teaching approach. Some children find it difficult to study about language because they lack the linguistic maturity to do so. For these students, adapt the exploratory activities suggested in the chapter. Another trouble spot is that some children simply are not interested in language study. You can create interest by concentrating on language concepts they can apply to their own speaking and writing, by letting them see the whys of language study activities.

THOUGHT QUESTIONS

1. How do children's established language functions (used before they reach school age) influence the instructional program?
2. Is language wholly learned or innate?
3. What is the difference between
   a. phonology and morphology?
   b. syntax and semantics?
4. How is language systematic?
5. Which language concepts seem most important (to you)
   a. at the primary level?
   b. at the intermediate level?
6. How would you integrate the informal study of language concepts in the instructional program?

LEARNER RESPONSE OPTIONS

1. Interview a child and an adult on the topic "What are the uses of language?" Compare the responses.
2. Tape-record the speech of a three- to four-year-old child. Use the data on pages 32–34 to make statements about the sample speech. Do the same for a five- to six-year-old child and for a seven- to eight-year-old child.
3. Develop a teaching plan to demonstrate to a child or group of children the idea that language changes.
4. Prepare an introduction to a lesson tracing the development of the English language.

5. Develop a chart of examples of local variations in pronunciation, vocabulary, and syntax.
6. Choose a library book that will help children learn more about language, and plan a presentation using the book. Give your presentation to a small group of children or to students in your class.

References and additional readings

Bolinger, Dwight L. *Aspects of Language.* 2d ed. New York: Harcourt, Brace and World, 1975.
Boyd, Gertrude. *Linguistics: Grammar, Usage, and Semantics.* Itasca, IL: Peacock, 1975.
Dale, Philip. *Language Development: Structure and Function.* 2d ed. New York: Holt, Rinehart and Winston, 1976.
DeStefano, Johanna S. *Language, the Learner, and the School.* New York: Wiley, 1978.
DeVilliers, F. A., and J. G. DeVilliers. *Early Language.* Cambridge, MA: Harvard University Press, 1979.
Fromkin, Victoria, and Robert Rodman. *An Introduction to Language.* New York: Holt, Rinehart and Winston, 1974.
Halliday, M. A. K. *Explorations in the Functions of Language.* London: Edward Arnold, 1973.
Hook, J. N. *History of the English Language.* New York: Ronald Press, 1975.
Lamb, Pose. *Linguistics in Proper Perspective.* 2d ed. Columbus, OH: Merrill, 1977.
Langacker, Ronald W. *Language and Its Structure: Some Fundamental Linguistic Concepts.* 2d ed. New York: Harcourt, Brace and World, 1973.
Lindflors, Judith W. *Children's Language and Learning.* Englewood Cliffs, NJ: Prentice-Hall, 1980.
Loban, Walter D. *Language Development: Kindergarten Through Grade Twelve.* Urbana, IL: National Council of Teachers of English, 1976.
Malmstrom, Jean. *Understanding Language: A Primer for the Language Arts Teacher.* New York: St. Martin's, 1977.
Pflaum-Conner, Susanne. *Development of Language and Reading in Young Children.* 2d ed. Columbus, OH: Merrill, 1978.
Piaget, Jean. *The Language and Thought of the Child.* 3d ed. New York: Humanities Press, 1962.

Pinnell, Gay S. *Discovering Language with Children*. Urbana, IL: National Council of Teachers of English, 1980.

Reed, C. E. *Dialects of American English*. Rev. ed. Amherst, MA: University of Massachusetts Press, 1977.

Rosen, Connie. *The Language of Primary School Children*. New York: Penguin, 1973.

Savage, John F. *Linguistics for Teachers: Selected Readings*. Chicago: Science Research Associates, 1973.

Tough, J. *The Development of Meaning*. New York: Wiley, 1977.

Vygotzky, Lev. *Mind in Society*. Cambridge, MA: Harvard University Press, 1978.

———. *Thought and Language*. Trans. Eugenia Hanfmann and Gertrude Vakar. Cambridge, MA: MIT Press, 1962.

Wood, B. *Development of Functional Communication Competencies: Pre-K–Grade 6*. Urbana, IL: National Council of Teachers of English, 1977.

CHAPTER 3 : *Grammar*

OVERVIEW

This chapter describes three approaches to the study of grammar: the traditional or prescriptive, the structural or descriptive, and the transformational-generative approaches. It goes on to describe, within the framework of instructional guidelines, the grammar concepts commonly found in English textbooks. The chapter ends with a detailed section of exploratory and systematic lessons in parts of speech, basic sentence patterns, and sentence combining.

KEY VOCABULARY

grammar

traditional (prescriptive) grammar

parts of speech

sentence function

sentence structure

parsing

structural (descriptive) grammar

form classes

function words

sentence patterns

sentence expansion

transformational-generative grammar

competence

performance

surface structure

deep structure

transformation

kernel sentence

phrase structure rules

tree diagram

transformation rules

basic sentence patterns

sentence combining

expansion

restructuring

LANGUAGE AND GRAMMAR

Language is a human communication system; grammar describes that system—it describes the ways we communicate. There are three widely accepted approaches to grammar. The *traditional* approach is *prescriptive*. It defines socially preferred ways of communicating. There is "good" grammar and "bad" grammar; there is a "correct" way to speak and an "incorrect" way to speak.

The *structural* approach is *descriptive*. It describes the ways we communicate and our arrangement of the elements of communication—words, or, more precisely, sounds, and units of meaning. Structural grammar has very little to do with rules for good or proper grammar; in fact, its earliest proponents even substituted new terms for traditional parts of speech. Speech, for the structural grammarians, is the primary language; writing and nonverbal communication, secondary.

The *transformational* (or transformational-generative) approach defines grammar as the set of rules that we all intuitively know and use in order to communicate. In a very different approach from those of traditional and structural grammarians, the transformational school focuses on language as an "underlying form that can be expressed *through* speech and *through* writing."[1] Grammar, then, becomes our understanding of language. Each of us knows intuitively what is "grammatical" (that is, what communicates meaning) and what is "ungrammatical" (what does not communicate meaning).

KINDS OF GRAMMARS

Traditional grammar has its foundations in the eighteenth century, in the works of Priestly and Lowth. Structural grammar, which held sway in the United States from about 1925 to 1960, is generally based on Bloomfield's theories.[2] The transformational movement began in the late 1950s with Noam Chomsky's work.[3]

Most language arts teachers have studied traditional grammar but are unfamiliar with structural and transformational grammar. Because each kind of grammar has implications for the teaching of English, contemporary textbooks in the field incorporate some of each.

1. Richard E. Hodges and E. Hugh Rudorf, eds., *Language and Learning to Read: What Teachers Should Know About Language* (Boston: Houghton Mifflin, 1972), p. 5.
2. Leonard Bloomfield, *Language* (New York: Holt, 1933).
3. Noam Chomsky, *Syntactic Structures* (The Hague: Mouton, 1957).

Traditional (Prescriptive) Grammar

Traditional grammar is a collection of grammatical principles and rules based on and developed from Latin grammars. Its emphasis is on terminology and rules.

Parts of Speech There are seven to ten parts of speech, depending on the taxonomy of different grammarians: noun, pronoun, verb, adjective, adverb, preposition, conjunction, article, infinitive, and interjection. The definitions of these elements are not systematic. For example, nouns and verbs are defined according to *meaning*; prepositions, adverbs, and adjectives, according to *function*.

Parts of speech serve several different functions. A noun can be a subject, a direct object, a subjective complement, an indirect object, or an object of a preposition.

Larger Units Traditional grammar combines the parts of speech in phrases, clauses, and sentences (particularly the subject-predicate concept of sentences). Sentences are categorized according to *function* (declarative, interrogative, imperative, exclamatory) and *structure* (simple, compound, complex). Sentences themselves are expanded through modification, subordination, and coordination.

Diagramming See the example.

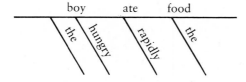

Parsing Parsing means analyzing a word's form and function in a sentence. For example, *ate* in the diagram is an irregular transitive verb, active voice, indicative mood, past tense, singular number, and third person; its subject is *boy*.

Structural (Descriptive) Grammar

The components of structural grammar are quite different.

Sound The smallest distinctive sound element in a language is a *phoneme* (/b/ in *bit, /p/* in *pit*). About forty vowel and consonant phonemes have been identified in the English language.

In addition to vowels and consonants, English uses *secondary phonemes* of stress, pitch, and juncture. (Examples: stress: I said *NO*; pitch: She is a *tiny* girl; juncture: *A jar* kept the door *ajar*.)

Meaning The smallest meaningful units of language, *morphemes*, range from noun plurals to larger units (*boy, house*). The word *worker* is made up of two morphemes: *work*, a free-form morpheme, and *er*, a bound morpheme. (A bound morpheme cannot stand alone as a meaningful unit.)

Form Classes Form classes resemble the four major parts of speech: nouns, verbs, adjectives, and adverbs. Form class is determined by the function a word performs in a sentence. Form class words can change form to indicate a change in meaning (*boy, boys*).

Function (Structure) Words These include noun markers or determiners (articles, possessives, demonstratives: *a, my, this*); prepositions; auxiliary verbs (*am, are, is*); modals (*may, can, will*); intensifiers or qualifiers (*very, considerable*); and conjunctions (coordinating and subordinating).

Definitions According to Position, Form, and Function For example, a *noun* is a word that

takes certain endings (to show plural number or possession).
often appears with certain function words (determiners) preceding it.
occupies a certain position (after a determiner or before a verb).

   Similarly, a verb can be described in terms of changes in position, form, and function. A *verb* is a word that

can change form by adding *-s* for the present tense or agreement and *-ed* for the past tense. (There are also a great many irregular verbs.)
is usually located after the noun that is the subject of the sentence.
can be preceded by auxiliaries (*am, were*) and modals (*can, would*).

An *adjective* is a word that

usually changes form to show comparative and superlative (by adding *-er* and *-est*) when the adjective contains one or two syllables. (Adjectives with more than two syllables usually change form by adding a structure word such as *more* or *most*.)
often appears before the noun it modifies.
often follows an intensifier (*very, quite*).

An *adverb* is a word that

can change form, like an adjective, by adding *-er* or *-est* (or *more* or *most*).
is often found at the end of a sentence but can be moved.
often follows an intensifier.

We can define function words as follows:

A *noun marker* signals that a noun is coming.
A *preposition* always patterns in phrases with nouns.
An *auxiliary* patterns with verbs and signals that a verb is coming; it can change form to show changes in tense and number.
An *intensifer* patterns with adjectives and adverbs.

A *coordinating conjunction* (*and, but*) connects two sentences or sentence parts of equal weight.

A *subordinating conjunction* (*although, after, since, because*) is used to insert one sentence into another.

Below is a group of sentences containing some nonsense words. Using your knowledge of position, form, and function, can you identify the nonsense words as "nouns" or "verbs"? Can you tell whether the verb is transitive or intransitive and how the noun is used (subject, direct object, indirect object, or predicate noun)?

A bargung moppels its ritbuck.

Several bargungs moppeled their ritbucks.

Two doolers gave the gotgoing some lavery.

Every brark is an unboodle.

A brark can opperlize those gratorps.

Sentence Patterns Structuralists speak in terms of sentence patterns—the regular appearance of form class words in specific relationship to one another. Below is one set of patterns, proposed by Lefevre and Lefevre:[4]

Pattern One:

N-V (noun-verb): *The balloon descended.*

N-V-ad (noun-verb-adverb): *Mary drove slowly.*

N-V-adj (noun-verb-adjective): *The man turned purple.*

Pattern Two:

N-V-N (noun-verb-noun): *The cowboy saddled his horse.*

Pattern Three:

N-V-N-N (noun-verb-noun-noun): *Dad called Mary a tomboy.*

N-V-N-adj (noun-verb-noun-adjective): *Ruth painted the room white.*

Pattern Four:

N-Lv-N (noun–linking verb–noun): *My boss is an Irishman.*

N-Lv-ad (noun–linking verb–adverb): *Anne has been here.*

---

4. From *Writing by Patterns,* by Helen F. and Earl A. Lefevre. Copyright © 1965 by Helen F. Lefevre and Earl A. Lefevre. Reprinted by permission of Alfred A. Knopf, Inc.

N-Lv-adj (noun—linking verb—adjective): *The apples were sweet.* (Other words commonly treated as linking verbs include *feel, seem, appear, look, become, remain, taste, smell, sound.*)

Sentence Expansion Sentences can be expanded by compounding, modification, or subordination.

Diagramming One method of diagramming involves a series of boxes to show the relationship and functions of words in a sentence. The subject and predicate are identified first, in the outerboxes; then smaller boxes are drawn inside to show more specific analysis.

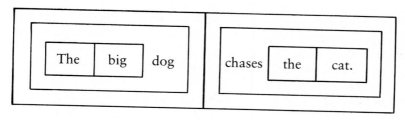

The *immediate constitutents* (ICs), or major parts, are *the big dog* and *chases the cat.* The *ultimate constitutents* (UCs), individual morphemes, are *the, big, dog, chase, s, the* and *cat.*

Additional Concepts Structuralists emphasize three concepts: Language is systematic, every language has its own grammar, and a living language changes. Their focus on speech as the primary form of language highlights the differences between spoken and written language. They also distinguish between the speech patterns unique to an individual (*idiolect*) and those belonging to a geographic region and social class (*dialect*), and among various levels of usage (standard, nonstandard, and so on). And finally, they recognize functional varieties—suiting language to the situation.

Transformational-Generative Grammar

The transformational school proposes the concepts of language competence and performance. *Competence* refers to the individual's unconscious knowledge of grammar:

The ability to understand grammatical sentences and to detect ungrammatical sentences: *Wash the dishes before leaving* versus *Leaving before dishes the wash.*

The ability to interpret sentences even where elements are missing: *Bill was a good athlete and so was Tom* (a good athlete).

The ability to recognize that two or more sentences may have the same meaning: *The attorney did the work* and *The lawyer did the work.*

The ability to understand that a sentence can be ambiguous: *Flying planes can be dangerous.*

Performance, on the other hand, signifies the actual use people make of this knowledge at any particular stage of their development.

Surface structure and *deep structure* are two important terms in transformational grammar. The form of a sentence—what you read or hear—represents the surface structure. The meaning of a sentence is the deep structure—the underlying set of semantic relationships expressed in the sentence. For example, the surface structures of *He refused to tell the story because he was afraid to* and *He refused to tell the story because he was afraid to tell the story* are different, but both sentences have the same deep structure. The surface structure *Bill was puzzled by Marie* has an underlying deep structure, or *kernel sentence, Marie puzzled Bill. Transformations* have converted the deep structure into the surface structure—in the latter case a passive transformation. This transformation interchanged the noun phrases *Bill* and *Marie*; *was,* a form of *be,* has been introduced; and the preposition *by* was inserted before *Marie. Marie* is the deep subject of the structure; *Bill* is the surface subject.

Phrase Structure Rules The basic tenet of transformational grammar is that all languages possess a finite set of rules that describe the operations by which basic structures are combined and modified into an infinite number of sentences. A sentence is composed of two parts: the *noun phrase* and the *verb phrase.* Phrase structure rules state ten ways in which the components of a sentence can be written:

1. Sentence ⟶ Noun Phrase + Verb Phrase (S ⟶ NP + VP).
   A sentence consists of a noun phrase plus a verb phrase.

2. NP ⟶ { Determiner + Common Noun
            Proper Noun
            Pronoun[5] }

   A noun phrase can be made up of a determiner (article, demonstrative, or possessive) and a noun (count, mass, collective, concrete, or abstract); a proper noun; or a pronoun (personal or indefinite).

---

5. Braces indicate only one choice. Each choice can be further elaborated with modifiers of various kinds.

3. VP ⟶ Auxiliary + Verb Expression
   A verb phrase can be written as an auxiliary and a verb expression. (The VP may contain a variety of combinations as noted below.) Simple, declarative, active sentences can be described by the phrase structure rules above. Basic sentences follow patterns like these:

   The girl laughed.

   The girl is a nurse.

   The girl frightened her brother.

   The girl has a bicycle.

   Apples are good.

   Father bought the boy a coat.

   The gymnast seems tired.

   Basic sentences have a fixed order: The subject is followed by the predicate. We could diagram (using a *tree diagram*) the basic sentence *The girl laughed* like this:

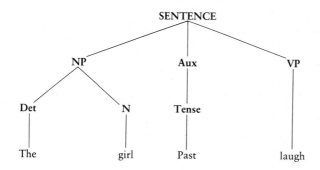

4. Auxiliary ⟶ Tense + (Modal) + (Aspect)[6]
   The auxiliary may only be an indicator of tense, or it may include a modal aspect.

5. Tense ⟶ $\begin{cases} \text{Present} \\ \text{Past} \end{cases}$

6. Modal ⟶ (*can, may, will, shall, must, could, might, would, should*)

7. Aspect ⟶ (*have* + *-en*) + (*be* + *-ing*)
   The *-en* form refers to a form of the verb or *be* when *have* + *-en* is added to a VP (that is, a past participle such as *eaten*). The *-ing* form

6. Parentheses indicate optional use.

is the form of the verb or *be* when *be + -ing* is added to a VP (that is, a present participle such as *playing*).

8. Verb expression $\longrightarrow$ $\begin{cases} \text{Verb nontransitive} \\ \text{Verb transitive} \end{cases}$

9. Verb$_{\text{nontransitive}}$ $\longrightarrow$ $\begin{cases} \text{Verb}_{\text{intransitive}} \\ \text{Verb}_{\text{linking + complement}} \end{cases}$

V_i, or verb intransitive, is a verb that needs nothing else to make a VP (*walk, go, run, stand*). V_l, or verb linking, is a verb (*remain, seem, is, feel*) that is followed by an adjective.

10. Verb$_{\text{transitive}}$ $\longrightarrow$ V + NP

V_t, or verb transitive, is the way a verb (*see, kick, hit, throw*) is used when followed by an object NP. Thus the tree diagram:

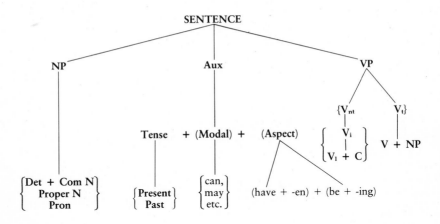

Transformation Structure Rules More complicated structures are described by means of transformation structure rules. See how the deep structure (QUESTION) *The girl* (tense) *laugh* is transformed into a surface question, *Did the girl laugh?*

1. Q + NP + tense + VP (deep structure)
2. Tense + NP + VP (inflection adjustment: *laughed* to *laugh*)
3. Tense + *do* + NP + VP (addition of *do*)
4. Did the girl laugh? (question transformation)

Transformations consist of additions, deletions, rearrangements, substitutions, or combinations.

From the kernel sentence *The boy sells papers,* we can make the following transformations:

(KERNEL) The boy sells papers.
(NEGATIVE) The boy does not sell papers.
(PASSIVE) Papers are sold by the boy.
(NEGATIVE-PASSIVE) Papers are not sold by the boy.
(QUESTION) Does the boy sell papers?
(NEGATIVE-QUESTION) Doesn't the boy sell papers?
(NEGATIVE-PASSIVE-QUESTION) Aren't papers sold by the boy?

Other common transformations include:

(REQUEST) You do the dishes. → Do the dishes.
(THERE) A cat is on the bed. → There is a cat on the bed.
(POSSESSIVE) John has a cat. The cat is lively. → John's cat is lively.

THE WHY AND HOW OF GRAMMAR STUDY

Research indicates that knowing grammar does not improve speaking or writing ability.[7] But recent reports suggest (the evidence is far from conclusive) that the transformational approach may prove helpful to the writing program.[8]

The most effective program for the elementary school, it now seems, emphasizes experience with language; formal grammar analysis, with its concentration on terminology, is undesirable. Language, then, should be studied as a vehicle, not an end. Undue emphasis on formal grammar must not displace valuable instruction and practice in the use of language. Each component of the language arts program should be viewed in terms of its relation to the total program. And there are far too many useful elements in the total program to spend an inordinate amount of time on formal grammar.

This is not to say there is no place for grammar instruction in the language arts program. Some think a basic understanding of grammar

7. Robert L. Ebel, ed., *Encyclopedia of Educational Research* (New York: Macmillan, 1969), pp. 450–451. Also see the fifth edition, published in 1982.
8. J. C. Mellon, *Transformational Sentence Combining* (Urbana, IL: National Council of Teachers of English, 1969); and Frank O'Hare, *Sentence Combining: Improving Student Writing Without Formal Grammar Instruction* (Urbana, IL: National Council of Teachers of English, 1973).

helps in discussing speech and writing. Others believe that "the only justifiable reason for teaching grammar is to lead children to want to explore their language and discover how it works."[9]

In a program where language is recognized as a tool, focus should be on the child's use of that tool—manipulating sentence parts, creating sentences by combining parts, forming sentences by adding words or phrases to fragments, and changing sentences by adding words or by modifying the words that already form the sentence. In this last phase, grammar concepts can be useful, but the primary focus here is on production and revision, not on analysis.

Grammar instruction at the elementary school level, then, should be an exploration of how our language works. Children's own language (oral and written) is possibly the best source of material for studying this aspect of grammar; an exploratory approach, the best method for teaching it. Let students make their own observations (through guided questioning), share their findings, and finally form their own tentative generalizations or "rules." This active involvement, creates not only a good learning situation but also a sound basis for evaluation.

INSTRUCTIONAL PRACTICES

The materials and lessons here are summaries or reviews of general areas, encompassing many more concepts than would usually be presented at any one time. Most are more appropriate for intermediate-level students than for primary-level children. Exceptions are noted.

Parts of Speech

> WORKSHEET: *Noun*
>
> Examine the five sentences. Decide how the underlined words are alike or different.
>
> The <u>boy</u> sings well.
> The <u>girls</u> ran fast.
>
> *Continued*

9. John M. Kean and Carl Personke, *The Language Arts: Teaching and Learning in the Elementary School* (New York: St. Martin's, 1976), p. 313.

The man's <u>coat</u> was gray.

His <u>glasses</u> were broken.

Those <u>cats</u> purr loudly.

1. What does the -s or -es added to some of the words mean?
2. What does the -'s added to one of the words mean?
3. Why do some of the words "fit" in certain positions but not in others?
4. Would any of the underlined words fit in the blank below?
   The _____ was (were) lost.
5. Could any of the underlined words sensibly replace the word *oogle* in the sentence *The oogle ran fast?*
6. The underlined words are all nouns. Try to define a noun.
7. Write five sentences and underline the nouns in each sentence.

ACTIVITY: *Singular Plural Nouns*

1. Add -s or -es to indicate more than one. Remember, nouns ending in -s, -z, -x, -ch, or -sh add -es.

girl	race	box	buzz
town	studio	sash	gas
toy	ski	cross	torch

2. Nouns ending in -y preceded by a consonant usually change to -i and add -es to form plurals. Write the plural form of the following:

army	courtesy	sky	pony

3. Some nouns change the medial vowel(s) to form plurals (*foot, feet*). Change the following to form plurals:

goose	man	tooth	woman

4. A few nouns change even more or not at all. Write the plurals of these nouns:

ox	child	deer	mouse

ACTIVITY: *Noun Possessives*

An apostrophe is used to show ownership. Look at the phrases below. What general statement can you make about showing possession of singular and plural nouns?

boy's coat   boxes' content
torches' blaze   state's population
teeth's enamel   women's coats

Pronoun The lesson plan below is a systematic, or mastery, type. It would follow exploratory lessons on the pronoun.

LESSON PLAN: *Pronouns and Their Antecedents*

Performance Objective

Given pronouns and their antecedents in written expression, the pupil indicates understanding of the concept by stating the sentence relationship it signals.

Pretest

Give the pupils several sets of sentences such as *The girl is a good student. She is also a fine athlete.* Ask them to indicate to whom or what the *pronoun* refers in each case. The idea here is that the pronoun can stand for and mean the same thing as another word in the preceding sentence. Criterion for mastery is 100 percent.

Teaching Suggestion

List at least five pronouns on the board: *they, she, himself, it, we,* for example. Ask their meanings. Establish that pronouns refer to or replace nouns or other pronouns.

Mastery or Posttest Suggestions

1. Write five sets of sentences like these: *The boy is a good student. _____ is also a fine athlete.* Ask students to fill in the blanks with a pronoun.
2. The suggestion provided in the pretest can also be used for the posttest.

Continued

Reteaching Suggestions

1. Prepare short sentences in which each pronoun has an antecedent. Circle each pronoun and ask the learner to underline the word for which it stands.
2. Using sentences like those above, underline the antecedents and ask the pupils to circle the pronouns that stand for the antecedents.
3. Write several pronouns. Ask for things each pronoun could stand for.

Other pronoun concepts include the pronoun as a subject, as a direct object, and as the object of a preposition and pronoun contractions.

ACTIVITY: *Pronoun Contractions*

Some pronouns can be combined with verbs to form contractions. An apostrophe indicates that one or more letters have been left out.

Match the contractions in Column 1 to their meanings in Column 2 by drawing a line from each contraction to its meaning.

Column 1	Column 2
you've	let us
we've	we have
I'm	she is
she's	we are
you're	I will
we're	you are
I'll	I am
let's	you have
he'd	he would or he had

WORKSHEET: *Verb*

The children walk to school each day.

1. Use Kevin's suggestion to show you understand what he means.
2. Write three other forms of *walk*, as Sue suggested, to show you understand her idea.
3. Does Sue's idea work with a word such as *move*?
4. Can *walk* be used in the blank in Jenny's test sentence?
5. To what form class does the word *children* belong? How does this help suggest the function of *walk*?
6. What other clues might Jim tell if *walk* is a verb?
7. Write two sentences to show that some words (*walk, love*) can be used as either nouns or verbs.
8. Does an irregular verb, such as *see*, form the past by adding *-d* or *-ed* to the stem?
9. How many forms do the following irregular verbs have? What are they?

Stem	*Sing.*	*Past*	*Pres. Part.*	*Past Part.*
set	sets	set	setting	set
sit	sits	sat	sitting	sat
do	does	did	doing	done

10. What is the difference between regular and irregular verbs?

ACTIVITY: *Verb Tense*

1. How does this set of sentences differ in terms of time? That is, which tells of a present action? past action? future action?
   a. Joe is washing the dog.
   b. Joe washed the dog.
   c. Joe shall wash the dog.
2. Write each of these sentences in three tenses: past, present, and future.
   a. Betty (climb) the tree.
   b. The cat (chase) the toy truck.
   c. He (pull) on the rope.

ACTIVITY: *Subject-Verb Agreement*

If the subject is singular, the verb should be singular; if the subject is plural, the verb should be plural.

	Singular		**Plural**	
	Present	*Past*	*Present*	*Past*
I	am	was		
you	are	were		
he, she, it	is	was		
we			are	were
you			are	were
they			are	were

Use the verb form that agrees with the subject.

1. They (is, are) leaving the house.
2. The boys (was, were) late for school.
3. Jim (is, are) a good basketball player.
4. Jill and I (is, are) friends.
5. I (am, was) sick yesterday.
6. You (was, were) not there.

The same kind of systematic lesson plan can be used to explore other parts of speech—adjectives, adverbs, and prepositions.

WORKSHEET: *Adjective*

1. What other words could replace the underlined words to make sense in these sentences?
   A. The old house was vacant.
   B. The house is very old.
2. Both sentences above begin with *the*, which is an article. What is a more general term for *article*?
3. Between what two kinds of words does the adjective come in Sentence A?
4. What is the function or purpose of an adjective?
5. An adjective can change form or add a structure word to show comparative or superlative value. For example:

Positive	Comparative	Superlative
old	older	oldest
beautiful	more beautiful	most beautiful

   What is added to *old* to form a comparative? a superlative?
6. What structure word was added to show the comparative form of *beautiful*? the superlative form?
7. In Sentence B, the verb *is* is a linking verb—its function is to join the subject (*house*) with the adjective (*old*) that follows. Other linking verbs are *become, seen,* and *remain.* Which words are used as adjectives below?
   a. The roses are beautiful.
   b. The water seems warm.
   c. John became tired.
8. In what two positions are adjectives found?

ACTIVITY: *Irregular Adjectives and Adverbs*

Most adjectives and adverbs form the comparative and superlative by adding *-er* or *-est*, or by using the words more and most. These are exceptions:

Continued

Adjectives

Positive	Comparative	Superlative
good	better	best
bad	worse	worst
much	more	most
little	less	least
far	farther	farthest

Adverbs

Positive	Comparative	Superlative
well	better	best
badly	worse	worst

Compose sentences using the comparative and superlative form of the exceptions above.

WORKSHEET: *Adverb*

Which of the words in parentheses fit the blank in the sentence?
Betty did her work _____.
(quickly, yesterday, pretty, here)

1. Which of the four words make sense in the sentence?
2. Which one tells "how"? "in what way"? "where"? "when"?
3. Can any of the adverbs (*quickly, yesterday, here*) be compared as adjectives are compared?
4. Does the adverb come before or after the verb in the sentence?
5. What statement can you make about the position of adverbs after studying these examples?
   a. Joe opened the package *carefully*.
   b. Joe *carefully* opened the package.
   c. *Carefully*, Joe opened the package.
6. Here is a test for adverbs: *Tom rode his bike* _____. What are some adverbs that could be used to fill in the blank?
7. Use the three adverb tests suggested in Exercises 2, 3, and 4 to see whether the words you suggested in the test sentence in Exercise 6 are used as adverbs.

Continued

8. One pupil said he sometimes had trouble telling an adjective from an adverb. He studied the sentences below written by the teacher.
   The girl is tall.
   The girl is here.
   Which underlined word is an adjective and which is an adverb?
   The candy is hard.
   Bill plays hard.

Notice that the concept of modification has many different ramifications. For example, in addition to nouns being modified by adjectives, nouns can also be modified by nouns, present participles, past participles, and prepositional phrases. Verbs, which are modified by adverbs, can also be modified by prepositional phrases, nouns, and other verbs. See the following sentences:

Joe ran *rapidly*. (adverb)   Joe ran *home*. (noun)
Joe ran *over the bridge*. (prepositional phrase)   Joe came *running*. (verb)

WORKSHEET: *Preposition*

After Tim made his statement, three children asked questions about prepositions. What do you think is the answer to each question?

Continued

1. Write nine sentences using a different preposition in each one.
2. Amy wrote this sentence to help her answer her question:
   Mother went to the store.
   Write enough sentences to help you decide on an answer.
3. One classmate said *no* to Amy's questions and wrote these sentences on the board:
   Soon Bill came *by*.
   Then he came *in*.
   What would you say about Amy's example sentence?
4. What is the noun in the prepositional phrase in Phyllis's sentence?
5. Why is it important to know the answer to Phyllis's question?
6. One pupil wrote this sentence to help him answer Tony's question:
   The car in the garage was bright red.
   a. What noun is modified by the prepositional phrase?
   b. What is the position of this noun in relation to the prepositional phrase?

Basic Sentence Patterns

In the beginning school years, sentence patterns should be taught by example rather than by linguistic description. Teach the order and function of words in a sentence informally, by starting with a simple statement: *The car stopped.* Young children enjoy the challenge of describing where, when, how, and why the car stopped. Children learn to sense the "nounness," "verbness," and descriptive qualities of words as the words function in expressing their ideas.

The worksheet below indicates the nature of sentence pattern activities in recently published language arts textbooks for primary-level children.

WORKSHEET: *Subject-Predicate*

Question of the Day

Using the sets of words in Box A, how many sentences can you make? for Box B? for Box C?

A

NP	VP
Snow	is green.
Bill	was hit by the ball.
The tree	is sweet.
He	is white.
Sugar	works.

B

NP	VP
Girls	ride horses.
Some cars	are pretty.
They	are here.
The cats	work.
The boys	are in the street.

Continued

C

NP	VP	
He	sings	a car.
A bird	were	down the street.
The ducks	wants	outside.
A girl	are	softly.
They	lives	happy.

At the intermediate level, children can be asked to identify sets of sentences according to patterns or to build fragments into sentences according to some particular pattern, like the ones here:

S–V (subject–verb)
S–linking verb–adj./adv.
S–V–direct object
S–V–two subjective complements
S–linking verb–subjective complement

Exercises can be developed that compare and contrast sentences with different patterns, and excerpts from articles and stories can be examined in terms of the sentence patterns used. Excerpts from students' own writings can be studied for examples of sentence patterns too.[10]

ACTIVITY: *Simple and Complete Subject and Predicate*

In these sentences, the complete subject is underlined once; the complete predicate is underlined twice. The simple subject is circled; the simple predicate appears in a box.

The very tall (boy) [walked] quickly down the street.

1. Write a complete subject and predicate for these simple subjects and predicates.
   a. girl ran
   b. dog raced

Continued

10. Pose Lamb, *Linguistics in Proper Perspective*, 3d ed. (Columbus, OH: Merrill, 1977), pp. 92–100.

2. Supply a simple subject and predicate in this sentence.
   The large brown _____ almost _____ the race.
3. Some sentences have compound subjects and others have compound verbs.
   Bill and I are friends.
   They ran and played for hours.
   a. Write a sentence using a compound subject.
   b. Write a sentence using a compound verb.

ACTIVITY: *Compound Sentences*

Compound sentences are composed of two or more sentences that could stand alone and that are joined by a conjunction (*and, but, for, or, nor*) or a semicolon. For example:
   The boy ate ice cream and the girl ate cake.
   The boy ate ice cream.
   The girl ate cake.

1. Look at the sentence below. There are two sentences in it that could stand alone. What are they?
   Betty went to the movies, but Jane watched television.
2. Write a compound sentence using the conjunction *for*.

Sentence Combining: Expansion and Restructuring

One of the most effective exercises to help children's language development is sentence combining. In fact, "In more than 30 studies, the conclusion was reached that sentence-combining had a significant effect on productive language growth."[11]

In their early school years, children enjoy taking basic noun phrases and verb phrases and testing various sentence patterns. The basic subject and verb—*Rabbits hop*—can be expanded by adding descriptive elements to both the noun phrase (*The big gray rabbits*) and the verb phrase (*hop*

11. Stanley B. Straw, "Grammar and Teaching Writing: Analysis Versus Synthesis," in *Research in the Language Arts: Language and Schooling*, ed. Victor Froese and Stanley B. Straw (Baltimore: University Park Press, 1981), p. 153. For a detailed discussion of the theory and practice of sentence combining, see J. C. Mellon, "Issues in the Theory and Practice of Sentence-Combining: A Twenty-Year Perspective," in *Sentence Combining and the Teaching of Writing*, ed. D. A. Daiker, A. Kerch, and M. Morenberg (Akron, OH: University of Akron Press, 1979).

merrily through the grass). The result: *The big gray rabbits hop merrily through the grass.* You can use any basic subject-verb elements (*The car crashed, Horses gallop, The boy climbs*) for expansions.

At the intermediate level, pupils can provide their own basic sentences and then experiment with expanding them through modification. For example, *The girl saw a dog* can be expanded into *Yesterday, the tall girl, who lives next door, saw Bob's dog, Spotty, in the park.* The children can discover open points in the basic patterns before the subject, after the subject, and after the verb—where modifiers can be inserted.

Sentence combining (combining two or more related sentences into one sentence) can start in the primary years. Begin with a set of sentences like the following displayed on an overhead projector or the board:

The boy was young. ⎫
The boy fell down. ⎬   The young boy fell down.
                    ⎭

Ask the children to describe what you've done. Then give them a series of short sentences (*The dress had pockets, The dress was red,* and so on), and call on them individually for combinations. When the point seems clear to most of the children, they can respond in unison.

Once students understand the concept of combining simple sentences, use the same approach to teach compounding the predicate:

The man put out the light. ⎫   The man put out the light and went
The man went to bed.   ⎬   to bed.
                            ⎭

THE SLEEK GRAY HORSE GALLOPED AROUND THE TREES AND THROUGH THE MEADOW

Even without knowing the term *relative clause,* children can respond to combining sentences like these:

| The dog barked. }
The dog was sitting at the door. } | The dog, who was sitting at the door, barked. |

Additional combining could include possessives and appositives:

| Bill has a dog. }
The dog is gentle. } | Bill's dog is gentle. |

| Clara is my youngest sister. }
She went to California. } | Clara, my youngest sister, went to California. |

At the intermediate level, coordinators, subordinators, and sentence connectors can be used. *Coordinators,* or coordinating conjunctions, include such words as *and, but, for, nor, or, and, yet.* Some pairs (*both . . . and, either . . . or, neither . . . nor, not only . . . but also*) are sometimes called *correlatives. Subordinators,* or subordinating conjunctions, include such words as *after, as if, because, before, if, since, so that, than, unless, until, when, whether,* and *while. Sentence connectors* are words like *however, moreover, nevertheless,* and *therefore.* To show combining through coordination, use an example like this:

| The phone rang. }
No one answered it. } | The phone rang, but no one answered it. |

Subordination:

| The wind was strong. }
The leaves fell to the ground. } | The leaves fell to the ground because the wind was strong. |

Sentence connection:

| I am not going to the movie. }
I am going to the dance. } | I am not going to the movie; however, I am going to the dance. |

On page 79 is an activity that even very young children enjoy.

> ### ACTIVITY: *Sentence Restructuring*
>
> Sentence elements can be reordered in many different ways.
>
> 1. Cut out seven cards and write each of the following words on a separate card.
>   *sometimes   I   eat   when   I   go   home*
> 2. Mix the cards and hand them out to seven children.
> 3. Have the children stand in the front of the room and make as many different sentences as they can.

SOME INSTRUCTIONAL CONCERNS

There are three major questions at issue here. First, how much time should we devote to grammar study in the elementary school years? Research shows that formal grammar study, which focuses on definitions, terminology, and rules, has little or no effect on children's language production. Obviously, then, our primary attention during these years must be on oral and written expression.

Second, what are the most effective techniques for teaching grammar at this level? Remember that the role of grammar is not to *prescribe* correct usage, but to *describe* language as it is used. This is the key to early instruction. Students should arrive inductively at generalizations—from functional situations. For example, certain grammar concepts can be incorporated at the intermediate level when children are in the process of revising compositions, searching for ways to rearrange or combine sentences, or to add phrases and clauses. The point is to keep instruction informal, and, more important, relevant to students' own language experiences.[12]

Finally, what areas of grammar should the early program emphasize? It helps to consider grammar study more broadly, as language study, to explore the varieties of usage in different places and situations. Discuss dialects and idiolects. Point out how the same object may have several different names in different geographic areas. (*Creek, bayou,* and *stream* all mean the same thing, for example.) Or discuss how language changes in social situations: We don't talk to our friends in the same way we might

---

12. For informal ways of exploring language with children, see Gay S. Pinnell, *Discovering Language with Children* (Urbana, IL: National Council of Teachers of English, 1980).

present a talk at a club meeting. Or talk about changes in usage that the children can recognize from talking to their parents and grandparents or from reading books and stories from different periods of time.

Remember, grammar is difficult for many children. It requires a level of abstract thinking often beyond the cognitive level of elementary school students. If we are going to successfully match grammar study with cognitive level, then it makes sense to use children's own language as the source of that study.

THOUGHT QUESTIONS

1. How does the study of grammar relate to the language material presented in Chapter 2?
2. What are the advantages of each of the three kinds of grammars?
3. What role should grammar play in the elementary school?
4. How can a grammar concept help children improve their sentence construction?

LEARNER RESPONSE OPTIONS

1. Examine an elementary school language arts textbook. What is the nature (topics, scope, sequence, teaching suggestions) of the grammar content?
2. Plan a lesson for one grammar concept related to each of the following. Present it to a group of your classmates.
   a. Parts of speech
   b. Basic sentence patterns
   c. Sentence combining

REFERENCES AND ADDITIONAL READINGS

Elgin, Suzette Haden. *A Primer of Transformational Grammar for Rank Beginners*. Urbana, IL: National Council of Teachers of English, 1975.
Framkin, Victoria, and Robert Rodman. *An Introduction to Language*. 2d ed., New York: Holt, Rinehart and Winston, 1978.
Herndon, Jeanne H. *A Survey of Modern Grammars*. 2d ed., New York: Holt, Rinehart and Winston, 1976.
Malmstrom, Jean. *Grammar Basics*. 2d ed. Rochelle Park, NJ: Hayden, 1977.

O'Hare, Frank. *Sentence Combining: Improving Student Writing Without Formal Grammar Instructions.* Urbana, IL: National Council of Teachers of English, 1973.

Weaver, Constance. *Grammar for Teachers.* Urbana, IL: National Council of Teachers of English, 1980.

PART III: THE YOUNG CHILD,

LISTENING, AND SPEAKING

CHAPTER 4: *Language Arts Experiences for Children Five and Under*

OVERVIEW

This chapter surveys the content of language arts programs in early childhood classrooms and some of the activities used in those classrooms. Most children now receive some type of early schooling; no longer is the first grade their first formal school experience. To be more effective, then, primary-level teachers must understand the content and methods of that early schooling.

KEY VOCABULARY

finger plays

body poems

sound stories

spontaneous conversation

facilitated conversation

sharing

story telling

picture reading

explaining

directing

comparing

evaluating

reading readiness

writing readiness

learning center activities

OBJECTIVES

The language arts program for young children focuses on oral expression and, to a lesser extent, listening. This emphasis on oral language and listening does not suggest that the program is narrow in either purpose or activities. On the contrary, a well-planned, well-executed program can incorporate a much wider range of activities and experiences than is open to a teacher at higher grade levels.

Young children spend a large part of their school day speaking and listening, but this does not mean that the objectives of the language arts program are automatically met. Unless these experiences are organized—for unity and continuity—speaking and listening cannot provide children with necessary understandings and learnings. And even a structured program cannot be effective unless it adheres to appropriate objectives.

The objectives of a typical early language arts program are unique in many ways—but not in all. The beginning program is the foundation for future instruction: It must share many elements, then, with the overall program.

What are the major objectives in the early years?

Listening: The ability to listen and to comprehend; development of concepts and vocabulary; discrimination among sounds; and the ability to follow directions.

Speaking: Oral language facility; speech with others and before groups; the introduction of new words to the speaking vocabulary; and the ability to relate experiences in order.

Literature: Curiosity about printed language; knowledge of basic stories, poems, and other literature forms; and increased enjoyment in listening and desire to read.

Reading Readiness: Prereading skills and an increased desire to read.

Writing Readiness: Coordination in preparation for writing; recognizing manuscript letters that are important to the child; left-to-right direction; and an increased desire to write.

CLASSROOM ACTIVITIES

Because young children are very active and because they are also very curious, teachers must plan, develop, and present activities that build on these natural traits. Vitally important, here too, is selecting activities that allow individual students to perform at their own ability and experience levels.

Listening

The research presented in Chapter 2 shows that we learn speech sounds by imitating the sounds in the environment around us. Our first "speech," then, depends in many ways on our listening skill. Here we know what comes first: listening, then speaking.

One of the main goals of early-childhood educational programs is to develop listening skills. This is done by giving students opportunities for listening: lessons on following directions, games played by oral rules and directions, daily storytime, work centers set up with tapes and records, and time to let children think about what they have heard.

The primary focus of the program is on comprehension—understanding oral communication. If we can teach listening comprehension, we can teach children to follow directions, to learn new information, to enjoy stories, and to participate in all kinds of group activities, at school and at home.

Teachers play a very important role in developing children's listening ability. It is their responsibility to plan activities that demand a variety of listening skills yet allow for youngsters' limited attention spans; to observe and evaluate student listening ability; and to act as model listeners, showing children how listening is done.

Listening is not an end in itself; it is a tool through which children learn to follow directions, to let others talk, to interrupt less frequently, and to improve their own oral sentence patterns. And it is not simply a language arts tool; it is a skill that is essential to every part of the curriculum.

Following Directions Because young children are active and enjoy physical activities, finger plays are an ideal way to involve them individually or in a group.

The Beehive

Here is a beehive. (*Hold up clenched fist.*)
Where are the bees?
Hiding away where nobody sees.
Look! They are coming out! (*Loosen fist slightly.*)
They are all alive!
One! Two! Three! Four! Five! (*Spread fingers.*)[1]

1. *Handbook for Language Arts: Pre-K, Kindergarten, Grades One and Two,* 1966, p. 33.

A *body poem,* in which children supply appropriate movements, involves more than the fingers:

On My Head

On my head my hands I place,
On my shoulders, on my face,
On my hips and at my side,
Then behind me they will hide.
I will hold them up so high;
Quickly make my fingers fly;
Hold them out in front of me;
Swiftly clap—one, two, three.[2]

Some favorite finger plays are "My Turtle," "Ten Fingers," "The Bus," "The Train," "Itsy, Bitsy Spider," and "Five Little Squirrels."[3]

Sound stories—where children supply appropriate sounds—is another way to involve even the shyest child at a very young age. Teachers and children working together can devise all sorts of sound games and stories that demand attentive listening. In the simple story that follows, the dashes represent the places where sounds should be supplied by students.

Ann and Robin lived on a large ranch where they heard many animal and bird sounds ———. Early in the morning the sounds would begin very softly ——— and grow ——— and grow ———. One cold day the wind howled ———, the thunder banged ———, and the rain pattered ———. A neighbor boy dashed into their barn for shelter. His teeth chattered ———, and to warm his hands he clapped them together ———. To warm his feet he stamped them on the floor ———. Ann and Robin went to the barn to help him. As they went, they heard the wind ——— and the thunder ——— and the rain ——— and the boy's teeth ——— and his hands ——— and his feet ———. They gave him a raincoat and took him into their house. After the storm they could again hear the animal and bird sounds ———. The sounds began very softly ———, and they grew ——— and they grew ———.

Answering Questions After reading a story (or simple paragraph) to the class, the teacher can ask several questions about the main ideas or characters presented. This should develop children's cognitive processes and

---

2. Ibid.
3. There are several good sources for both finger plays and body poems. See M. Josephine Colville, *The Zoo Comes to School: Finger Plays and Action Rhymes* (New York: Macmillan, 1978); Daphine Hogstrom, *Little Boy Blue: Finger Plays Old and New* (Racine, WI: Western, 1976); Emilie Poulssen, *Finger Plays* (New York: Hart, 1977); and Patricia Shely, *All Occasion Finger Plays for Young Children* (Cincinnati: Standard, 1978).

oral language skills as well as their listening skills. The questions should require more than yes-no answers (yes-no answers provide very little stimulus for thinking or speaking). Here is an example of a paragraph and appropriate questions:

> The boy quietly tiptoed to the door and peeked through. His mother was frosting a chocolate cake. Looking at the cake made him very hungry. He could hardly wait, for today was his birthday.
>
> 1. What was the first thing the boy did?
> 2. What does *frosting* mean?
> 3. What happens when you have a birthday?

Solving Riddles The teacher describes a prominent object in the classroom. The children listen to the description and take turns telling what they think it is. Soon, some children are describing objects and other children are guessing what they have described. Later, the teacher can select an object or a person not in the classroom—a circus animal, a policeman, a jet plane, or a busy city street—for the children to guess.

Completing Rhymes Simple rhymes and jingles are often used to draw attention to similarities in sentence endings. The teacher reads all but the last word in the rhyme and lets the children take turns filling in the rhyming word. For example:

> Jack be nimble, Jack be quick,
> Jack jumped over the _____.

> Mary had a little lamb,
> Its fleece was white as snow;
> And everywhere that Mary went
> The lamb was sure to _____.

Detecting Unrhyming Words To give children an opportunity to develop another listening skill, the teacher recites four or five rhyming words and adds one that does not rhyme. For example: *cat, lap, nap, lip,* and *map,* or *stop, throw, shop,* and *chop.* Then the children pick out the odd word.

Distinguishing Sounds The teacher records several familiar sounds (a typewriter, a telephone bell, a dismissal bell, an airplane, running water); then runs the tape and has students identify the sounds. (Children can be told in advance what sounds are on the tape.) Another practice—listening for the right word—helps build readiness for reading and spelling. The teacher uses simple sentences or questions ("Do we play ball with a *pat* or a *bat*?" or "Do we wear a *cap* or a *lap*?"), and students choose the correct word.

Speaking

Three-, four-, and five-year-old children are constantly talking. In fact, many teachers spend hours admonishing children to stop talking. Of course, the object of teaching young children is not to stop their oral expression but to direct it to constructive ideas and content—to develop their skills and to give teachers an opportunity to observe and record the needs and growth of individual youngsters.

Conversing Young children learn the techniques of conversation from other children and from adults. Often their communication with each other is jumbled, sporadic, and brief, and is always marked by constant interruption. (In a Piagetian view, the inability to delay speaking when others are talking is a developmental characteristic.) Because conversation is important in all social situations teachers must find time to talk with students individually or in small groups. A casual or informal setting is used, and the child sets the direction of the talk. (This is not the time to correct usage or sentence structure.)

There are two types of conversation: spontaneous and facilitated. Children use *spontaneous conversation* throughout the day, at home, at school, at play. Where spontaneous conversation is informal, *facilitated conversation* is directed and formal. It gives the teacher an opportunity to observe and evaluate oral skills; it gives children an opportunity to express their own ideas and to think about the ideas of others. Although facilitated conversation is organized, it can be easily incorporated in the classroom, as children plan or evaluate activities and trips, talk about classroom problems, or discuss how to care for materials and equipment.

Sharing More than a simple speech opportunity, sharing is an effective way to draw even shy children into classroom activity. Basically, there are two kinds of sharing activities: telling about something made or done during class and sharing out of school experiences or realia brought from home. Different art activities—drawing, painting, clay modeling—provide opportunities of the first kind; trips, pets, and toys, materials for the second. Most programs schedule a daily sharing time for young children, although some teachers prefer to hold it twice weekly or only occasionally. In some programs, where children understand that they can share whatever they have at any time, there is no set sharing period. Today, efforts are being made to broaden the situations in which sharing (often called *show* *and tell*) is involved. At times children may want to share their talents by telling a story, singing a song, or reciting a poem. One child may have a new book; another, a new record to share with the group. Another may want to explain a newly learned game or some simple science equipment. Sharing in these ways brings new ideas and experiences into the classroom.

Teacher involvement in sharing periods varies. Certainly, there is a responsibility to keep the periods reasonably short, in line with children's attention spans. There is also an occasional need for questions, either to start a shy child off or simply to start the session. The teacher can also encourage intellectual growth by asking questions and emphasizing sequence, recall, and generalization.

Storytelling and Picture Reading There are several ways to stimulate young children to tell stories in the classroom situation. *Picture reading* is a strong foundation for the development of visual literacy. Children can analyze and interpret the illustrations, discovering significant characters, main ideas (or actions), details, mood, and anticipated action. Gradually, they develop finer discrimination, for shape, size, place relations, and arrangement of visual details.

There are three levels of picture interpretation by children:

Level 1: Enumerating the items in a picture.
Level 2: Interpreting the events shown.
Level 3: Creating a story suggested by a picture.

Picture files (see Chapter 1) and story books are good source material for picture reading and story telling. There are several excellent wordless (or textless) books available, among them:

Mitsumasa Anno, *Anno's Journey* (Cleveland: Collins, 1978).
Raymond Briggs, *The Snowman* (New York: Random House, 1978).
Diane DeGroat, *Alligator's Toothache* (New York: Crown, 1977).
John S. Goodall, *The Surprise Picnic* (New York: Atheneum, 1977).
Brinton Turkle, *Deep in the Forest* (New York: Dutton, 1976).
Paul Winter, *The Bear and the Fly* (New York: Crown, 1976).

Dramatic play, puppetry, and picture stories are other ways to encourage students to tell stories. Each is an informal and simple activity that produces individual, creative responses.

Children love to dramatize and often become quite adept at playing roles and making up dialogue as they act out a familiar story. There should be no rehearsing. Children should take turns portraying different characters, and both their actions and speech should be spontaneous.

Puppetry not only creates a wonderful opportunity for speaking, but also is an excellent way to introduce shy children to storytelling.[4]

ACTIVITY: *Glove Puppets*

Objective

To improve interpretation and create greater self-assurance on the part of shy children.

Materials

"The Duel" by Eugene Fields
Old gloves
Scissors
Scraps of paper and cloth
Felt-tip markers
Glue
Cassettes and a tape recorder

Procedure

1. Read the poem and discuss the emotions, characters, and actions. Then reread it.
2. Divide the children into pairs. Each pair designs a dog and a cat by taking an old glove and decorating it with scraps of paper or cloth, or with colored-on features.
3. Let each pair listen to a recording of the poem on a cassette, and plan their puppets' actions.
4. Have those students who want to show their version before the class. (If they just want to do it by themselves, don't force them to perform.)

Picture stories, simply and colorfully painted or drawn, stimulate originality in the presentation of a story. Five-year-olds will often paint or

4. For puppet making and use, see Richard Cummings, *101 Hand Puppets* (New York: McKay, 1962); Frieda Gates, *Easy to Make Puppets* (New York: Harvey House, 1976); Shari Lewis, *Making Easy Puppets* (New York: Dutton, 1967); Lewis Mahlmann and David C. Jones, *Puppet Plays for Young Players* (Boston: Plays, Inc., 1974); and Laura Ross, *Hand Puppets—How to Make and Use Them* (New York: Lothrop, Lee & Shepard, 1969), and *Finger Puppets—Easy to Make, Fun to Use* (New York: Lothrop, Lee & Shepard, 1971).

draw several small pictures on one sheet of paper, portraying different events in the story and presenting the ideas of the story in sequence.

Explaining, Directing, Comparing, and Evaluating Oral expression is an integrating activity. Explaining, directing, comparing, and evaluating skills, then, are easily integrated into science, social studies, mathematics, art, and other content areas.

Explaining: Children describe why some objects float and some sink, why plants die, what a turtle eats, or what makes an airplane fly. Any explanations like these demand specific language. The teacher should allow time for pupils to ask questions that require simple explanations. This lets the teacher act as an adult model.

Directing: Giving directions should not be confused with explaining. Directions do not tell how to mail a letter; they are a sequence of steps. Children go from one place to another by listening to the teacher (and then a child) give directions. The locations should be inside the building (the principal's office or the lunchroom), and the teacher could have the children repeat the route verbally. Or, children direct the step-by-step procedure for an activity (cutting a valentine or preparing cookies for a party).

Comparing: An essential process in thinking, the basis for accurate concepts, is the ability to recognize similarities and differences. The classroom environment provides a multitude of situations for comparing. Different kinds of blocks can be compared by size, weight, and color. Several kinds of animals can be observed, and similarities and differences in skin and size considered. Or fabrics can be compared for texture, weight, and use.

Evaluating: The teacher helps children evaluate experiences by asking questions: "How do you think Jimmy felt when he fell in the mud? Why?" or "Do you like this music? Why?" Questions like these lead to others: "How could we have painted the chair another way?" or "What else should we do to the chair?" or "Why should we paint it this way?" The children not only attempt to evaluate experiences; they also try to solve problems.

Units and Projects Children's interests and questions should guide the teacher in selecting and developing short- or long-term units and projects. (Units and projects should evolve from a central theme.) The experiences of a group study provide a wealth of opportunities, not only for new ideas to talk about, but also for reading and writing readiness, artistic expression, and social amenities.

Other Activities Very young students will probably have been given many opportunities for activities to build experiential background and oral language. The following are very often included in their experiences:

Field Trips: Trips through the school to meet the principal, the cooks, the secretaries, and custodians, and to see the various rooms (music room, art room, library); walks around the playground, in the neighborhood, and to nearby stores; visits to fire stations, factories, and parks—all provide background for discussion and group experience stories.

Resource People: There are many people—parents too—who can be invited to school to share their expertise or interests.

Classroom Pets: Children learn a great deal by observing and caring for fish and pets.

Topic Days: Two or three times a week, discussions of particular topics are held. Topics are selected from the children's interests—pets, holidays, television shows, and surprises, for example.

Sequence of Pictures or Cartoon Strips: The pictures are displayed, and children tell a story about them. A similar activity can be done with filmstrips, slides, or motion pictures with the sound turned off.

Talking Bag: Several objects are put in a bag. The children try to describe them by how they feel.

Hide and Seek: A picture of an animal or object is covered with posterboard. Then three-sided flaps are cut in the posterboard to form doors. The flaps are opened one at a time to reveal different sections of the picture. Children use these clues to discuss the picture.

Experience Charts and Stories: The development of experience charts and stories is another integral part of the speaking program for young children. For a detailed description, see Chapter 7.

Literature

Literature is probably the best understood part of the language arts program for children under six.[5] Teachers read to children; talk to them about the characters and events in stories; teach them poems, rhymes, and jingles; and take them to the children's department in the public library. (For many children this is the norm at home, but there are many others who

5. For additional information, see Joan Glazer, *Literature for Young Children* (Columbus, OH: Merrill, 1981); and Linda Lamme, *Learning to Love Literature: Preschool–Grade Three* (Urbana, IL: National Council of Teachers of English, 1981).

have not had the opportunity to participate in these activities. Therefore, the emphasis of literature programs in early-childhood settings is on these types of experiences.)

Children who have had these opportunities at home branch out from fairy tales, to poetry, folk tales, myths, and more realistic stories. These children tend to be more receptive to book corners, rocking chair reading, and beanbag chair picture book reading. Creative teachers have extended the fun of "reading" by providing tepees, pup tents, old bathtubs, and jailhouses (a card table covered with a white sheet painted with black stripes). The special places or get-a-way spots seem to motivate children to look at picture books, to retell a story to themselves or to a friend, or to make up a story.

The literature *teaching center* in an early childhood room is established to teach traditional literature. Although many of the stories and poems will be read over and over in a large group setting, the teacher *teaches* the literature in this center. The procedures require the format of a *lesson plan*, and because of the small number of children involved it is almost a one-on-one situation. Young children need to be orally involved in learning literature for the best comprehension of the characters, setting, and events of a story. The procedures for teaching literature are discussed in Chapter 12; a list of books for young children begins on page 103.

Reading Readiness

In most early-childhood classrooms, reading readiness is developed through activities that involve listening, speaking, and writing. The specific elements of the program are as follows:

Experiential Background: Concepts and vocabulary are developed through sensory experiences, listening to stories and poems, and using learning centers.

General Language Facility: Speaking ability is developed through conversing, sharing, storytelling, problem solving, work units, drama, learning center activities, and the like. Listening comprehension is developed through following oral directions, answering questions, retelling in sequential order, solving riddles, listening center activities, and the like.

Concepts of Reading: Concepts about reading are developed through listening to stories and poems; picture reading; telling, interpreting, and relating stories and poems; composing experience charts; and experiences at the library.

Visual Discrimination: This factor is developed through recognizing and writing alphabet letters.

Auditory Discrimination: This factor is developed through completing rhymes, detecting unrhyming words, distinguishing sounds, and the like.

These elements are taught to individuals, to small groups, and, when the skill is part of another activity, to the whole group. A reading center (or library center) may be provided to keep children interested in learning to read printed materials. A library center usually consists of a small selection of picture or easy-to-read books collected in one area of the room. There may be bookcases, a rug on the floor, and a small rocking chair, floor cushions, or a beanbag chair. Here the children look at illustrations, "read" aloud a story to a friend, or "tell" themselves or others a story they have heard many times.

Field trips, picture interpretations, and other experiences are subjects for dictated stories. The teacher may write or type the stories and display them on charts or on the board. These stories can be used to teach children top-to-bottom and left-to-right progression, and other ideas. Moreover, they help children realize that writing is recorded speech. (Dictated story experiences provide an excellent opportunity to introduce the coordinated language-experience approach discussed in Chapters 7 and 11.)

All of the experiences in this chapter are related either directly or indirectly to prereading. They build background, vocabulary, and listening and speaking skills—experiences bound together by language. And reading is an extension of this process. Kindergarten children should be challenged and encouraged to grow toward reading, but they do not have to be involved in a formal program of reading instruction.[6]

Writing Readiness

Writing demands a physical readiness and a psychological one. The factors that prepare children to write, then, center on coordination and motivation:

1. The child shows an interest in writing and a desire to write.
2. The child has adequate visual acuity.
3. The child understands the concept of left-to-right progression.
4. The child has adequate muscular control.
5. There is proper bone development of the arm.
6. Hand dominance has been developed.
7. The child demonstrates social, emotional, and language maturity.
8. The school's writing program is suitable for the child's level of maturity.[7]

To help children develop the physical readiness to write, teachers provide activities that strengthen small and large muscles and eye-hand coordination. These include jumping, climbing, hammering, sawing, finger painting, finger play, shaping clay, tying shoes, dialing phones, easel painting, and coloring. Simple activities help develop left-to-right concepts; stories, games, blocks, comparisons, and dances work to develop top-to-bottom, shape, and long-and-short concepts.

Some activities translate directly to actual writing. Circles and ovals and horizontal, vertical, and slanted lines are the elements of letter forms. Children can copy or make the shapes or practice drawing lines as they color or paint. Doors, windows, fences, and ladders are good practice for horizontal and vertical lines; tepees and triangles, for slanted ones.

---

6. See "Reading and Pre–First Grade: A Joint Statement of Concerns About Present Practices in Pre–First Grade Reading Instruction," *Language Arts* 54 (April 1977): 460–461.
7. Mildred R. Donoghue, *The Child and the English Language Arts*, 3d ed. (Dubuque, IA: William C. Brown Co., 1979), pp. 211–215.

Motivation usually begins with children's own names. First they come to recognize their names on large labels over their coat hooks and private storage places or on name tags. Then the teacher provides pencils and paper (unlined or manuscript) and help (how to hold the pencil or where and how to put the paper).

In another motivational activity—one that reinforces the value of writing—the teacher records students' ideas in manuscript form on the board, on charts, or on individual drawings, and then (most important) reads what has been written.

In much the same way that toddlers "play" with sounds when they learn to speak, young children experiment with writing. Scribbling is a stage in learning to convey meaning. By inference from the writing system around them, children see that writing has direction, is linear, and is placed on the page in a certain way.

A young child may make *F* and say, "That's my name, Fred." This is an important discovery for a child—recognizing that print, in conventional forms, conveys meaning. Functional situations for writing—signing a name to a drawing, for example—help keep alive the motivation to learn those conventional forms. It is very important, then, that teachers react to early writing efforts (through display or praise or both) and treat them as serious attempts at communication ("Tell me what your note says" or "Read that to me").

The classroom should be a conducive environment for writing. Materials—unlined paper, felt pens, pencils, chalk, and crayons—must be readily available. More than this, children should be able to see both the teacher writing and many examples of written language in the classroom.[8]

Motivation—the psychological readiness to read—can be used as a vehicle for teaching letter names, for demonstrating that words are composed of letters, for introducing the idea that letters represent sounds, for pointing out that the writing (spelling) of a word is related to its sound, and for beginning instruction of some letter-sound associations.

LEARNING CENTER ACTIVITIES

Centers allow children to learn at their own rate and at their own level of maturity; they also allow for varying lengths of attention. Because nursery school and kindergarten children learn through activity, the approach is a very effective one for language arts experiences.

8. Sharon Thomas, "Making Connections," *Language Arts* 59 (January 1982): 3–6.

Table 4.1 lists the kinds of materials used and skills developed in learning centers for teaching the language arts to young children.

TABLE **4.1:** *Learning Center Materials and Skills*

Type of Center	Materials	Skills
Art	Easels, paint, crayons, clay, brushes, paper, scissors, paste, glue, pencils, chalk, felt-tip markers	Oral composition: vocabulary building (e.g., words for color) Handwriting: large and small arm, hand, and finger muscles; eye-hand coordination Creative writing: creativity, free expression, oral responses
Listening	Tape recorders and tapes, record player and records, television, radio, headphones and jacks, slide projectors (individual and large group), filmstrip viewers (individual and large group) and filmstrips, Language Master and strips,* System 80 and strips,† and Hoffman Readers and records‡	Oral composition: vocabulary (word meaning and usage) Listening: following directions, comprehension Spelling: distinguishing sounds and correct pronunciation

* Charles E. Merrill (Bell and Howell), Columbus, OH.
† Borg-Warner Educational Systems, Niles, IL.
‡ Hoffman Information Systems Division, Electronic Corporation, Acadia, CA.

Table 4.1 *(continued)*

Type of Center	Materials	Skills
Library	Books, magazines, filmstrip stories with records, recorded stories, taped stories	Reading: picture reading; introduction to fables, fairy tales, poetry, rhymes, traditional and modern stories Listening: oral comprehension Oral composition: vocabulary building, sharing, modeling of pronunciation, sentence structure, sequence
Family	Play kitchen equipment, doll bed, dolls, doll clothes, rocker, chairs, dress-up clothes, mirror, empty cans and food packages	Oral composition: role-playing, sharing, conversing, vocabulary development Listening: following directions
Block and large truck	Unit blocks, cardboard blocks, cars, trucks, boards, small blocks, wheelbarrow, toy people and animals	Oral composition: role-playing, discussion, sharing, vocabulary Listening: following directions Handwriting: large and small arm, hand, and finger muscles
Drama or role-playing	Old clothes, costumes, puppets, flannel board and flannel characters, false television screen, video tapes for taping action, camera	Oral composition: role-playing, directing, explaining, conversing, vocabulary (for example, words for textures)

TABLE 4.1 *(continued)*

Type of Center	Materials	Skills
Science	Magnets, animals, magnifying glass, plants, clock, thermometer, locks and keys, charts, games, minerals	Oral composition: vocabulary (for example, words for temperature), problem solving, explaining, classifying, comparing, sharing
Mathematics	Geometric shapes, small blocks, colored disks, dominoes, scales, balances, beads, counting rods, games, measuring cup, yardstick, rulers, money	Oral composition: vocabulary (for example, words for shapes, forms, and numbers); problem solving; explaining; comparing; sharing Handwriting: fine-motor development, eye-hand coordination
Manipulative	Games, puzzles, sewing boards, pegs and boards, patterning cards, cutouts, hammers, nails, boards, parquetry sets, dressing frames, buttons, snaps, lacing materials	Oral composition: sharing, explaining, discussing, problem solving, vocabulary development Handwriting: large and small muscle development, eye-hand coordination, visual discrimination
Special	Holiday materials, special interest materials, introductory unit or project materials, "mystery" box	Oral composition: introducing new words, sharing, comparing, explaining, directing Spelling: labeling materials, chart making Handwriting: manuscript form

MATERIALS

Early childhood teachers have a wealth of materials available to them. The references here are just the beginning of an extensive list of resources.

Trade Books

Imaginative Stories

Laurent DeBrunhoff, *Babar and the Wully-Wully* (New York: Random House, 1975).

Syd Hoff, *Barkley* (New York: Harper & Row, 1975).

Robert Kalan, *Blue Sea* (New York: Greenwillow, 1979).

Arnold Lobel, *A Treeful of Pigs* (New York: Greenwillow, 1979).

Dr. Seuss, *Oh, the Thinks You Can Think* (New York: Random House, 1975).

Animal Adventures

Harry Allard, *I Will Not Go to Market Today* (New York: Dial, 1979).

Frank Asch, *Moon Bear* (New York: Scribner's, 1978).

Ezra Jack Keats, *Maggie and the Pirate* (New York: Four Winds, 1979).

Beatrix Potter, *The Tale of Benjamin Bunny* (New York: Warne, 1977).

Ron Roy, *These Ducks Went Wandering* (New York: Seabury, 1979).

Marjorie Weinman Sharmat, *The 329th Friend* (New York: Four Winds, 1979).

Alphabet Books

Janet Ahlberg and Allen Ahlberg, *Each Peach Pear Plum: An "I Spy" Story* (New York: Viking, 1979).

Mitsumasa Anno, *Anno's Alphabet* (New York: Crowell, 1975).

Ed Emberley, *ABC* (Boston: Little, Brown, 1978).

Kate Greenway, *A Apple Pie* (New York: Warne, 1975).

Richard Scarry, *Early Words* (New York: Random House, 1976).

L. Weisgard, *My First Picture Book* (New York: Grosset & Dunlap, 1977).

Folk Tales and Fables

Verda Aardema, *Why Mosquitoes Buzz in People's Ears* (New York: Dial, 1975).

Emily Kingsley, David Korr, and Jeffrey Moss, *The Sesame Street Book of Fairy Tales* (New York: Random House/Children's Television Workshop, 1975).

Anita Lobel, *King Rooster, Queen Hen* (New York: Greenwillow, 1975).

Humor

Frank Asch, *Sand Cake* (New York: Parents Magazine Press, 1978).

Lenore Blegrad, *This Little Pig-a-Wig, and Other Rhymes About Pigs* (New York: Atheneum, 1978).

Rosamond Dauer, *Bullfrog and Gertrude Go Camping* (New York: Greenwillow, 1980).

David McPhail, *Bumper Tubbs* (Boston: Houghton Mifflin, 1980).

Christine Tanz, *An Egg Is to Sit On* (New York: Lothrop, Lee & Shepard, 1978).

Picture Books for Beginning Readers

Frank Asch, *Just Like Daddy* (Englewood Cliffs, NJ: Prentice-Hall, 1981).

Donald Crews, *Light* (New York: Greenwillow, 1981).

Tana Hoban, *Take Another Look* (New York: Greenwillow, 1981).

Arnold Lobel, *On Market Street* (New York: Greenwillow, 1981).

Jean Marzollo, *Amy Goes Fishing* (New York: Dial, 1980).

P. K. Roche, *Webster and Arnold and the Giant Box* (New York: Dial, 1980).

Elizabeth Winthrop, *Sloppy Kisses* (New York: Macmillan, 1980).

Concept Books

Lucille Clifton, *Everett Anderson's Year* (New York: Holt, Rinehart and Winston, 1973).

Tana Hoban, *Circles, Triangles, and Squares* (New York: Macmillan, 1974).

Mary O'Neill, *Hailstones and Halibut Bones: Adventures in Color* (New York: Doubleday, 1961).

Harlow Rockwell, *The Supermarket* (New York: Macmillan, 1979).

Peter Spier, *Crash, Bang, Boom* (New York: Doubleday, 1972).

Counting Books

Marc Brown, *One, Two, Three: An Animals Counting Book* (Boston: Little, Brown, 1976).

Tana Hoban, *Count and See* (New York: Macmillan, 1972).

Jan Pienkowski, *Numbers* (New York: Harvey House, 1975).

John Reiss, *Numbers* (New York: Bradbury, 1971).

Easy-to-Read Books

Dick Gackenback, *Hattie Rabbit* (New York: Harper & Row, 1976).

Wilson Gage, *Down in the Boondocks* (New York: Greenwillow, 1977).

Lillian Hoban, *Arthur's Prize Reader* (New York: Harper & Row, 1978).

Arnold Lobel, *Mouse Soup* (New York: Harper & Row, 1977).

Marjorie W. Sharmat, *Mooch the Messy* (New York: Harper & Row, 1976).

Transitional Books
Joanna Hurwitz, *New Neighbors for Nora* (New York: Morrow, 1979).
Laurence Hutchins, *Follow That Bus!* (New York: Greenwillow, 1977).
Seymour Simon, *Einstein Anderson: Science Sleuth* (New York: Viking, 1980).
John Wallner, *Aldo Applesauce* (New York: Morrow, 1979).

Mother Goose Collections
Brian Alderson, *Cakes and Custard: Children's Rhymes* (New York: Morrow, 1975).
Alice and Martin Provensen, *The Mother Goose Book* (New York: Random House, 1976).
Brian Wildsmith, *Brian Wildsmith's Mother Goose* (New York: Watts, 1964).

Storytelling Books
Paul Galdone, *The Gingerbread Boy* (New York: Seabury, 1975).
Arnold Lobel, *How the Rooster Saved the Day* (New York: Greenwillow, 1977).
Jay Williams, *One Big Wish* (New York: Macmillan, 1980).

Verse and Poetry Anthologies
May Hill Arbuthnot, *Time for Poetry*; now incorporated into *The Arbuthnot Anthology of Children's Literature*, 5th ed. (New York: Lothrop, Lee & Shepard, 1980).
Beatrice DeRegniers and others, *Poems Children Will Sit Still For. A Selection for the Primary Grades* (New York: Citation, 1969).
Stephen Dunning, *Reflections on a Gift of Watermelon Pickle . . . and Other Modern Verse* (Chicago: Scott, Foresman, 1966).
Stephen Dunning and others, *Some Haystacks Don't Even Have Any Needles* (New York: Lothrop, Lee & Shepard, 1969).
David Kherdian, *If Dragon Flies Made Honey* (New York: Greenwillow, 1977).
Nancy Larrick, *Bring Me All of Your Dreams* (New York: Evans, 1980).
David MacKay, *A Flock of Words: An Anthology of Poetry for Children and Others* (New York: Harcourt Brace Jovanovich, 1969).
David McCord, *One at a Time* (Boston: Little, Brown, 1977).

Records, Tapes, and Cassettes

Angus and the Ducks, Weston Woods (LTR 039; cassette PBP 109/109c).
Bruno Munari's Zoo, Weston Woods (LTR 097; cassette LTR 097c).
Caps for Sale, Weston Woods (LTR 012; cassette 104c).
A Child's Garden of Verses, Caedmon (TC 1077; cassette CDL 51077).
Curious George Rides a Bike, Weston Woods (LTR 017; cassette PBC 105c).
Frank Luther Sings Lois Lenski Songs, Wack (WA 1A–1B)
Happy Birthday to You and Other Stories (Dr. Seuss), Caedmon (TC 1287; cassette CDL 5187).
Little Bear's Visit, Weston Woods (LTR 083; cassette LTR 083c).
Little Toot, Weston Woods (LTR 016; cassette LTR 016c).
The Mother Goose Treasury, Weston Woods (LTR 109; cassette LTR 109c).
Peter and the Wolf (Leonard Bernstein), Educational Record Sales (record or cassette).
The Tale of Peter Rabbit, Caedmon (TC 1314; cassette COL 51314).
Three Little Pigs and Other Fairy Tales, Caedmon (TC 1129; cassette COL 51129).
Whistle for Willie, Weston Woods (LTR 065; cassette PBP 116c).

The following companies offer lists and catalogs of their products:

Caedmon Records and Tapes
D. C. Heath and Company
2700 North Richard Avenue
Indianapolis, IN 46219

Educational Record Sales
New York, NY 10007
Weston Woods Records and Tapes
Weston Woods Studios, Inc.
Weston, CT 06880

Source Books

Doreen J. Croft and Robert D. Hess, *An Activities Handbook for Teachers of Young Children,* 3d ed. (Boston: Houghton Mifflin, 1981).
Sandra N. Kaplan et al., *A Young Child Experiences: Activities for Teaching and Learning* (Pacific Palisades, CA: Goodyear, 1980).

Programs and Kits

Children's World (New York: Holt, Rinehart and Winston).
Crossties (Oklahoma City: Economy Company).

Discoveries for Young Americans (Chicago: Rand McNally).

Distar Language (Chicago: Science Research Associates).

Early Childhood Curriculum: A Piaget Program (Boston: American Science and Engineering).

Early Childhood Discovery Materials (New York: Macmillan).

Language Experiences in Early Childhood (LEEC) (Chicago: Encyclopaedia Britannica Educational Corporation).

The Language and Thinking Program (Chicago: Follett).

Learning Language Skills (Manchester, MO: Webster/McGraw-Hill).

Peabody Early Experience Kits (Circle Pines, MN: American Guidance Service. (Also *Peabody Language Development Kits*.)

Playway: An Interest Center Approach to Initial Education (New York: Winston Press).

Some instructional concerns

Teachers of young children have to make several decisions in setting up their instructional program: how to match the developmental status of the children with activities and materials; how to balance between directed and less formal activities; and how to relate their program to later programs in the elementary school.

Although primary-level teachers encounter developmental and balance decisions too, the real issue for them is the third decision—the relationship of the early program to their own. That early program is the foundation for later growth. (Scribbling isn't just the child's need to communicate; it's a step toward composing.) Ideally, then, nursery and kindergarten teachers recognize this, and create programs that can function as the bases of later programs. But the responsibility is not theirs alone. To be effective, primary-level teachers must understand the content and methodology of instruction used with children before first grade.

Thought questions

1. Why is picture reading important?
2. What are the differences among *explaining, directing, comparing,* and *evaluating*?
3. What reading opportunities should be provided for young learners?
4. How are writing experiences incorporated in the program for young children?

5. In what ways do early writing experiences relate to reading?
6. How can learning centers be used to enhance language abilities?

LEARNER RESPONSE OPTIONS

1. Design a bulletin board that describes a language arts program for kindergarteners.
2. Interview several early-childhood educators about their language arts programs. Compare their answers to the following questions:
   a. What materials do you use to teach the language arts?
   b. How many hours a week do you devote to language arts activities?
   c. Which skills do you consider basic skills that require instruction in centers or on an individual basis?
3. Select one of the elements of a language arts program for young children and tape a classroom session devoted to teaching that element.
4. Visit a public library, an elementary school library (or material center), and an early childhood classroom library. List the advantages and disadvantages of providing literature experiences for young children in each setting.
5. Select an elementary school language arts textbook and compare the activities suggested for primary-level students to the early-childhood activities described in the chapter.

REFERENCES AND ADDITIONAL READINGS

Broman, Betty L. *The Early Years in Childhood Education*. 2d ed. Boston: Houghton Mifflin, 1982.

Cazden, Courtney, ed. *Language in Early Childhood Education*. Rev. ed. Washington, DC: National Association for the Education of Young Children, 1981.

Croft, Doreen J., and Robert D. Hess. *An Activities Handbook for Teachers of Young Children*. 3d ed. Boston: Houghton Mifflin, 1981.

Hendrick, Joanne. *The Whole Child: New Trends in Early Education*. 2d ed. St. Louis, MO: Mosby, 1980.

Hildebrand, Verna. *Guiding Young Children*. 2d ed. New York: Macmillan, 1980.

Lamme, Linda. *Learning to Love Literature: Preschool–Grade Three*. Urbana, IL: National Council of Teachers of English, 1981.

Leeper, Sarah Hammond; Dora Sikes Skipper; and Ralph L. Witherspoon. *Good Schools for Young Children.* 4th ed. New York: Macmillan, 1979.

Lundsteen, Sara, and Norma Tarrow, *Guiding Young Children's Learning,* Chap. 10. New York: McGraw-Hill, 1981.

Seefeldt, Carol. *A Curriculum for Preschools.* 2d ed. Columbus, OH: Merrill, 1980.

Stewig, John W. *Language Arts in Early Childhood.* New York: Holt, Rinehart and Winston, 1982.

Yawkey, Thomas D., et al. *Language Arts and the Young Child.* Itasca, IL: Peacock, 1981.

CHAPTER 5: *Listening*

OVERVIEW

Listening comprehension is a skill critical to every part of the language arts program and to every area of the curriculum. The text emphasizes these relationships in its discussion of effective listening instruction. It goes on to describe activities and materials and evaluative techniques for assessing listening performance.

Listening and oral language are closely related, and the reader is encouraged to look ahead at the oral composition chapter for information and correlated activities. (Listening as a comprehension skill is also closely related to reading as pointed out in Chapter 11.)

KEY VOCABULARY

listening comprehension
literal listening
interpretive listening
critical listening
creative listening
hearing acuity
auditory discrimination

auditory memory
interrelated listening activities
directed listening activities
listening learning center
persuasive language
propaganda techniques

LISTENING COMPREHENSION

Hearing is a physical ability. Listening is more than the physical act of hearing: It demands thought.

Listening is a critical part of learning. To teach it effectively, we must know which environmental factors have positive or negative influences on a child's learning to listen and must recognize poor listening habits that are already established. As an evaluator, then, the teacher must understand the characteristics of effective listening.

There are four levels of listening: literal, interpretive, critical, and creative. *Literal listening* is the easiest for children to learn. Literal skills include being able to identify main ideas, describe details, and recognize cause and effect relationships and sequence. All of these are foundation skills for the more complex listening skills.

One of these more complex skills, *interpretive listening,* involves drawing conclusions, making generalizations, recognizing the objective of speech content, and identifying implied main ideas. Interpretive listening develops as children mature and expand their knowledge of word meanings.

Critical listening is another complex listening skill. With age, children begin to recognize a speaker's bias and propaganda techniques (where they are used); to determine whether a speaker is qualified to talk on a given topic and whether the data being presented are appropriate or accurate; to understand how the information gained meets their own needs; and to differentiate fact from opinion. Obviously these skills cannot be mastered at primary or intermediate levels. But they can be introduced and then reinforced throughout the elementary school years.

The last of the four listening levels is *creative listening.* This too is a complex skill, one that takes years to master. Creative listening requires the imagination to produce new ideas based on what has been said. Good creative listeners must understand cause and effect relationships; can visualize events; can make value judgments about actions within the speech, and are able to solve problems, predict outcomes, elaborate on or modify what was heard, and use what was heard to create new ideas. The skills here are very complex. To teach them successfully demands well-planned lessons, clear goals, and extensive evaluation.

LISTENING AND THE OTHER INSTRUCTIONAL AREAS

All of the language arts require skilled listening. Listening provides the vocabulary, the sentence patterns, and the auditory discrimination that build a foundation for children to speak, read, spell, and compose.

There are two classic listening time studies for elementary-aged children. Wilt determined the percentage of the school day elementary school children are expected to listen; she also discovered that teachers were not aware of the amount of time they expect children to listen.[1] Teachers estimated that children learned by listening on the average of 74.3 minutes a day, but classroom observations showed they listened 158 minutes— more than half the time they were in class. In fact, more time was spent in listening than in any other single classroom activity. The largest percentage of the time the children were "supposed to listen" was the time spent listening to the teacher talk; the next largest, the time in which they listened to questions asked by the teacher and answered by one child. Children were expected to listen less to each other than to the teacher. Obviously, many teachers are unaware of the amount of time they expect pupils to listen. This suggests that teachers need to become more sensitive to the importance of listening as a factor in communication and as a learning experience.

In another classic study, Herman revealed that children spend 75 percent of the time during their social studies classes in listening activities.[2] Over 42 percent of this time occurs during verbal interactions between children and teacher.

Devine, in a review of fifty years of research on listening, found that aspects of listening were measurable and teachable.[3] He stated that teachers should consider the findings of Wilt and others who emphasize the amount of time children spend listening.

Devine also examined the research to see if listening is influenced by intelligence. Although he reports a correlation between scores on listening tests and intelligence tests, he found enough variance to conclude that listening involves something besides intelligence. He also found that little to no attention is given to listening instruction despite the fact that data revealed a scope and sequence for that instruction. Devine derived from the research three ways listening is related to reading:

1. Listening and reading are both concerned with the intake of communication.
2. The mental processes for both listening and reading are similar.
3. Listening and reading are each a complex of related skill components.

1. Miriam E. Wilt, "A Study of Teacher Awareness of Listening as a Factor in Elementary Education," *Journal of Educational Research* 43 (April 1950): 626–636.
2. Wayne L. Herman, "The Use of Language Arts in Social Studies Lessons," *American Education Review Journal* 4 (March 1967): 117–124.
3. T. G. Devine, "Listening: What Do We Know After Fifty Years of Research and Theorizing?" *Journal of Reading* 21 (January 1978): 296–304.

Finally, asking "Is listening, then, simply thinking?" Devine answered, "No, not quite!" and concluded that the relationship of listening and thinking needed more research.

A special relationship exists between listening and reading. Listening and reading are, as Devine points out, *receptive* phases of language; speaking and writing, in contrast, are *expressive* phases. Without certain listening skills—direct association of sound, meaning, and word form—children cannot learn to read. The ability to identify sounds heard at the beginning, middle, or end of a word and to discriminate among sounds is essential to success in analyzing words phonetically. And from the standpoint of interpreting what is read, skillful listening is indispensable.[4] Listening and reading reach equivalence in both word-recognition rate and word-per-minute rate late in the elementary school years. Not until the latter part of the sixth or seventh grade is reading efficient enough to be preferred over the usual act of listening in many learning situations. It seems, then,

4. Thomas Jolly, "Listen My Children and You Shall Read," *Language Arts* 57 (February 1980): 214–217.

that oral instruction is more effective in the elementary school. Generally, advanced pupils prefer learning through reading; slower ones, through listening, particularly when the content is easy. (When content taxes their listening skill, slower students usually prefer reading.) Reading and listening are not identical, but there are many aspects in which they are alike. Knowing these similarities helps us teach efficiently.

As with reading comprehension, a measure of children's listening comprehension is their response to questions about a listening experience. Questions like the following can help children's development of listening comprehension through storytime:

Literal–Main Ideas: For example, without reading the story's title, ask at the end of the story, "What do you think would be a good title for this story?"

Literal–Detail: For example, before reading state, "Listen to see if you remember the things the puppet did in the story."

Literal–Sequence: For example, before reading "The Gingerbread Man" say, "Listen to see who ran after the Gingerbread Man first, second, third. . . ."

Interpretive–Inference: For example, before reading *Where the Wild Things Are* say, "Listen to see if at the end of the story you can think why you know Max's mother loves him."

Interpretive–Sensory Moods: For example, before reading *Peter's Chair* say, "Listen to see if you can tell how Peter felt at first about his younger sister."

Critical: For example, after reading two versions of "Jack in the Beanstalk" ask, "Why do you think these two stories are different?"

Practically all of the other content areas—mathematics, science, social studies, health, and so on—require reading, writing, speaking, and listening skills. Often the ability to follow oral directions in these subjects becomes the key to success in completing an assignment.

TEACHING LISTENING

Some teachers believe that listening develops naturally, that it requires no instruction. They believe that if experiences and situations conducive to listening are provided during the regular instructional program children will automatically learn how to listen. This is probably true to a degree, but research shows that children also need direct instruction in listening.[5]

In the primary grades the emphasis in teaching listening is on the skills of listening and an introduction of the general aspects of listening. First, children must be physically able to receive and process (think about) sound. This is called *hearing acuity*. Second, they must be able to give meaning to the spoken word (*comprehension*). Third, children must be able to discriminate likenesses and differences in sounds (*auditory discrimination*). Fourth, they must learn to remember what they have heard, (*auditory memory*). Fifth, they must learn to be attentive to listening activities. And sixth, children must develop a need or a reason for listening. These last two are usually established at the same time, and are highly correlated. Of course, although the primary teacher introduces and teaches these aspects of listening, they are not mastered and must be continually taught throughout the elementary grades.

In the intermediate grades the listening act becomes an even stronger force in influencing attitudes, furnishing information, and forming opinions. The variety of listening experiences is wide; the need for listening skills, great.

Real purposes and evaluation make listening more directed. Pupils listen more effectively when they have certain things to listen for. For example, before an oral report a pupil can state the issues the report will cover. The teacher could also prepare questions as a check before and after the report. This procedure not only is a good follow-up but also stresses speaking along with listening.

Discussions can be held about practices that encourage better listening. These discussions could center around questions like the following:

Why is listening important?
How can we increase auditory comprehension?
How can we learn and understand more through better listening?
How can a person help others to be good listeners?
How does a person use the information learned through listening?

To emphasize the importance of careful listening, ask students to rephrase an answer to a question or to restate an assignment that you have given orally only once. (They will make considerable progress in hearing the instructions the first time if you establish a businesslike, efficient

5. Sara W. Lundsteen, *Listening: Its Impact at All Levels on Reading and the Other Language Arts*, rev. ed. (Urbana, IL: ERIC/RCS and the National Council of Teachers of English, 1979).

atmosphere. Asking an individual in the class to repeat his or her idea of the assignment not only tests how well the student listened but also checks the effectiveness with which the teacher communicated.) You can use test items based on oral reports, reject "repeat" comments by members of a class, and occasionally administer oral tests. (Oral testing may be time consuming, but it does provide crucial practice in following directions.)

Furthermore, you must be aware of the possible effects of your questions on listening and subsequent thinking. For example, notice the difference between the following two questions, each asked after an oral reading selection: "How many tickets were sold?" and "When did you get the first hint that the ticket sale was going to be a success?"

Other ideas for bringing listening to the attention of children include keeping a record of all listening activities for one day, evaluating class conversation, dramatizing selections presented as listening activities, telling "chain stories," and cooperatively devising rating sheets for listening to radio and television. Some teachers have found the tape recorder an effective tool for developing habits of concentrated attention when presenting certain types of material (for example, number facts or spelling words).

MAJOR INSTRUCTIONAL APPROACHES

Interrelated Activities

A listening curriculum should provide sequential experiences that are integrated within the entire instructional program (social studies, mathematics, science, art, music, physical education, health, and the language arts). The following activities for children can be varied to fit the needs of different age groups, the content of the material, and other activities that are a part of the modern curriculum.

Social Studies Activities

1. List the conversations heard in the lunchroom that show how people work together.
2. Find out the meanings of unknown terms used in a report on pioneer candle making.

Mathematics Activities

1. Write a paragraph about how numbers are used in radio and television commercials.
2. Listen for mathematical terms in everyday conversations.

Science Activities

1. Listen to directions for making a paper pinwheel to test wind direction.
2. Make a daily chart of conversations or sounds heard during the day.

Art and Music Activities

1. Use pastels for drawing scenes of listening at home.
2. Match sounds with musical instruments (from the record *Instruments of the Orchestra*).

Physical Education Activities

1. Listen to recorded directions for performing a folk dance.
2. Take turns giving and listening to directions for playing new games.

Health Activities

1. Listen to oral reports on the care of the body.
2. Watch a film on a child's daily diet and then write a short paragraph about it.

Language Arts Activities

1. Speaking
   a. Listen to poems and repeat them.
   b. Listen to tapes that have good, average, and poor speaking skills recorded on them.
   c. Tape oral reports, and then listen for ways to improve them.
2. Reading
   a. Listen to another child read a short tall tale.
   b. Listen to recordings of several children's stories.
   c. Listen to good and poor oral reading techniques, and then analyze the differences.
3. Writing
   a. Listen and record in writing a dictated paragraph.
   b. Listen and write the sounds heard as you write.
   c. Write a paragraph describing a musical selection.
   d. Listen to part of a story and then compose a new ending.
   e. Listen to a record of sounds of the city and then compose a short story.
   f. Listen to a conversation at the dinner table and then compose a paragraph on "Dinner at Home."

4. Spelling
   a. Listen to spelling tapes and write each word.
   b. Listen to spelling rules and write an example for each.
   c. Pair off and listen to each other spell words orally.

Directed Listening Activities

A formal listening lesson might consist of material to be read to a small group, followed by a set of written questions. The material could be from some other content area—science or social studies, for example. It should be material at a higher level than the group normally reads (there is usually a discrepancy in favor of listening over reading). The outline below summarizes the steps in a DLA:

1. Preparation for listening
   a. Creating interest
   b. Building an experience background
   c. Introducing new concepts and vocabulary
   d. Setting up purposes for listening
2. Listening
   a. Listening to understand the selection read
3. Checking comprehension
   a. Answering questions
   b. Clearing up confusion through discussion
   c. Noting main ideas, details, and inferences
   d. Relating to real experiences
4. Related skills and abilities
   a. Focusing on listening skills needed by the group
5. Extension
   a. Listening to other supplementary materials
   b. Viewing or listening to films
   c. Listening to records
   d. Participating in activities related to the selection (writing opinions, further research, and so on)

Grouping for Instruction The most effective way to teach listening is to put students into homogeneous groups on the basis of their listening ability, and to present appropriate-level lessons to the different groups. At present there is a shortage of instructional material for use with different listening levels within a class, yet it is obvious that children with superior listening ability are especially in need of challenging materials. There is also a need for interesting material that fits the needs of children with lower listening achievement. If homogeneous grouping is to be of value, materials designed to take advantage of the potential of such groups are essential.

One weakness of grouping is the possibility of an unfortunate, invidious attitude being created by the teacher's selection of a group. In an effort to overcome or to minimize that attitude, some teachers allow pupils to choose the group in which they want to participate. This works well when the difficulty of materials is readily apparent. One way to convince students that they should work with the less difficult material is to have them check their ability by explaining one of the more difficult exercises to classmates. Of course, the teacher attempts to guide the choice of appropriate material through conferences and discussion. But it is important that individuals select their own set of exercises.

Planned Lessons Some children may require systematic lessons in listening. These lessons should center on specific skills, and should include the use of various media (films, recordings, radio, tapes, television, and so on). They should also cover various types of listening activities: listening to a speaker; listening to a conversation; listening to several speakers in a discussion session or a panel presentation; and listening to groups report, tell stories, read together, speak, or take part in creative drama. Also important are note taking during listening situations and outlining afterwards. (See LESSON PLAN.)

Listening Learning Center

The learning center approach is an excellent way to individualize part of the listening program, particularly the skills aspects, by allowing for differences in ability, learning rate, mode of learning, and interest.

The teacher goes through several steps in planning a learning center:

1. Identifying the content area
2. Pretesting to diagnose strengths and weaknesses of pupils in the area
3. Determining the skills or learnings to be treated at the center
4. Establishing the sequence of tasks from easiest to most difficult
5. Identifying different kinds of instructional materials to use and devising different ways to present these in tasks of graduated difficulty
6. Posttesting to evaluate each major segment of the center

Teachers can evaluate children's listening through standardized tests, informal checklists, or recorded tapes. Some evaluative activities would be for individuals; others, for pairs or small groups.

LESSON PLAN: *Listening (Main Ideas)*

Performance Objective

Read a short informational paragraph; then have learners state the main idea.

Pretest

Select a short informational paragraph appropriate to the students' listening level. Carefully read it aloud. Then ask, "Can you tell me what this paragraph is about *in one word?*" This sets the task for the learners. Next say, "Can you tell me what this paragraph is about using *less than six words?*" (Six is an arbitrary number to limit learners to the main idea.) Criterion for mastery is your judgment regarding how well students have grasped the main idea.

Teaching Suggestion

Select a well-written informational paragraph. In such a paragraph, the first sentence is often the topic sentence. Number all the details and write them in short phrases on the board; then direct students to study each phrase and make a sentence that expresses the main idea of the details.

Mastery or Posttest Suggestions

1. Ask the pupils to listen to a paragraph for the main idea and, if you want, the supporting details. Have them write down their answers.
2. The suggestions provided for the pretest can be adapted to the posttest.

Reteaching Suggestions

1. The main idea can be taught in narration or story writing. Here you have learners listen to a story and create a good title. If carefully thought out, the title will be the main idea or point of the story.
2. Outlining is a good tool for teaching the main idea of an informational selection. Even as early as second grade, learners can be told, "There are three important ideas in this listening lesson. See if you can hear them as I read to you." Later, you can put the ideas on the board, and discuss how each learner determined what an important idea was.

Table 5.1 lists examples of tasks and materials that could be part of a primary-level listening center focusing on listening awareness. Each task must be preceded and followed by several similar tasks in order to ensure mastery. And, of course, the teacher must evaluate and revise the tasks as they are used by the children.

TABLE 5.1: *Listening Skills and Materials for the Primary Grades*

Skill: Listening Awareness	Tasks	Materials Needed
Sounds heard in nature	Record sounds in the immediate environment	A quiet place outside, paper, pencils
	Identify sounds made by farm and other animals	Commercial record, checklist, the book *Gobble, Growl, Grunt* by Spier, paper, pencils
	Make animal sounds for a partner to guess	Quiet area, set of animal pictures for response by partner

Continued

TABLE 5.1 *(continued)*

Skill: Listening Awareness	Tasks	Materials Needed
	Recognize bird calls	Record of bird calls, time outdoors where birds might be observed and heard, a short list of local birds to check
Sounds made by machines	Detect danger signals	Tape of fire siren and screeching car brakes; police whistle; checklist
	Identify sounds of common machines	Tape of car motor, tractor and phone ringing; list of machines to number order of sounds on the tape (or use paper and pencil to record sounds of machines heard on a television or radio program)
	Describe sounds made by machines	Tape of machine sounds, list of words to choose from for each sound
Sounds made by people	Recognize voices of classmates	Blank tapes to record class members, time to present tape to a small group
	Differentiate ages of speakers	Tapes of speakers of different ages, pictures to paste by each number after listening
	Identify emotional states of speakers	Tapes of people to illustrate sorrow, joy, fear, and other emotions

Some examples of tasks and materials to be used in a listening center focusing on literal, interpretive, and critical listening skills are in Table 5.2. These tasks and materials are appropriate for middle-level students.

Activity Teaching

We can also teach the four levels of listening using different activities. Some of these activities should be taught individually, some in small groups, some in large groups, and some in listening centers. Use the list below to help you develop your own activities.

Literal Listening

Read a short paragraph. Ask the children to write a good title for the paragraph they've just heard.

Read a poem that has one major idea. Ask the children to listen for that idea.

Read an oral description of a character, building, or scene. Ask the children to draw the character, building, or scene.

Read a short story. Ask the children to recall the order of events.

Give each child a picture of items in a familiar story. Ask them to tell their portion of the story in proper sequence.

Give children oral directions to follow in sequence. For example, "From Fernville (on a road map), travel south to Route 77 to Route 12, then east to the intersection with Route 133. What town is located there?"

Give oral arithmetic exercises. For example, "Take 10, add 7, subtract 3, and divide by 2. What are you?"

Using graph paper, ask the children to follow a series of oral directions. The result? A design or a picture.

Interpretive Listening

Read a short paragraph or story, omitting the end. Ask children to make up an ending.

Read selections written from various points of view (informative, persuasive, entertaining). Ask the children to identify the author's purpose for each selection.

Read a paragraph from which a generalization can be made. Then ask the children to write the generalization.

TABLE 5.2: *Listening Skills and Materials for the Intermediate Grades*

Skills	Tasks	Materials Needed
Detail	Find answers to specific questions	Tapes of graded difficulty, questions to answer
Sequence	Establish sequence	Set of sequential pictures to arrange according to a taped story
Directions	Construct according to directions	Arts and crafts materials, set of directions to be read aloud by a student
Rhyme and rhythm	Mark stress in a sonnet	Poetry record, copy of poem to mark stressed and unstressed syllables
Images	Illustrate or describe the "picture" communicated	Lyric poem read aloud by a student
Moods	Contrast poems written in differing moods	Poetry tape, crayons, finger paint, paper
Bias or prejudice	Compare reports of the same incident	Teacher-made tape from two newspaper accounts
Validity of information	Analyze commercials on television	Television, list of "bandwagon" techniques
Fact or opinion	Detect clues for opinion	Television documentary, clues to "opinions"

Critical Listening

Read a series of statements, some fact and some opinion. As each is read, ask children to write *F* for fact and *O* for opinion.

Read about characters or situations, some of which may be real and some of which are definitely make-believe. Have the children indicate the make-believe ones.

After hearing a taped commercial, ask the children to identify the appeal of the speaker's language apart from the message.

Read aloud a human interest article that is slanted in its presentation. Ask the children to discuss the incidents in the story as reported.

Creative Listening

Let children make sounds on cue as a sound story is read aloud (example story: Gerald McBoing-Boing.)

Let children listen to records (for example, *I Went for a Walk in the Forest*, [Young People's Record]), which can be dramatized after close listening.

Read a story and then ask questions that will cause children to make value judgments about the actions of the characters.

Read a story to the children. Ask them to write another episode for the story.

LISTENING AND VIEWING

The mass media—radio, television, movies, records, tapes, magazines, and newspapers—convey identical messages to large numbers of people. Two of these media, television and movies, require listening and viewing. Does this combination of viewing with listening increase listening skills? Data on the use of television to improve listening skills, and the effect of television on those skills, are still controversial.[6] Research shows that children watch an average of 20 to 36 hours a week until eleven years of age; after that viewing time decreases.[7] Two reports present evidence that listening does improve to some degree, but the evidence isn't strong enough to demonstrate a definite improvement in listening ability.[8]

There remains a controversy about the effect of television viewing on achievement in school. In reporting on several studies, Newman concludes that, compared to other important factors such as heredity and family environment, the number of hours of television watched appears to exert only a minor influence on reading achievement. She does point out that there are other concerns about television viewing; the effect of television

6. Susan B. Newman, "Television: Its Effects on Reading Achievement," *The Reading Teacher* 33 (April 1980): 801–805; and Neil Postman, *Teaching as a Conserving Activity* (New York: Delacorte, 1979).
7. Mariann Pezzella Winick and Judith S. Wehrenberg, *Children and TV II: Mediating the Medium* (Washington, DC: Association for Childhood Education International, 1982), p. 8.
8. Devine, "Listening," pp. 296–304; and Lundsteen, *Listening*.

violence on children's behavior, for example. The formidable challenge television presents has also been addressed by Postman, who analyzed today's competing learning systems—the schools and television. The difference between the two, he says, is in the timing of rewards. Television emphasizes immediate gratification; schools put learners on "hold."

Research on listening improvement from watching and listening to films is negligible. Many teachers who use educational films have improved comprehension skills by developing a procedure for using films in the classroom:

1. Previewing the film.
2. Developing background information on film content.
3. Presenting the concepts and vocabulary of the film to students.
4. Letting the students know why (objectives) they are going to see and hear the film.
5. Showing the film.
6. Reviewing, discussing, and evaluating children's learning from the film.
7. Using follow-up activities to reinforce the objectives for viewing the film.

Teachers should stay informed about the content and nature of tapes, records, movies, and television and radio programs that children hear and see, so they can discuss media and programs with them. Occasional sharing of favorites can help improve children's tastes, stimulating them to watch and listen to some of the more constructive fare for their age group. You can encourage independent critical judgment using cooperative activities like these:

Calling attention to programs of quality.

Formulating standards of selection dealing with purpose, consistency, presentation, and effects of particular productions.

Discussing, evaluating, and analyzing programs.

Analyzing radio, television, and film advertising—descriptions, appeal, truth, and slogans.

Reading and writing reviews of radio and television programs and movies.

Comparing film and television productions with the books on which they are based.

Displaying books related to tapes, films, records, radio and television programs.

Preparing an advance list for parents of good children's programs.

Another aspect of television that needs to be taught is recognition of the persuasive language used by advertisers, lecturers, or participants in panels and forums. These *propaganda techniques* fall into seven general categories:

Name Calling: Using derogatory labels (*yellow, reactionary, troublemaker*) to create negative impressions of a person without providing evidence to support those impressions. (Example: Mr. Brown is a scheming trouble-maker.)

Glittering Generalities: Using vague phrases to influence a point of view without providing necessary specifics. (Example: Billy Stone believes in this school; let's show that this school believes in Bill Stone.)

Transfer Technique: Associating a respected organization or symbol with a particular person, project, product, or idea (thus transferring that respect). (Example: Karen Martin, tennis superstar, uses our new improved _____.)

Plain Folks Talk: Relating a person (for example, a politician) or program to the common people in order to gain their support. (Example: Elect Thomas Moore, a man of the people, who has had to work all of his life for his living.)

Testimonial Technique: Using a highly popular or respected person to endorse a product or proposal. (Example: Max Baker, the most outstanding basketball player in the country, says, "I wouldn't be without my _____.)

Bandwagon Technique: Giving the impression that everyone else is participating in a particular activity. (Example: Everybody is buying _____. You buy some too!)

Card Stacking: Telling only one side of a story (ignoring information favorable to the opposing point of view). (Example: This car is the only one to buy because it has power steering, power brakes, AM-FM radio, stereo tape player, air conditioner, radial tires, and plenty of room for seven people to ride in comfort.)

Critical listening and viewing skills are necessary if listeners are going to make intelligent decisions about which political candidate to support or which products to buy or which movie to go to or which television program to watch or whatever. Because children are faced with many of these decisions early in life, instruction in critical listening and viewing must be offered early.

Teachers can foster critical skills by encouraging students to listen and watch with a questioning attitude.

Why is the speaker saying this?

Does the speaker know what he or she is talking about?

Is the speaker likely to be biased? Why?

Is the speaker approaching the subject logically or emotionally? What emotional words are being used?

Is the speaker employing any propaganda techniques? Which ones? How are they used?

Is the speaker implying things that he or she does not directly state? What? What is he or she saying that makes you believe this?

Here is a sample activity that focuses on persuasive language.

ACTIVITY: *Propaganda Hunt*

Objective

To increase critical-listening skills.

Materials

7 shoe boxes (or other boxes)
7 labels

Directions

Label the boxes with the names of the seven propaganda techniques listed in the text. Have students find examples of these techniques in television commercials, make a note of them, and drop their examples in the boxes. Then, evaluate with the class the appropriateness of each example to its category.

SPECIAL INSTRUCTIONAL MATERIALS

There are many materials on the market for teaching listening skills. The materials are adaptable for use in a listening center and for small- or large-group instruction. Listening lessons are also integrated in basal reading texts (in reading lessons) and spelling texts. Any time children read orally and a teacher checks comprehension either orally or in writing, an evaluation of listening skills takes place. Dictated spelling words or dictated writing lessons demand listening skills; tapes, records, television, "talking" machines, and films and sound filmstrips all require children to listen.

The following materials are generally available.

Books and Other Media

A Game a Day Book (Sterling).
Follow the Reader (Old Greenwich, CT: Listening Library). Books are
    available for young and older children. Each title has four copies, a
    cassette tape, and a teacher's guide—ideal for listening centers.
Language for Meaning Series (Boston: Houghton Mifflin).
Listen (a book of activities) (Stevensville, MI: Educational Service).
Listening to the World (Circle Pines, MN: American Guidance Service).
Multisensory Tutorette Audiocard System (Audiotronics).
Yearling Books (New York: Dell).

Filmstrips

How to Listen (Chicago: Society for Visual Education).
Listening, Looking, and Feeling (Los Angeles: Bailey Film Associates).

THE COMPUTER AND LISTENING

The most important use of the computer in teaching listening is for checking comprehension. The teacher gives directions or asks questions orally,
and responses are entered into the computer for storage. This kind of
exercise reviews the accuracy of responses, completeness of responses, and
content knowledge. A checklist for evaluating listening comprehension
would contain these three aspects with precise questions related to the
content of the activity.

EVALUATION

Listening skills should be evaluated by both teacher and children. The
teacher must be a good listener, providing a model for students. And
children must be aware of what makes a good listener, allowing them to
evaluate their own listening ability.

The Teacher

The teacher wears two hats—one as an evaluator of his or her own
methods of teaching listening and one as an evaluator of children's listening skills.

Self-Evaluator Experienced elementary school teachers have been teaching listening for a long time, whether it was called that specifically or not. They have asked themselves:

Do I serve as a model of good listening by being attentive to students and not interrupting them when they speak?

Do I ask thought-provoking questions that require attentive listening and encourage more than a single-word response?

Do I allow time for listeners to process their ideas before asking for a response?

Do I involve children in both conversational and presentational communication situations?

Do I make sure that the purposes of different listening activities are clear to students?

Do I relate listening to all areas of the curriculum?

Do I plan a variety of listening activities that involve children in diverse cognitive tasks?

Do I recognize differences in children's listening abilities and plan activities to meet individual needs?

Evaluator of Children's Skills Early in the school year, the teacher might evaluate the listening skills of the children by asking the following questions:

How well do students follow directions?

How often must I repeat instructions?

Do the children's responses reveal comprehension through listening?

Are the children able to recall information and describe elements accurately after a listening experience?

Good teachers, whether they are beginners or have many years of experience, realize the importance of skillful listening for more effective learning, but find it difficult to check the effectiveness of their efforts. One method for checking that effectiveness is the standardized *Durrell Listening-Reading Series* test, which attempts to answer these kinds of questions:[9]

9. *Durrell Listening-Reading Series* (New York: Harcourt, Brace and World, 1969).

Which children are limited in reading achievement because they don't understand spoken language?

How far above reading level is each child's listening comprehension?

Among the students who are candidates for remedial instruction, which have the highest learning potential?

The primary-level test (for Grades 1–2) is divided into four sections: vocabulary listening, vocabulary reading, sentence listening, and sentence reading. The intermediate-level test (for Grades 3–6) covers vocabulary listening, vocabulary reading, paragraph listening, and paragraph reading.

This test series, or a similar one,[10] gives the teacher a concrete basis for judging how well pupils are developing in this very significant area of the language arts. Still, observation and teacher-made tests are important parts of the evaluation program.

The Children

Children can evaluate their own listening skills by using informal checklists like the one below.

CHECKLIST: *My Listening Skills*

	Yes	No
1. Did I remember to get ready for listening?	———	———
a. Was I seated comfortably where I could see and hear?	———	———
b. Were my eyes focused on the speaker?	———	———
2. Was my mind ready to concentrate on what the speaker had to say?	———	———
a. Was I able to push other thoughts out of my mind for the time being?	———	———
b. Was I ready to think about the topic and call to mind the things I already know about it?	———	———

Continued

---

10. The 1981 *Stanford Achievement Tests* (New York: Harcourt Brace Jovanovich) contain a listening test for primary and intermediate levels. The Brown-Carlsen Listening Comprehension Test, the STEP Listening Test, and others are described in Lundsteen, *Listening*.

3. Was I ready for "takeoff"?
   a. Did I discover in the first few minutes where the speaker was taking me?
   b. Did I discover his central idea so that I could follow it through the speech?
4. Was I able to pick out the ideas that supported the main idea?
   a. Did I take advantage of the speaker's clues (such as *first, next,* etc.) to help organize the ideas in my mind?
   b. Did I use my extra "think" time to summarize and take notes, either mentally or on paper?
5. After the speaker finished and the facts were all in, did I evaluate what had been said?
   a. Did this new knowledge seem to fit with the knowledge I already had?
   b. Did I weigh each idea to see if I agreed with the speaker?

If you marked questions *no,* decide why you could not honestly answer them *yes.*

Source: O. W. Kopp, "The Evaluation of Oral Language Activities: Teaching and Learning," *Elementary English* 44 (February 1967): 117. Reprinted by permission of the National Council of Teachers of English.

SOME INSTRUCTIONAL CONCERNS

One usual problem area in teaching listening is the failure of teachers to use questions that promote higher-level listening comprehension and to gradually lead children to these same questioning techniques.

For *literal comprehension,* use the following types of questions: detail questions (for bits of information), main-idea questions (for central thoughts), vocabulary questions (for word meanings), and sequence questions (for order of events). For *interpretive comprehension,* use evaluative questions (asking for inferences, conclusions, and generalizations). Evaluative questions call for judgment. *Critical comprehension* is called into play by questions that focus on recognizing the speaker's bias and qualifications, the accuracy of information, and propaganda techniques, and understanding implied cause and effect relationships. For *creative comprehension,* use questions that stimulate ideas, that set up problem-solving situations, or that lead students to predict outcomes or elaborate on the material in other ways.

All of these kinds of questions apply to the total instructional program—not just the language arts. Remember, listening is an element of every part of the instructional program.

Students often fail to achieve full listening abilities because they do not recognize the habits that produce negative listening results. For example, some children think a topic is uninteresting before the speaker gets very far into the presentation; or think more about the speaker than the content; or listen only for facts, not ideas; or fake attention and spend listening time day-dreaming. Once students recognize that these kinds of behaviors affect their listening ability, they can begin (with the teacher's help) to correct them.

THOUGHT QUESTIONS

1. Why should listening be considered in terms of the overall instructional program?
2. What are the advantages and disadvantages of each of the major instructional approaches to listening instruction?
3. Should oral-composing activities be related to listening activities? Why or why not?
4. Why is teacher self-evaluation as a listener important?
5. How can the primary-level child be helped to evaluate his or her listening performance?

LEARNER RESPONSE OPTIONS

1. Keep a record of your listening activities for a typical day. Record the time, length, and category (conversation, discussion, lecture, music, news, directions) of listening. Compare your list with those of several of your classmates.
2. Visit a classroom and tape-record some of the oral activities. List the listening skills needed to comprehend the meaning of those activities.
3. Discuss with an elementary school child the kind of listening he or she does. Write a list as the child dictates.
4. Make a chart that shows the characteristics of a good literal or critical listener.
5. Prepare a systematic lesson plan for one of the listening skills in Table 5.1.

6. Develop a lesson plan using a learning center to teach a major listening skill and its related subskills.

REFERENCES AND ADDITIONAL READINGS

Cheyney, Arnold B., and Rosemary Lee Potter. *Video: A Handbook Showing the Use of Television in the Elementary Classroom.* Stevensville, MI: Educational Service, 1980.

Crowell, Doris C., and Kathryn H. Au. "Using a Scale of Questions to Improve Listening Comprehension." *Language Arts* 56 (January 1979): 38–43.

Koile, Earle. *Listening as a Way of Becoming.* Waco, TX: Word Books, 1977.

Lundsteen, Sara W. *Listening: Its Impact at All Levels on Reading and the Other Language Arts.* Rev. Ed. Urbana, IL: ERIC/RCS and the National Council of Teachers of English, 1979.

Potter, Rosemary Lee. *The Positive Use of Commercial Television with Children.* Washington, DC: National Education Association, 1981.

Russell, David H., and Elizabeth F. Russell. *Listening Aids Through the Grades.* 2d ed., edited by Dorothy Grant Hennings. New York: Teachers College, Columbia University, 1979.

CHAPTER 6: Oral Composition

OVERVIEW

This chapter proposes a planned oral language curriculum. First, it suggests instructional strategies in different areas of oral composition. Then, it examines several environmental and cultural differences found in different regions of the United States and relates them to the teaching of oral composition. Finally, it develops evaluation techniques appropriate for both children and teacher. The approach throughout centers on children—their development—and how they learn through talking, thinking, listening, and doing.

KEY VOCABULARY

round-table discussion
panel discussion
buzz groups
brainstorming
role-playing
flannel board
wordless books
anecdotes
movement stories
characterization
improvisation
literary dramatization

choral reading
echoic verse
line-a-child
refrain
antiphonal
unison
readers' theatre
usage
standard
nonstandard
dialectal differences

THE PLANNED CURRICULUM

By the time children come to school they have usually developed a large speaking vocabulary. The purpose of an oral language program, then, is not necessarily to get children to talk but to develop skills they already possess.

Language is personal; children's language is shaped by their environment. Language is social; it conveys information between people. And language is an active experience; it is learned more through use than through study.

Oral language involves both informational (that is, factual) use and fictional use. The factual uses of language include conversation, discussion, description, oral reporting, and conducting meetings and interviews. The fictional uses of language include storytelling and dramatization. Through experiences with both of these types of language, children become adept speakers.

To effectively teach spoken language, teachers must use a variety of methods and materials and relate speaking to the other language arts and other areas of the curriculum. But even more important, they must recognize that oral language demands systematic study. Yes, it's true students talk all through the school day, but if they are going to express themselves at their optimum level, oral experiences must be as well developed and organized as spelling or any other learning experience.

What kinds of elements do we include in a well-developed, well-organized oral language curriculum? Klein identifies three sets of factors that bear on communication situations:[1]

The Speaker: His or her personal experiences, language abilities, cognitive abilities, and attitudes.
The Kinds and Uses of Talk: Proposing, describing, explaining, inquiring, and exploring.
The Circumstances: Setting, subject, audience, and purpose.

To encourage the growth of each child's communication skills, we must develop oral expression exercises that incorporate these factors.

Planned instruction very definitely affects children's oral communication skills. In a review of research data, Mead states that children have very

1. Marvin L. Klein, *Talk in the Language Arts Classroom* (Urbana, IL: National Council of Teachers of English, 1977). Also see his "Designing a Talk Environment for the Classroom," *Language Arts* 56 (September 1979): 647–656.

few opportunities to listen to and practice practical types of oral language.[2] Stewart reinforces Mead's findings, claiming that the emphasis of teaching should change from form of speech to function.[3] To do this, she recommends the indirect method of oral language teaching through games, not labeling linguistic forms. In a related study about teaching oral language, Heath reports that teachers' questioning changes as group size changes.[4] When talking to a whole group, they ask questions that require brief answers; when talking to a small group, they ask questions that demand longer and more creative answers. Grambell agrees that group size changes the amount of oral language used, and goes on to report that it also changes speech style, from formal to informal depending on the setting (intimate, casual, or consultative).[5]

ORAL EXPERIENCES

The major oral language experiences include conversation; discussion; description, comparison, and evaluation; reporting; conducting meetings and interviews; storytelling; and creative drama. The experiences vary in complexity according to the abilities, interests, and motivation of both children and teacher. As a teacher you will need to plan for each of the experiences and evaluate the abilities of your students.

Conversation

Conversation is informal talk on a topic of common interest. It is a social activity.

During the school day, children should be encouraged to talk freely to one another as they play and work together in planning, constructing, and evaluating. Teachers must provide frequent opportunities for conversation so that every child can use the language skills necessary to develop the ability to present ideas in logical order, to fit the conversation to the

2. Nancy A. Mead, "Developing Oral Communication Skills: Implications of Theory and Research for Instruction and Training" (Paper delivered at the National Basic Skills Orientation Conference, Arlington, VA, September 1980).
3. Lea P. Stewart, "Language in the Classroom" (Paper delivered at the annual meeting of the International Communication Association, Acapulco, Mexico, May 1980).
4. Shirley Brice Heath, "Teacher Talk: Language in the Classroom," *Language in Education: Theory and Practice*, no. 9 (1976).
5. Trevor J. Grambell, "Talk Contexts and Speech Styles: Planning for Oral Languaging" (Paper presented at the annual meeting of the Canadian Council of Teachers of English, Halifax, Canada, August 1980).

occasion, and to change the topic of conversation at the appropriate time. Conversational skills should be taught and developed throughout the elementary school years.

Stimuli Often pupils need help starting a conversation. Help them by suggesting topics like the following:

Experiences: A garden, a stamp collection, building model airplanes, caring for and raising animals, trips, vacations, or field trips.

Media: A story, a picture, a movie, a television or radio program, newspaper and magazine articles, a poem, recordings, drawings, or tapes.

Objects: Apples, skates, gloves, toys, heirlooms, household products, a rock, or something they found.

School Situations: An assembly, a classroom talk, or conversations between teacher and pupil or pupil and pupil.

Procedures Several approaches have proved effective in teaching conversational skills. One method is to divide the class into interest groups and let each group converse on topics of special interest. A second approach is to randomly divide the class into groups (five or six members in each group), and let the conversation center on some theme or adventure that interests the entire class. A more direct way is for the teacher to select four or five topics and name students to each group. (A modification of this approach is to let students select their group and possibly the direction the conversation will take.) Another procedure is to divide the whole class into four or five groups and let two children in each group have a conversation while the others listen. Or, have five or six children hold a conversation while the rest of the class listens. All of these methods provide a far greater opportunity for each child to talk than if the entire class listens to two speakers having a conversation. Also, by dividing the class into small groups, you are helping the shy child who may not be ready to talk in front of the entire class.

Some teachers find a talk center useful. A center provides an area where small groups of children can sit and converse. Here they can share objects brought from home or discuss objects that the teacher has placed there in the "mystery" bag.

During conversations and sharing time, use questioning to encourage oral expression. For example, ask these kinds of questions:

Main Idea: Questions that ask the child to identify the central theme of an oral expression. (How did you become interested in coin collecting?)

Detail: Questions that ask for bits of information. (Where did you find this coin?)

Vocabulary: Questions that ask for the meaning of words used. (Why is that called a *rare* coin? What do you mean by *condition* of the coin? What is an *uncirculated coin*?)

Sequence: Questions that require knowledge of events in their order of occurrence. (Which were the first coins in your collection? Which are the newest?)

Inference: Questions that ask for information that is implied. (What problems might you have in filling your collection?)

Evaluation: Questions that ask for judgments about the item discussed. (What is the most unusual coin you have? What makes coin collecting fun?)

Creative: Questions that ask the child to create new ideas based on ideas presented. (If you could keep only three of your coins, which ones would you choose? Why?)

Other beginnings for growth-potential questions include "What could you tell other children about . . . ?" or "How can you tell . . . ?" or "How are . . . related?" or "How similar or different are . . . ?" or "What are some reasons for . . . ?" or "What could have caused . . . ?" or "What might happen if . . . ?" or "How would you summarize . . . ?"

Evaluation Once children have experience with conversations, they have a basis for developing the criteria of good conversations. The list of criteria in Chart 6.1 may help them develop their criteria.

CHART 6.1: *Conversation Guide*

1. Talk in a soft voice.
2. Help others take part. Do not talk all the time. One way to involve others is to ask questions ("I like that television show, too, Mike. What about you Lucy?"). Another way to keep a conversation lively is with remarks ("Yes, I know just how you felt").
3. Say "Excuse me" or "Pardon me" when you interrupt someone.
4. Support your opinions with reasons or examples.
5. Listen. Stick to the general theme. Don't introduce brand-new topics.
6. React politely to disagreement. "I hate it" is a poor way to respond to "That television show is really good."
7. When you haven't heard what someone has said, say so politely at the proper time and then ask the person to repeat it.

Discussion

Discussion is more formal than conversation. In conversation, people can move freely from one topic or idea to another; in discussion, we basically remain with the question at hand. Time creates another difference. A conversation can be picked up at all different times; a discussion should continue until its purpose has been met.

Experiences Many opportunities for discussion are inherent in classroom activities (how to organize the pet show, what should the class do for the book fair, what should be done about pupils who are racing across lawns in the neighborhood) and subject matter (history, geography, science). In fact the suggestions found in language textbooks for discussion topics are usually a poor second to actual classroom situations. Use them primarily for practice ideas when the main purpose of the lesson is to focus on specific discussion skills.

Stimuli Three major stimuli for discussion are current events, dilemmas or problems, and children's literature. News time is an excellent time to involve all members of the class at all levels of the elementary school. Radio and television enable the below-average reader to contribute accurate and important information to these discussions. Pictures in magazines and newspapers also help the poorer reader gain insight into background material on a topic. Usually news time is held once a week, unless important events occur more often. Some teachers use bulletin boards to display relevant materials that the children bring to class. A weekly newspaper for children is another basis for discussion of a topic or a few related news items. As criteria are developed for news discussion, the class members can focus on how to talk about news, what is reportable news, why current affairs should be discussed, and how to organize news reporting.

Dilemmas or problems are almost sure-fire discussion material, guaranteed to encourage original thinking. Try one of the following:

What would you do *if*

your pet followed you to school?
you lost your homework on the way to school?
you were lost in a store and couldn't find your mother?
you broke a neighbor's window during a ball game?
you saw a little boy crying with a cut finger?
your cat ran away from home?
you found an injured young bird?
you overslept past school time?
you punctured the tire of your bicycle on the way to school?
you lost the letter you were asked to mail?

Children's literature is a third stimulus for discussion. There are several books that lend themselves well to this type of experience: *Up a Road Slowly* and *Across Five Aprils* by Irene Hunt, *Onion John* by Joseph Krumgold, and *I'll Get There, But It Had Better Be Worth the Trip* by John Donavan.

Possien describes five different types of discussion experiences:

1. A *round-table discussion* involves a small group of from three to eight people, including a moderator. Its purpose may be simply to share ideas

or to deal with a particular problem in an informal manner. The moderator must guide the group so as to keep the discussion moving and on the topic. He or she helps the group summarize and evaluate results. The moderator, the members of the discussion group, and the audience, if there is one, need to have clear ideas of their responsibilities.

   The entire class may be divided into small groups and each group may simultaneously engage in round-table discussion, or one group may participate while the rest of the class listens as an audience. This is the best procedure to use until the class is thoroughly familiar with round-table discussion.

2. The *panel discussion* is similar to the round-table discussion, but the procedure is somewhat more formal and is more audience-oriented. An audience is always present for the panel discussion and is usually allowed to ask questions and participate when the discussion between the panel members is over. Panel members have a responsibility to be more than adequately prepared, for each is cast in the role of an authority on the subject.

3. *Buzz groups* constitute another type of discussion group and may be devised by dividing the class into a number of smaller subgroups of five and six members. A specific problem is given for consideration, and a limited amount of time is set for each group to arrive at an answer or a response.

   These groups may get out of hand and result in little more than wasted time unless clearly understood ground rules are laid in advance. The children need to keep their purpose firmly in mind and proceed in accomplishing their purpose with as little noise and confusion as possible.

4. *Brainstorming* is a way of getting a great many ideas from a group on a particular problem and is regarded as being a good means of releasing group creativity. This technique is based on four simple rules which must be followed for good results:
   a. No idea may be criticized, evaluated, or rejected during the brainstorming.
   b. All ideas are acceptable regardless of how improbable they may seem.
   c. Emphasis is placed on quantity of suggestion.
   d. Group members may add to, combine, or improve the ideas of others.

5. *Role-playing* is a form of creative dramatics which is very effective in encouraging children to think and to understand better another person's problem or point of view. Role-playing helps children to explore and develop different ways of solving problems. It is valuable in solving problems concerning human relationships and is very effective in helping children to develop a sense of involvement in problems of history.[6]

6. Wilma M. Possien, *They All Need to Talk: Oral Communication in the Language Arts Program* © 1969, pp. 62–64. Reprinted by permission of Prentice-Hall, Inc., Englewood Cliffs, N.J.

Instructional Procedures The key to a good discussion is preparation. To make a worthwhile contribution, children must have accurate information about the subject, be able to back up statements with facts, and give sensible reasons for their opinions. Through firsthand experience, reading and listening, asking questions, and sharing with others, pupils come to know about areas that can be intelligently discussed.

Several approaches are effective in teaching discussion techniques. One procedure is to divide the class into a number of small discussion groups on the basis of topics. Another possible arrangement is to have five or six students in turn demonstrate a discussion of a problem or issue before the other members of the class.

The teacher should not monopolize classroom discussions but may have to assume some direct leadership, especially with primary-level pupils or with groups of pupils who have had little experience in discussion. Use lead-in questions to stimulate discussion: "What do you think about that?" "Who has another idea?" "What else might be true?" "Can someone think of another explanation?" See that all pupils have an opportunity to participate. Help children to contribute according to their own special interests and abilities. And be sure the discussion comes to a satisfactory conclusion.

Sometimes during classroom discussions controversial topics arise. At first, young children generally do not express their own opinions on most topics. Their reactions are those of their families or other out-of-school associations. One procedure for teaching children to begin to think on their own is to encourage them to participate in discussion of a controversial topic.

When a controversial topic arises, write it on the board, get as many children as possible to express their viewpoint on the topic, and list each point of view on the board. Give all students an opportunity to select the point of view they agree with, and list their names under their selection on the board. Have one child copy all of the board information. Take this information and develop a small group on each side of the issue. Structure a learning center activity to teach each group of children how to present its side of the issue and how to react to the points of the other sides. Remember, a good lesson does not mean that all children agree or accept one idea; an effective lesson is one where children are thinking and expressing their thinking without feeling threatened, belittled, or wrong. These beginning steps of understanding controversial issues will have a bearing on students' lifelong approaches to differences of opinion.[7]

7. A children's book that may help spark a discussion is Clyde Ribert Bulla, *Last Look* (New York: Crowell, 1980).

Evaluation Use the list of discussion skills in Chart 6.2 to help students develop their own criteria for evaluating a good discussion. For students who need more practice with the agreed-upon criteria, use a tape recorder—play back a discussion or play an earlier discussion with a more recent one—to dramatize needed improvements.

CHART 6.2: *Discussion Guide*

1. Choose a topic and develop your own ideas about it.
2. Keep to the topic being discussed.
3. Listen closely to each speaker.
4. Participate in questions and answers during the discussion.
5. Help decide which ideas are the most useful.
6. Back up opinions with facts or valid reasons.
7. Ask for necessary explanations.
8. Contribute comments that will carry the thinking forward to a decision.
9. Draw shy members into the discussion.

Description, Comparison and Evaluation

An excellent way to promote and develop children's abilities to describe, compare, and evaluate is through the use of literature. For one activity, we've used two books as examples: *Sam* by Ann Herbert Scott and *Play with Me* by Marie Hall Ets.

Sam: Sam wants to play as all children do, but his family does not have time to play with him. His mother is cooking; his brother, studying; his sister, playing with paper dolls; his father, working. As Sam wanders from person to person, he is told to "go outside and play" or "go inside and play" or to never touch this or that again. Finally, he is so frustrated that he begins to cry. It is then that his family realizes Sam's problem and gives him the "job" of making a tart in the kitchen—a job that is just right for him.

Play with Me: The little girl in the story goes to the meadow to play. She asks various animals and insects to play with her, but they run away from her. Finally, she sits down at the pond and watches a bug. As she sits there quietly, the animals and insects return one by one and stay close to her. A fawn even comes up and licks her cheek. All of them are "playing" with her at the end of the story.

Because children's attention spans are short, it is best to read each story at a separate session and to discuss each separately. In another session, both books can be discussed in terms of describing, comparing, and evaluating.

ACTIVITY CARD

Session 1

Read *Sam* to the children. At the end of the story, ask the following questions:

1. Have you ever felt like Sam does in this story?
2. What was Sam's problem?
3. Did you ever have trouble getting your family to play with you? How did you solve your problem?
4. If you were Sam, would you have cried? Why or why not?
5. What else could Sam have done besides crying?

Session 2

Read *Play with Me* to the children. Then ask the following questions:

1. Why didn't the animals and insects play with the little girl at first?
2. Why did they finally return to her?
3. Have you ever tried to get an animal or insect to play with you? What happened?
4. Could this story really have happened? Why or why not?

Description Think back to the story *Sam*. If you had Sam for a friend and you wanted to tell your mother about him, what would you say? What does Sam look like? Who are the members of his family? How do they treat him? Judging from the pictures in the book, where does he live? In the story *Play with Me*, where does the little girl live? If she were your friend and you wanted to tell your mother about her, what would you say? What does she look like? What does she like to do? Can you tell your mother about her family? Why or why not?

Comparison What is Sam's problem? What is the little girl's problem? Are the two problems almost alike? How? What did Sam mean when he said he wanted someone to play with him? What did the little girl mean when she said that all of them (the animals) were playing with her? Do

Sam and the little girl mean the same thing when they say "play with me"? Why or why not?

Evaluation Which story did you like better? Why? (If a child says "because it's good," then ask, "What makes this story better than the other?") If you were going to give your friend a book for a birthday present, which one of these books would you choose? (Question as above.) In which book do you feel you belong? Do you feel more like Sam or the little girl when you say "play with me"?

Poetry lends itself to similar activity. Let children describe what a poem says, how it makes them feel, and what kind of picture it presents. Pairs of poems by different poets but on similar topics (for example, "April" by William Watson and "April" by Ted Robinson) are excellent for comparisons. Here, evaluation—the ability to express orally why they liked or did not like a poem—is probably the most important aspect.

Reports

In every classroom there are many opportunities for sharing information, and quite often this sharing is done through oral reports. It is not necessary to assign reports on topics unrelated to classroom work (for example, topics from a list in a language text) in order to give the necessary practice in reporting; instead, take advantage of natural classroom situations where reporting is indicated.

Describing a recent event.

Discussing new ideas discovered while reading, listening to the radio, or watching television.

Explaining procedures for constructing an object for a school or personal project.

Giving directions for games or exercises.

With guidance from the teacher during these situations, pupils learn a variety of ways of reporting. Sharing should have a definite purpose that is clearly understood by the child who is giving the report. The purpose helps determine the form the report will take.

A sequence of five steps is involved in preparing an oral report: (1) using reference sources, (2) taking notes, (3) preparing bibliographies, (4) organizing ideas, and (5) making an outline.

CHART 6.3: *Reporting Guide*

1. Choose a subject that interests you and those who will hear the report.
2. Gather information from various sources.
3. Take notes from your reading, putting them into your own words.
4. Select only the ideas essential to the subject. Arrange the ideas in logical sequence.
5. Prepare an outline, noting the main and supporting topics.
6. Begin the report with an interesting sentence. Look for varied ways to present material. Use examples, pictures, objects, and diagrams to make your points clear. Plan an interesting conclusion.
7. Use acceptable sentence patterns and vocabulary, and speak in a clear conversational tone.

An oral report should have a good beginning and a good ending, and must be developed in order to hold the attention of the audience. Examples should add interest and clarify meanings. Some of the material might be presented on a chart or graph. Pictures or realia can be part of a report. Unusual or pertinent vocabulary can be written on the board or presented on a chart. Group reports may take the form of a panel or dramatic presentation.

Scheduling oral reports is important. Nothing is more boring than listening to one presentation after another, all following a similar pattern. Let children give reports as the need arises. At some time, but not on the same day (or on the same topic) give every child a chance to participate.

Have pupils develop criteria to check against as they prepare oral reports. The performance objectives in Chart 6.3 can help you guide the children in developing their own criteria.

Effective instruction in report making demands four factors. The teacher must set a good example; good audience-speaker relationships must be maintained; planning must occur with the child before the performance; and opportunities must be provided for improving performance through diagnosis and evaluation of individual needs.

Conducting Meetings

There are many club meetings in the intermediate school years. During meetings, pupils find it useful to have a chart of parliamentary procedures on the wall for quick reference. The following information will help you develop this type of chart.

When motions are in order, members who want to speak stand and speak only when the chairperson calls on them. A member can call the group to vote on an idea by saying, "I move that . . . ." In order to be voted on, a motion must be seconded. Then the chairperson restates the motion and calls for discussion. Finally, he or she calls for a vote on the motion and announces the result. The chairperson plans the agenda and sees to it that the order of business is followed and that motions are made properly. The secretary is responsible for notices of meetings and records (lists of committee members, notes about unfinished business). Most important, the secretary keeps the minutes of what is done at the meetings, reporting date, place, time, and kind of meeting; the name of the person presiding; and all motions, whether carried or not.

CHART 6.4: *Parliamentary Guide*

1. Call the meeting to order.
2. Ask the secretary to read the minutes of the previous meeting.
3. Ask the members for any corrections or additions to the minutes. If there are no corrections or additions, say, "The minutes are accepted as read."
4. Call for and discuss reports from any committees.
5. Call for unfinished business. Ask for a motion, discussion, and vote.
6. Call for new business. Ask for a motion, discussion, and vote.
7. Turn the meeting over to the person in charge of the program for that meeting.
8. After the program, thank the persons concerned and ask for a motion to adjourn.
9. Call for a vote on the motion and tell the group that the meeting stands adjourned.

Conducting Interviews

Interviews can be conducted by individual or small groups of children. To be successful, an interview must be planned. Practice interview techniques in the classroom, with children role-playing as interviewer and interviewee.

Interview questions should be designed to bring out the information sought. Remind students to avoid extremely personal or embarrassing questions and to listen carefully and take notes as questions are answered.

The following bulletin board display suggests an instructional strategy as well as several interviewing activities.

CHECKLIST: *Interviews*

1. Have you heard or read interviews reported by
   a. television?
   b. radio?
   c. newspapers?
   d. magazines?
2. What do you think are some reasons for interviews?

Guidelines for Interviews

1. Make an appointment at the time most convenient for the person being interviewed.
2. Be polite.
3. Plan questions carefully and state them clearly.
4. Take notes on the answers.
5. Avoid taking too much of the person's time.
6. Thank the person for his or her kindness in granting the interview.

Interview

1. a visiting speaker to get information for the school paper.
2. a classmate who has received some unusual honor.
3. a specialist to get information to bring back to class.
4. the principal or a teacher in the school.
5. the person in the classroom or building you know least about.

Storytelling

Storytelling is an art, but one that can be learned by persistent effort. Teachers and children who master this art will find the rewards are well worth that effort.

Teacher The teacher should provide the children with a good model in use of voice, pacing, choice and pronunciation of words, and ways of beginning and ending. Teacher storytelling acquaints the children with literature and gives them good listening experiences.

What stories should you choose? Select stories that appeal to you—not just "classics" or those that happen to be recommended—or that meet your storytelling objectives. Remember, storytelling is an instructional activity. It can be used to increase knowledge, to impart values, to develop understanding of the spoken word, to develop a sense of humor, to broaden reading interests, to develop appreciation of literary forms as well as to entertain. Folk tales are especially good for telling, for they were told and told and told again long before they were ever captured in print. Myths, stories from the Bible, stories by Andersen and Kipling, even episodes from longer books can be adapted for telling. If you enjoy the telling, your audience will usually enjoy the listening.

Don't try to memorize every word, but keep in mind the original vocabulary and phraseology. As a general rule, read picture stories from the actual book, to share the illustrations as well as the story. Stories that depend on the exact wording of the author should also be read rather than told. But even if you plan to read a story, memorize parts here and there so that you can maintain eye contact with listeners.

After choosing a story with action, a closely knit plot, and lots of dialogue (and perhaps humor), think about the story's characters (there should be no more than four) and ways of developing them so that they come to life. Then begin to practice, following the guidelines below.

CHECKLIST: *Preparing to Tell a Story*

1. Read the story carefully.
2. Reread the story to get the incidents clearly in mind.
3. Reread to get a clear picture of details.
4. Use the tape recorder to practice telling the story. Use cue cards—opening lines, main points of the story, the climax, closing lines—if they help you.
5. Memorize essential parts that provide atmosphere or imagery ("Who's that tripping over my bridge?" roared the troll; or "In the high and far-off times, O best beloved . . . .").
6. Retape your story. Concentrate on improving pitch, range, and voice. Make sure you are enunciating clearly and that you are making good use of pauses.
7. Continue to practice telling the story. Use gestures sparingly; don't be overdramatic.

A flannel board is a simple and inexpensive tool to attract the children's attention and stimulate interest. Cutouts give concrete meaning to oral vocabulary and provide a picture of events large enough for the whole class to see.

Storytelling can also be enriched with props and characterization. Morrow, in an article filled with creative ideas, makes several suggestions:[8]

8. Lesley Morrow, "Exciting Children About Literature Through Creative Storytelling Techniques," *Language Arts* 56 (March 1979): 258–262.

> **CHECKLIST:** *Using a Flannel Board in Storytelling*
>
> 1. Memorize the story or write a brief outline.
> 2. Number each cutout in order of use.
> 3. Make a large flannel board—18 by 36 inches—so that several cutouts can be placed on the board at one time.
> 4. After a phase of the story has been told, remove all the cutouts and start on the next phase.
> 5. Use variety in speed, volume, and pitch of voice.
> 6. Remember to make objects as well as characters.
> 7. If a story has only one or two scenes, the background objects can be placed on the board at the beginning of the story.
> 8. Store cutouts in a labeled box or file for convenient use (yours and the children's).

Prop Stories: The storyteller uses a collection of materials representing characters and objects in the story.

Puppet Stories: Puppets are used as characters for the story being told.

Chalk Talks: The story is drawn on a chalkboard as it is told.

Photograph Stories: Photographs of people or objects, used to represent characters or things in the story, are shown as the story is told.

Sound Stories: The children and/or the storyteller provide sound effects as the story is told.

Music Stories: The storyteller chooses appropriate music for parts of or the whole story, and plays a tape of it as the story is told.

Cut Stories and Origami Stories: For both, paper is cut as the story is told. With cut stories, the characters are cut out of paper (usually the characters have already been drawn and colored) as each character is introduced in the story. Origami stories use a folded-paper technique; the characters or objects take form as the folded paper is cut.

Children Storytelling is one literary activity that does not depend on reading ability. Through the medium, all children can improve their speech patterns, their poise in speaking, and their ability to organize events in proper sequence.

Children soon learn the characteristics of a good "telling" story: an interesting plot (perhaps episodic, particularly for young children), characters so real that we really care what happens to them, and a mood that makes the story "live."

Let children tell the stories they enjoy and want to tell—not those assigned from a textbook or other sources. To keep the audience attentive, help them find a story that few or no other class members know. And don't interrupt during the telling of the story, no matter what mistakes the storyteller makes. Storytelling is primarily for enjoyment, and no other objectives of language instruction should infringe on this enjoyment.

Teaching Strategies Don't allow students to practice errors; the time for teacher help is in the preparation. Make sure pupils select a good beginning, know the sequence of details, use words that fit the meaning, and pronounce words correctly. These preventive procedures leave students with knowledge to apply in judging other performances.

After the initial individual approach, divide the class into groups of four or five children. Have each child, in turn, tell a story to his or her group. (At times, of course, students will have an opportunity to tell a story to the entire class.) In the small groups, each child should check his or her progress (with the help of other members of the group) at incorporating the suggestions made by the teacher and other class members.

Class discussion about the characteristics of good storytelling should bring out suggestions for improvement. Listening to good storytellers, either in person or on records, can help children recognize the qualities that attract listeners. The tape recorder can be used to good advantage here. By listening to their own performance, children can see where they need improvement. Specific "reminders" might include (1) the who, what, when, where, and why questions; (2) planning good beginning and closing sentences; (3) using interesting words; (4) having the characters exchange dialogue; (5) telling the events in order; and (6) keeping the outcome in doubt until the end of the story.

For children who are reluctant to tell stories, wordless (textless) books with pictures are a good way to elicit oral expression. Many children who are shy or who need additional experience talking have no hesitation telling aloud the story from these kinds of books. For younger children, try:

Mitsumasa Anno, *Topsy-Turvies* (Cleveland: Collins World, 1978).
Raymond Briggs, *The Snowman* (New York: Random House, 1978).
Diane DeGroat, *Alligator's Toothache* (New York: Crown, 1977).
For older children, try:
John S. Goodall, *The Surprise Picnic* (New York: Atheneum, 1977).
Fernando Krahn, *A Funny Friend from Heaven* (Philadelphia: Lippincott, 1977).
Lund K. Ward, *The Silver Pony: A Story in Pictures* (Boston: Houghton Mifflin, 1973).

Anecdotes or Personal Experiences In addition to literature stories, children quite often have amusing or interesting experiences to recount in anecdote form. An *anecdote* is a brief story about an interesting incident. Some children are able to tell their experiences clearly and concisely, placing events in the proper order, building up to the climax, and then quickly bringing the story to an end. Others clutter up the story with irrelevant details, relate events out of sequence, and prolong the narrative unnecessarily. The ability to tell a personal experience or a funny story in an interesting manner is a valuable asset. Children are naturally fascinated by this kind of language activity and should be given the opportunity to practice and improve their performance.

Children also need help in deciding which personal experiences are suitable for relating to the class. Good anecdotes can be developed from all kinds of sources. Try some of these: an incident observed on the way to school; something that happened "when I was very small"; an incident "when Mother was a little girl"; an unusual or amusing episode from the life of a famous person; or what happened during first attempts to do something, ("The first time I tried ice skating" or "The first pie I baked by myself").

In telling anecdotes or personal experiences, children must first be thoroughly familiar with all the details of the event, and must be able to recall them in proper sequence so that listeners are prepared for the climax. Once the climax is reached, the story should end quickly. Show students that unnecessary details can obscure the point and that drawing out the story makes it dull and boring. Encourage simple, spontaneous expression, and gestures, tone of voice, and facial expressions to make the event more interesting to listeners.

Drama

Creativity, action, and interpretation are all part of drama experience in the elementary school. We can list seven general values of dramatization: cooperating in a group and working together for a common purpose; learning to appreciate character portrayal and action in literature and increasing the pleasure in them by sharing them with others; encouraging leadership and organizational abilities; providing an outlet for emotions; developing creative imagination; fostering self-reliance in speaking; and promoting variation in voice quality and pitch and encouraging accurate enunciation and pronunciation.

In order for children to express themselves at their optimum level, drama experiences must not be casual events. They should be as well organized as any other language arts experience.

Drama activities must be planned sequentially, designed for the appropriate level, and based on past learnings. You could use a sequence like the following:

Primary Level

1. Simple pantomimes and dramatic play.
2. Dramatizing activities, favorite nursery rhymes, poems, songs and stories.
3. Using stick puppets, hand puppets, and flannel board figures.
4. Identifying self with characters in stories.
5. Preparing a class "radio" or "television" program.

Intermediate Level

1. Sharing the feelings and experiences of characters in a story.
2. Dramatizing stories and events.
3. Presenting short plays or scenes from longer plays.
4. Producing puppet shows.
5. Presenting original skits, dialogues, or monologues.

Evaluation is not a real concern with younger children. Drama here should be a game—one that encourages thought and imagination. With older pupils, make positive suggestions and ask questions (What did you enjoy most about this? Why? Whose acting could have been clearer? Who has a suggestion as to how we might put more spirit into the dramatization?). For all, it is the *drama process*—not the product—that is most important.

Even though a teacher plans thoroughly, some children may not want to perform before an audience. Don't force anyone to participate. Instead, let the fun of performing influence shy children to join in. Once children have performed successfully before the class, they will want to take part again.

Younger children dramatize for their own satisfaction; older students usually have to work before others to help them drop their self-consciousness. An audience of classmates works fine here.

The drama process can be categorized in six segments: sense awareness, movement, characterization, improvisation, role-playing, and literary dramatization.

Sense Awareness Close observation is a part of putting the senses into "high gear." For example, tell the pupils: "Let's look closely at the clouds. Are they moving? Which way are the clouds moving? Are they moving fast or slowly? What makes them move? Do they look different? I see some that look like white sheep. What do the clouds look like to you?" Sensitivity to sound, smell, taste, and touch needs sharpening too.

Movement Communication takes place through body action. In fact, an understanding of body action was acquired long before words became a means of communication.

Movement stories (or poems) delight children, and they are very easy for both teachers and children to create. Here is an example:

> Jim tried to move his body in every way possible. He began with three giant steps ———. He tried walking slowly ——— and then quickly ———. "I can roll," he said ———. And Jim could crawl ——— and slide ——— and leap ——— and spin ———.

The dashes show when the children should move.

Characterization *Characterization* is "being" an animal or another person. This form of drama demands observation and discussion of the physical attributes and feelings of animals or people. Let children reenact everyday events to promote their understanding of other people. One child can be the postal worker delivering the mail or the person receiving it; another might be a safety patrol helping children cross the street or the person who carries out groceries at the supermarket.

Improvisation In this form of drama, children act without a script. For example, children could use dialogue as they pretend to be (in order) the three Billy Goats Gruff crossing the bridge. You could set up a short scene in advance: "You three boys have stumbled on a valuable treasure, but then you hear some men's voices. They are coming toward you!"

Social studies is rich in opportunities for improvisation: "Pretend you are an astronaut setting foot for the first time on a new planet," or "Act out your favorite part of the Lewis and Clark expedition."

Role-Playing Useful in many situations, role-playing is especially helpful in problem situations. An argument on the playground can be reenacted in the classroom with participants playing themselves. Then the roles can be reversed so that each child gets an idea of what the others thought and felt. Other problems, both inside and outside the classroom, can be dramatized to help children understand other points of view or to find solutions.

Literary Dramatization   One of the most advanced drama experiences for children is dramatizing parts of stories, books, or poems. Most teachers find it helpful to begin with short vignettes.

There are several children's books suitable for dramatization:

Byrd Baylor, *The Way to Start a Day* (New York: Scribner's, 1978).
John Burningham, *Mr. Grumpy's Outing* (Holt, Rinehart and Winston, 1974).
Nancy DeRoin, *Jataka Tales* (Boston: Houghton Mifflin, 1975).
Dennis Lee, *Nicholas Knock and Other People* (Boston: Houghton Mifflin, 1977).
Tom McGowen, *The Spirit of the Wild* (Boston: Little, Brown, 1976).
Jack Prelutzky, *Nightmares: Poems to Trouble Your Sleep* (New York: Greenwillow, 1976).
Robyn Supraner, *Giggly-Wiggly, Snickety-Snick* (New York: Parents Magazine Press, 1978).
Jane Yolen, *The Mermaid's Three Wisdoms* (Cleveland: Collins, William and World, 1978).

Dramatization may be varied with puppets or shadow plays. Puppets can be simple hand puppets that the children have made or more complicated marionettes. Simple puppets—the hand puppet (head moves with the index finger; arms, with the third finger and thumb) or the rod puppet (controlled by one or more rigid rods to which the puppet is attached)—work best for most situations, but marionettes are often enjoyed by upper-level pupils. Puppets can be made from a variety of materials: paper sacks, Styrofoam, rubber balls, papier-mâché, socks, fruits or vegetables, sticks, and so on. Sometimes children have trouble working their hands and speaking at the same time. You can tape-record the script as the children read it or act it out and then play it back during the actual puppet or shadow play performance to help children concentrate on their hand movements until they can coordinate speaking and manipulating.

In shadow play, the puppets or child actors stay behind a screen that is lighted so that only their silhouettes are seen. This is another effective way to involve shy children in speaking experiences.

Other Drama Activities   *Choral reading or speaking* is a form of drama. One of the simplest kinds of choral reading is *echoic verse*. The reader says a line and the audience repeats it, word for word, intonation for intonation, sometimes even action for action. Echoic activities have an

CHECKLIST: *Selecting and Adapting Stories and Poems for Dramatization*

1. Choose a story that
   a. can be understood by the group.
   b. contains characters with whom the children can identify.
   c. has an uncomplicated plot.
   d. has a conflict that needs to be resolved.
2. When telling or reading the story
   a. be sure that you know the whole story in detail.
   b. speak and interpret the story enthusiastically.
   c. choose words that are meaningful to the age group.
3. When planning
   a. let the children help you.
   b. emphasize the main points of the story: how it starts, events for scenes, the climax, and how it ends.
   c. describe the main characters in the story.
   d. develop the setting of the story.
   e. discuss what will be needed for properties.
   f. encourage the children to try to understand the different characters.
4. When acting
   a. let the children act only when the main points of the story have been agreed on.
   b. allow for creative and spontaneous actions within the framework developed by the children.
5. When evaluating
   a. note the development of the agreed-on main points.
   b. discuss the portrayal of the characters in light of descriptions in the story.
   c. discuss the meaning of the story, in detail if appropriate.

advantage over other forms of choral reading because copies of the text are not necessary for the audience. "The Goat" is the kind of poem that can be used echoically.

The Goat

There was a man,
Now please take note.
There was a man
Who had a goat.

He loved that goat,
Indeed he did.
He loved that goat,
Just like a kid.

One day the goat
Was feeling fine,
Ate three red shirts,
From off the line.

That man he grabbed
Him by the back,
And tied him to
A railroad track.

But when the train
Pulled into sight
That goat grew pale
And green with fright.

He heaved a sigh,
As if in pain,
Coughed up those shirts
And flagged the train![9]

Two other poems that lend themselves well to echoic reading are "The Mysterious Cat" by Vachel Lindsay and "The Night Will Never Stay" by Eleanor Farjeon.

Choral activities give children the opportunity to develop their imagination (through interpretation) to improve their speech, to expand their creativity, and to take part in an active situation, not a passive one. With choral reading, the value of group achievement is of prime importance.

There are several types of choral reading or speaking arrangements:

Line-a-Child: Each child reads one or two lines individually. When the climax is reached, a few lines may be read in unison. At the primary level, a good poem to try is "The Goblin" by Rose Fyleman; at the intermediate level, "Pippa's Song" by Robert Browning. Here is another example:

There Were Two Blackbirds

Boy:	There were two blackbirds,
	Sitting on a hill,
Girl:	The one named Jack,
Boy:	The other named Jill;
Girl:	Fly away, Jack!
Boy:	Fly away, Jill!
All:	Come again, Jack!
	Come again, Jill!

Refrain: One individual reads or speaks the narrative part and the whole group joins in on the refrain. An example for the primary years is "The Wind" by Robert Louis Stevenson; for the intermediate years, "Shoes and Stockings" by A. A. Milne. "To Market, to Market" is another example:

9. From Ramon R. Ross, *Storyteller* (Columbus, OH: Charles E. Merrill, 1972), pp. 89–90. Reprinted by permission of Charles E. Merrill Company.

To Market, to Market

Solo: To market, to market, to buy a fat pig;
All: Home again, home again, dancing a jig.
Solo: Ride to market to buy a fat hog;
All: Home again, home again, jiggety jog.
Solo: To market, to market, to buy a plum bun;
All: Home again, home again, market is done.

Two Part or Antiphonal: Two groups of children (boys and girls, light voices and deep voices, questions and answers) each take a part. An example for the primary years is "Wishes" by Rose Fyleman; for the intermediate years, Psalm 24, or "There Was a Crooked Man."

There Was a Crooked Man

Boys: There was a crooked man
Girls: And he went a crooked mile
All: He found a crooked sixpence against a crooked stile.
Boys: He found a crooked cat,
Girls: Which caught a crooked mouse
All: And they all lived together in a little crooked house.

Unison: Unison speaking can be of two types: sequence and cumulative. In *sequence*, the individual or group is responsible for connecting the different phrases smoothly to make a finished whole. For the primary years, try "Poor Old Woman"; for the intermediate years, "Roads" by Rachael Fields. "One Misty, Moisty Morning" is another example.

One Misty, Moisty Morning

All: One misty, moisty morning
      When cloudy was the weather
      I chanced to meet an old man
        Clothed all in leather,
        Clothed all in leather,
      With cap under his chin . . .
      How do you do, and how do you do,
      And how do you do again?

Cumulative speaking begins with a few voices, adding more voices as the power of the poem develops. An example for the primary years is

"Trains" by James Tippett; for the intermediate years, "Jonathan Bing" by Beatrice Brown. "There Was an Old Woman" works well too.

There Was an Old Woman

Boys: There was an old woman
         Sold puddings and pies,
Girls: She went to the mill
         and dust flew in her eyes
All: While all through the streets,
         To all she meets,
         She always cries,
Solo: "Hot Pies—Hot Pies!"

In choral reading or speaking, three factors must concern the teacher: rhythm and tempo, color and quality of voice, and arrangement. To help develop rhythm and tempo, children can clap, sway, or beat out the rhythm. The rhythm can be described as happy or sad; the concept of tempo, fast or slow, becomes a part of the rhythmic pattern. Nursery rhymes are excellent for primary children to feel rhythm and tempo; intermediate-level children will find the lilting rhythms of the words of A. A. Milne, Rachael Field, or Eleanor Farjeon suitable for this purpose. Exciting, simple material can be used to help children develop sensitivity to pitch, inflection, and intensity (for example, "I Have Known Rivers" by Langston Hughes). The orchestration of the choral reading is a creative aspect of the project. Class members and the teacher should work together to find the best arrangement to convey the meaning of the poem.

Yet another activity is *readers' theatre,* a dramatic reading of a script. Any number of students can participate. Each character is portrayed by a reader; a narrator fills in details of the plot or setting. Action is minimal; and so are costumes and props (although a few simple props may be used for fun and effect). The readers' voices and expressions must project the emotion and characterization and ideas of the selection. These kinds of experiences expand oral expression, develop concepts and vocabulary, and serve as part of the foundation for written expression. Children's books, or scenes or episodes from them—try Beverly Cleary's *Ramona the Brave*—make good readers' theatre scripts. And the guidelines for the other oral activities can all be adapted to the method easily.[10]

10. For more detailed information about readers' theatre, see Irene Coger and Melvin White, *Reader's Theatre Handbook,* 3d ed. (Glenview, IL: Scott, Foresman, 1982).

ORAL EXPRESSION ACTIVITIES

We need additional activities to develop and refine practical speaking skills. Using the phone; making introductions; making announcements; giving messages, directions and explanations; and reviewing books, movies, and television programs are all basic skills that are introduced at the elementary school level and reinforced and developed in later grades.

Using the Phone

Children using practice phones in the classroom can enact the following situations to enable the teacher to observe their telephone usage.

Pam wants to call her friend. She does not know her phone number and needs to look it up in the phone book.

Jack wants to invite Ed to go to a movie with him. On his first try to reach Ed by phone, Jack gets a wrong number.

Sally wants to call a new friend who has just moved into her neighborhood. Because the phone number isn't in the current directory, she calls Directory Assistance. Peter is the operator.

Rebecca does not know the cleaner's telephone number. She finds the number in the Yellow Pages.

One primary-level teacher began a unit on the telephone by preparing a bulletin board that showed the parts of a phone and by using a teletrainer borrowed from the telephone company. (A teletrainer consists of two activated telephones and a speaker-control unit. It can simulate a dial tone, a busy signal, and a ringing signal.) A number of directories were available for class use.

"Many of you know how to make a telephone call, especially to call mother or father, and this is fine," the teacher began. "But some of you have trouble finding a number in the directory, and some of you get mixed up when you try to dial a number. There are several things that we need to know to use a phone correctly."

Instructions followed on how to look for and call a particular number: "Suppose we want to call Mrs. Mary Brown. How are the names in the telephone book arranged? Why is the street address helpful?"

After students located the number, attention was directed to how to dial it: "What are some things we have to do in order to call 842–4771?" The pupils and teacher prepared the following sequence of steps:

1. Pick up the phone and hold the receiver to your ear.
2. Listen for the dial tone, a steady humming sound. If you dial before you hear it, you may get a wrong number or no number at all.
3. When you hear the dial tone, place your finger in the hole on the dial for 8. Turn the dial to the right until your finger hits the finger stop. Remove your finger and let the dial go back by itself. It will make a clicking sound.
4. Place your finger in the hole for 4 and turn the dial until your finger hits the finger stop. Remove your finger and let the dial go back again. Continue to dial the numbers 2–4–7–7–1 in the same way.
5. When you finish dialing, wait a minute and you will hear a ringing sound. If you get a beep-beep sound, this means the line is busy and you must hang up and wait a few minutes before dialing again. If you hear the phone ringing, give Mrs. Brown time to answer; let it ring several times.
6. When Mrs. Brown answers the phone, tell her your name and why you are calling.

The children practiced in small groups calling Mrs. Mary Brown and other numbers. Their performances were discussed by the class and teacher. Each child also located and wrote the number for the police department, the fire department, the family doctor, and a neighbor.

Next the children examined the Yellow Pages. They located the names of plumbers, department stores, grocery stores, shoe stores, and other stores. Near the end of the period, the class discussed long-distance dialing and the use of area codes.

You may want to suggest the criteria in Chart 6.5 for phone skills and good manners in phoning.

Making Introductions and Observing Social Courtesies

One way to teach social courtesies is to entertain visitors in the classroom. Before visitors arrive, discuss with the class how to greet visitors at the door, how to make introductions, how to seat visitors, and how to serve refreshments.

CHART 6.5: *Telephone Guide*

1. Speak clearly.
2. When originating the call, give your name immediately.
3. State the purpose of the call.
4. Keep your message brief and to the point.
5. Answer calls as quickly as possible.
6. When another person is wanted, ask the caller, "Wait just a minute, please," and get the person asked for at once. If it takes a little more time for the person to reach the phone, explain, "Mother is out in the yard. She will be here in a minute or two."
7. Take any messages accurately or ask if they will please call later. The message should include the caller's name, phone number, and message, and the time the call was received.
8. If you get a wrong number, apologize to the person who answers: "I'm sorry, I have the wrong number." Be polite to anyone who reaches your number by mistake.

An excellent time to help children develop self-confidence in making introductions and being introduced would be during an open house or similar function. They should be able to put their learning to use in introducing their parents and friends to their teacher and classmates, and in replying when others are introduced to them.

Here is a list of suggestions for making social introductions:

1. Speak slowly and clearly so that the names can be understood easily. It's all right to ask for a name to be repeated if you didn't hear it the first time.
2. Tell something about the people you are introducing to help them start a conversation.
3. Say, "_____, I would like to introduce _____." Give the name of the person you want to honor first, perhaps a teacher, an older person, or a person of rank.
4. When being introduced, make a reply: "I'm very glad to meet you, _____."
5. To remember the name of a new acquaintance, use it when you speak to him or her.

A related, more formal situation involves introducing a speaker to a class or a group of people. A good introduction demands careful planning. It should include the name of the speaker; facts about the speaker (education, profession, experiences); what the speaker is going to talk about and why he or she is qualified to talk about it; and an expression of pleasure that he or she is going to talk. (Some of this information may come from the speaker; the rest may have to be researched in books, newspapers, and magazines.) The teacher can demonstrate two introductions (a good one and a bad one) and ask students to compare the kind of information they convey and how interesting they are.

The following dialogues can be practiced for other social courtesies:

How to Greet Visitors at the Door: "Good morning. It's good to see you" or "Hello. Won't you please come in?"

Offering Help: "May I take your coat?"

Seating Visitors: "Mrs. Smith, would you like to sit here?"

Serving Refreshments: "May I serve you?" or "Would you like some punch?"

Expressing Appreciation: "Thank you for showing us your rock collection" or "Mr. Brown, we appreciate your telling us about your trip to Europe."

Responding to Expressions of Appreciation: "You're welcome."

Social courtesies should be taught, not merely as conventional forms of behavior, but as genuine expressions of respect and regard for others. Help children to see that these courtesies make for good relationships with other people. Your attitude here is very important too: A teacher's sincerity does much to foster sincerity in children.

Making Announcements

Announcements of meetings or programs must include an adequate description of the event, who is invited, the date, the time, the place, and the price of admission if any. An announcement that something has been lost should describe the article clearly, tell when and where it might have been lost and to whom it should be returned, and mention a reward if there is one.

Here are examples of three different kinds of announcements:

A School Program

See Chapter 1 for a systematic lesson plan for this type of oral announcement.

An Out-of-School Function

The Girl Scouts will meet Monday, December 6, at 3:30 P.M., in the school cafeteria. Please bring fifty cents to pay for the Christmas wrappings and paint. Wear old clothes or bring a smock. We will be painting Christmas toys to put in Junior Red Cross boxes.

Lost Articles

Yesterday during the 2:00 P.M. recess, a yellow sweater with white buttons and a rolled collar was left on the ground by the swings. If you find the sweater, please return it to Alice Goodner in Miss Jones's room.

Messages, Directions, and Explanations

Messages, directions, and explanations must be organized and presented in clear, concise terms.

Group discussion helps in planning what information should be included and how it should be arranged. A child who carries a message from one person to another must know who is sending the message and who is to receive it, and must be able to state the message accurately.

In giving directions, children must learn to include, in order, all the steps necessary for another person to follow the procedure. Directions for getting from one place to another should be very specific ("turn left" not "turn that way"). Directions for making or doing something should always include the correct names for objects or materials (not "a little thing-a-ma-jig").

Explanations call for similar skills but also include reasons—telling why something is done in a certain way or how something works. For younger children, explanations may be mere enumerations of points; for older children, they include cause and effect relationships. Help children select the points necessary for a clear explanation, and to omit details that are irrelevant or confusing.

Book, Movie, and Television Program Reviews

Too many teachers think of book reports as proof of whether children have read a book, but they are much more than this. Book reports increase reading enjoyment, extend interests, and provide clues toward individual and group evaluation of literature. Reviews, then, reinforce understanding of setting, characters, and sequence of events; develop skills of analysis; and help students contrast literary experience with real-life experience.

Reviews of movies and television programs, in informal discussion or as formal reports, do much the same things, helping deepen understanding and improve tastes. Chapter 12 provides more information on book reports, which can be adapted to movie reviews as well.

USAGE

Usage refers to the way in which people speak. Effective usage is saying what we want to say as clearly as possible and in a tone suitable to the purpose of the communication.

Here we focus on particular language forms: words, idioms, and constructions. Two broad labels are applied to these forms: *standard* (socially accepted) and *nonstandard* (variant).

Dialectal Differences

Environmental and cultural differences affect how children use language. To understand their usage, then, teachers need some basic information about the linguistic features of each learner's dialect. (Don't confuse dialectal variations with the universals of language development discussed in Chapter 2.) Several sources are available for generalized findings.[11] But

---

11. For example, see Walter Laban, *Problems in Oral English* (Urbana, IL: National Council of Teachers of English, 1966), pp. 47, 49.

keep in mind that these findings are representative. As always, you're going to have to tailor your instruction to individual needs.

Urban Table 6.1 lists some of the characteristic speech patterns in urban areas. Other nonstandard forms involve subject expression (*John lives in New York* ⟶ *John he live in New York*); the future form of *be* [*He is sick* ⟶ *He sick* (at present) and *He be sick* (chronically)]; and the use of prepositions (*He is over at his friend's house* ⟶ *He over to his friend's house*).[12] These forms and the patterns in the table refer to differences in syntax.

Some elements of dialectal phonology include

r-lessness: /r/ is dropped or replaced with /ə/. For example, *foe* (four), *poe* (poor).

TABLE 6.1: *Speech Patterns Characteristic of Urban Children*

Written Expression	Linguistic Feature	Oral Expression
1. John's house	Possession	John house
2. John runs.	Third-person singular	John run.
3. ten cents	Plurality	ten cent
4. He jumped.	Past	He jump.
5. She is a cook.	Copula	She a cook.
6. He doesn't have any toys.	Negation	He ain't got no toys. He don't have no toys. He don't got no toys.
7. He asked if I came.	Past conditional question	He asked did I come.
8. Every day when I come he isn't here.	Negative *be*	Every day when I come he don't be here.

Source: Roger W. Shuy, "Some Considerations for Developing Beginning Reading Materials for Ghetto Children," *Journal of Reading Behavior* (Spring 1969): 37. Used by permission of National Reading Conference, Inc.

12. Walter A. Wolfram, *A Sociolinguistics Description of Detroit Speech* (Washington, DC: Center for Applied Linguistics, 1969). Also see William Lobov, *Language in the Inner City* (Philadelphia: University of Pennsylvania Press, 1973), and *The Social Stratification of English in New York City*, rev. ed. (Washington, DC: Center for Applied Linguistics, 1981).

l-lessness: Moves to a /*w*/ glide or disappears. For example, *toe* (toll), *haw* (haul), *awe* (oil).

Reduction of Consonant Clusters: Especially after stressed vowels. For example, *pass* (past/passed), *hole* (hold).

Weakening of Final Consonant: /*t*/ and /*d*/ mostly, and sometimes /*g*/ and /*k*/. For example, *boo* (boot), *see* (seed or seat).

Vowel Shifts: For example, *bear* (beer), *pail* (peel), *awe* (oil).

Rural One study of the speech patterns of Appalachian rural children found several features:[13]

1. Dropped endings (*goin', comin', seein'*).
2. No distinction in the sound of different vowels before *r* (*far, fir, car, cur*).
3. The elimination of subjects in sentence patterns (*'m goin' downtown, 'e's doin' his work*).
4. Nonstandard use of the objective case of pronouns in compound subjects (*me and you, me and my sister*).
5. The addition of *n* to possessive pronouns (*his'n, her'n*).
6. Unique pronunciations (*cidy* for *city*, *tank* for *thank*, *duh* for *the*, *tink* for *think*, *berry* for *very*).

Some Appalachian phonological and grammatical patterns overlap with other dialects:[14]

1. Vowel stress (*tahr* for *tire*).
2. Frequent deletion of unstressed syllables (*'fore* for *before*).
3. *a* prefix (come a-runnin').
4. Do and don't (It don't do no good).
5. Irregular verbs often regularized (*throwed* for *thrown*).
6. Past tense and past participle forms often reversed (*taken* for *took*).
7. Double or multiple negations (*I ain't got none no more*).

Language Differences

Children's native language influences their English language learning. The descriptions here show how that interference can occur.

---

13. William A. Stewart, *Appalachian Advance* 4 (September 1969): 12.
14. Walter Wolfram and Donna Christian, *Appalachian Speech* (Washington, DC: Center for Applied Linguistics, 1976).

Spanish-American Spanish-speaking children who have already learned the alphabet pronounce vowels differently than their English-speaking peers. The Spanish language does not use the voiced *th, z, zh,* or *j,* or *thr.* The tendency is to substitute the sound in the Spanish language that is most like the missing sound. The blend of *s* with other consonant sounds (*t, p, k, f, m, n,* and *l*) may present a problem, since Spanish words do not begin with the *s* + consonant sound. A vowel always precedes the *s* when it is followed by a consonant (as *estar* for *star*). Children may have difficulty pronouncing two consonants together in the final position (*wasp, disk, last*). Words ending in *r* + *d, t, l, p,* or *s* may be pronounced without the final consonant (*car* for *card*). The Spanish *h* is silent (*hotel* becomes *otel*). There are only two contractions in Spanish; stress is different; and the Spanish adjectives often follow rather than precede nouns (*The dress blue is pretty*).

Some other points of difficulty: negation (*Jim is no here*); adjectival agreement (*The two boys are bigs*); omission of subject pronouns (*Is here*); comparisons (*is more small*); omission of articles (*He is policeman*); subject-verb agreement (*The girls runs* or *The girl run*); possessive adjectives and pronouns (*the book of the boy*); and past tense (*He need help yesterday*).

Indian There are many different tribes in the United States. Obviously we haven't the space to examine the language patterns of them all. Instead, the text focuses on the largest tribe in the country, the Navajos, and the problems Navajo children may have with English. These problems cannot be generalized for speakers of all Indian languages.

Navajo speakers do not distinguish between the English /p/ and /b/, and usually substitute their own slightly different /b/ for both. This sound never occurs at the end of a syllable in Navajo, however, so they often substitute either a glottal stop or the Navajo /d/ for a final /p/ or /b/. This /d/, which sounds like the /t/ in *stop,* is also typically substituted for the English /t/ and /d/ when they occur at the beginning of words. In Navajo, there are no correspondents to /f/, /v/, /th/ and /ng/. Vowel length and nasalization are differentiated to distinguish meaning. The vowel sounds /ae/ (*a*) and /e/ (*u*) do not occur in Navajo, and are the hardest for pupils to learn. Children who speak Navajo must learn to distinguish among English /o/ (*o* as in *joke*), /u/ (*oo* as in *book*), and /uw/ (*oo* as in *loot*). Groups of adjacent consonants present a major problem, and often Navajo speakers will substitute similar clusters of their own. Tonal pitch in Navajo is the only distinctive feature that differentiates meaning between words like *nili* (you are) and *nili* (he is). Navajo uses participles to convey meanings expressed by intonation in English. For example, *-is* and *-sa* added to Navajo words signal questions.

Many features of English syntax are difficult for Navajo speakers to understand. Articles and adjectives are troublesome because, with a few exceptions, they do not exist in Navajo. Few Navajo nouns are changed to make the plural (*four dog*); the possessive *'s* is a problem because the Navajo pattern for *the boy's book* would be *the boy his book*. The Navajo *bi* translates as any of the third-person pronouns: he, she, it, they, them, him, her, his, its, their. The Navajo child is also faced with a semantic system that categorizes experiences in a very different way.[15]

Asian Several distinct aspects of the Chinese language may affect the Chinese learner. For example:

1. The verb has only one form—tenses are indicated by the use of auxiliaries placed before or after the verb form.
2. Nouns are not inflected to indicate plural form (*three book, many boy*).
3. Word order cannot be manipulated to change meaning as it can in English (*He is a policeman* cannot become *Is he a policeman?*).
4. The Chinese article *a* is very specific, referring to the noun that it modifies (*a book, a dog, a pencil*).
5. There is a tendency for Chinese speakers to drop, glottalize, or add a vowel sound to English endings in the consonants *t, d, s, l, p, b, k, f, g, r,* and *v*.
6. A tone system is used as a device for distinguishing word meanings. Words having the same pronunciation may have four or more different tones to represent four or more different meanings.

The Japanese and Korean languages also affect children's use of English:

1. Both use only function words (articles and auxiliary words), which follow content words; in English, a combination of function words and word endings are used to show distinctions.
2. The words *it* and *there* as introductory words in sentences (*It is raining, There are many people here today*) do not exist in Japanese and Korean.
3. The Japanese and Korean vowel systems do not distinguish between words like *bit* and *bite*, and *bet* and *bait*.

---

15. Items selected from Muriel R. Saville, "Providing for Mobile Populations in Bilingual and Migrant Education Programs," in *Reading for the Disadvantaged: Problems of Linguistically Different Learners*, ed. Thomas D. Horn (Newark, DE: International Reading Association, 1970) pp. 129–131.

4. When words or syllables terminate in certain consonant sounds, there is a tendency to insert a vowel sound (*striku* for *strike*, *collegi* for *college*, and *churchi* for *church*).
5. The schwa sound used in English for unaccented vowels does not exist in Japanese and Korean.
6. Several consonant sounds (*v, b, l*) are not distinguished.

The recent influx, particularly on the West Coast, of children speaking Khmer, Lao, or Vietnamese (from Cambodia, Laos, or Vietnam) adds these Asian languages to the list. Materials about the people, culture, and language of these students is available from the Center for Applied Linguistics.[16]

Instructional Program

The teacher's reaction to dialectal differences is critical to children's developing self-expression. If the teacher places immediate restrictions on that expression, students may feel insecure. Instead, encourage children to express themselves in whatever dialect they have, then lead them gently, by example, toward a more generally accepted (classroom, school, or standard) dialect. The program should be based on ideas like these:

Language is a form of human behavior and is subject to variations among its users and to continual change.

There are choices to make in the use of language (*isn't* or *ain't, as I did* or *like I did, he doesn't* or *he don't*) and varying social penalties for particular forms of usage.

There is usage for both formal and informal situations.

Usage can be more or less appropriate (in terms of the audience and the occasion) than arbitrarily right or wrong, or good or bad.

The teacher is probably the most influential speaking model for children outside their home environment. And this may well be the most effective tool we have to teach standard usage. Teach by example, not by continually saying no. Children are great imitators, and much of their language is "caught" as well as "taught." [17]

---

16. 3520 Prospect Street, Washington, DC 20007.
17. For additional information, see R. W. Shuy, "Learning to Talk Like Teachers," *Language Arts* 58 (1981): 168–174.

A common problem in usage instruction is the attempt to cover too many elements during the year. The program should center on just a few areas:

Irregular verbs (*do, see, come, eat, give, run*).
Pronouns (*I* and *me, we* and *us*).
Confusion (*lie* or *lay, sit* or *set, let* or *leave, well* or *good*).
Double negatives.
Subject-verb and agreement.

As you can see, we have not used grade placement in the list. Our reasoning is that forms should be emphasized as needed. Nonstandard usage is obvious. You can recognize it easily and deal with it whenever it appears, at whatever level.

Look for common (to group) and specific (to individual) usage on which to base instruction. One of the best ways to secure data on oral language patterns is to listen to children's uninhibited expression during free activity

---

TABLE 6.2: *Speech Forms for Intensive Teaching in Elementary School*

Verb Forms	Pronoun Forms
ain't or *hain't*	my brother, *he* (and other double subjects)
I *don't* have *no*	*him* and *me* went, Mary and *me* saw
learn me a song	
leave me go	
have ate, have went, have did, have saw, have wrote	*hisself, theirselves*
he *begun*, he *seen*, he *run*, he *drunk*, he *come*	*them* books, *this here* book, *that there* book
I *says*	it's *your'n, her'n, his'n, our'n*
he *brung*, he *climb*	
we, you, they *was*	
was *broke* (for broken)	
was *froze*	
knowed, growed	

Source: Robert C. Pooley, *The Teaching of English Usage* (Urbana, IL: National Council of Teachers of English, 1974), p. 183. Copyright © 1974 by the National Council of Teachers of English. Reprinted with permission.

CHART 6.6: *Analysis of Nonstandard Usage*

Pupils	Verbs	Subject Pronouns	Adjective/ Adverb	Negative	Redun- dancy	Illiteracies
Ann	have came	Betty and me	gooder	don't have no	John he	hain't
James						
Donnie						
Lisa						

periods or club meetings. Then use a chart, like Chart 6.6, to record problems.

Discuss common nonstandard usages with the class as a whole; specific nonstandard usage, with small groups or individuals. Focus on grossly inappropriate speech patterns (severe social penalty) before working on less serious ones.

Primary Level In the early school years, don't overreact when children use a nonstandard speech form. Instead, rephrase the statement so children have an idea of approved usage. Where you can anticipate a problem, use the approved form as a question before students have a chance to use the variant form. Above all, be sympathetic and understanding, suggesting standard substitutes rather than condemning existing usage. Remember, the objective here is to alter habitual language patterns without trauma.

Intermediate Level At this level, instruction becomes more formal—although activities are still informal. For example, you would still try to improve oral usage primarily through listening and speaking exercises, not written ones. (The tape recorder is an effective device for helping children hear the way they talk, for calling attention to usage patterns.)

Give children frequent functional practice using standard forms by letting them speak to the class, report to a group, tell stories, or participate in drama activities. Students should look on usage as an integrated part of every classroom activity, not as an isolated element to be practiced only in language periods.

You may find second-language techniques helpful, particularly when children recognize they use a nonstandard speech form and want to participate in activities that focus on the standard form. Of course, any techniques you use require some basic information about the linguistic features of the learners' dialect.

The following procedure (with a substitution of *f* for the voiceless *th* in the final position—*wif* for *with, mouf* for *mouth, paf* for *path*—example) shows how second-language techniques can be used.

1. Help children recognize that this nonstandard dialect and the standard dialect are different. (Use a tape recorder and point out that when we say *wif*, we're substituting a sound heard at the beginning of words like *fan, fat, fog,* and *fight.*)
2. Have children hear the standard sound being taught. (Give an oral list of words that contain the voiceless *th* in the final position—*with, mouth, path*—and ask them to discriminate these words from other words. Don't use *whiff, muff,* or *laugh* though.)
3. Help children discriminate between a sound in the standard dialect and the corresponding sound in the nonstandard dialect. (Identify which sounds are spoken twice in a series to discriminate the voiceless *th* from *f: with, wif, with; mouf, mouf, mouth; path, paf, path*).
4. Have children practice reproductions of the standard feature. (Use pattern practice—repeating a series of words like *with, mouth,* and *path,* after each is presented orally. Sentences may be repeated: *John ran down the path with his mouth wide open.* Later the interfering element /f/ can be included: *After he ran down the path with his mouth wide open, John began to puff, whiff, and laugh.*)
5. See that children use the standard feature in a meaningful situation. (Use short speaking situations where students can be particularly careful about the feature under consideration.)

You can use this same procedure to teach a syntactical feature, as shown in the lesson plan on page 177.[18]

---

18. For discussion of syntactical and phonological differences and principles of teaching a second dialect; see Diane Bryen et al., *Variant English: An Introduction to Language Variation* (Columbus, OH: Merrill, 1978); Bernice Cullinan, *Black Dialects and Reading* (Urbana, IL: National Council of Teachers of English, 1974); and Eleanor Thonis, *Literacy for America's Spanish Speaking Children* (Newark, DE: International Reading Association, 1976).

LESSON PLAN: *Usage (Syntactical Feature)*

Performance Objective

The learner adds *he plays fair* to the out-of-school *he play fair*.

Pretest

Prepare a list of nonstandard usage forms as children talk. Choose one specific form for direct attention.

Teaching Suggestions

1. Write and state both corresponding standard and nonstandard forms. Discuss the differences and help learners become aware of these differences. Have them show that they can discriminate between the two forms. For example, ask them to clap their hands when you say the standard form, or have them say both forms. Then have them reproduce the standard form orally.
2. Use patterns for concentrated repetition (*he plays fair, she plays fair, John plays fair*).

Mastery or Posttest Suggestion

Observe the linguistic pattern under consideration by having learners engage in a role-playing situation where they discuss the topic "fair play."

Reteaching Suggestions

1. Use the Language Master for pattern drill—a prerecorded sentence and then the child's repetition.
2. Allow students to help each other in modeling and practicing the language pattern.

Problems There are four procedures that lead to disappointing results in teaching standard speech forms. First, *teaching grammatic forms* (for example, the declensions of the pronoun to children who use the variant pronoun) contributes little to a change in speech habits. Second, *reliance on total class instruction*, regardless of whether nonstandard usage is common or specific, can waste hours of class time. Third, *teaching language as a subject* (rather than as a series of practical skills integrated in the overall program) produces disappointing results. And fourth, *depending on workbooks and seatwork* (filling in blanks and crossing out alternate forms) has little or no effect on proficient use of standard forms.

EVALUATION

Oral language is difficult to evaluate, but that does not mean that our evaluations should be subjective or cursory. We still must determine accomplishment, diagnose the product of individual effort, and base our judgments on the best possible measurements.

A tape recorder is probably the most effective evaluative tool we have. It allows us to compare speech skills and measure progress over time. Other evaluative devices include teacher-made tests and simple rating scales.

The most practical procedure to follow in evaluating oral expression is to make consistent use of checklists to compare expression in a particular situation with the objectives of speech in that situation. A checklist of objectives like the ones below might be used in terms of overall standards for improving speaking skills.

Ability to select and organize the content or ideas of a speaking situation.
Ability to speak with a sincere, courteous attitude and respect for the audience.
Ability to speak with a suitable voice and use appropriate forms of words that express ideas clearly and accurately.
Ability to use appropriate posture and body actions.

Some teachers have found flow charts helpful in maintaining a record of individual participation and skill strengths in all oral composition activities. One way to record this information is to place the names of each class member alphabetically on the left-hand side of a large sheet of cardboard. The first section of the chart could be labeled "Oral Composition Activities"; the second, "Skills." As children participate in the activities, a check could be placed beside their names in the appropriate activity square. This helps ensure that all children have an opportunity to participate in each activity, and that all children progress to a more advanced level as they succeed in the current one.

SOME INSTRUCTIONAL CONCERNS

A major challenge for teachers is balancing speaking opportunities. For any given talk activity, you should consider its potential in terms of the child, and the range and depth of possible situations (setting, audience, purpose, and talk use). Before using any talk activity, ask yourself these questions:

1. What is the setting range—ceremonial, informal, formal, intimate?
2. What is the audience range—self, personal you, unknown you?
3. What is the subject range— concrete, abstract, personal, etc.?
4. What is the purpose range—to inform, to describe, to explain, to entertain, to direct, to persuade?
5. What range and/or depth of talk-use interplay is there—proposing, inquiring, exploring, describing?
6. What does it require of the child's cognitive abilities—hypothetical reasoning, classifying, intensive inner speech?
7. What does it require of the child's language abilities—structurally complex sentences, if-then assertions, metaphoric expressions, extensive use of negation, relations of grammatical and temporal order?
8. What does it assume about the child's personal experiences—wealthy, poor, rural, urban, etc.?
9. Where does this activity stand in relation to activities Y and Z—in relation to the total talk curriculum picture? [19]

In brief, the framework of an oral composition program must be balanced and comprehensive, encompassing purpose, context, and planning. To see that it is, the teacher must keep accurate records of each experience.

A second problem, at the intermediate level, is the difficulty some children have in presenting oral reports in interesting ways. The issue really isn't adequate preparation, here; it's a question of presentation. Encourage children to use pictures, chalkboard diagrams, charts, graphs, or maps to illustrate what they want to say. Or make a bulletin board, table-top display, flannel board, or overhead projector available. If several children have worked together on a topic, let them present their report at a round-table discussion or in an original play or puppet show.

Thought questions

1. What is a planned oral language curriculum?
2. What are some common elements of the proposed teaching strategies for conversing, phoning, making introductions, and interviewing?
3. Why is the drama process an important avenue for speech development?

19. Klein, *Talk in the Language Arts Classroom*, pp. 37–38.

4. Why should standard English be acquired by the dialect speaker?
5. How would you respond to a critic who says "Most of the oral activities in the language arts program should be eliminated. The time should be used to teach basic reading and writing skills."

LEARNER RESPONSE OPTIONS

1. Prepare a set of questions to guide an oral report about a hobby. Try to use each of the seven major question types listed on page 141.
2. List (with reasons) the best procedures for teaching and evaluating conversational skills.
3. Tape a panel discussion about ways to help children develop their oral expression. Play it for a group of your classmates.
4. Use the five discussion experiences described on pages 143–144 to solve a problem situation.
5. Practice the storytelling suggestions in the chapter, and then present a selection to a small group of classmates. With them, evaluate your performance.
6. Use the techniques suggested in the chapter to tell a story to a small group of children.
7. Make a flannel board and cutout characters for telling a story.
8. Give a child a wordless picture book, and ask him or her to "tell" the story of the pictures.
9. Use one of the components of drama to teach a small group of children.
10. With a small group of classmates, prepare a choral reading selection for an elementary school audience.
11. Teach one type of choral reading or speaking to a small group of children or peers.
12. Give an oral report on the speech characteristics of people in your area of the country.
13. Visit a school in a low-income area and one in a middle-income area. Tape children's conversations at both. Compare the speech characteristics of each group to standard English characteristics. Then design a second-language outline for one nonstandard feature.
14. Prepare a checklist for evaluating one of the oral language experiences presented in the chapter.

References and additional readings

Baker, Augusta, and Ellin Greene. *Storytelling: Art and Technique.* New York: Bowker, 1977.

Briggs, Nancy C., and Joseph A. Wagner. *Children's Literature Through Storytelling and Drama.* 2d ed. Dubuque, IA: Brown, 1979.

Broughton, G., et al. *Teaching English as a Foreign Language.* Boston: Routledge & Kegan Paul, 1980.

Chambers, Dewey. *The Oral Tradition: Storytelling and Creative Drama.* 2d ed. Dubuque, IA: Brown, 1977.

Hatch, E., ed. *Second Language Acquisition: A Book of Readings.* Rowley, MA: Newbury House, 1978.

Klein, Marvin L. *Talk in the Language Arts Classroom.* Urbana, IL: National Council of Teachers of English, 1977.

Kroll, Barry M., and Roberta J. Vann, eds. *Exploring Speaking-Writing Relationships: Connections and Contrasts.* Urbana, IL: National Council of Teachers of English, 1981.

McCaslin, Nellie. *Creative Dramatics in the Classroom.* 3d ed. New York: McKay, 1980.

Nenfro, Nancy. *Puppetry and the Art of Story Creation.* Austin, TX: Nenfro Studios, 1979.

Pinnell, Gay S., ed. *Discovering Language with Children.* Urbana, IL: National Council of Teachers of English, 1980.

Rodrigues, Raymond J., and Robert H. White. *Mainstreaming the Non-English Speaking Student.* Theory and Research into Practice (TRIP) Booklet. Urbana, IL: National Council of Teachers of English and ERIC/RCS, 1980.

Ross, Ramon. *Storytelling.* 2d ed. Columbus, OH: Merrill, 1980.

Segal, M., and D. Adcock. *Just Pretending: Ways to Help Children Grow Through Imaginative Play.* Englewood Cliffs, NJ: Prentice-Hall, 1981.

Siks, Geraldine. *Drama with Children.* New York: Harper & Row, 1976.

Stibbs, Andrew. *Assessing Children's Language.* Urbana, IL: National Council of Teachers of English, 1979.

Wolfram, W., et al. *Dialects and Educational Equity.* 5 vols. Washington, DC: Center for Applied Linguistics, 1979.

PART IV: WRITTEN

COMMUNICATION

CHAPTER 7: Written Composition

OVERVIEW

This chapter stresses three important areas in teaching children to write: early writing experiences; creative writing; and effective expression. Instructional procedures are offered for special writing experiences, including letter writing, report writing, and other practical writing situations. The conventions of writing (capitalization, punctuation, sentence sense, paragraph sense, and manuscript form) are described. The chapter concludes with suggestions for analyzing compositions, giving particular attention to revision and proofreading.

KEY VOCABULARY

experience chart writing

language-experience approach

patterned writing

writing center

sustained silent writing

text (story) grammar

free verse

couplet

triplet

quatrain

limerick

haiku

cinquain

lanterne

septolet

tanka

directed writing activity

sentence sense

subordination

manuscript form

revision

proofreading

BASES FOR COMPOSING

For the past two decades, listening and reading have been emphasized in the communicative arts, rather than speaking and writing. We should give balanced attention to all the language arts in the curriculum and should cultivate each area from the time children enter school. In order to nourish the writing program, we must provide adequate time to encourage children to write and to provide instruction on how to write; they must have time to practice writing and evaluating their work and to learn the conventional writing skills. This chapter suggests the wide variety of forms and functions of writing. Graves has stressed that written composition is a fundamental skill for the literate individual.[1] Cramer has cited the positive influence writing can have on the development of the skills of reading comprehension, word recognition, spelling, handwriting, the mechanics of written English, oral language, and listening.[2]

The development of written expression must be considered in relationship with other elements of the language arts program. The abilities and skills needed for oral language experiences can be transferred to writing situations. The same holds true for vocabulary development, grammar, and literature. In brief, helping children to write effectively involves all language activities.

As indicated in Chapter 4, young children begin to write what is meaningful to them at an early age. This initial writing is a natural stage in their progression toward more mature writing. As Clay[3] and Holdaway[4] suggest, beginning writers bring many resources to the writing process (such as an oral language base, invented spelling, story conventions, and the like). These are the foundations for later explicit and elaborated writing. Teachers can build on this foundation by observing and listening to children, by providing a risk-free classroom environment filled with talking and writing, and by using instructional practices that motivate children to write and support their efforts.[5] Additionally, teachers can participate in

1. Donald Graves, *Balance the Basics: Let Them Write* (New York: Ford Foundation, 1977).
2. Ronald L. Cramer, *Children's Writing and Language Growth* (Columbus, OH: Merrill, 1978), Chapter 11.
3. Marie Clay, *What Did I Write? A Study of Children's Writing* (New Zealand: Heinemann Educational Books, 1975).
4. Don Holdaway, *The Foundations of Literacy* (Sydney, Australia: Ashton Scholastic, 1979).
5. Glenda L. Bissex, "Growing Writers in Classrooms," *Language Arts* 58 (October 1981): 785–791.

the act of writing along with children. This is one of the best ways to remain sensitive to the challenge and stimulation that writing presents.[6]

CHILDREN'S WRITING DEVELOPMENT

Just as children play with sounds in learning to speak, young children experiment with letters, words, sentences, and the forms of discourse. From the beginning, they write to express meaning in functional situations of their daily life. Starting from scribbling, children, wanting to express their thoughts through writing, set about discovering more and more about the writing process. Teachers need to provide many opportunities for children to explore writing as a means of learning about writing.

6. Marvin L. Klein, "Teaching Writing in the Elementary Grades," *Elementary School Journal* 81 (May 1981): 319–326.

DeFord[7] suggests that, although the steps are not always sequential, the following stages characterize children's progress in the writing process. At first, they begin with scribbling or aimless marking on paper. Gradually, they become aware of the difference between "drawing" and "writing." "I'm drawing you a picture" may be spoken by the child, as opposed to "I'm writing a letter to Aunt Grace." Through being read to and watching others write, children learn the concept of writing left to right and top to bottom on the page. Later may come the development of letter-like shapes, when children try to write a message. Refinement with letters and letter-like shapes comes with copying or tracing letters. A bit later, one may expect to see combinations of letters, possibly with spaces, indicating the child understands units (letters, words, sentences). The letters, however, may not necessarily reflect letter/sound correspondence. Example: Santa Claus

OHOG X

Gradually, children begin to write clearly isolated words, often using sound/letter correspondence. Example: Easter Rabbit

eStt RBBTT

Then simple sentences may be written with invented spellings. Example: He bringed money

He BBRE-MOINE

From this point, children may combine two or more sentences with periods and capitalization.

This information suggests what teachers can expect from students at various stages, which will perhaps help them facilitate children's learning to write. To assist in this development, a number of procedures should be considered by the teacher. For example, a wide exposure to written language should be provided within the classroom—books, personal letters, signs, charts, newspapers, and magazines. Teachers serve daily as models of reading and writing activities. Although some learning about writing is self-taught, some comes about through imitation. Learning experiences should be planned in which children see a need to write, such as writing about a field trip, preparing a report about a topic of interest, or writing notes to parents and friends.

Children should be encouraged to write in a risk-free environment, where they can test their knowledge of language. Avoid overcorrecting

7. Diane E. DeFord, "Young Children and Their Writing," *Theory into Practice*, 29 (Summer 1980): 157–162.

during the initial writing stages. This practice often inhibits a child's speaking, and it may discourage a child's writing efforts as well. Most students are interested in trying to spell words they want to use. Note the progress from one-letter spelling (such as *g* for *girl*) to some medial and final consonants (*btr* for *brother*), the use of blends (*trk* for *truck*), the use of morphologic markers (*ed, ing, s*), the use of common words (*we*), and finally the gradual establishment of the vowel. Sometimes patterns are overgeneralized, like using *reecht* for *reached*. Such miscues signal a movement toward standards.[8]

WRITING CREATIVE PROSE

Creative writing can be a powerful instructional tool. Immensely rewarding in itself, creative writing can heighten students' awareness of and pleasure in reading, instill knowledge of good writing and effective communication, provide interesting and delightful opportunities to develop spelling and handwriting skills, and increase interest in almost every other facet of the language arts. We all have within us certain creative impulses, and many of us have specific talents. Teachers in elementary schools can uncover these talents and exploit these impulses through an imaginative creative writing program.

As they teach creative writing, teachers must initiate early writing experiences, encourage written expression, and help students better formulate written expression. These three areas are discussed in turn.

Early Writing Experiences

Two ways of starting children in writing experiences are constructing charts that recount actual experiences and interrelating writing with other language arts skills.

8. Some references on early development of writing include the following: Marie Clay, *What Did I Write? A Study of Children's Writing* (New Zealand: Heinemann Educational Books, 1975); M. Dehn "Strategies in Learning to Read and Write: An Examination of the Learning Process," *Reading Teacher* 33 (December 1979): 270–277; Mary Anne Hall et al., "Writing Before Grade One—A Study of Early Writers," *Language Arts* 53 (May 1976): 582–585; Martha King and Victor Rentel, "Toward a Theory of Early Writing Development," *Research in the Teaching of English* 13 (October 1979): 243–253; and Charles Read, "What Children Know About Language: Three Examples," *Language Arts* 57 (February 1980): 144–148; and Shirley Haley-James, "When Are Children Ready to Write," *Language Arts* 59 (May 1982): 458–463.

Experience Charts Experience charts are recognized as a useful way of preparing children for reading. They also serve in preparing children for written expression; they are cooperative compositions that require planning what to say, organizing a logical sequence, and choosing the words to convey the exact meaning intended.

When the writing aspects of making a chart are emphasized, the teacher directs the work with comments and questions like the following:

How shall we start the chart?
Can someone think of another way?
Do you like that way of saying it?

The teacher develops a sense of organization by asking other leading questions:

What do we do next?
How should we end?
What title shall we put at the top of the chart?

Further discussion of the composition aspects of this writing experience involves the expression of ideas. The teacher develops this aspect by asking directive questions:

Have we said what we mean?
Is there more that should be said?
Have we put the items on the chart in the proper order?

Through experience charts, children build favorable attitudes toward writing and gain practical experience in such matters as unity of subject matter, organization of thought, choice of words and phrases, and fluency of expression. Although the primary emphasis should be upon these matters, the teacher may call attention to capitalization and punctuation, also.

Experience writing should be just what the name implies; children writing about their experiences. The classroom must be a laboratory where pupils have the opportunity to increase and enrich the range and variety of their storehouse of experiences. Experience writing should be built on class trips, activities, letters the children dictate, discussions, mock news reports, and group and individual literary efforts.

Little attempt should be made to control the children's vocabulary or to provide for repetition of words. This results in one of the chief values of the writing. It enriches the vocabulary as children brainstorm and experiment with new words.

To start the written composing process, the teacher should record (in writing) the children's oral expression. Dictation may be done individually as well as cooperatively by a group of five or six children. Sometimes a teacher may invite individual pupils to compose stories and then dictate them privately. As each child is telling the story, the teacher may write or type it, placing it on a chart or on the chalkboard. The dictated composition may merit duplication and distribution for reading and analysis by the class. To increase exposure and ease classroom management, younger children can dictate to older children; parents and aides can be used as scribes. Children's stories can be bound as "books" and be illustrated.

At the beginning, the written materials should reflect accurately the grammatical, syntactic, and vocabulary features of the child's own dialect. For example, when a child dictates "The dog he look like he sick," this should be recorded exactly as given and not rewritten as "The dog looks sick." Furthermore, Chomsky and Halle lend support to the notion that nonstandard dialectal and phonological features can be adequately represented (perhaps even optimally) with conventional spelling.[9] That is, no attempt should be made to use "eye" dialect, such as *wuz* for *was*. When divergent speakers of English read stories written in standard English, they should be allowed to read these materials in their own dialect. Changing the child's language destroys its integrity and implies that this language is inferior and hence the child must be inferior too. "Correcting" the child's language here may also cause a reluctance to dictate or read stories aloud. The language of the classroom constitutes only a fraction of the child's total language environment. Consequently, if classroom language instruction is to make an impact, language modification must be viewed as a long-range objective. This objective cannot be effectively implemented by destroying children's images of the communicative effectiveness of the language they bring with them to school.[10]

Language-Experience Approach In the language-experience approach, no distinction is made between the reading program and the program for

9. Noam Chomsky and Morris Halle, *The Sound Pattern of English* (New York: Harper & Row, 1968).
10. See Virgil E. Herrick and Marcella Nerbovig, *Using Experience Charts with Children* (Columbus, OH: Merrill, 1964). This small book shows many effective ways to help pupils understand that words, phrases, and usage conventions are the most expressive and efficient forms of communication.

CHART 7.1: *Experience Chart*

Our New Book

We have a new book.
Mrs. Jones, the librarian,
read it to us on Monday.
Its title is <u>Petunia</u>.

The story is about a
goose who thought she
could learn to read by
carrying a book under
her wing.

How does it end? We
won't tell!

developing the other language arts skills.[11] Full development and growth in any one of these skills hinges upon full development and growth in the other skills. The teacher encourages creative work with crayons, pencils, and paints as well as through the medium of speech. As a child gains self-expression through oral language, the teacher summarizes in a sentence or two a story first dictated by a child; this short composition is then written by the teacher as the child watches. Group compositions are also recorded as the children observe. While writing, the teacher calls attention to items that are important to reading and writing, such as letter formation, association of sounds with symbols, repetition of the same sounds or symbols, and the functions of capitalization and punctuation. These group compositions are used as a basis for discussion, as well as the children's own individual compositions.

As soon as pupils express the desire to write their own compositions, they are given the opportunity to do so. As children reach an independent level in handwriting, they are provided with basic word lists. Soon they develop control over a basic vocabulary through their writing experiences. When children develop in reading ability, they are given increasing opportunities to read from books for interest and research purposes and to do more writing.

Simply stated, the language-experience approach uses this rationale:

What I can think about, I can talk about.
What I can say, I can write.
What I can write, I can read.
I can read what I can write and what other people write for me to read.

Thus it can be seen that writing skills grow directly out of the procedures employed to develop reading facility. Developing facility in writing, in turn, makes a positive contribution to facility in word recognition, speaking, and spelling. Oral language facility increases through reading and writing by means of the dictation of stories and the discussion that is part of the storytelling process. Listening, fostered by reading good prose and poetry to the children, helps them develop a sensitivity to language forms.

Inability to spell the words they wish to use may be frustrating to young writers, particularly if teacher expectations include "correct" spelling at this time. However, some tips can be given to young writers, such as:

11. Mary Anne Hall, *Teaching Reading as a Language Experience*, 2d ed. (Columbus, OH: Merrill, 1981).

1. Leave a space for the unknown word and continue with writing.
2. Write as much of the word as you can.
3. Write the probable spelling on a slip of paper. If it looks correct, use it.
4. Think through the story before beginning to write, and ask the teacher to list difficult words on the chalkboard.

After a first draft has been finished, there are a number of ways of providing help for those who need it. The teacher may write down any word requested, either on the chalkboard or on a piece of paper on the child's desk. The child should be encouraged to look up unknown words in a picture dictionary or in a reader where the word may be found.

The children may keep a spelling notebook with a separate page devoted to words that they use frequently.[12] Additionally, charts of frequently used words may be displayed on the bulletin board or other accessible place.

Encouraging Written Expression

First-Hand Experiences As indicated in the preceding discussion, first-hand experiences can be the spark that ignites an idea. Close observation, followed by describing or explaining details and relating reactions to an experience, is a foundation stone in composing. Sense awareness is a very important component of expressive composition—listening, looking, touching, tasting, and smelling. Questions such as the following may be useful for stimulating sensory awareness:

What is the most beautiful thing you have ever seen?
What is the most beautiful sound you have ever heard?
How does an onion, pepper, candy, ice cream, or a sour pickle taste? Try to describe each.
How many different textures can you discover in the classroom? Try to describe them.
What is your favorite aroma? Try to describe it so that another person knows what you are describing.

Objects An example of objects used to stimulate writing would be a collection of hats brought into the classroom: that of a firefighter, a sailor,

12. For further detailed suggestions, see the chapters "Dictated Experience Stories" and "Creative Writing" in Russell G. Stauffer, *The Language Experience Approach to the Teaching of Reading* (New York: Harper & Row, 1970).

or a baseball or football player. Encourage the children to think about the possible stories associated with, say, the fire fighter's hat. Ideas can be expressed orally. Then each child may select one of the other hats to write about.

Pictures and Films A teacher who is adept at photography could take 35-mm slides of a waterfall. When showing them, the teacher could suggest that the children describe the sounds they would hear if they were in the picture. Art reproductions may also be used, as well as the children's own art work. Films like *Paddle to the Sea* (based on the book by Holling C. Holling)[13] may suggest further adventures. Children can react by inventing what might happen next, or at least summarize the story as presented. Sound filmstrips like *Lentil*[14] can be used in much the same fashion. In addition, filmed materials like the following are designed to encourage children to have inventive ideas.

A City Awakens, Churchill Films, 662 N. Robertson Blvd., Los Angeles, CA 90069 (16-mm film, color)

And Then What Happens? A First Experience in Creative Writing, Warren Schloat Productions, Inc., 150 White Plains Rd., Tarrytown, NY 10591 (five sound color filmstrips, cassettes, teacher's guide)

Let's Write a Story, Churchill Films, 662 N. Robertson Blvd., Los Angeles, CA 90069

Magic Moments, Encyclopaedia Britannica Educational Corporation, 425 N. Michigan Ave., Chicago, IL 60611 (twenty 16-mm sound films)

Millions and Millions of Bubbles, Churchill Films, 662 N. Robertson Blvd., Los Angeles, CA 90069 (16-mm film, color)

Pulcinella, Connecticut Films, Inc., 6 Cobble Hill Rd., Westport, CT 06880 (16-mm sound film, color)

Tchou Tchou, Encyclopaedia Britannica Educational Corporation, 425 N. Michigan Avenue, Chicago, IL 60611 (16-mm film, color)

Thoroughbred, Pyramid Films, Box 1048, Santa Monica, CA 90404 (16-mm film, color)

Titles At times, a title suggestion may be sufficient to release the flow of ideas. Some possible titles are: "Things I Dislike," "A Conversation with My Dog," "My Three Wishes," "What Happiness Means to Me," "My Most Pleasant Evening at Home," or "My Latest Dream." Some children

13. National Film Board of America, 680 Fifth Ave., New York, NY 10019.
14. Weston Woods Studio, Weston, CT 06880.

may like imaginary biographies, such as "My Life as a Goldfish"; others like topics closer to them, such as "My Favorite Pet."

More often, however, sets of related words or story beginnings and endings may prove more stimulating than titles. An example of a set of related words would be: *bump, dog, bandage, bicycle,* and *smiles.* From these words, children may evolve many different stories.

An example of a story beginning might be: "Bill and Jean were digging for clams. All at once Bill's shovel hit something that made a hollow sound. It was a shiny, hard object." A story ending: "Bob's older sister said, 'Well, I guess that will be a lesson you will not soon forget.'"

Literature A story such as *Pippi Longstocking*[15] can be followed by written ideas about what else could happen to Pippi. Or a teacher can read a story to the class and stop before reading the end and ask, "What do you think is going to happen? Let's write our own ending." Or children can describe a character in a book, such as Sara in *The Summer of the Swans.*[16]

After reading *Whistle for Willie,*[17] the teacher might try to stimulate writing by asking, "What if Peter woke up one morning and could not whistle for the dog?" "Someday" may be a natural title for an essay after children have heard or read *When I Am Big*[18] or *Someday.*[19] Different beginnings, different endings, changing of characters, changing of locale—all are opportunities for written expression. Sometimes, simply the display of a set of book jackets will serve as a starter for a story. And *Summer Diary*[20] is a book that hasn't been written as yet—the young child is supposed to do just that!

After hearing and reading make-believe stories, pupils can be encouraged to tell or write their own fantasy stories. For example, following the presentation of Kipling's *Just So Stories,* children often like to tell or write their own accounts of "why" or "how"—such as how the crow got its caw. With Paul Bunyan or Pecos Pete providing a stimulus, intermediate-level children frequently tell or write their own tall tales. After reading and discussing many fables and studying their characteristics (brevity, animals for characters, presentation of a moral), children may wish to try fable writing. Similarly, the reading and study of myths may lead children to write their own myths. Older children may be introduced to the idea of writing autobiographies by reading a book such as *Life Story.*[21]

15. Astrid Lindgren, *Pippi Longstocking* (New York: Viking, 1950).
16. Betsy Byars, *The Summer of the Swans* (New York: Viking, 1970).
17. Ezra Jack Keats, *Whistle for Willie* (New York: Viking, 1964).
18. Robert Paul Smith, *When I Am Big* (New York: Harper & Row, 1965).
19. Charlotte Zolotow, *Someday* (Harper & Row, 1964).
20. Ruthven Tremain, illus., *Summer Diary* (New York: Macmillan, 1970).
21. Virginia Lee Burton, *Life Story* (Boston: Houghton Mifflin, 1962).

Patterned writing also depends upon literature. To understand what is meant by patterned writing, see the following example.

What Is Red?

Red is a sunset
Blazy and bright.
Red is feeling brave
With all your might.
Red is a sunburn
Spot on your nose,
Sometimes red
Is a red, red rose.
Red squiggles out
When you cut your hand.
Red is a brick and
A rubber band.
Red is a hotness
You get inside
When you're embarrassed
And want to hide. . . .

What Is Red?

Red is sunburn
Ouch! What a hurt!
Red is Martha's shirt
With a spot of dirt.
Red is Joe's hair
Or underwear with a tear
(Mind you a t-shirt with
A lot of skin bare.)
Red is the sun
And something else.
"Red is my dad's name"
Sam said that himself.
This is red: ☐
If you color it so
Best of all
Red is a rose.

The poem on the left is from *Hailstones and Halibut Bones* by Mary O'Neill.[22] The one on the right was written by a third-grade boy.

Patterned writing helps children to write, imitate, and innovate story forms. They find it challenging and motivating, and writing success occurs for most. The procedures for using a poem or story for pattern writing includes close study of the model, discussion about the model, questions about patterns in the model, and other features. You may begin by having the whole class contribute, then move to small groups, and finally to individuals. First drafts may be refined and the patterned story or poem illustrated—and an illustrated typed copy may be made into a "book." Below are a few representative books of stories and poems that some teachers have found useful when teaching patterned writing.

Pascale Allamand, *The Animals Who Change Their Colors* (New York: Lothrop, Lee, & Shepard, 1979).
Frank Asch, *Monkey Face* (New York: Parents Magazine Press, 1977).
Sarah E. Barchas, *I Was Walking Down the Road* (New York: Scholastic, 1975).
Eric Carle, *The Grouchy Ladybug* (New York: Crowell, 1977).

22. Excerpt from "What Is Red?" Copyright © 1961 by Mary Le Duc O'Neill from the book *Hailstones and Halibut Bones* by Mary O'Neill. Reprinted by permission of Doubleday and Company, Inc. and World's Work Ltd.

Bernadine Cook, *The Little Fish That Got Away* (Reading, MA: Addison-Wesley, 1976).
Maggie Duff, *Rum Pum Pum* (New York: Macmillan, 1978).
Edward Emberley, *Klippity Klop* (Boston: Little, Brown, 1974).
Paul Galdone, *The Gingerbread Boy* (New York: Seabury, 1975).
Merra Geinsburg, *The Strongest One of All* (New York: Greenwillow, 1977).
Anita Lobel, *A Treeful of Pigs* (New York: Greenwillow, 1979).
Mercer Mayer, *Just for You* (New York: Golden Press, 1975).
Maria Polushkin, *Mother, Mother, I Want Another* (New York: Crown, 1978).
Robert Quackenbush, *Skip to My Lou* (Philadelphia: Lippincott, 1975).
Diane Wolkstein, *The Visit* (New York: Knopf, 1977).
Margot Zemach, *Hush, Little Baby* (New York: Dutton, 1976).

The Writing Center This is simply a place where students can go to write. Usually located in a quiet space within the classroom, the writing center is often stocked with thought-stimulating objects and pictures. For example, one fourth-grade teacher placed the following materials in the center:

A set of pictures
A "finish me" card file (unfinished stories)
Varied, interesting objects in a box
A chart with cartoons and short newspaper/magazine articles
A box of stationery containing interesting letterheads: MGM Studios, NASA, Dr. Albert Einstein, Queen Elizabeth Shipping Lines
Notebook paper and ballpoint pens in assorted colors, typing paper, a typewriter
Dictionaries and reference books
File folder (for work completed at the center)

Near the writing center should be a bulletin board which could occasionally display a theme to serve as the focal point for a composition. Other material for a writing center should include basic writing tools and resources, such as picture dictionaries and elementary school dictionaries, a thesaurus, perhaps an encyclopedia, and certainly various format items: handwriting charts, and forms for friendly letters, business letters, poems. Teachers may direct the activity in writing centers by placing worksheets there. See the primary-level example presented here.

WORKSHEET: *Shapes Around Us*

1. Go to the viewing center and watch the filmstrip called "A Circle in the Sky!" (Chicago: Coronet Instructional Films, 1970).
2. Listen to the tape of a story called "The Wing on a Flea," *A Book About Shapes* by Ed Emberley. The book is beside the tape recorder, and you may look at the pictures while the teacher reads.
3. Go to the art center and get some construction paper scraps.
4. Go to your seat and cut out some shapes that look like the shapes on the bulletin board. Make them different colors and sizes.
5. Paste your shapes on a sheet of paper. Put some on top of each other and try to make an object that looks like an animal or a person.
6. Look at your finished shape and write three sentences about it on a sheet of writing paper.
7. Put your name on the back of both papers and put your shape picture and story on the bulletin board.
8. Read at least three other stories on the bulletin board.
9. Take your picture down and turn it upside down on your desk. Look at it for five minutes and think of things that it reminds you of.
10. Now write three sentences about what it looks like.
11. Put your first story in your folder.
12. Share your second story with others by going to the reading circle and reading it aloud. Put your second story and picture in your folder.

Another item commonly found at the writing center is a set of independent composition activity cards. These may be commercial sets or sets developed by the teacher. An example of one of these cards is illustrated here.

ACTIVITY CARD: *Independent Composition—Story Writing*

Two boys are running through a field. They are running very fast. The wind is slapping against their faces. Use the following questions to get some ideas for a story.

Why are they running?

Where are they running from or to?

Are they happy or are they frightened?

Is something or someone chasing them?

Independent composition activity cards may be developed around a host of ideas: writing a descriptive paragraph about the texture of things pasted on the cards; writing a limerick after studying a sample limerick and its characteristics on a card; completing a story whose first paragraph is given on the card followed by some questions (as illustrated); using a picture and sentence on the card to begin a story; writing a paragraph that gives a good word picture of a photograph on the card; or writing in response to a problem situation, as illustrated in the card.

SSW (Sustained Silent Writing) This idea is based on the concept of SSR (Sustained Silent Reading) which gives learners time to silently read material of their choice. Some teachers set aside a five- or ten-minute period (possibly at the end of the school day) once or twice a week during which students write about whatever they wish. The teacher may read aloud certain writings, providing positive comments. Papers may be turned in for analysis by the teacher, but they are not graded or corrected. The teacher notes individual writing needs and later provides differentiated instruction, based on needed skills. An activity like SSW focuses on the

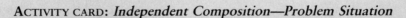

ACTIVITY CARD: *Independent Composition—Problem Situation*

1. If you were Joe's father, what would you tell him?
2. Why might Coach Dowell not have selected Joe for the first team?
3. Does Joe gain anything by continuing to play even though he isn't chosen for the first team?
4. Is there something you cannot do well? What should you do about it?
5. What things do you do poorly that you would like to do well? Why?
6. Write a paragraph about how you learned to do something well that you now enjoy doing.

whole process of writing, rather than attending solely to isolated components. Thus it helps students become more fluent writers.[23]

Diaries or Journals Each child may have a blank notebook that is his or her personal "book." Children may be encouraged to write on any topic or idea of their choice when they wish to do so. The diaries or journals may be taken home for out-of-school writing. Children, if they want, may share what they write with friends or others.

Additional Comments The above strategies are some ways to encourage creative prose writing. When a composition has been completed, be sure that it is shared with someone. One way to do this is by displaying it for others to enjoy.

More Effective Written Expression

Some time must be given to specific aspects of the writing process in order to improve the quality of writing. Here, as in other skill development, teachers should build on student strengths instead of focusing on their weaknesses. We suggest that teachers build instructional writing strategies with a general plan for the composing process, effective use of words, ways of describing, features of organization, and characterization.

General Plan Children in all grades should see composition as consisting of at least three important phases—prewriting, writing, and revision.[24] *Prewriting* refers to play activities, drawing, talking, viewing, and daily experiences for generating written language. *Writing* refers to the more or less sustained production, interrupted only by contemplation or physical movements. *Revision* is an attempt to improve the quality of the written product.

In discussing these three elements of a general instructional sequence, Norton[25] writes of the prewriting phase as the stimulation and motivational phase. Here the children use ongoing class activities in brainstorming ideas, posing questions, and clarifying ideas. Art is encouraged as a visualization of thinking before writing. During the composing period, Norton

23. Richard Allington, "Sustained Approaches to Reading and Writing," *Language Arts* 52 (September 1975): 813–815.
24. Donald Graves, "An Examination of the Writing Process of Seven-Year-Old Children," *Research in the Teaching of English* 9 (Winter 1975): 227–241. Also see Donald Graves, "Research Update," *Language Arts* 56 (October 1979): 829–835.
25. Donna Norton, *The Effective Teaching of the Language Arts* (Columbus, OH: Merrill, 1980), p. 237.

recommends the individual dictation of stories to a teacher, individual (independent) writing, teacher interaction to help clarify ideas, and other teacher assistance when asked. The writing phase is followed by sharing, involving such ideas as reading to others, developing a sense of audience, making permanent collections of the writing, or perhaps extending the writing to some form of creative drama. The revision, or postcomposing, activities suggested by Norton include keeping writing folders, holding writing conferences, and teaching the conventions of writing through the writing process.

Words A writer needs words and needs to delight in their use. Many exercises are possible to help children become sensitive to words. Discussion of tired, overworked words, such as *nice, good, pretty,* can bring forth suggestions of more specific words to substitute for them. Lively verbs can help in description. For example, the sentence "The girl walked down the street" could be improved by substituting a more descriptive verb, such as *stumbled, dawdled, ambled,* or *fluttered.* Vivid adjectives and adverbs also help to paint a clear word picture and can be developed as children suggest words associated with sight, sound, taste, touch, and smell. Newspaper and magazine advertisements use many descriptive words. They can be used to focus attention upon words that appeal, as suggested by the following task card.

Word charts can be developed with such titles as "Fun Words," "Quiet Words," "Fast Words," "Sleepy Words," or "Words about Sports." Attention can be focused on synonyms and antonyms; word families (*heart, hearty, heartily, heartless, heartache*); and foreign language words (*sombrero, petite, salon*). Worksheets may be prepared for words with different meanings: "I rose from the bed." "He smelled the red rose." Word lists may be developed of occupations (*farmers, mechanics*) or settings (*hospital, sports arena*). Refer to the section about word files in Chapter 1.

TASK CARD: *Descriptive Words*

Study the two advertisements placed on the bulletin board. Pick out the descriptive words used to make the reader want to try the product.

Pretend you are in advertising and must write an advertisement for a new product. It may be something to eat, drink, or wear; a game to play; or some cleaning product. See if you can make it sound like something the reader just cannot do without. Give it a name and illustrate it if you want.

Unusual words children glean from their reading can be placed on the bulletin board. Trade books, such as *Fooling Around with Words*[26] or *Teapot, Switcheroo, and Other Silly Word Games,*[27] can be used for playing with words. Use of alliteration, personification, simile, and metaphor add impact. Fresh images may be encouraged by having pupils complete comparisons (as red as . . . , as bold as . . . , as big as . . . , kittens are like . . . , the beating of the rain is like . . . , the scream of the fire siren is like . . .). Similes and metaphors may be found in all good literature.

Description In their writing, children often attempt to give a "picture" of what they are describing. It might be a description of an object, a place, an animal, a person, or an event. The questions to ask about effective description are the "sense" ones: "Can you see it? (hear it? taste it? feel it? smell it?)." Sensory-oriented exercises are recommended; write your clearest description of the appearance of your bedroom, the sound of the song of a bird, the taste of lemonade, the feel of sand on your toes, and the smell of frying bacon at breakfast.

Specific attributes may be developed for an object, place, animal, person, event. For example, as children describe an object, attributes may be listed on the chalkboard: color, shape, size, weight, texture, temperature, aroma, taste. Attributes for a place might involve animate or inanimate objects in the place and their spatial arrangements, temperature, colors, shapes, and so on. For persons, attributes might include size, weight, facial features, clothing, body characteristics. Similar observation guides may be prepared for animals and events.

Organization In developing students' organizational skills in writing, teachers should suggest that students choose an interest-arousing and suitable topic, give an interesting title reflecting the major idea or perhaps a key phrase used in the story, plan a good beginning sentence or two that will arouse attention and let the action begin to take place, and prepare a concluding sentence that sums up the experience or sharply ends the action. More specifically, children may avoid such beginnings as "One day . . ." or "Once upon a time . . ." by using a variety of phrases.

It was Bill's chance to . . .
As Susan opened the door to the house . . .
Tom never dreamed that this was going to be a special day . . .

26. Ruthven Tremain (New York: Greenwillow, 1976).
27. Ruthven Tremain (New York: Greenwillow, 1979).

Stories can begin with a conversation, with a question, or with other techniques to set the stage for action.

A study of children's literature reveals ways for the writer to "invite" the reader into the story. For example, the pupil might study beginning sentences in such works as *Charlotte's Web* ("Where's Papa going with that ax?"),[28] *Roosevelt Grady* ("The Opportunity Class. That's where the bean pickers got put."),[29] or *It's Like This, Cat* ("My father is always talking about how a dog can be very educational for a boy. That is one reason I got a cat.").[30] After such study, one sixth-grade girl started a story in this fashion: "Can you remember when you were so little that you could not reach anything? Well, this is just the problem this small boy is having."

There must be something in an action that reveals what, when, where, why and how things happen. From this one piece of action several actions in a sequence (one idea per paragraph) can build to a complete story. Pupils must decide on the most important details. Putting the events in an order that makes one want to know "what happens next" heightens the suspense value. Before putting together the various pieces of action, the writer must decide whether the story is best told from the point of view of the writer (as a participant in the story), of an observer, or of one of the characters.

Text grammars have been developed to describe how a story scheme is organized into categories of information. In general, the grammar defines a *story* as a series of problem-solving episodes centering on the main character's (or characters') efforts to achieve a major goal. Although various authors label components of the story differently, any grammar usually includes some form of the following major types of information:

Setting: Introduces characters, time, and place
Initiating Event: Leads main character to formulate major goal and starts sequence of actions and events
Goal: Major desire of main character
Number of Attempts: Actions of the characters
Series of Outcomes: Events or states produced by characters' actions
Internal Responses: Subgoals, thoughts, and feelings of characters leading to actions

28. E. B. White, *Charlotte's Web* (New York: Harper & Brothers, 1952).
29. Louisa R. Shotwell, *Roosevelt Grady* (Cleveland, OH: World Publishing, 1972).
30. Emily C. Neville, *It's Like This, Cat* (New York: Harper & Row, 1963).

Reactions: Thoughts or feelings produced by the outcome of actions[31]

Children should hear and read many types of stories before trying to write one of a particular type. Time should be devoted to analyzing such features as: beginning, middle, end of a story; characters; setting; action; dialogue; and title.

Characterization To bring characters to life, the writer needs to tell, among other things, how they look, what they do and say (and how), what other persons think about the characters, and what goes on in the characters' own thinking. Such information can reveal the motivation for the characters' actions. Use of conversation helps to make characters seem real and alive. Characterization may be developed in several other ways. The narrator or other characters may simply state a fact: "The boy is selfish." Or the character can explain how he or she acts, or describe an event that proves the point. Storytellers often compare characters with each other—readers will sense just how good or bad a character is through such comparisons.

WRITING CREATIVE POETRY

Poetry writing can help children gain a better understanding of language and writing in general; it involves looking at things accurately, experiencing them acutely, and expressing them lucidly.

The strongest foundation for a poetry writing program is a planned poetry reading and study program that includes a balance of poems of various characteristics, topics, and forms. Through such a program, children become familiar with what poetry is and its various themes and forms. They sense that poems can be about activities (work, play, special occasions); surroundings (home, neighborhood); reflections (issues of our time, personal concerns); or the arts. They see that varied forms are possible (couplets, triplets, quatrains, limericks).

Five steps may be recommended as a general procedure for preparing pupils to write poetry.

1. Reading and studying a well-known poem. (Put it on the overhead projector or the chalkboard.)

---

31. Stephanie H. McConaughy, "Using Story Structure in the Classroom," *Language Arts* 57 (February 1980): 157–165.

2. Reading a child's poem (perhaps from a previous year) to convince the children that they too can do it.
3. Asking questions to discuss the form under consideration.
4. Pooling experiences and opinions by the class members to gather ideas for their own poems.
5. Writing suggested, distinctive words, phrases, and ideas on the chalkboard.

At this time, children are invited to try writing their own poems.

Free Verse

Examples of free verse include such poems as "Mouse" by Hilda Conkling and "Fog" by Carl Sandburg. Sources of free verse include *Prayers from the Ark*[32] and *The Creature's Choir*.[33]

Through wide exposure to poetry, along with analysis of the poet's craft, the child comes to recognize what free verse is and how it differs from prose. It is brief, focuses on a specific theme, and demands precise use of words that appeal to the senses as well as convey meaning. Words are patterned in a rhythmic manner (and also sometimes in a rhyming manner) and placed in lines for effect.

Free verse is unrhymed poetry. There are no restrictions as to metrical pattern or recurrence of stress. The writer is free to decide upon rhythm or meter, where a new line begins, what content or imagery to use, and the like. Children should be encouraged to write free verse about their daily experiences.

Poems should appeal to the senses, and poems about "sensations" should be read to children. Sharpness of perception is required.

What do you see in this picture?
What sound do you hear in the school corridor as we sit silently in our seats?
Describe your favorite flavor of ice cream, and let's see if we can guess it.
Let's talk about the feel of a slippery bar of soap.
Can you describe the smell of these plants and blossoms?

Perhaps the teacher will want to initiate some free-verse writing by discussing a topic like "rain." The pupils would be encouraged to think

32. Carmen B. De Graztold, *Prayers from the Ark,* trans. by Rumer Godden (New York: Viking, 1962).
33. Rumer Godden, *The Creature's Choir* (New York: Viking, 1965).

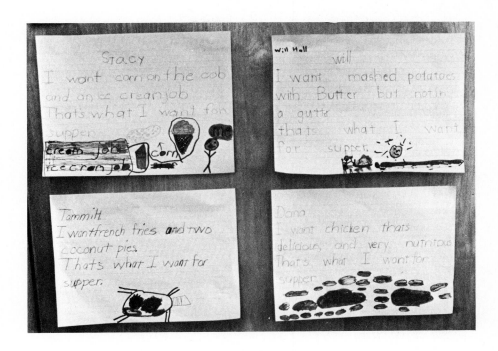

of some ideas and images, which can then be written on the chalkboard. The teacher may demonstrate how a poet smooths and condenses ideas and arranges them in the form of a poem.[34]

Here is an example of a free verse by a group of second-grade children.

Rain

Rain is water.
It is like taking a bath.
Rain is sometimes warm and sometimes cold.
It is like going swimming.
Rain is wet.

Free-verse writing should precede the writing of rhyming or syllabic poetry, so that the child first focuses on ideas and thoughts.

---

34. See Moira Dunn, "Writing Poetry in the Elementary School," *Elementary English* 45 (March 1968): 337–341. See also Denis Rodgers, "A Process for Poetry Writing," *Elementary School Journal* 72 (March 1972): 294–303.

Rhyme Arrangements

Couplet A couplet is a simple, two-line, rhymed pattern. A model from literature might be taken from "Cats Have Kittens" or "Jump or Jiggle," both by Evelyn Beyer. Another model might be Christina Rossetti's "What Is Pink?" From the first model, a couplet such as the following might result.

> If dogs have pups
> Do saucers have cups?

From the second Beyer model, noun pairs might be presented for consideration, such as:

> Boys _____
> Girls _____

"Color" couplets abound in Rossetti's work. For example:

> What is brown?
> The color of the ground.

Triplet A triplet (or tercet) is a three-line poem that conveys humor and tells a brief story. Following is a triplet prepared by an eight-year-old.

> There was a kite
> Tied to a light.
> Oh, what a sight!

Quatrain A quatrain contains four lines with an a, b, a, b rhyming pattern. After reading and study of a number of quatrains ("The Pasture" by Robert Frost is an example), one child wrote:

> A bear is funny,
> He likes to climb trees,
> He likes the honey,
> But not the bees.

Limerick The rhyme pattern of a limerick is a, a, b, b, a. Three metrical beats are given in lines 1, 2, and 5, and two beats in lines 3 and 4, as noted in the following example.

There was a young lady of Lynn
Who was so exceedingly thin
    That when she essayed
    To drink lemonade
She slipped through the straw and fell in.

Syllabic Arrangements

Haiku The classical Japanese haiku consists of seventeen syllables in three lines; the first and third lines have five syllables, the second seven. There is no metrical pattern and lines do not rhyme. It contains at least some reference to nature (other than human nature); refers to a particular event (that is, it is not a generalization); and presents that event as happening now, not in the past. As yet, there are no generally accepted criteria for English haiku. It seems obvious, however, that it cannot be exactly the same as Japanese haiku if only because of the difference in language. There is no rule compelling one to follow classical Japanese standards for haiku, but beginners should conform to Japanese standards as far as it is practicable. If the pupils choose simple topics and write naturally, their own actual experiences serve as subjects for their haiku. The following poems represent average fifth- or sixth-grade haiku attempts.

Snow falling till dawn
Early skiers having fun.
Winter has begun.

Water trickling over rocks
bringing life to the forest
for the bountiful land.

White snow on the ground
beautiful, so beautiful.
Then it goes away.

Three books of haiku that may be helpful are:

Ann Atwood, *My Own Rhythm: An Approach to Haiku* (New York: Scribner, 1973).
Harry Behn, *More Cricket Songs* (New York: Harcourt Brace Jovanovich, 1971).
Richard Lewis, ed., *The Way of Silence* (New York: Dial, 1970).

Cinquain The cinquain, though not Japanese, was perhaps influenced by haiku. One excellent book of cinquains is Lee Bennett Hopkins, comp., *City Talk* (New York: Alfred A. Knopf, 1970).

Cinquain is a syllabic verse form, but the pattern involves gradually increasing the number of syllables in each line until the last, which returns to two syllables:

2 syllables
4 syllables
6 syllables
8 syllables
2 syllables

Here is an example:

The night
Bright, twinkling stars
Milky way, galaxies
Dark skies, midnight blue, shining moon
Silence

Teachers often alter the form, using this pattern: first line, one word giving the title; second line, two words describing the title; third line, three words expressing an action; fourth line, four words expressing a feeling; fifth line, another word for the title. An example might be:

Colt
　　　All legs
　　　　　Wobbling, shaking, kicking
　　　　　　Curious, full of life
　　　　　　　Pony.

Lanterne Here the five lines contain the following number of syllables, respectively: 1, 2, 3, 4, 1. Note the visual shape of the Japanese lantern in the following example.

The
red ball
rolls quickly
down the long steep
hill.

Septolet The seven lines contain the following number of syllables, respectively: 1, 2, 3, 4, 3, 2, 1. For example:

Quick
Blue-eyed
Pussycat
Frightening jays
From the yard
Proudly
Fast.

Tanka The tanka is somewhat like an extension of haiku, with a 5, 7, 5, 7, 7 syllable pattern; rhyme and meter are not used. The following poem is an example of this form.

Footprints in the sand
Side by side, the large and small,
Across the damp beach
Tell me that father and son
Have left behind the mother.

Other Arrangements

Diamond Poem

Day
Warm, new
Dawning, waiting, rushing,
Work, activity, rest, sleep,
Closing, thinking, planning,
Cool, quiet
Night

Five-Sense Poem

Happiness is the color of rainbows.
It tastes like a triple ice-cream cone.
It sounds like the slosh of waves.
It smells like fresh bread baking.
It looks like a newborn baby.
It makes me feel warm and good.

Blotz Poem

This is a hysteriadae
Hysteriadaes live in Hawaii, Havana, or Hickory Hollow

Hysteriadaes eat haddock, halfbacks, hamburgers, and hedges
Hysteriadaes like havoc, hiccups, hearses, and harpoons
Hysteriadaes hurl horrid hogwash and hang husky humans
A hysteriadae hoaxed me into haggling with a hairy hillbilly for a horrid
   harmonica.

Evaluation

When trying to make valid judgments about children's work, one must
know their ages and something about their maturity, background, and
experiences. What is considered good poetry for a child of eight may be
too immature and unthinking in form and idea for a child of twelve. An
expression that is unsatisfactory for a child of wide experience may be
judged excellent for an underprivileged child or a child of limited experience. A poem which may seem to have no value may show by comparison
with the child's earlier work the very sort of individual growth for which
the teacher is striving.

Although standards must be flexible and adapted to the age and grade
of the child or group, there are some specific items to look for that will
help the teacher: originality of thought and expression; choice of words;
reflection of what the writer really thinks and feels; clear description of a
central thought, idea, or pattern; and pleasing cadence to the language. If
a child's poem has even one of these characteristics, it indicates that the
poetic spirit is at work and should be respected.

The child's work must be handled carefully. Pride in work can be
developed through praise. Growth takes place in individual or small group
conferences where questions are raised.

How do you feel about this?
What is a way to narrow the topic?
Would it be better if the last three words were on a line by themselves?
What more specific word could be used for this rather vague one?
What needless words could be deleted?

After such an evaluation session, the child is encouraged to rewrite a final
copy if there is to be an audience.[35]

---

35. See Chapter 11, "Dignifying Children's Poetic Composition," *Poetic Composition
Through the Grades* by Robert A. Wolsch (New York: Teachers College Press, Columbia
University, 1970). Also see Ronald Cramer, *Children's Writing, Reading, and Language
Growth* (Columbus, OH: Merrill, 1978), Chapter 7.

FUNCTIONAL WRITING

A child whose writing experiences are only stories and poetry has a restricted composition program. Such a program neglects the writing of expository prose. Teachers must strive for a balance between creative writing and functional writing. Each has a significant place in the composition program.

Some situations at the primary and intermediate levels that lend themselves to functional writing include:

Letters: friendly letters; business letters; social notes of thanks, invitation, sympathy, congratulations

Card writing and postcards

Reports in content subjects

Announcements and notices of events, articles for the school newspaper, items for the bulletin board and exhibits

Records of class plans: class activities, events, club minutes, room histories or diaries

Forms such as registration slips, examination blanks.

In a classroom where many learning experiences enrich the curriculum, good reasons for writing are not difficult to find. Pupils are actively writing weather reports, making lost-and-found announcements, listing plans, reporting on facts learned, describing how a project was undertaken, writing minutes of club meetings, and the like.

Letter Writing

Since letter writing is a fundamental job in written composition, it deserves special consideration. Teachers can use real situations when teaching letter writing, even for practice periods to provide for specific or technical difficulties. There are many situations calling for real letter writing: pupils who are ill or who have moved away, requests for materials, and so on.

Friendly Letters Informal discussion should precede letter writing at the primary and intermediate levels. This discussion could cover questions relating to content and form. Though form is important, it should be considered of secondary importance to content. The pupils ought to know that courtesy, informality, humor, expression of opinions and feelings, cheerfulness, and clearness make interesting, friendly letters. They need to know that they should write letters naturally, just as they would speak. A letter is an "on-paper" visit and should sound as if the writer is actually visiting. Pupils should be encouraged to bring their letter writing to school. If they want to write letters to friends, the teacher ought to make them feel that at school they can get the help they need.

The mere copying of "standard" letters from a language textbook or workbook seems like a waste of time to children and usually should be avoided. If proper forms of letters are available during a letter-writing activity, these models may be used for discussing the meanings behind the form. Children should be encouraged to do the job correctly under the teacher's guidance and to develop high standards that come from within so the goals will not be laid aside when they write without the teacher's supervision.

Checklists posted on the bulletin board or chalkboard can be helpful in bringing pupils' attention to mechanical features of letter writing. Information such as the following can be provided for the primary years.

> **CHART 7.2:** *Friendly Letter Guide (Primary Years)*
>
> A friendly letter has five parts:
>
> Heading
> Greeting
> Body
> Closing
> Signature
>
> 1. Begin the first word in a greeting with a capital letter.
> 2. Begin each proper name with a capital letter.
> 3. Put a comma after the last word in the greeting.
> 4. Begin the first word in the closing with a capital letter.
> 5. Put a comma after the last word in the closing.

Business Letters The sample business letter here shows its six parts and the required capitalization and punctuation.

When the time comes to write a business letter, the teacher may distribute mimeographed addresses from *1001 Valuable Things You Can Get Free* (Mort Weisinger, Bantam Books, 1968) or some other source. Business letter writing should include experience with ordering things by mail.

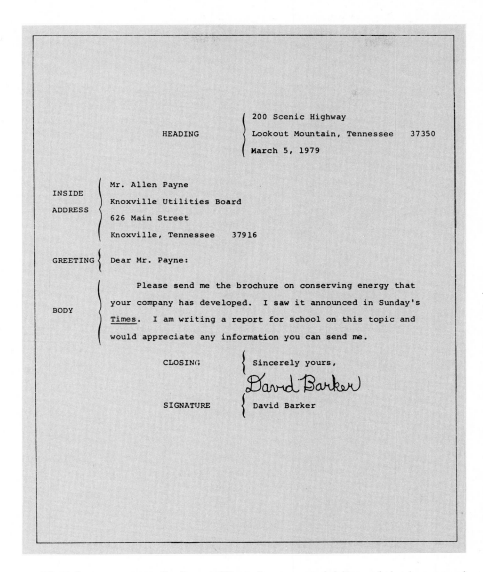

```
                                  ⎧  200 Scenic Highway
                   HEADING        ⎨  Lookout Mountain, Tennessee    37350
                                  ⎩  March 5, 1979

                                  ⎧  Mr. Allen Payne
        INSIDE                    ⎪  Knoxville Utilities Board
        ADDRESS                   ⎨  626 Main Street
                                  ⎩  Knoxville, Tennessee    37916

        GREETING ⎨  Dear Mr. Payne:

                                  ⎧      Please send me the brochure on conserving energy that
                                  ⎪  your company has developed.  I saw it announced in Sunday's
        BODY                      ⎨  Times.  I am writing a report for school on this topic and
                                  ⎩  would appreciate any information you can send me.

                     CLOSING      ⎨  Sincerely yours,

                                         David Barker

                     SIGNATURE    ⎨  David Barker
```

When letters are ready for mailing, the proper folding of the letter and addressing of the envelope need attention. Approaches to addressing envelopes, with proper punctuation and capitalization, should be illustrated and models provided for the pupils. (Other practical occasions require letter writing, such as giving our opinions. Examples would be writing to the editor of a paper or writing to a company to complain about a particular product.)

Social Notes One of the first courtesies a child is taught is to say "Thank you" for gifts or kindnesses. Expressing appreciation is a way of showing consideration for others. It is very easy to say "Thank you" in person; when it must be written, it seems more difficult. Pupils can be helped to understand that they may put in a letter just what they would say if the person were present. A letter of thanks should mention the thoughtfulness of the other person. For example, William may tell how much he likes a gift he received and what use he is making of it. If Maria should happen to receive a gift she does not like, she can still sincerely express appreciation for the kindness that prompted the gift and avoid mentioning her true feeling about the gift itself. There is no excuse for rudeness. Thank-you notes promptly and graciously written indicate good manners and consideration for the feelings of others. Even when thanks are expressed personally, a follow-up note at a later date is a thoughtful gesture.

Letters of invitation should be sincere and cordial. They need to be specific as to the event for which the invitation is issued (party, program, visit to the class) and always give the time, place, and host or hostess.

When a friend is ill or has had a misfortune, a good way to show sympathy is to write a cheer-up letter. Such a letter should have at least two content items. It should say something to show that the writer is sorry the friend is ill and hopes he or she will be well soon. It should mention only things that will cheer or amuse the recipient—not discuss the illness or the illnesses of others or unpleasant news that might worry the friend.

Children have many opportunities to do the kind thing and write a note of congratulations to a friend who has won a contest, received an honor, or had some other good fortune. Children should be aware of such rules as: mention the honor that has been received, say something that shows you are glad he or she received it, and don't say anything that suggests he or she was unworthy of it or might have done better.

Card Writing Card writing is a variation of letter writing. Initial instruction may be followed by independent activity at a card-writing station, as suggested here.

Although there are no specific rules concerning writing postcards, three points might be suggested:

Postcards are less formal than letters.

Complete headings are not needed on postcards.

Postcards should not be used for very personal or very private messages.

ACTIVITY CARD: *Card-Writing Station*

Materials

Large box marked "Thank-You Cards," another marked "Cheer-Up Cards," and a third labeled "Congratulations Cards." Construction paper, crayons, pens, etc.

Directions

1. Plan a thank-you card for a gift you have received. Fold a piece of construction paper in the form of a card and write the message. Illustrate your card.
2. Plan a cheer-up card for someone who is ill. Design the card. Write the message and put the finished card in the "Cheer-Up" box.
3. Plan a congratulations card for someone who has had some good fortune. Say something that shows you are happy for the person.

Reports

Children's written work in the content areas (particularly science and social studies) will often take the form of reports. What is usually involved in writing a report? A topic is assigned or chosen, information must be gathered, and the ideas must be organized with major points and supporting details. A need to use reference sources and a bibliography often occurs with report writing. After the first draft is written, it will usually need to be revised and proofread before the final product is prepared.

Blake and Spennato[36] believe that the Directed Reading Activity (DRA), a useful technique for developing reading ability, could be adapted into a Directed Writing Activity (DWA) for helping children become better writers. Their suggestion is to provide a structure for important phases of prewriting, writing, and revision. The plan is especially pertinent to report writing.

The steps include the following and may take several days to complete.

1. **Prewriting:** Here children are helped to select a topic, collect and organize information, develop vocabulary, and the like.

---

36. Howard Blake and Nicholas A. Spennato, "The Directed Writing Activity: A Process with Structure," *Language Arts* 57 (March 1980): 317–318.

2. **Framing the Writing Assignment:** In this step, children develop questions that are relevant to the topic and then decide which of the questions interest them most and are most related. These questions will serve as a guide to the writing if they have sufficient information to answer the questions.
3. **Writing:** The writer organizes the information, answering the questions. Then the writer reads the draft aloud to a classmate or the teacher who listens for clarity of thought and fluidity of language. Using the listener's reactions, the writer moves to the next step.
4. **Revising the Draft:** Here attention is given to the substance and syntax of the draft, not to the mechanics.
5. **Editing:** In this step, pupils check for all mechanics (punctuation, capitalization, spelling, and so on). The teacher or another student reads the draft to help further refine mechanical errors.
6. **Final Draft:** Using the information from all sources, the author edits the writing, proofreads it, and submits a finished draft.

(See Chapter 10 for information on helpful organization skills, such as note taking, outlining, and summarizing.)

Announcements and Notices

Various school activities call for written announcements and notices. Such announcements should always include all the information necessary to enable the reader to respond appropriately. The child should always check written announcements or notices to see if they answer these important questions: Who? What? When? Where? Why? An interesting caption helps to arouse interest. Careful attention must be given to handwriting, for a notice serves no purpose if it is illegible. Moreover, a notice that is attractive in appearance is more likely to be read than a sloppy, carelessly written one.

Notices and announcements should be posted only in places set aside for this purpose and in a manner that does not deface property. They are not to be posted until permission has been granted by the proper authorities. Requesting such permission provides for functional language teaching and learning.

The example of a systematic lesson on oral announcements presented in Chapter 1 may be adapted to a written announcement.

Two related writing activities are news articles and want ads for the school or class newspaper. Both are direct and to the point. A good guide to writing a news account is to answer the questions: *Who* is the story about? *What* has happened? *When* did the event occur? *Where* does the action take place? *Why* did it happen? *How* did it happen?

For want ad writing, the children may study the columns in the classified ad section of the newspaper. When writing an ad, pupils should include information potential buyers will need; they should give directions for locating the seller, either by phone or by mail.

Also, composing a lost and found ad helps develop students' ability to include important and specific details in their writing. Important facts to include: specific description of the item, where it was lost or found, name of the owner or finder, telephone number of the owner or finder, and rewards, if offered.

Children might begin writing for rhetorical purposes (to convince or persuade) by writing a paragraph listing the reasons for or against something, such as "Why I Should Have a Bicycle" or "Why I Do Not Want to Take Piano Lessons." Students should elaborate on their reasons to support their idea.

Records

Several types of records are kept by elementary school children. Some are group efforts—a class diary or an account of a project or experiment; others are individual records—a record of progress in spelling or of books read. Record keeping can be a valuable learning experience if it is not so lengthy and detailed as to become burdensome.

In a class diary, all pupils assume a share of the responsibility. Since everything that happens cannot be recorded, pupils must learn to choose the really important items. They learn to be accurate and specific, giving dates and pertinent details. In keeping records of experiments or the weather, or similar accounts, each entry should be dated and the information clearly stated in terms meaningful to others. Records should be simple but accurate. Entries ought to be made regularly in the form agreed upon by the pupils and the teacher.

Conventions in writing

Some mechanics of written expression are considered in this section. They include capitalization, punctuation, sentence sense, paragraph sense, and manuscript form.

Capitalization

Capitalization is a mechanical element of written language. Courses of study and textbooks in language arts are often quite definite in listing grade requirements in the area of capitalization. However, such listings are merely guides for the introduction of these items; within a classroom there will be considerable variation in capitalization skills. This means that items of capitalization generally listed in the primary years should be mastered before items that are listed for the intermediate years.

Instructional Items A guide to capitalization skills is needed by teachers. The following list of minimal capitalization skills takes into account the needs of children in writing.

Capitalization	Example
The word *I*	
First word in a sentence	He sings in the chorus.
Title of people	Our speaker was Ms. Jones.
Important words in book or story title	
Proper nouns (cities, states, streets, months, day, and so on)	Boston, Lee School, Monday
Proper adjective	It is a Japanese car.
First word in a direct quote	Ted said, "Move over."
First word in letter greeting	Dear Tony,
First word in a letter closing	Your friend,
Initials	R. C. Thomas

Instructional Procedures Capitalization skills can be developed in a number of ways. Certainly the teacher will want to observe the written work of the pupil, noting errors made and possibly tabulating the types of errors as a basis for further teaching and study. Chart 7.3 suggests one method of tabulating.

Self-diagnosis of difficulties should be taught. Group and individual dictation drills emphasizing capitalization items that seem difficult for the pupils to master may be used. Pupils should be called upon to check on their use of capital letters on numerous occasions. This acquaints the child not only with irregularities in practice but also with sources commonly used as standards. Group correction of a paper with special reference to capitalization is possible through the use of an overhead projector or the chalkboard. Short, diagnostic tests on the major capitalization skills may

CHART 7.3: *Analysis of Capitalization Items*

Pupils' Names	First word of a sentence	Proper nouns	Days, months places, holidays	Titles	First word in a poem	Salutation/ closing of a letter	Official organizations	Brand names	First word of a quoted sentence	Proper adjectives

be given periodically, followed by practice periods devoted to specific needs. Finally, a five-minute, individualized practice period (proofreading exercise) near the end of the day may be devoted to capitalization errors observed during the day.

Punctuation

Punctuation errors are common mechanical mistakes pupils make in written composition. The following is a suggested list of punctuation items that should receive instruction in the elementary school.

CHECKLIST: *Punctuation*

Punctuation	Example
Period	
at end of sentences	Bill threw the ball.
after abbreviation	Feb.
after initial	T. R. Brown
Question Mark	
at the end of a question	May I go?
Exclamation Mark	
at the end of an exclamation	Oh! What a surprise!
Comma	
after friendly letter greeting	Dear John,
after letter closing	Your friend,
after initial yes or no	Yes, I can go.
between city and state	Birmingham, Alabama
between month and year	January, 1980
before direct quotation	Todd said, "We can do it."
after words in a series	The basket held many oranges, bananas, and apples.
after noun of direct address	Dick, will you go?
Apostrophe	
contraction	I'm
possession	Bob's dog is missing.
Miscellaneous	
quotation around direct quotation	Lisa said, "Try your best."
underlining book titles	*Little House on the Prairie*
colon before list	There were many different kinds of fruit in the basket: apples, grapefruit, tangerines.
colon after business-letter greeting	Dear Ms. Jones:
colon in writing time	5:30 P.M.

Some activities that may be used to provide meaningful practice with punctuation are as follows:

1. Teach students that commas help the reader understand what a sentence means
   a. Ronny can't hear, Dan. Ronny can't hear Dan.
   b. "If you drive George we can all go to the movies," said Alice. (Is someone going to drive George somewhere? Is Alice talking to George?)
   c. Pat made chicken salad sandwiches and apple pie. (How many different things did Pat make? Did Pat make chicken salad sandwiches?)
2. Ask students to correct the punctuation in a passage or series of sentences and to indicate the reason.
3. Read passages to students, providing each student with a copy. The student inserts marks of punctuation as the teacher reads.
4. Supply each student with a copy of a letter with no punctuation marks. When the letter is read orally, students name the punctuation marks that are missing.
5. Provide the students with pictures. Ask students to write direct dialogue, using quotation marks and commas. (For example, a picture of two girls playing might evoke this sentence: Betty said, "Let me show you how to jump the rope.")

The teacher, by studying pupils' papers, will note errors made and keep a record, such as Chart 7.4, as a basis for providing needed instruction. (See Chapter 13 for diagnostic/corrective worksheets for punctuation items.)

Children can improve their writing ability if they understand that the language they are writing is related to the one they have spoken all their lives. For advanced pupils in written composition, more detailed instruction in the use of intonation can be obtained from various sources.[37] However, writing is not simply "talk written down." Writing has its own norms, as described by Smith and others.[38]

37. See J. N. Hook, *The Teaching of High School English*, 4th ed. (New York: Ronald, 1972), pp. 319–349.
38. Frank Smith, "Myths of Writing," *Language Arts* 58 (October 1981): 792–798.

CHART 7.4: *Analysis of Punctuation Items*

Pupils' Names	Period	Comma	Semicolon	Colon	Quotation Mark	Apostrophe	Question Mark	Hyphen	Underlining

Sentence Sense

Sentence types are often classified according to purpose: declarative, interrogative, exclamatory, and imperative. Or they may be categorized according to structure: simple (contains subject and predicate); compound (combines two or more simple sentences, or independent clauses, joined by such words as *and, but, or,* and *nor*); and complex (consists of one or more independent clauses to which is attached a dependent clause that acts as a modifier and begins with a connective such as *if, when,* and *since*).

Beginning Instruction It is not unusual to find children who, at the conclusion of elementary school, do not understand what a sentence is and therefore have difficulty writing good sentences. Yet teachers can begin early to help children learn what a sentence is. In kindergarten or primary years when children dictate stories to the teacher, emphasis can be placed on sentence sense. Suppose the children are telling about a walk in the park. One child may say, "Today we went for a walk in the park." The teacher, while writing these words on the chalkboard, says, "That's a good beginning sentence. What should our next sentence be?"

"We saw some squirrels in the park," suggests another child.

The teacher remarks, "Jan has told one thing about our trip. Who can tell something else?"

"The squirrels were eating nuts," says Bill.

"That is another sentence," comments the teacher. "We will begin it with a capital letter and put a period at the end."

Oral reading also helps pupils to develop sentence sense. As they listen, children discover that changes in pitch and juncture indicate the beginning and ending of sentences.

Constant comparison between what children read and what they report helps them to sense the concept of one idea separated from others by an initial capital letter and a terminal mark of punctuation. This is the writer's way of showing where pauses would occur between ideas if one were talking instead of writing. The teacher, writing at the children's dictation, can do much to strengthen their grasp of completeness in sentences.

One-sentence compositions are also helpful. Children may be asked to tell one thing (one sentence) about a picture or object, a pet, a trip, or some topic like "My New Shoes," "My Baby Sister," or "My Favorite Toy." From the one-sentence composition, move to the two- and three-sentence composition as sentence skill develops.

Pupils can be asked to write model sentences based on basic sentence patterns and to experiment with expanding these basic patterns by adding descriptive words, words denoting time and place, and so on. They can be led to discover how meaning and emphasis are influenced by the position of words in the sentence. For example, "The dog chased the cat" can be expanded into "Yesterday, the black dog chased the white cat, Tommy, down the street." Without getting technical about prepositional phrases, infinitives, participles, and so on, children can detect open points in the basic patterns where subordinate units and modifiers can be inserted. (See Chapter 3 for review of these ideas.)

Further Suggestions Other suggestions for developing sentence sense throughout the elementary school program have been selected from Petty and Jensen:

Provide children with ample opportunity for oral composition, especially in the primary grades.

Encourage oral expression to form habits of using sentences that make sense, that are clear and complete.

Encourage considerable group composing and dictating of letters and other forms of written expression.

Encourage children to answer questions with the expression of one complete thought.

Provide exercises in which class members are required to distinguish between fragments and complete sentences.

Insist on pupils proofreading their own writing.

Provide exercises for making sentences out of nonsentence groups of words.

Use matching exercises made up of short lists of complete subjects in one column and complete predicates in another.

Provide exercises for breaking up run-on sentences into correct sentences.

Provide exercises for the organization of sentence elements into their proper relationships.[39]

Despite such experiences, some children complete the elementary school years still writing fragments. One reason for this is they are often misled by the practices of speech. In speech, sentences lacking the full structure of the pattern are frequently uttered. For example, in reply to the question, "Who is that fellow?" the oral answer might well be "My brother." When an advanced pupil cites a fragment in the work of a professional writer, it can be pointed out that the professional is working on a more subtle and complicated level than the pupil is yet capable of handling. The professional diverges from the norm intentionally—not insecurely or haphazardly or out of ignorance. He or she does this in particular situations in order to achieve calculated effects. The teacher must emphasize the conventional practices and tell children that eventually they will learn how and when to depart from the norm.

Some Sentence Difficulties The *and* fault, the run-on sentence, and the choppy sentence are difficulties frequently found in the writing of children. For example, the National Assessment of Educational Progress Results[40]

39. Walter Petty and Julie M. Jensen, *Developing Children's Language* (Boston: Allyn and Bacon, 1980), pp. 280–281.
40. National Assessment of Educational Progress, *What Students Know and Can Do* (Denver, CO: Education Commission of the State, 1977), pp. 17–19, 25–28, 34–35. Also see Constance Weaver, "Welcoming Errors as Signs of Growth," *Language Arts* 59 (May 1982): 438–444.

indicated that sentence fragments or run-on sentences appeared in about half the papers written by nine-year-old children. Run-on sentences tended to appear more often than sentence fragments. The judges concluded that nine-year-olds understand more clearly what a sentence is than how to punctuate it, but the lowest level papers suggested that some children have only the barest notion of what a sentence actually is. Lower quality papers from thirteen-year-olds suggested that their writers were unaware of the differences between written and spoken language (their writings were attempts to record their thoughts as if they were saying them.)

Some suggestions for correcting the *and* fault include:

1. Use exercises for developing sentence sense since this fault results from lack of understanding of the sentence.
2. Read aloud or write on the chalkboard a group of sentences joined by *and*s. Let the children point out where each sentence begins and ends. Read again with the *and*s eliminated.
3. Have pupils write paragraphs of three to four sentences. In preliminary discussion, encourage them to be sure to indicate the pause at the end of each sentence.
4. Provide experiences with building sentences of discernible parts; that is, give the pupils kernel sentences, such as "Betty ate," and encourage them to add elements of expansion that tell what, when, where, why, and how the action took place. Pupils might gradually evolve such a statement as "Yesterday while we were at the movies, Betty ate so much popcorn that she became ill." Help them to see how some parts of what they want to say can be put into subordination so that all necessary elements are incorporated in a closely knit sentence of fewer words: "After eating so much popcorn at the movies yesterday, Betty became ill."

Children should be aware of three ways of adjusting run-on sentences: by writing two separate sentences, by adding a sentence connector, and by subordination. The run-on sentence, "Mr. Jones is a good speaker he was chosen to deliver the address," could be adjusted accordingly:

Mr. Jones is a good speaker. He was chosen to deliver the address.
Mr. Jones is a good speaker; therefore, he was chosen to deliver the address.
Since Mr. Jones is a good speaker, he was chosen to deliver the address.

Some suggestions for avoiding choppy sentences include:

Giving practice in improving poor sentences: for example, exercises in which two short sentences are combined into one sentence

Reading aloud and writing on the chalkboard a composition composed of choppy sentences (let the pupils suggest ways of improving it.)

Teaching use of connectors other than *and* to add variety to sentences

Paragraph Sense

The following dialogue might serve as a good introduction to paragraph writing.

Bill: The sentences in a paragraph tell about one topic.
Betty: Then won't all the sentences be alike?
Teacher: How would you answer Betty's question?

The paragraph indicates the interrelationship of sentences. Through the primary years, the child tells, hears, and sees brief paragraphs—and writes them. As with the sentence, the pupil learns the concept of the paragraph through practice. Teaching activities in the intermediate years often focus on ideas such as the following in providing samples of related sentences: finding the main topic, arranging sentences in logical order under the topic, noting quotations in paragraph form, studying paragraphs for key words, and finding details in a paragraph.

Other suggested activities for developing paragraph skills include:

Reading paragraphs from science or history books; selecting the topic sentence and main idea

Writing one-paragraph compositions telling the story of a cartoon, a picture graph, or a comic strip such as "Peanuts"

Clipping and mounting paragraphs from a magazine (the pupils may read them and write the titles and topic sentence on another sheet of paper.)

Writing a good beginning sentence for a well-constructed paragraph with a deleted first sentence

Writing a good ending sentence for a well-constructed paragraph with a deleted last sentence

Presenting a paragraph that includes a sentence that does not help to explain the topic and asking the children to find the unrelated sentence

Reading an interesting, correctly written letter to the class; then rereading it for dictation to see if the pupils can put it into paragraphs correctly

Providing opportunities for discussing and listing blocks of ideas before children write a news report

Manuscript Form

Neatness, appropriate spacing, even margins, and attractive arrangement of items on the page make written work more pleasing to the eye and more legible. Each year the teacher and children should develop, through discussion, a manuscript form guide. It should vary according to the age and skill of the children involved. The following guide, intended for the pupil's use, suggests a manuscript form that was developed in one classroom.

CHART 7.5: *Manuscript Form Guide*

1. Write your name at the right on the top line of your paper.
2. Write the date at the left on the top line of your paper.
3. Center the title of your report on the third line. Remember to capitalize the important words in your title.
4. Begin the first paragraph of your report on the fifth line.
5. Indent the first word of each paragraph about one inch from the left margin of the paper.
6. Keep a straight margin, about one inch wide, along the left side of your paper. Try to keep about the same margin on the right side.
7. Avoid crowding words at the end of the line.

Usage

The reader should review the section on usage in the chapter on oral composition. Nonstandard verb items often are used in written situations, particularly if they are a part of the oral usage of the student. Additionally, there are several usage items that need particular attention in written expression.

Pronouns	Adjective/Adverb
they're, their	two, to, too
it's, its	their, there
you're, your	good, well
who's, whose	good, bad

These items are better taught as separate morphology or spelling lessons and then applied in written situations.

EVALUATION OF WRITTEN EXPRESSION

Several methods may be used to evaluate children's compositions. Certainly, the use of standards developed cooperatively by the teacher and children, as suggested throughout this book, can be effective in establishing goals for any writing task.

Depending on the age and maturity of children, peer evaluation may be utilized. Here children react to papers prepared by others. Two students with much the same ability can read papers to one another and offer suggestions for improvement regarding problems of content, organization, or mechanical errors. Or small groups can study the writing of a student who has agreed to submit his or her paper for evaluation. The students can be given duplicated copies, or the teacher may project the paper on an overhead projector after preparing a transparency of it. Group members would be encouraged to comment, discussing the good points of the writing and later offering ideas that could improve the paper. Either approach can sharpen evaluation skills, with children having an opportunity to learn from each other's writings. Moreover, the child learns to write for an audience other than the teacher.

Perhaps the most effective way to help children improve their writing is through teacher-student conferences about selected writing tasks. In this situation, a student's writing is evaluated by the teacher while the student is present. Such conferences can be arranged while others are writing; at a special conference time within a class or a period of time; on an occasional basis, perhaps once a month or more often; or on a sign-up or request basis. The primary advantages of individual conferences are that evaluation can be adjusted to the child's specific needs and that the teacher *and* the student can determine those needs.

The major components of compositions to be evaluated at the elementary school level include the following:

1. **Ideas:** Conveys thoughts successfully
2. **Organization:** Arranges ideas in sequential order
3. **Sentences:** Uses complete and varied sentences
4. **Word choice and usage:** Uses vivid, descriptive words and effective details
5. **Mechanics:** Uses capitals correctly; uses correct punctuation; spells correctly; and writes neatly

If the *meaning* or message of the composition has been conveyed in the first draft, then attention can be focused on *form*. (If not, questions can be raised to clarify purpose of meaning. Of course, teachers may have provided assistance with meaning during the writing stage.) In directing attention to form, as well as meaning, a first step would be to ask the child to read aloud the composition. In this way, clarity of the thoughts would be highlighted along with attention to sentence style, adjectives or adverbs, and capitalization and punctuation conventions.

Capacity for evaluating grows with maturity, so more attention to editing should be given in the intermediate years than in the primary years. It may be enough for primary-level children to ask, "Did I say clearly what I meant to say?" and "Did I say it in an interesting way?"

Finally, it is hoped that self-evaluation will become a part of each writer's personal habits. Therefore attention should be devoted to proofreading and revision with class members.

REVISION AND PROOFREADING

Individual revision and proofreading to correct and improve writing is often an onerous task to the child, yet in the final analysis, it is a valuable experience.

Revision

The teacher may write a paragraph on the chalkboard to serve as a model for illustrating the process of revision. The teacher asks the questions that the pupils should be asking themselves when they examine their own papers with a view toward revision, as suggested in Chart 7.6.

CHART 7.6: *Revision Guide*

1. Does the entire composition keep to the subject?
2. Does every paragraph contain one main idea? Are the sentences related to the main idea? Are they presented in logical order?
3. Is a variety of sentence patterns used?
4. Are exact words and specific details used?
5. Are there descriptive words that appeal to the senses?
6. Is there a good beginning sentence, a good ending sentence?

All these items need not be attended to in one session. One revision item may be taken up at one time and another at a later time.

Proofreading

As with revision, proofreading will not be effectively taught in one lesson but needs to be repeated at intervals. Again, pupils must ask themselves pertinent questions as they examine their own papers. The use of the phrase "their own papers" is used advisedly; little progress is gained by having the teacher proofread the pupils' papers or by having pupils mark one another's papers. The job of proofreading belongs to the child who wrote the composition, and help from others should come only after each has made initial efforts to improve his or her own paper. Merely mentioning the term *proofreading* or occasionally reminding children to check their work is insufficient—one must give practical and specific suggestions about what to look for, as in the proofreading guide, Chart 7.7.

CHART 7.7: *Proofreading Guide*

1. As the teacher (or another pupil) reads the sentence, listen and look at each group of words to be sure it is a good sentence. Make sure that you have no run-on sentences.
2. Listen and look for mistakes in punctuation. Be sure that you have put in punctuation marks only where they are needed. Did you end sentences with the mark required?
3. Listen and look for mistakes in word usage. Be sure that you have said what you mean and that each word is used correctly. Is there any incorrect verb or pronoun usage?
4. Look for mistakes in capitalization. Did you capitalize the first word and all important words in the title? Did you begin each sentence with a capital letter?
5. Look for misspelled words. Use the dictionary to check the spelling of any word about which you are not sure.
6. Check legibility of writing and items such as margins, title, indents, etc.

The pupils may find it helpful to reread their compositions several times with a different purpose in mind each time. For example:

Reading for sentence sense
Reading for punctuation and capitalization

Reading to make vague words clearer
Reading for misspelled words
Checking such items as margins, title, and the like.

(Again, these items may be considered over a period of time.)

One way to improve proofreading ability is the group correction lesson. The teacher may select a few sentences from pupils' papers (or sentences composed by the teacher) that have errors and copy them on the chalkboard. The same purpose can be served by using the opaque (or overhead) projector or by mimeographing sentences and paragraphs for class discussion and evaluation. Of course, the teacher should include in the presentation the kinds of errors he or she wishes to bring to the pupils' attention. Then with a group of children, or the entire class, the teacher uses the sentences as a basis of instruction, helping the group to see how to improve them.

Pupils may keep a notebook of rules for punctuation, capitalization, and spelling conventions, and this set of rules may be used to help with proofreading. The notebook may be developed as pupils encounter the items during the year; items should, for optimum use, be grouped under such headings as "Capitalization," "Paragraphs," and "Punctuation." Each rule should be stated in precise language, and a sample illustrating the rule should be included. For example, "Use a capital letter to begin the first word, the last word, and each important word in the title of a piece of writing: *The Wind in the Willows*."

Furthermore, the teacher should use the findings revealed by proofreading experiences to help each individual with particular needs. One way is to prepare a checklist of technical skills. Opposite each item, the child may tally each time a certain error occurs in written work. When errors recur, it is important for the teacher to plan instruction so that appropriate help can be provided. For those needing unusual help (the very slow or the very able), individualized checklists may be provided. Small instructional groups may be organized when only four or five children need help in the same area; and class lessons may be given on skills that appear to be needed by all.[41]

One of the more effective ways to encourage revision and proofreading is to demonstrate to pupils that progress has been made over a period of time in the skill of written composition. To accomplish this, pupils might

41. See the following source for an example of an editing workshop: Ronald Cramer, *Children's Writing, Reading, and Language Growth* (Columbus, OH: Merrill, 1978), Chapter 9. Also see Richard Koch, "Syllogisms and Superstitions: The Current Stage of Responding to Writing," *Language Arts* 59 (May 1982): 464–471.

keep notebooks or folders in which samples of different kinds of written work are filed periodically, with the dates recorded on the papers. Pupils are strongly motivated when they compare papers written in September with those written the following December and can see improvement.

THE COMPUTER AND WRITING

Hennings[42] has proposed an instructional context in which the word processor computer may be useful in composing skills. (A microcomputer consists of a typewriter-like keyboard, a television-like screen (monitor), a memory component, and sometimes a printer.) The idea is to use the word processor in the recording and editing of experience stories in the primary years. Rather than printing children's dictated sentences on a chart or the chalkboard, the teacher types their sentences into the computer, which displays them. The story can be read from the monitor, suggestions can be made for revisions, and the appropriate commands can be given the computer to make the changes. If a printer is a part of the equipment, the microcomputer can produce one or more paper copies of the edited piece, which can then be read or treated as any other printed copy. The composition may also be placed in the memory of the micro-computer and used at a later date. The same idea may be implemented in the intermediate grades for group writing situations. Some students at the upper elementary school levels may be able to work at the computer alone without teacher guidance.

Computers can also be used to analyze written compositions. In this use, student papers are typed on computer cards. Data banks for the composition are created by the teacher, and the papers are analyzed on the basis of these data. The data banks may include such things as number of words (length of composition, number of different words in the composition, sentence length, number of connectors, usage, capitalization rules, and the like. The computer does not judge style or organization, nor does it evaluate the composition. It provides information that may be useful to teachers following up lessons.

The cost factor is probably the greatest disadvantage of the classroom computer now, but with time, this will likely be less of a disadvantage. Advantages often attributed to the use of computers in writing programs include (1) the motivational aspects, (2) the saving of time, and (3) the fact that children become computer literate.

---

42. Dorothy Grant Hennings, "Input: Enter the Word-Processing Computer," *Language Arts* 58 (January 1981): 18–22.

SOME INSTRUCTIONAL CONCERNS

A challenge similar to that mentioned in the preceding chapter faces the teacher. A comprehensive writing program includes a range of activities that take into consideration the different purposes of writing (to inform, to describe, to explain, to persuade, to entertain); the variety of writing forms (stories, poems, journals, notes, letters, reports, and the like); and the different audiences for writing (self, known readers, and unknown readers). Translated into practice, this suggests teachers must understand writing as being more than just the transmitting of information; writing will provide opportunity for self-expression as in music, art, or other media.

The teacher must plan so that children have the opportunity to write for various purposes in order to develop skills unique to each purpose. Writing forms are related to writing purposes, and imaginative use of form can be effective in achieving an important purpose. The teacher must help the writer become sensitive to different audiences and to adjust writing style and content to fit each. This can become more prominently a part of the intermediate program, since young children generally write primarily for themselves, according to developmental psychologists such as Piaget and Vygotsky. As the writer moves increasingly outward from self, he or she can consider the more detailed and formal aspects required in written products for an unknown audience. Again, a record-keeping plan can be helpful in providing a balanced writing program.

Additionally, teachers must not restrict the writing program to the "English" period. Writing should permeate all content area instruction. For example, young children can study sketches prepared by the teacher in the mathematics class to write their own word problems. "Two children were flying kites. Three children were jumping rope. How many more children were jumping rope than flying kites?"

Results from the National Assessment of Educational Progress in Writing suggest that nine-year-old and thirteen-year-old children possess a reasonable mastery of the conventions of written language but show less competence in sentence construction, development of ideas, and relating ideas successfully. These factors are closely related to composition revision.

In terms of student difficulties, revision is often misunderstood. Graves has provided some characteristics of young children and their revision efforts.

1. Beginning writers do not revise.
2. Statements of feelings are revised only if the child senses the feeling is not accurate.

3. Eight-year-old children find it easier to revise topics about personal experiences than about the experiences of others.
4. Revisions begin when children choose their own topics.
5. Children who can quickly list personal topics for writing demonstrate a strong capacity for revision.
6. Peer audiences have an effect on children's revisions.
7. Children who write quickly are more likely to revise in larger units and sustain a single composition for a longer period of time than those who write slowly.[43]

Such information seems to indicate the place of revision in the writing process and suggests the most effective methods for encouraging writing: Do not expect many efforts at revisions at the beginning writing level; ask children if they told about their true feelings; encourage children to write about personal experiences; permit children to choose many of their writing topics; and so on.

At the intermediate level, some children still look upon revision as little more than correction of spelling and punctuation. Attention must be devoted to taking a sentence and experimenting with its word order in various ways, examining possibilities for adding or deleting particular words, and rearranging sentences for a better effect; in this way, teachers will convey to children a sense of what is involved in the revision process.

THOUGHT QUESTIONS

1. What is one instructional sequence for a creative writing lesson?
2. Should children be exposed to early types of writing experiences? Why or why not?
3. What strengths and weaknesses do you believe exist in the Sustained Writing Program?
4. How might part of the writing program be integrated with other subject areas of the elementary school curriculum?
5. Why should poetry writing be introduced to children?
6. How may written compositions be evaluated with the goal of improvement?

43. Donald H. Graves, "What Children Show Us About Revision," *Language Arts* 56 (March 1979): 312–319.

LEARNER RESPONSE OPTIONS

1. Study an English textbook for children at one grade level. Which of the experiences suggested in this chapter are present? Are there some that do not appear in the listing?
2. Tape record an experience story dictated by a child or group of children. Type the story and share with your peers.
3. Write a patterned poem or story, providing the original and your own.
4. Organize an oral presentation with the purpose of motivating creative writing.
5. Prepare an independent composition activity card.
6. Develop a lesson for a child or group of children, involving word study of a particular type (for example, descriptive verbs). Use it with peers or children.
7. Introduce one form of rhyming or syllabic poetry writing to a child or class. Evaluate your performance.
8. Prepare a lesson outline for teaching a particular type of letter writing.
9. Make an outline of the section on report writing. Give an oral report to your peers from your outline.
10. Report to the class how the trade book, *How to Write a Report*, can be used with a group of children.
11. Prepare a lesson for announcements and notices of events.
12. Develop a systematic lesson (as for "announcement") for either record writing or filling in forms.
13. Develop an exercise, the purpose of which is to review or introduce one or two principles of capitalization.
14. Study one or more of the references cited at the conclusion of this chapter. Discuss its use as a resource for extending the ideas of this chapter.

REFERENCES AND ADDITIONAL READINGS

Carlson, Ruth Kearney. *Writing Aids Through the Grades*. New York: Teachers College Press, 1970.
Carlson, Ruth Kearney. *Sparkling Words: Three Hundred and Fifteen Practical and Creative Writing Ideas*. Rev. ed. Urbana, IL: National Council of English, 1979.

Cooper, Charles, and Lee Odell. *Evaluating Writing: Describing, Measuring, Judging.* Urbana, IL: National Council of Teachers of English, 1977.

Cramer, Ronald L. *Writing, Reading and Language Growth: An Introduction to Language Arts.* Columbus, OH: Merrill, 1978.

Ebenson, Barbara J. *A Celebration of Bees: Helping Children Write Poetry.* Minneapolis, MN: Winston, 1975.

Graves, Donald. *Writing: Teachers and Children at Work*, Exeter, NH: Heinemann Educational Books, 1982.

Haley-James, Shirley, ed. *Perspectives on Writing in Grades 1–8.* Urbana, IL: National Council of Teachers of English, 1981.

Hennings, Dorothy G., and Barbara M. Grant. *Written Expression in the Language Arts: Ideas and Skills.* 2d ed. New York: Teachers College Press, 1981.

Jackson, Jacqueline. *Turn Not Pale, Beloved Snail.* Boston: Little, Brown, 1974.

Larrick, Nancy. *Somebody Turned on a Tap in These Kids: Poetry and Young People Today.* New York: Dell, 1971.

Livingston, Myra C. *When You Are Alone, It Keeps You Capone: An Approach to Creative Writing with Children.* New York: Atheneum, 1973.

Petty, Walter T., and Mary E. Bowen. *Slithery Snakes and Other Aids to Children's Writing.* New York: Appleton-Century-Crofts, 1967.

Pratt-Butler, Grace K. *Let Them Write Creatively.* Columbus, OH: Merrill, 1973.

Sealey, Leonard, et al. *Children's Writing: An Approach for the Primary Grades.* Newark, DE: International Reading Association, 1979.

Smith, Frank. *Writing and the Writer.* New York: Holt, Rinehart and Winston, 1981.

Stewig, John Warren. *Read to Write: Using Children's Literature as a Springboard to Writing.* 2d ed. New York: Holt, Rinehart and Winston, 1980.

Temple, Charles, et al. *The Beginnings of Writing.* Boston: Allyn and Bacon, 1982.

CHAPTER 8: *Spelling*

OVERVIEW

This chapter presents a comprehensive survey of spelling instruction. It begins with a discussion of selecting words for the spelling program. The semantics and the sound bases of spelling are discussed, and a table of English phoneme-grapheme correspondences is presented. Specific procedures for teaching spelling are suggested, including the test-study plan, dictation exercises and procedures, and instilling positive pupil attitudes. Guidelines for spelling games are provided, and an inductive approach is described for presenting important spelling rules or generalizations. Grouping for spelling instruction, determining levels, and providing special techniques are explored as means for achieving greater individualization of the spelling program.

KEY VOCABULARY

social utility theory

basic words

phoneme-grapheme correspondences

semantic base of spelling

spelling patterns

test-study plan

corrected-test technique

dictation exercises

spelling consciousness

spelling rules

cloze procedure

instructional level

kinesthetic learner

phonologically irregular word

spelling notebook

How Children Appear to Acquire Spelling Understanding

During children's early writing efforts, teachers must recognize that spelling acquisition is a gradual process.

One of the first major studies designed to examine the beginning efforts of children to spell was conducted by Read.[1] Among his subjects were approximately twenty preschoolers who were able to identify and name the letters of the alphabet and to relate the letter names to sounds of words. These children "invented" spellings for the words they wrote. Read found that, even at this age, children are able to use their knowledge of the phonetic characteristics of words (how sounds are articulated).

More recent studies of students' spelling have been made by Henderson and his students.[2] They looked at the kinds of spelling done by children in free writing situations and concluded that young spellers go through various spelling stages with written language.

By encouraging young children to spell on their own, without too much pressure at the beginning for correct spelling, teachers can assist children in their acquisition of skill in this area. These stages appear in the following order.[3]

1. Writing the first letter (or phoneme) of each word or syllable (*F* for *Fred* or *sb* for *sandbox*)
2. Adding the final phoneme of the word or syllable, but omitting the short vowel sounds (*fl* for *fill* or *kn* for *kitten*)
3. Using vowels that "say their names" (*se* for *sea* and *cot* for *coat*)
4. Using blends (*ch, sh, bl, tr*) and bound morphemes (*ed, ing, s*)
5. Separating a short vowel sound from surrounding consonants (*bint* for *bent*) long vowel sounds (*raette* for *rate*)
6. Spelling frequently used words in the standard form (*we, do*)
7. Moving toward standard form (*leavz* for *leaves, plat* for *plant, cookt* for *cooked, sawd* for *sawed, bodm* for *bottom*)
8. Standard form

Obviously, young children apply their understanding of English sounds as they begin to write. This information provides some implications for spelling instruction:

1. Charles Read, *Children's Categorization of Speech Sounds in English*, National Council of Teachers of English Research Report no. 17 (Urbana, IL: National Council of Teachers of English, 1975).
2. Edmund H. Henderson and James W. Beers, eds. *Developmental and Cognitive Aspects of Learning to Spell* (Newark, DE: International Reading Association, 1980).
3. Anna D. Forester, "Learning to Spell by Spelling," *Theory into Practice* 19 (Summer 1980): 186–193.

1. Spelling development should be promoted within the context of general language study, such as early writing opportunities in which children explore the ways in which their knowledge of spoken language is related to writing. One specific vehicle for this development is the language-experience approach as explained earlier. Cramer[4] compared the informal language-experience approach with formal teaching of spelling in the first grade and found that the language-experience group performed significantly better in both regular and irregular spelling. This finding points up the benefit of emphasizing written expression and paying less attention to standard spelling at this time.

2. Children should have wide exposure to charts, books, and other meaningful printed materials in their classroom environment. Frequent writing is needed also to encourage use of the spelling strategies children have developed and to provide opportunities to learn more about sound and letter correspondences, letter sequence, word-building features, and the like. In early writing, encourage children to spell words as best they can, which is frequently termed *invented spelling*. With some freedom to explore written language, children will advance toward the conventions of English orthography. Writing makes spelling meaningful.

3. According to newer insights about spelling, it should not be viewed as a mere rote memorization process. As children write, they generate and test patterns of spelling against their present understandings. Spelling ability develops with opportunities to verify one's own spelling efforts. By acquiring knowledge about spelling generalizations that govern English spelling, standard spelling can be achieved for many words. Also note that most spelling textbooks provide more than lists of spelling words. They include dictionary study, vocabulary study, language history, proofreading, and the like.

4. Many opportunities should be provided to play with words. Word games focusing on letter-sound associations, tongue twisters, word-building exercises, word searches and puzzles, and the like help children gradually begin to understand the system. Activities dealing with a dictionary are equally useful. (See Chapter 10 for ideas about dictionary study.)

5. Handwriting has a special relationship to spelling, since illegible letter formation causes words to appear to be misspelled. (See Chapter 9 for attention to handwriting.)

6. Spelling instruction should not be restricted to a specific series of spelling textbooks or a spelling period. Too much dependence is often placed upon these alone for the improvement of spelling. Since spelling is a language-based process, it develops through ongoing interaction with

4. Ronald C. Cramer, "An Investigation of First Grade Spelling Achievement," *Elementary English* 47 (February 1970): 230–249.

written language. Spelling growth is influenced by the quality of the reading program, the written composition program, the handwriting program, and the content areas program. Through actual reading and writing, children derive a functional knowledge of the system of their language.

SELECTION AND GRADE PLACEMENT OF WORDS

Most of the word lists in today's spelling books are structured to make full use of two important factors: frequency of use in writing and sound-letter relationships. These factors are discussed in turn.

Utility

Some spelling programs are based on the theory of social utility; that is, words are selected on the basis of their importance in the different spelling activities of life. There are a number of investigations about spelling vocabulary, but perhaps the most important one is by Ernest Horn.[5] He studied letters of bankers, excuses written to teachers by parents, minutes of organizations and committee reports, letters of application and recommendation, the works of well-known authors, letters written in magazines and newspapers, personal letters, business letters—a total of 5 million words and 36,000 different words. From this, the most important 10,000 words were selected as basic words, according to these criteria:

1. The total *frequency* with which the word was used in writing
2. The *commonness* with which the word was used by everyone, regardless of sex, vocation, geographical location, educational level, or economic status
3. The *spread* of the word's use in different kinds of writing
4. The *cruciality* of the word as evidenced by the severity of the penalty attached to its misspelling

5. Ernest A. Horn, *A Basic Writing Vocabulary—10,000 Words Most Commonly Used in Writing*, University of Iowa Monographs in Education, First Series, no. 41 (Iowa City: University of Iowa Press, 1926). See also Henry A. Rinsland, *A Basic Vocabulary of Elementary School Children* (New York: Macmillan, 1945). This is a basic writing vocabulary as determined by words used most often by children in and out of school situations. Also see James A. Fitzgerald, *A Basic Life Spelling Vocabulary* (Milwaukee, WI: Bruce, 1951). This is a basic spelling vocabulary of 2,650 words that are used most often by children in and out of school and words that will be used by them as they develop from childhood to adulthood. This list is of great value to curriculum makers; it should interest those who wish to evaluate the vocabularies of their spelling books or who desire a valid core spelling vocabulary.

5. The probable *permanency* of the word's use
6. The *desirability* of the word as determined by the quality of the writing in which it was used.

Horn suggested three criteria for introducing these basic words in the spelling program:

The most important words should be introduced in the beginning grades and those of lesser importance in the later grades.

The simplest words should be introduced in the beginning grades and the more difficult words in the later grades.

Those words that are used often or needed in the curriculum activities of children should be introduced when appropriate.

Words may vary greatly in their degree of difficulty for different pupils. Data in this area are insufficient at present; the best answer is determined through prestudy tests for each pupil, which reveal just which words each should study among those of greatest importance. Also, there is a need to adjust the spelling load to the ability of the learner.

Justification for the social utility approach to selection and grade placement of words is evident when two factors are considered: the permanence of the words and the amazingly small number of words in the average person's writing vocabulary. In attempting to determine how long the 5,000 words most commonly used in writing had been in existence, Horn stated:

Less than 4 percent of these words have come into the language since 1849, and less than 10 percent have come in since 1749. More of these words were in the language before 1099 than have come into the language since 1799.[6]

The data in Figure 8.1 indicate approximate percentages of total words in writing accounted for by a certain number of words.

The data in Figure 8.1 suggest that an increase in the number of words beyond 3,000 does not result in a proportional increase in spelling power in writing done by the average child or adult.

So which words should be studied and learned? Normally, those in a basic spelling list, supplemented by individual lists based upon needs and errors. No one spelling book can adequately fulfill the spelling requisites of written composition, but most leading spelling books contain words

6. Ernest A. Horn, "The Validity and Reliability of Adult Vocabulary Lists," *Elementary English Review* 16 (April 1939): 134.

FIGURE 8.1: *Approximate Percentage of Total Words Commonly Used in Writing*

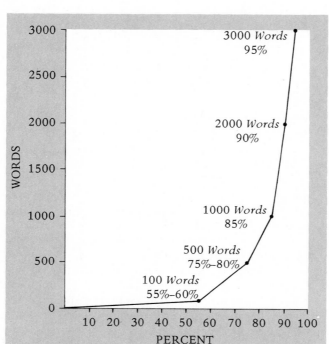

that are selected with care.[7] As shown in Figure 8.1, a pupil must know the spelling of about 3,000 words in order to know how to spell about 95 percent of the words that will be needed in writing. Content area words that are important and are used frequently in writing should be presented as a part of the spelling curriculum.

The Bases of Spelling: Sound and Meaning

Research on spelling since the late 1960s has increasingly revealed the very complex nature of spelling—both of English orthography (the written representation of words) and of the ways we know how to spell. An understanding of phoneme-grapheme correspondence (the correspondence

---

7. Hillerich has pointed out a lack of agreement among spelling textbooks on which words should be included for instruction and their grade placement. See Robert Hillerich, *Spelling* (Columbus, OH: Merrill, 1976), p. 17.

of the sounds of the language and the letters used to represent them) is crucial to the spelling process. More and more, however, linguists have come to stress the importance of understanding that spelling is also based on semantics. We can spell, for example, *knowledge* because we are aware of its semantic relationship to *know* and we can recognize this relationship even though we pronounce the first syllable of *know*ledge differently from the way we pronounce the word *know*. As Frith reports, "English orthography reflects knowledge sometimes on the level of sound and sometimes on the level of meaning or syntax."[8]

As explained earlier, most linguists now believe that the acquisition of spelling abilities, very much like the acquisition of language itself, is developmental; the ability to spell increases as the child progresses through the developmental stages and mentally (or cognitively) matures. And perhaps most important for our everyday teaching of spelling, most linguists believe that spelling ability is facilitated through the child's "interactions with written language";[9] that is, learning to spell must actively involve the students with writing and reading in general and not merely with rote memorization of words and word lists.

Although the analysis of spelling shows it to be a complex subject, we should not be discouraged about teaching it. After all, the research shows that we learn how to spell in a variety of ways and that we learn from many sources.

Because it seems at present the most widely used strategy, we will discuss here teaching spelling according to phoneme-grapheme correspondence. We urge, at the same time, that the lessons and activities used in the classroom involve students in the active exploration of language. In the words of Hodges, "Learning to spell is a complex enough task to warrant formal study, but its relationship to written language generally should be recognized. Spelling instruction needs to provide pupils with opportunities to use emerging spelling skills in written contexts."[10]

Phoneme-Grapheme Correspondences

Mastery of the correspondence of sounds (phonemes) of the language and letters (graphemes) used to represent them is, as we said, considered essential to the spelling process. Symbols for the smallest distinct mean-

8. U. Frith, "Spelling Difficulties: An Annotation," *Journal of Child Psychology and Psychiatry* 19 (July 1978): 280.

9. Richard E. Hodges, "The Language Base of Spelling," in *Research in the Language Arts: Language and Schooling*, ed. Victor Froese and Stanley B. Straw (Baltimore: University Park Press, 1981), p. 218. We are indebted to Hodges for his careful review of spelling research.

10. Hodges, "The Language Base of Spelling," p. 221.

ingful units of sounds are called phonemic symbols. Not all linguists agree on the identification and number of the sounds—the linguists are, of course, influenced by their own pronunciation. Furthermore, as a study of various dictionaries will quickly reveal, there is a lack of agreement in sound symbolism.

A chart of sound-spelling, or phoneme-grapheme, correspondences is provided in Table 8.1. Although the data will not be correct in all details for all dialects of English, it may be used to gain some idea of the major spelling patterns of English. Some common variant spellings of the English sounds can be detected from this chart as well.

To some linguists, many English words are spelled in a regular manner; that is, they find the phoneme-grapheme correspondence reliable.[11] Hodges and Rudorf report data suggesting that the phonemes of the 3,000 words most frequently used in children's writing are regularly represented by certain graphemes approximately 30 percent of the time.[12]

In a spelling program focusing upon phoneme-grapheme correspondences, much attention is given to patterns and principles. Lamb presents five spelling patterns often recommended by linguists for study by elementary school children (see Table 8.2). Exceptions (and many are very common words) are noted in the table to caution the reader. After the generalization is operational for most of the children, the exceptions, their frequency, and their significance can be discussed. No pattern should be taught as foolproof.

SUGGESTED PROCEDURES FOR TEACHING SPELLING

Within the specific spelling instruction period, an efficient program gives consideration to the manner of presenting new words to be taught, the pupil's study procedures, review and testing, and helping the child acquire and maintain an interest in spelling.[13]

Presenting New Words

A preliminary test of the words in the lesson should be given before the pupil begins direct study. It is important that the child make no alterations

11. Richard E. Hodges and Hugh Rudorf, "Searching Linguistics for Cues in the Teaching of Spelling," *Elementary English* 42 (May 1965): 527–533.
12. But see Hodges, "The Language Base of Spelling," for an insight into the controversy surrounding this issue.
13. The suggestions that follow are based on a solid research foundation, as cited by Thomas D. Horn, "Spelling," in *Encyclopedia of Educational Research*, 4th ed. (New York: Macmillan, 1969), pp. 1282–1299.

TABLE 8.1: *Productive Phoneme-Grapheme Relationships*

Phoneme	Grapheme		Example
Vowels			
/ĭ/	*i*	all positions	hit
/ĕ/	*e*	medial positions	bet
/ă/	*a*	all positions	sat
/ŏ/	*o*	all positions	lot
/ə/	*u*	all positions	luck
/ī/	*i*	medial positions when next phoneme is word-final	lime
/ē/	*e*	syllable final position	legal
/oi/	*oy*	word final position	boy
/ou/	*ow*	all positions	sow
/o/	*o*	all positions	loss
/ú/	*u*	all positions	full
Consonants			
/b/	*b*	all positions	bat
/p/	*p*	all positions	put
/t/	*t*	initial positions	tie
/d/	*d*	all positions	doe
/g/	*g*	all positions	gone
/th/	*th*	all positions	the
/v/	*v*	all positions	leave, vote
/ks/	*x*	all positions	box
/l/	*l*	all positions	lump
/le/	*le*	all positions	fable
/m/	*m*	all positions	map
/n/	*n*	all positions	now
/ng/	*ng*	word final positions	king
/r/	*r*	all positions	ran
/hw/	*wh*	all positions	where
/h/	*h*	all positions	how
/ch/	*ch*	all positions	church, nature
/w/	*w*	all positions	wax
/zh/	*si*	all positions when followed by /ə/	vision

Source: Paul R. Hanna, Richard E. Hodges, and Jean S. Hanna, *Spelling: Structure and Strategies*, pp. 86–93. Copyright © 1971 by Houghton Mifflin Company. Adapted by permission.

TABLE 8.2: *Spelling Patterns Recommended for Elementary Level*

Pattern	Examples	Exceptions
C-V-C (short vowel)	cat drip dent	
C-V-C + e (long vowel, silent e)	save hive drove	love have give come
C-V-V-C (long first vowel)	rain leaf coat need	relief break brief bear
C-V + r (controlled, preceding vowel)	far bird clear bore	heard burn third
C-V (long vowel)	go be by	to do too

Source: Pose Lamb, *Linguistics in Proper Perspective*, 3d ed. (Columbus, OH: Charles E. Merrill Publishing Company, 1977), pp. 67–72.

in the first spelling, for until one can spell a word correctly on the first attempt and without hesitation, one does not sufficiently know the word. This teaches children how to test their own spelling ability adequately.

Test-Study Plan The test-study plan of spelling instruction has proved to be very effective. It consists of the following features.

1. A preliminary term or monthly test is given to determine the general level of spelling achievement of individuals within the class.
2. A test on each weekly (or other instructional period) assignment is given before instruction is begun on that assignment. Sometimes the test is preceded by the teacher pronouncing each word as the pupils

look carefully at it. Following this, the pupils pronounce the words themselves.

3. The words that each pupil misspells on this pretest are identified by the child and become his or her study list for the lesson.
4. In learning to spell each word, each child uses the steps that have been worked out by the class or by the teacher and the child if modifications have been necessary to fit his or her particular needs.
5. A mid-lesson test is given to determine progress made since the pretest. A final weekly or lesson test shows the total progress made during the lesson and identifies words for later review.
6. Each child keeps a record of spelling achievement on a chart or similar device.
7. Any words that the child misspells on the final test are recorded by him or her in a special review word list.
8. Each child studies the words in the review list in the same manner as they were studied in their original presentation.
9. At regular intervals, testing of the review words for each child is done until all such words are mastered.
10. A final term or monthly test is given to measure the progress made since administration of the first test.[14]

Corrected-Test Technique According to Thomas Horn, the corrected-test technique alone will contribute from 90 to 95 percent of the achievement resulting from the combined effect of pronunciation exercise, corrected test, and study.[15] If this is true, the corrected test appears to be the single most important factor contributing to achievement in spelling. This procedure requires the teacher to spell aloud slowly—letter by letter—each word administered on the pretest. The pupils follow with their eyes, marking each word either as correct or incorrect. The corrected-test technique is advocated to provide maximum learning opportunities, not to make less work for the teacher. Since the corrected test appears to be so potent a learning factor, it should be utilized during spelling periods in such ways as to ensure its maximum effect.

In the corrected-test approach, children check their spelling of each word as the teacher presents it orally on a letter-by-letter basis. This provides children with the opportunity to use the auditory sense in developing a perception of the correct spelling. However, with the increased

---

14. Walter Petty and Julie M. Jensen, *Developing Children's Language* (Boston: Allyn and Bacon, 1980), pp. 499–450.
15. Thomas D. Horn, "The Effect of the Corrected Test on Learning to Spell," *Elementary School Journal* 47 (January 1947): 277–285.

emphasis on the use of multisensory experiences in the development of a perceptual image, it seems logical to add to this procedure the opportunity to use the visual sense in the corrected-test approach to help develop a more accurate perception of each word. One way this might be done would be to present each word on an overhead projector, asking children to check their spelling against the word appearing on the screen. If the word is misspelled, it is checked wrong. After checking the spelling of a word, children are instructed to look at the word on the screen and carefully follow along as the correct spelling is read by the teacher.[16]

Pupils' Study Procedures

The teacher must give careful attention to the pupils' methods of study and their use of the study period. The study period should be a learning period. Only those children who made errors in the pretest should be required to study spelling words, but the others need not be excused from

16. Jerry N. Kuhn and Howard H. Schroeder, "A Multi-Sensory Approach for Teaching Spelling," *Elementary English* 48 (November 1971): 865–869.

subsequent tests. Effective study requires that each child work only on his or her own difficulties; locating the difficulties then is the first thing to do. The checklist provides a series of steps the children might follow when studying the spelling of a word.

CHECKLIST: *Study of a New Spelling Word*

1. Pronounce the word clearly to yourself.
2. Carefully copy the word, noting how the sounds in the word are represented by the letters.
3. Look at your copy and say the letters twice.
4. Cover the word or close your eyes. Pretend you are writing the word on paper twice.
5. Write the word on paper without looking at your book or the copy you made.
6. Check your word. Did you spell it correctly?
7. If you missed the word, go over all the steps again. When you are sure you can spell the word, study the next word.

Effective study exercises should be utilized on the days following the pretest and prior to the final test. The sample lesson plan provides a five-day plan.

Review and Testing

Review periods are needed in the teaching of spelling. Pupils should voluntarily review words that they misspell frequently (words they have in their spelling notebooks), and provisions need to be made for incidental review.

Testing is also important. There can be several tests in connection with each lesson. A single correct spelling must not be taken as a true measure of the ability to spell a word. Dictation is one way to test spelling. A dictation exercise, such as a group of sentences, a story, a description, or an explanation, should include the most basic and commonly used words. Words are not used by themselves in actual practice, but in context; therefore, sentence or paragraph dictation may be a satisfactory type of practice that will establish the spelling of a word as an unvarying habit. Some dictation may be given every day, even if it is only three or four brief sentences.

LESSON PLAN: *Five-Day Spelling Plan*

Monday
Pretest and corrected-test technique

Tuesday
Give exercises that attach meaning and imagery to the spelling words. Phrasing exercises (the writing of each word in two or three phrases) are helpful. For example, if the word is *cover*, phrases might be *box cover* or *cover the answers*. Another type of exercise would be to provide the phrase and then have the pupils write only the spelling word. They could also practice adding affixes to the word, making a list of these words (*covering, covers, covered, uncover,* and so on).

Wednesday
Written expression. Sentences may be composed, using each word in the lesson in a sentence. Sentences may be expanded or shortened by adding or subtracting modifying words. Self-testing is also an effective exercise.

Thursday
Partners. Pupils could dictate each word to their partners and vice versa. Then they would correct their spelling words together, recording and studying all misspelled words.

Friday
Final test. Misspelled words are correctly written in the pupils' spelling notebooks for continued review and testing. Achievement is marked on a progress chart.

Dictation can begin in the primary years by soliciting several short sentences from the children as they study a picture. Dictate short sentences for the children to write, such as:

Tim is a big boy.
Tim hit the ball.

The children are asked to correct their own papers as the teacher writes the sentences on the board and spells each word orally.

In the intermediate years, children enjoy writing riddles from dictation.

Some words to be used in the riddles may be written on the board for the children to refer to, if needed. Here are a couple of examples:

I won't tell if you hit me
But if you poke me with a pin
I'll go pop.   (A Balloon)

It has a head.
It has a tail.
But it does not have a body.   (A Coin)

Pupil Interest

Each child should develop a "spelling consciousness" and an interest in spelling. Following are some suggestions for maintaining spelling interest.

The teacher's attitude emphasizes the importance of spelling.

The teacher uses efficient, business-like methods in teaching spelling.

A spirit of mutual pride and cooperation in spelling achievement is encouraged by the teacher.

Each pupil is provided with a definite and efficient method of learning to spell words.

The teacher insists upon careful, exact, neat work.

Each pupil sees his or her progress and maintains an individual progress chart.

The teacher calls attention to the importance of accurate spelling in ordinary daily life.

Opportunities to spell in written work are provided.

SPELLING GAMES AND ACTIVITIES

Games and activities can help children learn many basic ideas about components of the language arts. They give children variety in the way they handle a topic, allow them to participate actively in the learning process, and provide repeated exposures without becoming tiresome. Related learnings include following directions, becoming observant, and cooperating. Games are most effective when they meet a specific objective or purpose, are planned for a small group of children, and are a part of the program, rather than a reward.

One excellent source for spelling games is Anderson and Groff's *Resource Materials for Teachers of Spelling*.[17] Commercial "Spelling Learning Games" kits are also available.[18]

Some books containing word games include:

Candy Carter and Zora Rashkis, eds., *Ideas for Teaching English in the Junior High and Middle School* (Urbana, IL: National Council of Teachers of English, 1980).

Willard Espy, *Another Almanac of Words at Play* (New York: Potter, 1980).

Willard R. Espy, *The Game of Words* (New York: Grosset and Dunlap, 1972).

Margaret E. Mulac, *Educational Games for Fun* (New York: Harper and Row, 1971).

17. Paul S. Anderson and Patrick J. Groff, *Resource Materials for Teachers of Spelling* (Minneapolis, MN: Burgess, 1968).
18. Chicago: Rand McNally.

Reader's Digest editors, *Word Power* (New York: Berkley, 1980).
Joseph R. Shipley, *Word Play* (New York: Hawthorn, 1972).

For students:

Harold H. Hart, *Grab a Pencil* (New York: A. and W. Publishers, 1980).
Edward Horowitz, *Word Detective* (New York: Hart, 1978).
Richard B. Manchester, *The Mammoth Book of Word Games* (New York: Hart, 1976).
Richard B. Manchester, *The 2nd Mammoth Book of Word Games* (New York: Hart, 1978).
Maxwell Nurberg, *Fun with Words* (Englewood Cliffs, NJ: Prentice-Hall, 1970).

Several spelling-type games are available commercially, such as:

Scrabble (Selchow and Righter, 2215 Union Blvd., Bay Shore, NY 11706)
Scrabble Crossword Cubes (Selchow and Righter)
Spill and Spell (Parker Brothers, 190 Bridge St., Salem, MA 01970)
Perquackey (Lakeside Games, 4440 W. 78th St., Minneapolis, MN 55435)
Cross Up (Milton Bradley, 1500 Main St., Springfield, MA 01101)
Four-Letter Words (Lakeside Games)

SPELLING RULES

The trend in the elementary school has definitely been one of teaching fewer spelling rules. Most of today's spelling programs group words by their spelling patterns in order for pupils to induce rules or generalizations about English spelling patterns.

Ernest Horn suggests that the only spelling rules to be taught are those that apply to a large number of words and have few exceptions. For example:

1. Words ending in silent e usually drop the final e before the addition of suffixes beginning with a vowel, but they keep the e before the addition of suffixes beginning with a consonant. Illustration: *make—making; time—timely.*
2. When a word ends in a consonant and *y*, change the *y* to *i* before adding all suffixes except those beginning with *i*. Do not change *y* to *i* in adding suffixes to words ending in a vowel and *y* or when adding

a suffix beginning with *i*. Illustration: *baby—babies—babying; play—played—playing*.

3. Words of one syllable or words accented on the last syllable, ending in a single consonant preceded by a single vowel, double the final consonant when adding a suffix beginning with a vowel. Illustration: *run—running; begin—beginning*.
4. The letter *q* is always followed by *u* in common English words. Illustration: *quick, queen, quiet*.
5. English words do not end in *v*.
6. Proper nouns and most adjectives formed from proper nouns should begin with capital letters.[19]

A "cloze procedure"[20] can be used for testing knowledge and application of Horn's six rules through use of such sentences as:

1. The girl was mak _____a cake.
2. Bill was play _____with a ball.
3. Susan was run _____down the street.
4. Two pints is the same amount as one q _____art.
5. Do you believ _____that story?
6. The new boy's name is _____ack.

In teaching the few important rules, Brueckner and Bond suggested the following sequence of steps:

1. Select a particular rule to be taught. Teach a single rule at a time.
2. Secure a list of words exemplifying the rule. Develop the rule through the study of words that it covers.

19. "Spelling" by Ernest A. Horn. Reprinted by permission of Macmillan Publishing Co., Inc., from *Encyclopedia of Educational Research*, 3d ed., Chester W. Harris, ed., © American Educational Association, 1960. Also see Theodore Clymer, "The Utility of Phonic Generalizations in the Primary Grades," *The Reading Teacher* 16 (January 1963): 256–258; Robert Emans, "The Usefulness of Phonic Generalizations Above the Primary Grades," *The Reading Teacher* 20 (February 1967): 421–423; Mildred Bailey, "The Utility of Phonic Generalizations in Grades One Through Six," *The Reading Teacher* 20 (February 1967): 415–417; and Mildred Bailey, "Utility of Vowel Digraph Generalization in Grades One Through Six," in *Reading and Realism*, ed. Allen Figurol (Newark, DE: International Reading Association, 1969), p. 656.
20. Idea is adapted from the cloze procedure—use of context clues—in checking reading comprehension. In a reading passage, every "nth" word is omitted, the reader supplying the missing word. In spelling, particular letters are omitted. For further information on the cloze technique, see Eugene Jongsman, *Cloze Reading Research: A Second Look* (Newark, DE: International Reading Association, 1980).

3. Lead the pupils to discover the underlying generalizations by discussing with them the characteristics of the words in the list. If possible, the pupils actually should formulate the rule. Help them to sharpen and clarify it.
4. Have the pupils use and apply the rule immediately.
5. If necessary, show how the rule in some cases does not apply, but stress its positive values.
6. Review the rule systematically on succeeding days. Emphasize its use and do not require the pupils to memorize a formalized statement.[21]

We include here a review exercise for the four ways to spell the past tense by adding -ed.

CHECKLIST: *Spelling Review*

Look at the four ways to spell the past tense by adding -ed

1. look   looked
2. hop   hopped
3. chase   chased
4. try   tried

Decide how you would spell the past form (-ed form) of each of these words. Then write the spelling pattern number as indicated above before the words.

_____a. jump   _____e. joke
_____b. cry   _____f. ship
_____c. fog   _____g. wax
_____d. jam   _____h. dry

PROOFREADING

Proofreading exercises are designed to develop a firm habit of attention to detail. Proofreading should begin early; a more formal approach to proofreading can be presented at the intermediate level. Kean and Personke

---

21. Leo J. Brueckner and Guy L. Bond, *The Diagnosis and Treatment of Learning Difficulties* © 1955, p. 373. Reprinted by permission of Prentice-Hall, Inc., Englewood Cliffs, NJ.

have suggested a fourteen-lesson program for developing proofreading habits.[22]

Proofreading for spelling is a visual task that focuses on the spelling errors of the writer. Sufficient time should be provided for proofreading, and it should be an integral part of instruction, perceived as important by teachers and children. Additional emphasis can be focused at times by declaring "Special Proofreading Week" or "Special Proofreading Day." An individual teacher focusing on this skill may produce some improvement, but to be most effective, the proofreading program should be school-wide.

What are some instructional procedures for proofreading spelling? One or two common difficulties may be appearing in a number of papers, such as *who's—whose* and *they're—their*. The words would be written on the chalkboard with examples, such as:

whose—belonging to   as in "Whose desk is that?"
who's—who is   as in "Who's going?"
their—belong to   as in "Their cat's friendly."
they're—they are   as in "They're playing."

Several sentences would be placed on the chalkboard with one word missing. The children would decide which of the four words (*whose, who's, their, they're*) would correctly complete the sentences. Then the children would be asked to correctly rewrite a paragraph, spelling the misspelled homophones correctly. The children may be asked to write several sentences, using each of the homophones correctly. Then they would be asked to check some recent papers to see if they had correctly spelled each of the four words.

GROUPING FOR SPELLING INSTRUCTION

As one observes the wide differences in spelling achievement within a single grade level of children (in a fourth-grade class, for example, there may be a range of five or six grade levels in spelling achievement), it is evident that the teacher must give serious consideration to ways of adjusting instruction to meet the varying needs of the children. Fortunately, spelling lends itself well to individualization.

22. John M. Kean and Carl Personke, *The Language Arts: Teaching and Learning in the Elementary School* (New York: St. Martins, 1976), pp. 277–281.

Why do children have such differing levels of spelling skills? Several factors are responsible: ability, ways of learning, and rates of learning. Each factor must be considered in designing a more individual program. One type of program calls for arranging the children in groups for the poor spellers, the average spellers, and the above-average spellers.

Determining Levels

It is not difficult to determine a child's spelling level, since evidence can be found in almost every piece of written work that is turned in to the teacher. Standardized tests are certainly unnecessary in the primary years and are not essential at the intermediate level.

Another way of finding individual instructional levels has been proposed by Burrows and others. First, a spelling list from each grade's speller is needed. A sample of 20 to 25 words is selected from each. (If there are 250 words in the grade's total list, selecting every tenth word provides an unbiased sample of 25 words, for example.) Second, in testing the class to determine spelling levels, each child should have sheets of paper with room enough for 20 to 25 words in a column. Each word on the first-grade list is pronounced once, the pupils writing it on their paper. Third, children who spell 70 percent or more of the first-grade words correctly are tested again, using the second-grade-level list. Testing continues (perhaps on other days) until all children spell less than 70 percent of a list correctly. The following distribution represents a likely occurrence in a second-grade classroom:

Number of Children	Instructional Level
5	1
12	2
8	3
5	4

This means there would be four spelling groups, with each assigned to an appropriate level.[23]

A list of words for an informal spelling inventory is taken from the *Word Book Spelling Program* (Chicago: Rand McNally, 1976). The list appears here as Chart 8.1.

23. Alvina T. Burrows, Dianne Monson, and Russell L. Stauffer, *New Horizons in Language Arts* (New York: Harper & Row, 1972), pp. 245–248.

CHART 8.1: *Word Lists for Informal Spelling Inventory (ISI)*

Grade 1	Grade 2	Grade 3	Grade 4
1. bit	1. ate	1. another	1. bank
2. cane	2. birds	2. before	2. blowing
3. date	3. by	3. called	3. calling
4. egg	4. day	4. city	4. check
5. fog	5. eat	5. cry	5. colored
6. gum	6. for	6. dresses	6. dance
7. home	7. glad	7. feet	7. eaten
8. jam	8. he	8. friend	8. finger
9. joke	9. I	9. great	9. gathered
10. lamp	10. likes	10. heard	10. happened
11. lot	11. me	11. into	11. joke
12. mop	12. not	12. left	12. large
13. nip	13. over	13. merry	13. luck
14. page	14. rabbit	14. never	14. naughty
15. pole	15. second	15. orange	15. pages
16. rid	16. store	16. presents	16. pitcher
17. sad	17. they	17. Santa Claus	17. pushed
18. sore	18. train	18. ship	18. rice
19. tin	19. we	19. skin	19. scared
20. wax	20. would	20. started	20. skated
		21. supper	21. steal
		22. through	22. tail
		23. upon	23. tramp
		24. wear	24. upstairs
		25. woods	25. whose

Instructional Procedures

A general procedure, based on levels of achievement, could include the following seven steps:

1. Spelling instruction would be initiated, using the test-study and corrected-test (self-correction) techniques. On Monday, each group is administered a list of twenty words taken from the master spelling list. The teacher has four lists (grades 1, 2, 3, and 4) and reads one word from each list in turn. The children in group 1 spell the first word; the group 2 children spell the second word; those in the third group spell the third word; and those in the fourth group, the fourth word.

CHART 8.1 *(continued)*

Grade 5	Grade 6	Grade 7	Grade 8
1. autumn	1. anybody	1. amusing	1. amateur
2. behind	2. bareheaded	2. badly	2. argument
3. button	3. bracelet	3. budget	3. bodies
4. chance	4. carried	4. commercial	4. cashier
5. colony	5. community	5. controversy	5. comfortable
6. dairy	6. dancing	6. definitely	6. controllable
7. drill	7. during	7. disappointed	7. decoration
8. excited	8. expect	8. enable	8. difference
9. follow	9. form	9. envy	9. doubtless
10. giving	10. grapevines	10. familiar	10. equipment
11. history	11. honey	11. fortune	11. extension
12. inside	12. jellyfish	12. guardian	12. funeral
13. leaving	13. let's	13. hygiene	13. hemisphere
14. March	14. massive	14. interviewed	14. innings
15. motor	15. mule	15. locate	15. justice
16. nurse	16. office	16. mighty	16. lover
17. perfume	17. pioneer	17. notify	17. molecule
18. possible	18. principal	18. peaceable	18. olives
19. queen	19. region	19. practicing	19. peculiar
20. route	20. seal	20. purchase	20. possibility
21. scratch	21. sixth	21. republic	21. pronunciation
22. shower	22. spaceship	22. security	22. reception
23. special	23. straight	23. sorrow	23. resources
24. surprise	24. theater	24. submit	24. serviceable
25. umbrella	25. treat	25. through	25. sufficient

2. When the four lists are dictated, the corrected-test technique is begun. Each child is given a typed copy of the words he or she was asked to spell (group 1 must have five copies of the list and so on). The child checks spellings against the list, finding his or her own misspellings.

3. Each misspelled word is studied immediately, as previously suggested.

4. On Wednesday, the procedure for Monday is repeated. (All pupils spell the same words again even if they had no misspelled words on Monday.) A child who spells all words correctly on both days is finished for the week. A child who misses the same word on Wednesday that was missed on Monday studies it again on Thursday.

5. The test is given again on Friday for those who do not spell all words correctly on both Monday and Wednesday.

6. Additional delayed-recall checks are made monthly. (The words missed in the preceding four weeks are used again in the test-study procedure.)

7. Instruction is varied by giving the more able spellers supplementary words for spelling or they are given a new list on Fridays. For the slowest learners, reduction of the number of words per week is recommended (one-half or fewer of the lesson words).

The Poor Speller Seven special points should be considered in teaching the poor speller.

1. Present a limited number of words each week (perhaps five to ten).

2. For the spelling words, use only the most common words in writing, the most basic words. These are the words that appear earliest in a graded spelling textbook series. A list proposing the words of highest frequency use is presented in Chart 8.2.

Particular attention should be given to Horn's list. Three little words—*I, the,* and *and*—account for 10 percent of all the running words in print. Anyone who spells these three words correctly is automatically a 10 percent correct speller. Only ten words—*I, the, and, to, a, you, of, in, we,* and *for*—account for 25 percent of all the running words in the average adult writing vocabulary. One hundred words—the words listed by Horn—account for 65 percent of the running words written by adults.[24]

3. To supplement a list of basic words—or replace it if deemed desirable by the teacher—each child should develop an individual word list. Each child keeps his or her own spelling notebook, with the pages alphabetically labeled. Some appropriate kinds of words for the notebooks are:

Words the child asks the teacher how to spell in writing tasks
Words the child has to look up to use in writing
Words misspelled on papers turned in
Special content words (for writing purposes, not spelling mastery).

4. Check the child's method of learning—visual, auditory, kinesthetic—and teach the child to study the word lists in the most productive way for each individual. The *Mills Learning Method Test* is designed to compare

24. See also Rinsland, *A Basic Vocabulary of Elementary School Children* for the first 254 words of highest frequency use.

CHART 8.2: *First 100 Words in Order of Frequency*

1. I	21. at	41. do	61. up	81. think
2. the	22. this	42. been	62. day	82. say
3. and	23. with	43. letter	63. much	83. please
4. to	24. but	44. can	64. out	84. him
5. a	25. on	45. would	65. her	85. his
6. you	26. if	46. she	66. order	86. got
7. of	27. all	47. when	67. yours	87. over
8. in	28. so	48. about	68. now	88. make
9. we	29. me	49. they	69. well	89. may
10. for	30. was	50. any	70. an	90. received
11. it	31. very	51. which	71. here	91. before
12. that	32. my	52. some	72. them	92. two
13. is	33. had	53. has	73. see	93. send
14. your	34. our	54. or	74. go	94. after
15. have	35. from	55. there	75. what	95. work
16. will	36. am	56. us	76. come	96. could
17. be	37. one	57. good	77. were	97. dear
18. are	38. time	58. know	78. no	98. made
19. not	39. he	59. just	79. how	99. glad
20. as	40. get	60. by	80. did	100. like

Source: Ernest A. Horn, *A Basic Writing Vocabulary* (University of Iowa Monographs in Education, First Series, no 41; Iowa City: University of Iowa Press, 1926).

the effectiveness of various learning methods: visual, auditory, kinesthetic, and combined.[25]

The study procedures presented earlier in this chapter as a checklist indicate ways to study from a visual or auditory mode. These include "picturing" the words by the visual learner; for the auditory learner there is heavy emphasis upon saying the word aloud, writing what the child says, underlining syllables, learning unphonetic parts, and the like.

For the kinesthetic, or motor, learner, Fernald advised the teacher to write the word with a crayon in big letters on a piece of paper, using the "tracing" technique described below.[26]

25. Robert E. Mills, *Mills Learning Method Test* (Ft. Lauderdale, FL: The Mills Educational Center, 1970).
26. Grace M. Fernald, *Remedial Techniques in Basic School Subjects* (New York: McGraw-Hill, 1943), Chapter 13.

Keeps two fingers in contact with writing (index and second finger, fingers kept stiff)

Says the word

Says each part without distortion on the initial stroke of each syllable as each syllable is traced

Crosses *t*'s and dots *i*'s from left to right

Says each syllable as each syllable is underlined

Says the word

Repeats the above six steps until the child appears ready to imitate the technique

The child traces the word, following the procedure noted, until the word can be written without the copy. Then he or she checks the word against the original copy. If it is correct, he or she writes the word again and checks it again. The child is encouraged to write the word correctly two successive times. If unsuccessful, the child should keep trying until it is correct. He or she should always rewrite the entire word if an error is made; erasures or other corrections are not permitted. Retention of the word is checked the following day.

Kinesthetic learners should not have words spelled aloud to them nor should they be asked to spell orally. They should be discouraged from copying a word from the chalkboard but should learn it first by tracing. Parents should be informed of the procedure used at school so they may follow the same routine at home.

5. Try to categorize the types of spelling errors made by the poor speller—not just isolated misspelled words. For a rapid method of collecting samples of a pupil's tendencies to spelling errors, Spache's spelling errors tests are recommended.[27] Two separate tests for use in grades 2 through 4 and 5 through 6 are offered. Each test provides opportunities for committing twelve common types of spelling errors:

Omission of a silent letter (*bite* ⟶ *bit*)

Omission of a sounded letter (*and* ⟶ *an*)

Omission of a double letter (*arrow* ⟶ *arow*)

Addition by doubling (*almost* ⟶ *allmost*)

Addition of a single letter (*dark* ⟶ *darck*)

Transposition or reversal (*ankle* ⟶ *ankel*)

Phonetic substitution for a vowel (*bead* ⟶ *beed*)

27. George D. Spache, *Spelling Errors Test* (Gainesville: University of Florida, n.d.).

Phonetic substitution for a consonant (*bush* ⟶ *buch*)
Phonetic substitution for a syllable (*flies* ⟶ *flys*)
Phonetic substitution for a word (*bare* ⟶ *bear*)
Nonphonetic substitution for a vowel (*bags* ⟶ *bogs*)
Nonphonetic substitution for a consonant (*bottom* ⟶ *botton*).

6. Maintain individual spelling error charts in order to further individualize the work. For example, the twelve common types of errors suggested in number 5 could be charted showing the child's name and error type or types.

7. Maintain a high level of interest and a desirable attitude toward spelling. Earlier in this chapter, in the section on procedures for teaching spelling, we suggested some important ideas about pupil interest which must be convincingly presented to the poor speller. Some evidences of interest and attitude toward spelling have been delineated by Brueckner and Bond.[28] Evidences of lack of interest include:

Avoidance of writing or reluctance in writing
No apparent effort to check the spelling of new words
Reluctance to use a dictionary to look up spellings about which the pupil is uncertain
Resentment of criticism of spelling in other written work

Evidences of a good attitude toward spelling include:

Experimenting by writing words on scratch paper
Requests by a pupil for help in spelling difficult words
Proofreading to detect slips, lapses, and misspellings
Eagerness and promptness with which the study of new words is begun
Satisfaction with evidence of improvement in spelling

The Average Speller The average speller uses the regular instructional program. The following five specific points may be incorporated as features of the program.

1. Use pairs of pupils with similar spelling achievement; they should also be able to study together words missed from the basic list. Again, good study procedures should be emphasized, including the corrected-test technique.

---

28. Brueckner and Bond, *The Diagnosis and Treatment of Learning Difficulties*, p. 353.

2. Maintain individual word files (or notebooks) of words that need to be studied. This file may include other content area works, personal word "demons," and other words the learner may want to learn to spell. The words should be reviewed frequently.

3. Check for the types of errors made. Knowledge of the most common types of errors at the various school levels is important to keep in mind. For example, common errors made in the primary years are:

Mispronunciation (*pospone* for *postpone*)
Confusion of words similar in sound (*were* for *where*)
Omitting or inserting "silent" letters (*stedy* for *steady*)
Transposition of letters (*form* for *from*)

Certain kinds of spelling errors require different correctional procedures. For example, visual image should be stressed when a pupil misspells a phonologically irregular word. These are words, such as *again* or *guess*, that are not spelled the way they sound. Incorrect spelling of homonyms (*their, they're, there; your, you're; know, no*) suggests a need to emphasize meanings and perhaps to teach by word groups. Lack of knowledge of important rules may cause incorrect spelling of such words as *coming, getting, studying,* and *tired*. Accurate speaking and listening would be stressed with words such as *February, which, athlete, pin*. Visual image and pronunciation may be helpful procedures when transposition of letters could occur (*girl, goes, first, from* written as *gril, gose, frist, form*). *Stars* may appear incorrectly as *stors* due to poor handwriting. Errors involving double consonant letters likely can be improved through stressing visual imagery, and errors with medial consonant letters would suggest a need to emphasize pronunciation and learn about unstressed vowels.

4. Record types of errors to pinpoint specific weaknesses and give direction to individual and small-group instruction.

A chart like Chart 8.3 could be kept of types of spelling errors made by pupils.

The types of spelling errors on the left side of the chart could be adjusted to the types of spelling words presented. A study of the marked chart would indicate the needs of particular students and provide a basis for small-group instruction. When needed, systematic lessons may be presented. The example shown in the lesson plan is for one particular type of spelling error—the silent *e*.

5. Provide much practice or use of spelling words through written expression and maintain a progress chart to indicate improvement that is taking place.

CHART 8.3: *Types of Spelling Errors*

	Jim	Sandy	Joe	Linda
Consonant error				
Consonant cluster error				
Consonant digraph error				
Schwa error				
Long vowel error				
Vowel digraph or diphthong error				
Root/affix error				
Silent letter error				

The Above-Average Speller The above-average speller requires several modifications in this program. The teacher may:

1. Excuse from formal spelling instruction the child who can spell 90 percent or more of the month's or semester's word list correctly.
2. Have the pupil keep a word file for his or her writing purposes.
3. Permit the pupil who so desires to continue into higher-level basic word lists or to study some specialized writing vocabulary (social studies, science)
4. Challenge the child in such ways as the following:
   a. Assigning bonus lists of words not included in the basic spelling list (Such words, though not used as frequently as the words selected for the basic spelling list, are important for the capable

LESSON PLAN: *Spelling—Silent* e *Principle*

Performance Objective

Given a word illustrating the silent *e* principle, the learner spells other words illustrating this principle.

Pretest

Use sets of words like the ones provided below as a spelling test. The word in parentheses is to be used as a model by the child as he or she spells the other words in the row.

(ride)	1. wide	2. slide	3. five	4. drive
(ate)	1. late	2. plate	3. gave	4. save
(cake)	1. fake	2. rake	3. shake	4. take
(home)	1. nose	2. close	3. rope	4. rode

Criterion for mastery is 100 percent correct.

Teaching Suggestions

1. If the learner is unable to meet the criterion in the pretest, write the sets of words in vertical columns on the chalkboard. Tell the child to pronounce each word, then ask: "What vowel letter is in the middle of each word in the set?" "Is the vowel sound long or short?" "What letter is at the end of each word?" "Does the letter at the end represent any sound?" Lead to the generalization that when a one-syllable word ends in silent *e*, the preceding vowel is a long sound.
2. Direct the learner's attention to the following arrangement of words, noting similarities and differences in spelling and pronunciation.

not	Tim	mad	hid	rid	rod	slid
note	time	made	hide	ride	rode	slide

Mastery or Posttest Suggestion

The pretest can be used as the posttest, using the same procedures and criterion for mastery.

Reteaching Suggestion

Direct the learner's attention to the similarities in the sets of words in the pretest.

speller who is likely to do more than an average amount of written work.)

b. Encouraging the child to make extensive use of spelling in functional and creative writing

c. Encouraging the child to take part in interesting and worthwhile diversions in the field of linguistics (for example, exercises could focus upon word origins, which are absorbing to children)

d. Listing spelling words that may be spelled correctly in more than one way, as *catalog, catalogue*

e. Keeping individual lists of new words the child would like to learn how to spell

f. Using words in written sentences to show varied meanings of words in the spelling list

g. Finding the root words in larger words

h. Adding prefixes and suffixes to root words and writing an explanation of their effect on meaning

i. Making charts of synonyms, antonyms, homonyms, contractions, and abbreviations

j. Listing derivatives of words found in the weekly spelling list

k. Learning the spelling of words from units of work

l. Preparing dictation exercises for the class

m. Learning plurals, particularly of troublesome words

n. Selecting and marking out "silent" letters frequently mispronounced

o. Compiling a list of words with different *gh* sounds (for example, *enough, graph, though, sleigh, taught, night*)

THE COMPUTER AND SPELLING

Today inexpensive spelling computers can give children practice with words. Nolen[29] describes one such computer system that asks a user to spell a word which is clearly pronounced. As the user types a response, each letter is converted into audible speech patterns through an integrated circuit synthesizer. If the completed word is correct, the unit provides praise and a new word. If the response is in error, the unit asks for a second trial before providing the correct spelling. Such practice provides a learner with a clear visual image as well as some attention to sound relationships.

29. Patricia Nolen, "Electronic Aids in Spelling," *Language Arts* 57 (February 1980): 178–179.

SOME INSTRUCTIONAL CONCERNS

Some teachers wish to individualize spelling instruction beyond grouping. One fourth-grade teacher further individualizes her program in this manner. She provides a small notebook for each child; this is the child's speller. The pages are lettered alphabetically and tabbed to indicate the letters. When a child asks for a word, the teacher writes the word under the correct letter. When children have to check the dictionary for the spelling of a word, they enter the new word in the speller. Words that are corrected on children's papers are also included in the speller. During the next week or so, these are the words studied by the child with the teacher's assistance. As children do daily writing, the teacher keeps a notebook of spelling difficulties common to the class as a whole or to many of the students. These give the teacher material for lessons on various spelling concepts. At times, spellers check each other or the teacher does so while other children are studying. Such a program helps develop interest in spelling, keeps the good speller from being slowed down by others, and prevents the poor speller from experiencing undue pressure and repeated failure. Such a program, by drawing words from the children's daily writing, also emphasizes spelling as an element of written composition.

Some students have difficulty in proofreading for spelling errors. They must understand that proofreading procedures for spelling are different from those used in checking for capitalization and punctuation errors. Whereas oral reading is helpful in determining where punctuation is needed and a scanning process—looking at the beginning of sentences and searching for proper nouns and adjectives—is best for checking capitalization, the proofreading of spelling requires that words be looked at individually. After marking any questionable spelling, the student should refer to the dictionary for accuracy.

THOUGHT QUESTIONS

1. Knowing how children appear to acquire spelling understanding, would you recommend a strictly phonics-based spelling program?
2. What factors should be considered in selecting words for the spelling program?
3. How can the language arts areas be further integrated, as for example in the development of spelling ability and in reading comprehension?
4. How may children be encouraged to become good spellers?
5. How would you present an important spelling generalization to children?

LEARNER RESPONSE OPTIONS

1. Prepare a list of spelling words on the basis of some phoneme-grapheme relationship. State the generalization to be achieved.
2. Study a spelling textbook at a grade level of your choice. Identify the phonological and morphological generalizations presented in it. What types of lessons are used: phoneme-grapheme, word building, historical study, analysis of words?
3. Present a list of spelling words to a class or a small group of children, using the test-study and corrected-test techniques.
4. Prepare a set of four to six study exercises to accompany the spelling list in Learner Response Option 3.
5. Interview a child about his or her spelling ability, methods of study, and attitude toward spelling. Write an analysis on the basis of your findings.
6. Prepare a spelling game, stating objectives, materials, and procedures.
7. Using one of the ways suggested in this chapter, determine the level of spelling material appropriate for an individual.
8. Collect written papers from an elementary school classroom. Analyze the most common kinds of errors.
9. Plan a systematic (mastery) lesson for one of the kinds of errors identified in Learner Response Option 8.

REFERENCES AND ADDITIONAL READINGS

Allred, Ruel. *Spelling: The Application of Research Findings.* Washington, DC: National Education Association, 1977.

Fitzsimmons, Robert J., and Bradley M. Loomer. *Spelling Research and Practice.* Des Moines: Iowa State Department of Public Instruction, 1977.

Henderson, Edmund H., and James W. Beers. *Developmental and Cognitive Aspects of Learning to Spell.* Newark, DE: International Reading Association, 1980.

Hodges, Richard E. *Learning to Spell.* Urbana, IL: National Council of Teachers of English, 1981.

Hillerich, Robert L. *Spelling: An Element in Written Expression.* Columbus, OH: Merrill, 1978.

Read, Charles, and Richard E. Hodges. "Spelling." In *Encyclopedia of Educational Research.* New York: Macmillan, 1982.

Thomas, Ves. *Teaching Spelling.* Buffalo. NY: Gage, 1974.

CHAPTER 9: *Handwriting*

OVERVIEW

This chapter is a comprehensive study of handwriting programs for the elementary school. It stresses the importance of handwriting, the need for legibility, and the recognition of individual styles. The focus is on functional handwriting instruction in all curricular areas. Early in the chapter, attention is directed to basic features of a handwriting program: writing readiness, use of commercial materials, and handedness as it affects recommended paper-and-pencil positions. In the study of manuscript and cursive writing, the following topics are treated: initial instruction, use of the chalkboard, practice activities involving perceptual-motor learning, and common errors and difficulties. The chapter concludes with a detailed description of the handwriting learning center as means of furthering individualized instruction, ways of maintaining interest in handwriting, and evaluation procedures (standardized and informal).

While studying this topic, the reader should recall and relate previous discussions of writing in the chapter dealing with the young child, the written composition chapter, and the spelling chapter.

KEY VOCABULARY

writing readiness	hand dominance
manuscript	size
perceptual-motor	upper-loop letters
reversals	lower-loop letters
cursive	retrace
nonslant cursive	check stroke
looped strokes	letter form
nonlooped strokes	spacing
overcurves	alignment
undercurves	slant
baseline	line quality

273

SOME BASIC PREMISES IN THE TEACHING OF HANDWRITING

A handwriting program that meets children's needs takes into account four basic premises regarding the purpose of handwriting, the attention that should be paid to it, the objectives of teaching, and individual styles in handwriting.

The primary purpose of handwriting is to express meaning. The pupil should have a purpose for writing, even in the earliest stages of writing instruction. Pupils may at times need help and practice on specific letters, but the basic motivation for improving their skill is a strong desire to express and communicate. (Direct handwriting instruction or practice periods need not be too long—15 to 20 minutes per day at the primary level and about 10 to 15 minutes per day at the intermediate level.)

Because handwriting is a skill that is used in all other curricular areas, attention must be given to it as needed throughout the school day. Special handwriting periods are usually desirable to reach and maintain the desired efficiency level, but the instruction and practice provided should be based on the needs of children in practical writing situations.

The objectives of handwriting instruction include helping pupils recognize and accept the importance of good handwriting, develop pride in and a critical attitude toward their own handwriting, acquire suitable speed in handwriting (adjusting speed to purpose), and develop habits of neatness and orderly arrangement in written work.

Individuality in handwriting is to be respected, though courtesy requires enough conformity to prevent inconvenience and misunderstanding on the part of the reader. Improving handwriting does not necessarily destroy individuality. The teacher should help each child find and develop the style of handwriting that is best for him or her.

GROWTH PATTERNS AND READINESS IN HANDWRITING

The physical growth of children should be taken into consideration in planning the program of handwriting instruction. The growth patterns of children as they relate to handwriting may be briefly summarized as follows:

Ages five to seven: Handedness has usually been established by ages five and seven. Most children in this age group, however, have not fully developed coordination of the smaller muscles of the hands and fingers. Some irregularities in handwriting may be expected, and standards should

not be unreasonably high. Frequent use of large areas, such as the chalk-board, permits use of the better coordinated large muscles.

Ages eight to ten: Coordination of smaller muscles has improved by the time the child reaches the ages of eight to ten. Writing is reduced in size and it becomes more uniform in quality.

Ages eleven to thirteen: By the end of the elementary school years, the average child can produce handwriting of good quality at an acceptable rate of speed.

Although these considerations should influence your expectations and evaluations, a study by Niedermeyer[1] concludes that there is no physio-logical reason to delay handwriting instruction and that early instruction contributes to a positive attitude toward school. Since the growth patterns

1. F. C. Niedermeyer, "Kindergarteners Learn to Write," *Elementary School Journal*, 74 (December 1973): 130–135. Reported by Victor Froese in "Handwriting: Practice, Prag-matism, and Progress," *Research in the Language Arts* ed. Froese and Stanley B. Straw (Baltimore: University Park Press, 1981), p. 233.

of children vary, not every child will be ready for handwriting instruction at exactly the same time. The teacher should be able to identify and help the child who is ready.

HANDWRITING MATERIALS

Appropriate use of commercial handwriting materials for teachers and pupils can do much to promote interest in handwriting. Every teacher should have a teacher's handwriting manual. General teaching procedures, goals to be achieved, chalkboard writing, analysis of letters, and sample lesson plans are discussed in most teacher guidebooks. The reader should know that a large number of writing systems is available and, most important, that there is a fairly wide range of discrepancies among those systems. The Zaner-Bloser examples we reproduce in this chapter are among the most widely used of such systems. Until instructional material that is more suitable to the individualized approach proposed in this chapter is available, the teacher is obliged to *adapt* the material found in the manuals. Teacher guidebooks, too often designed for formal, whole-class work, contain helpful and important suggestions, but they are not to be used in a slavish, word-for-word manner and should not be so interpreted. Too, some commercial handwriting materials stress repetition over application.

The teacher should also secure a copy of the scope-and-sequence chart that often accompanies basic material adopted for pupil use. A close study of this kind of chart will reveal an overview of many features of the handwriting program for the various books (grades K–8):

Kinds of writing
Basic habits
Paper rulings
Writing tools
Elements of legibility
Letter forms
Rhythm-fluency
Applied uses
Refinement skills
Evaluation

The teacher can use this information to get a brief overview of the handwriting program at one particular level, as well as the programs in the preceding and following levels. With this information, the teacher can diagnose what should have been learned previously and what still needs attention, and thus can provide the kind and amount of instruction needed to accommodate the varied differences found among pupils.

The pupil's handwriting workbook is a convenient source of practice materials. The teacher, after an inventory of the pupils' individual needs, may use the parts of the workbook that provide instruction on particular difficulties. There is little justification for assigning the same practice lesson to all pupils unless it is actually needed by all. There is less justification for assigning pages in the workbook to be completed while the teacher is busy with other chores. In such cases, the pupils are simply slavishly using "copybooks" and little or no instruction is taking place. Published handwriting materials are useful, but they do not relieve the teacher of the basic responsibility of instruction.

TEACHING MANUSCRIPT

Manuscript is a writing form that uses simple curves and straight lines to make unjoined letters. (See Chart 9.1 for Manuscript Alphabet.) Cursive is a writing form with the strokes of the letters joined together and the angles rounded. (See Chart 9.2 for Cursive Alphabet.) Manuscript came to the United States from England in the 1920s.[2]

After much discussion and study of the relative merits of manuscript and cursive writing, most authorities agree that manuscript writing has definite advantages for initial instruction and that the addition of cursive writing should be made before the beginning of the fourth grade. According to Herrick, there are three major arguments supporting the use of manuscript symbols for initial instruction.[3] First, the motor development and eye-hand-arm coordination of young children enable them to form straight vertical lines and circles (the basic forms of manuscript writing) more rapidly and legibly than the complex cursive forms. Second, the manuscript writing symbols are similar to those the children are learning to read, so there is no need for them to learn to read two forms of written

2. Froese, "Handwriting: Practice, Pragmatism, and Progress," in *Research in the Language Arts*, p. 239.
3. Virgil E. Herrick, "Children's Experiences in Writing," in *Children and the Language Arts*, ed. Herrick and Leland B. Jacobs (Englewood Cliffs, NJ: Prentice-Hall, 1955), pp. 271–272.

CHART 9.1: *Manuscript Alphabet*

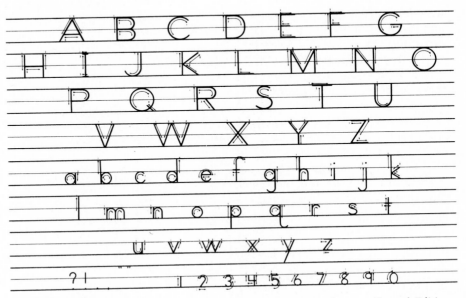

Source: Used with permission from *Creative Growth with Handwriting*, Second Edition. Copyright © 1979. Zaner-Bloser, Inc., Columbus, OH.

language at a time when their responsibilities for learning are already overwhelming. Finally, although there is no agreed-upon definition of *legibility*, it is generally agreed that manuscript writing is more legible than cursive writing.

Virtually all schools teach a form of manuscript writing in the primary grades, according to Petty and Jensen[4] and many other language arts specialists.

Initial Instruction

Primary-level teachers are responsible for giving children a good start in handwriting and for helping them develop desirable attitudes toward it.

4. Walter T. Petty and Julie M. Jensen, *Developing Children's Language* (Boston: Allyn and Bacon, 1980), p. 478.

The following ten suggestions, modified from a list by Shane, Mulry, Redding, and Gillespie, may prove helpful in overall planning for writing instruction in the primary years.

1. Beginning handwriting attempts should be characterized by large, free strokes rather than being confined within narrow, lined spaces. Chalkboards, easels, or large sheets of paper may be used. Since the small-muscle control of most five- and six-year-olds is limited, the use of the large muscles in these initial handwriting attempts should be encouraged to avoid fatigue.

2. Folds, between which letters are to be formed, may be made on unlined paper until children become adept at writing between lines.

3. As skill increases, lined paper may be introduced for those children who are coordinated enough to use it. The beginning space between lines is usually about 1 inch. Some teachers like to use commercially available paper that has a dotted or light-colored line as a guide for the height of the lower-case letters.

4. When children are working at their desks, they should have a sample of the handwriting task before them. Since eye-hand coordination in these early stages is still developing, too much strain is imposed by looking up and down and back and forth at the chalkboard. As children become more skillful, they may copy from the chalkboard, but they should be seated near the sample and facing it.

5. When pupils begin to write on lined paper, they may use a large beginner's pencil. Research suggests that standard-sized pencils are all right to use, too, depending on the teachers' and pupils' preferences.

6. It is important that the teacher's handwriting be firm, bold, and exact. Teachers who lack certainty and ease in manuscript writing should try to perfect this skill.

7. Primary rooms should have a permanent alphabet and a sample of Arabic numerals visible for easy reference. These may be printed on tagboard by the teacher or purchased commercially.

8. The teacher studies the children's written work for clues to their needs and progress, providing practice situations to help children cope with troublesome letters. The teacher often works with small groups on several different writing tasks and gives individual help when needed.

9. Attention should be given to spacing between letters and words in each writing experience.

10. The same general procedures that are followed in teaching manuscript forms may be employed in teaching children how to write numerals. As they do their arithmetic lessons, number pages in their booklets,

write telephone numbers or dates, or make calendars, children should be taught where to start and how to form the numerals.[5]

As mentioned earlier, young children have natural curiosity and excitement about writing. Teachers should help them direct these feelings into actually beginning writing.

It is also important that handwriting procedures be individualized from the beginning. Children should be helped to evaluate their own work, find their own errors and build on their strengths. They should not be required to practice repeatedly forms they have already mastered. Only errors made by practically everyone should be taken up by the entire class.

5. Harold G. Shane et al., *Improving Language Arts Instruction in the Elementary School* (Columbus, OH: Merrill, 1962), pp. 372–374.

Chalkboard Writing

Writing on the chalkboard is enjoyable for the children and easily supervised by the teacher. Guidelines ruled on the chalkboard are helpful. Capital letters may be made about 3 inches high, with proportionally sized lower-case letters. The following suggestions for chalkboard writing should prove helpful.

Checklist: *Chalkboard Writing*

1. Face the chalkboard and stand comfortably.
2. Stand far enough back to allow good arm movement and to allow adequate visualizing of letters and words.
3. Hold an eraser in the left hand for easy use (right hand for left-handed children).
4. Keep the writing near eye level. (If the chalkboard in the room is too high, a low platform or stepstool may be needed so children can reach it.)
5. Hold the elbow close to the body.
6. Use a half-length piece of chalk. Hold the chalk about 1 inch from the writing end between the thumb and first and second fingers. The second finger will rest upon the chalk, differing somewhat from holding a pencil. The inner end of the chalk will point to the center of the palm of the writing hand.

Practice Through a Functional Approach

The handwriting needs of young children include writing their own names, addresses, and telephone numbers; writing dates; keeping records, such as a weather chart; writing labels and captions for objects, charts, and pictures; and writing letters, notices, announcements, and simple stories. The functional approach to teaching beginning handwriting generally produces better results than work with individual letters.

This approach does not rule out instruction concerning letter forms; it also takes into account pupil difficulty with individual letters. The sample lesson plan which follows represents a mastery of systematic type lesson for the manuscript letter *g*.

LESSON PLAN: *Manuscript: Lowercase* g

Performance Objective

Given a known word including the letter *g*, the learner forms the letter according to instructions for good manuscript form.

Pretest

Write (in manuscript) the word good on the chalkboard. Ask the learner to write it carefully several times on paper. If the learner's *g* is of medium or poor formation, continue with the teaching suggestions.

Teaching Suggestions

1. Have the learner visually analyze the *g* on the chalkboard, answering such questions as: "Which part is made first?" "Which way do you move your pencil to make the circle?" "How wide is the lower part?" "Where does it finish?"
2. Have the learner make four or five *g*'s, describing the process as he or she writes.
3. Ask the child to analyze *g*, *j*, and *g*, answering such questions as "Which two letters are alike?" "How are *g* and *q* different?" Then the learner can make *g*, *j*, and *q*.

Mastery or Posttest Suggestions

The learner, after making four or five *g*'s, may analyze these letters by answering such questions as, "Am I moving my pencil the right way to make the circle?" "Is the lower part as wide as the circle?" "Does the lower part end high enough?"

Reteaching Suggestions

1. Instruct the learner to write the words *glad* and *age* after they have first been written on the chalkboard by the teacher.
2. Ask the learner to write the sentence *I am going to go*, after it has been written on the chalkboard.

Perceptual-Motor

Furner described a program of primary-level handwriting instruction in which the perceptual-motor nature of learning is emphasized. Her main point is that instruction in handwriting should build perception of letters and their formation as a guide for motor practice, rather than emphasizing only the motor aspect. The following points summarize her specific instructional recommendations.

1. Involve pupils in establishing a purpose for each lesson.
2. Provide many guided exposures to the formation of letters; for example, focus attention upon different aspects of the formational process in subsequent trials in order to assist the child in building a mental image of the letter form.
3. Encourage a mental as well as a motor response from each child during the writing process; for example, have the child describe the process while writing, or have the child visualize or write a letter as another child describes it. This procedure makes use of multisensory stimulation.
4. Stress self-correction by emphasizing comparison and improvement rather than writing many samples.
5. Provide consistent letter-form models. The teacher's writing should conform to the style adopted by the school.
6. Keep expectations regarding the quantity of writing consistent with what the children can realistically produce. (For example, Furner found that the average first grader can write only 16 to 17 letters per minute. This amounts to only about 30 words in ten minutes.)[6]

Frequent Types of Manuscript Errors and Difficulties

Lewis and Lewis reported a study of errors in the formation of manuscript letters by first-grade children.

Frequency of Errors In general, errors were most frequent in letter forms in which curves and vertical lines merge: J, U, f, h, j, m, n, r, u. Errors were least frequent in the letter forms constructed of vertical lines or horizontal and vertical lines: E, F, H, I, L, T, i, l, t.[7]

Size The most frequent type of error was *incorrect size*. Although this error was distributed among all letters, it was most frequent with the descenders, p, q, y, g, and j.

Examples: ___p q y g j___

6. Beatrice Furner, "Recommended Instructional Procedures in a Method Emphasizing the Perceptual-Motor Nature of Learning in Handwriting," *Elementary English* 46 (December 1969): 1021–1030; 46 (November 1969): 886–894; and 47 (January 1970): 61–70.
7. Edward R. Lewis and Hilda P. Lewis, "Which Manuscript Letters Are Hard for First Graders?" *Elementary English* 41 (December 1964): 855–858.

Forms The letter forms most frequently *reversed* were N, d, q, s, and y.

Examples:

Omission *Partial omission* occurred most frequently in *m*, *U*, and *I*.

Examples:

Additions These were most frequent with *q*, *C*, *k*, *m*, and *y*.

Examples:

Incorrect Relationship of Parts This fault was generally common, occurring most frequently with *k*, *R*, *M*, and *m*.

Examples:

Incorrect Placement Relative to Line This was a common error with descenders and a less frequent error with the other letters.

Examples:

Incorrect Shape The letter forms most frequently misshaped were *j*, *G*, and *J*.

Examples:

Observation has shown that in manuscript form, common *reversal* problems involve *d* and *b*, *q* and *g*, *s*, *y*, and capital *N*. Most reversals can be avoided by careful initial teaching and by supervised early writing attempts. Instruction calls for emphasizing the correct beginning point, correct direction of motion, and correct sequence of multipart letters. Chalkboard practice is highly recommended for the elimination of possible reversal errors. In addition, the confusion caused by presenting similar letters such as *d* and *b* is easily reduced by separating by a week or more the teaching of these two letters. Other teaching suggestions include:

Associate a strong *b* and *d* sound with words as the letter is taught: *b* in *boy* and *d* in *dog*.
Build a close association between formation of *a* and *d*.
Make the letter *b*, saying "b right."

Associate lower-case *b* with capital *B*. (Capital B is seldom reversed.)
Associate formation of lower-case *h* with *b* (seldom confused with *b*).
Use the kinesthetic approach—tracing of letters.
Associate forming capital and lower-case *c,* capital and lower-case *s*.
Accompany the *N* with "sharp top always to the left."

Teaching cursive writing

A few school systems continue to teach only manuscript writing in the intermediate years, but before the beginning of the fourth grade, the transition has usually been made from manuscript to cursive. The evidence concerning the alleged superiority of cursive writing over manuscript writing is inconclusive. It is argued that cursive writing can be done with greater speed than manuscript writing, but it has also been shown that legibility decreases with great increases in speed. Some handwriting experts assert that there is not as much opportunity for individuality in the manuscript form as in cursive. Social pressures favor the teaching of cursive forms, however, for many adults feel that manuscript is "printing" and not really "writing." A sample of cursive letters recommended by one commercial system of handwriting is shown in Chart 9.2.

Initial Instruction

There is no generally accepted agreement concerning the exact time when cursive writing should be introduced. Strickland says that the second grade appears to a number of people to be too early for two reasons. First of all, children still have not developed enough muscular coordination to master cursive writing easily; therefore, an excessive amount of time must be spent learning it. Secondly, children have just reached the stage in which they can enjoy manuscript writing and are beginning to be prolific writers. Adding a new form of writing at this time cuts off interest in creative writing as it is beginning to flower and makes the whole problem of writing more difficult.[8] Herrick says that, in general, the time necessary for making the transition decreases as the transition period is postponed from second grade to third grade.[9]

8. Ruth G. Strickland, *The Language Arts in the Elementary School*, 3d ed. (Boston: D. C. Heath, 1969), p. 380.
9. Herrick, "Children's Experiences in Writing," p. 273.

CHART 9.2: *Cursive Alphabet*

Source: Used with permission from *Creative Growth with Handwriting*, Second Edition. Copyright © 1979. Zaner-Bloser, Inc., Columbus, OH.

There is a readiness for the transition just as there is for beginning writing. Not all pupils are ready at the same time; some will be by the middle of the second grade, whereas others should wait until the latter part of the third or the beginning of the fourth grade. Most children, however, develop a readiness for cursive writing sometime during the second or third year of school. Three clues that indicate this readiness are the ability to write manuscript letters well from memory, the ability to read cursive writing from the chalkboard and from paper, and a desire to learn cursive writing.

Many teachers begin teaching pupils to read cursive writing early in the second school year by writing a few words on the chalkboard in cursive form—names, the date, the days of the week, or a simple sentence. While doing this, the teacher may point out the following differences between cursive and manuscript writing:

In cursive writing, the letters of each word are joined and the pencil is not lifted until the end of the word.

The letter *t* is crossed and the *i* and *j* are dotted after completion of the word in cursive writing instead of after completion of the letter as in manuscript writing.

In cursive writing, spacing between letters is controlled by slant and connective strokes, not by the shape of the letters, as in manuscript.

Cursive writing has slant, whereas manuscript is vertical.

The writing paper may be placed straight on the desk for manuscript, but the paper is slanted for cursive writing.

Four to six weeks of daily instructional periods of 15 to 20 minutes are usually sufficient for the transitional instructional period. Some teachers have found the following more specific suggestions helpful in initial lessons with cursive letters.

1. Start with one type of stroke, such as used in the words *cat, in, cup,* or *it,* and indicate four steps from manuscript to cursive.

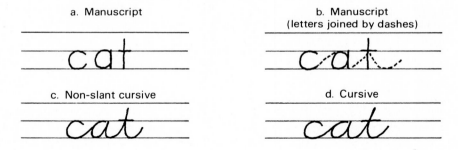

2. Begin with words containing letters that are practically alike in both alphabets except for beginning and ending strokes: for example, the lowercase letters *a, c, d, g, h, i, l, m, n, o, p, q, t, u,* and *y* and the capital letters *B, C, K, L, O, P, R,* and *U.*
3. Give attention to letters that do not follow regular manuscript strokes, like *s* and *r*; also *b, e, f, k,* and *z*, which do not join easily with other letters.
4. Devote some time to crossing *t*'s and *x*'s and dotting *i*'s and *j*'s.
5. Use the chalkboard for much initial work. The suggestions for chalkboard writing in the previous section are applicable to cursive writing as well as to manuscript; the only exception is that for cursive writing, pupils write directly in front of the right shoulder (or in front of the left shoulder, if left-handed).

6. Use pupil spelling words for practice in handwriting class, giving a much greater proportion of time to lower-case letters than to capitals. (Ninety-eight percent of the letters that pupils write will be lower-case.)

During this transitional period, the children may continue to use manuscript writing for some work, especially that done without close supervision by the teacher. Skill in manuscript should also be maintained throughout the elementary school years and used when this style of writing is more appropriate for the work being done. The continued use of manuscript even through adulthood is becoming more and more prevalent.

The D'Nealian Handwriting System (see Chart 9.3) is a new form of manuscript that is readily learned, provides for easy transition from manuscript to cursive, and is said to be effective with special populations (children with learning problems).

Frequent Types of Cursive Errors and Difficulties

Several findings, observations, and techniques are useful in helping children correct errors and illegibilities in handwriting.

Newland found that four types of errors are responsible for most illegibilities:

Failure to close letters

Closing looped strokes (*l* like *t*; *e* like *i*)

Looping nonlooped strokes (*i* like *e*)

Straight-up strokes rather than rounded strokes (*n* like *u*; *c* like *i*; *h* like *b*).[10]

Four letters, *a*, *e*, *r*, and *t*, cause about 45 percent of errors of illegibility. The Arabic numerals 5, 0, and 2 are most often written illegibly.[11] Other problem numerals are 7, 9, and 6.

One research includes *n*, *o*, *s*, and *v* in the group of letters causing difficulty.[12] Still another research indicates that *h*, *i*, *k*, *p*, and *z* represent 30

10. T. Ernest Newland, "An Analytical Study of the Development of Illegibilities in Handwriting from Lower Grades to Adulthood," *Journal of Educational Research* 26 (December 1932): 249–258.
11. T. Ernest Newland, "A Study of Specific Illegibilities Found in the Writing of Arabic Numerals," *Journal of Educational Research* 21 (March 1930): 177–185.
12. S. L. Pressy and L. C. Pressy, "Analysis of 3000 Illegibilities in the Handwriting of Children and Adults," *Educational Research Bulletin* 6 (September 1927): 270–273; Donald H. Rollistin, "A Study of the Handwriting of College Freshmen" (Master's thesis, University of Iowa, Iowa City, 1949).

CHART 9.3: *D'Nealian Handwriting*

D'Nealian™ Manuscript Alphabet

a b c d e f g h i j k l m
n o p q r s t u v w x y z

A B C D E F G H I J K L M
N O P Q R S T U V W X Y Z

D'Nealian™ Cursive Alphabet

a b c d e f g h i j k l m
n o p q r s t u v w x y z

A B C D E F G H I J K L M
N O P Q R S T U V W X Y Z

D'Nealian™ Numbers

0 1 2 3 4 5 6 7 8 9

Source: Used by permission of Scott, Foresman and Company, Glenview, IL.

percent of all illegibilities. Horton found that 12 percent of errors occur with *b, c, i, l, m, n, u, v,* and *x.*[13]

Often it is not individual letter formation that causes difficulty, but letter combinations. Some difficult combinations are:

  b (followed by *e, i, o, r,* or *y*)
  e (followed by *a, i, s*)
  f (followed by *r*)
  g (followed by *r*)
  n (followed by *g*)
  o (followed by *a, c, i, s*)
  v (followed by *e, i*)
  w (followed by *a, c*)

Finally, some teachers have found that cooperatively developed teacher-pupil charts, such as Chart 9.4, are helpful in summarizing special points to check in cursive writing.

RIGHT- AND LEFT-HANDED CHILDREN

Manuscript

Wide-spaced paper is advisable for the beginning writer. It is sometimes recommended that both right- and left-handed pupils place the paper straight on the desk in front of them and pull the downstrokes toward themselves. Enstrom has found that many teachers feel this placement is not natural, interferes with visibility, and causes pupils to turn their hands over on the side, tilt their heads excessively, and hunch over their work. He suggests four procedures to aid in preventing these practices. Have the right-handed pupil slide the horizontally placed paper somewhat to the right on the desk. Instruct the pupil to hold back approximately 1 inch on the pencil with one finger resting on top. Be sure that the desk is not too high for the pupil. Have the paper for the left-handed pupil slanted to the right at about a 30-degree angle.[14]

---

13. Lowell W. Horton, "Illegibilities in the Cursive Handwriting of Sixth Graders," *Elementary School Journal* 70 (May 1970): 446–450.
14. Eric A. Enstrom, "Paper Placement for Manuscript Writing," *Elementary English* 40 (May 1963): 518–522.

CHART 9.4: *Handwriting Guide*

1. When joining *b*, *c*, *o*, and *w* to another letter, you do *not* come to the baseline before beginning the next letter.

   Examples: *be on welcome*

2. Be sure the lower parts of *y* and *z* extend the same distance below the baseline (also *f*, *g*, *j*, *p*, *g*).

   Examples: *zoo yes*

3. The letters *r* and *s* have tips that make them a little taller than letters like o or e.

   Example: *rose*

4. The letter *f* is the only one that has a lower and upper loop.

   Example: *fall*

5. Remember that *d* and *t* are taller than *a* and shorter than *l*.

   Examples: *bad late last*

6. When you write *a*, *d*, and *g*, be careful to close them (also o, p, q, s).

   Example: *adage*

7. The letters *b*, *f*, *h*, *k*, and *l* have tall loops and are about the same height as capitals.

   Examples: *b B f F h H k K l L*

8. When these capitals begin words, they do not join the next letter: D, F, L, O, P, Q, T, U, W, and X.

   Examples: *Don Frank Louise*

Continued

9. Letters beginning with overcurves are *m, n, v, x, y,* and *z.*

   Examples: *m n v x y z*

10. Letters beginning with undercurves are *e, i, p, r, s, t, u,* and *w.*

    Examples: *e i p r s t u w*

11. Letters that begin above the baseline are *a, c, d, g, o,* and *q.*

    Examples: *a c d g o q*

12. Letters that extend below the baseline are *f, g, j, p, q, y,* and *z.*

    Examples: *f g j p q y z*

Cursive

Almost every classroom will have at least one and possibly two or three children who are left-handed.[15] Our system of handwriting has been developed for the majority who are right-handed. As a result, the left-handed child will often develop improper handwriting habits that impede both speed and quality. This need not happen if the teacher will make adjustments for the left-handed child and will make the following suggestions to the child:

Place the writing paper clockwise about 30 degrees or more. (This is more crucial than any other factor in determining success or failure in writing with the left hand.)

Keep the elbows reasonably close to the body.

Direct the blunt end of the pencil or pen so that it points to the left shoulder.

Hold back from the writing point at least ¼ inch farther than a right-handed writer. (A rubber band or other marker placed around the pencil or pen at this point will serve as a reminder.)

15. H. Howell, "Write On, You Sinistrals," *Language Arts* 55 (October 1978): 852–856.

Sit at a desk that is adjusted comparatively low so that it is possible to see where the point of the pencil or pen touches the paper.[16]

In addition, the authors of this book would like to suggest two further procedures that may help the left-handed writer to make the proper adjustments from the beginning. First, the writing paper should be placed toward the left side of the desk for both manuscript and cursive writing. Second, if it seems impossible for the writer to slant the writing to the right, he or she should be permitted to write vertically or to slant to the left.

In a few cases, the teacher may be faced with the problem of determining hand preference when handedness is not firmly established. If handedness is established, there is little justification for attempting to change it; but an unsure or ambidextrous child should be carefully encouraged to use the right hand for ease in social and work situations. A child who has established awkward left-handed habits should be helped to improve; if the poor habits are firmly entrenched, a great deal of help may be necessary. In such cases, the pupil may need lots of writing practice at the chalkboard. He or she may have to be excused from most of the paper work for a while to avoid reversion to old habits that seem at the time to be more efficient.

HANDWRITING LEARNING CENTER

A Fourth-Grade Example

One fourth-grade teacher decided to utilize aspects of the learning-center approach to provide some of the handwriting instruction for a period of six weeks. The materials used and some of the activities associated with these materials should provide many ideas for those interested in further development of this approach.

Activities and Materials

Activities, instruments, and materials used in this learning center are supported by research in handwriting done in the past decade.[17]

16. Eric A. Enstrom, "The Extent of the Use of the Left Hand in Handwriting and the Determination of Relative Efficiency of the Various Hand-Wrist-Arm-Paper Adjustments," *Dissertation Abstracts,* 27, no. 5 (Ann Arbor: University of Michigan, 1957).
17. For example, see Joseph S. Krzesni, "Effect of Different Writing Tools and Papers on

Folders Folders were provided for each child so that the children had a specific place to store their writing activities. Inside each folder were three sets of evaluation sheets for maintaining a record of the formation of each letter of the alphabet (lower and upper case) as well as of each numeral. These evaluations occurred at the beginning, middle, and conclusion of the six-week period. The folder also contained a sheet for recording the score on three writings of the standard evaluation scale that accompanied the basal handwriting series. Finally, the folder contained a checklist for the pupils to evaluate their own handwriting, such as the one presented here.

Transparencies Three transparencies, showing the entire alphabet (upper and lower case) and numerals were provided. Three sheets of paper, corresponding to the lines on these transparencies, were included in each child's folder. Each child could place the transparency over his or her own alphabet writing and check.

Three other transparencies were available to use in checking the pupils' handwriting on regular notebook paper. These consisted of three separate paragraphs. The pupil wrote one of these paragraphs and then placed the transparency over the paper to see how nearly the writing coincided with the sample.

Another transparency with about 30-degree diagonal lines was available so that the pupils could check their slant and spacing.

Handwriting Booklets A copy of the grade-level handwriting booklet was separated and each page placed inside a clear plastic envelope. A pupil

---

Performance of the Third Grades," *Elementary English* 48 (November 1971): 821–824. (He found the use of ballpoint or felt-tip pens improved performance of third-graders by 33 percent.) Two outstanding bibliographies of research in handwriting cite references that confirm other ideas proposed for the center: Lowell Horton, "The Second R: A Working Bibliography," *Elementary English* 46 (April 1969): 426–430; and Eunice Askov, Wayne Otto, and Warren Askov, "A Decade of Research in Handwriting: Progress and Prospect," *Journal of Educational Research* 64 (November 1970): 100–111. (Ideas confirmed in these two references include the use of evaluation scales by both teachers and pupils; the selection of appropriate practice materials based upon exhibited, individual needs revealed through diagnostic evaluation; attention to image-development of the letters and numerals; relating of letters and numerals on the basis of common elements; provision for various modes of learning—tracing, copying, "feeling"; the effects on writing performance of specific positions of the parts of the body; and the emphasis upon functional reasons for handwriting, with considerable attention paid to motivational aspects.) Another interesting medium for handwriting instruction is described by Mary Anne Strahan in "Film Loops to Teach Handwriting," *Instructor* 80 (May 1971): 70–71. Also see the chapter on handwriting in H. G. Shane and James Walden, *Classroom-Relevant Research in Language Arts* (Washington DC: National Education Association, 1978).

CHECKLIST: *How Well Do I Write?*

A. Here is how I write when I am in a hurry: (Write: "This is a sample of my writing when I am in a hurry.")

B. Here is how I write when I do my best writing: (Write: "This is a sample of my best writing.")

C. I would grade my hurried writing: (Circle one.)
        excellent   good   fair   poor
I would grade my best writing: (Circle one.)
        excellent   good   fair   poor

D. Here is my analysis of my handwriting:
(Put a check in the appropriate blank.)

		YES	NO
1.	**Slant** Do all the letters have the same slant?	____	____
2.	**Spacing** Are the spaces between letters and words uniform?	____	____
3.	**Size** Are all letters with tall loops almost a space tall (b, f, h, k, and l)?	____	____
	Are d, p, and t about ⅔ space tall?	____	____
	Are other lower-case letters approximately ⅓ space tall?	____	____
4.	**Alignment** Do all the letters touch the baseline?	____	____
5.	**Loops** Are b, f, h, k, and l (upper-loop letters) well formed?	____	____
	Are g, j, p, y, and z (lower-loop letters) well formed?	____	____
6.	**Closing** Are a, d, g, o, p, q, and s closed?	____	____
7.	**Roundness** Are h, m, n, v, x, y, and z rounded on top?	____	____
8.	**Retraces** Are a, d, i, m, n, r, s, t, u, v, and w retraced?	____	____
9.	**Endings** Do all my words end with good finishing strokes?	____	____

Source: My Handwriting Quotient (Madison, WI: W. A. Sheaffer Pen Co., 1960).

with a particular need would use the appropriate page of the handwriting booklet.

File Cards A box of file cards, entitled "Points to Remember About Each of the Letters," was prepared. Each letter (upper and lower case) and numeral (0–9) was written on a card. In this way, several pupils could make use of the file at the same time. File card samples are provided here for one letter and one numeral.

FILE CARD: *Cursive* a

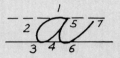

1. Begin at the headline.
2. Curve back and down.
3. Touch the baseline.
4. Curve up to the headline.
5. Pause.
6. Slant down to the baseline.
7. Curve up to the midline.

Source: Used with permission from *Creative Growth with Handwriting*. Second Edition. Copyright © 1979. Zaner-Bloser, Inc., Columbus, OH.

Activity Cards A file of activity cards stressing the different strokes and features of letters (as noted in the preceding checklist) was available in the center. Each card contained the name of the stroke or letter feature, an illustration of the stroke, letters or groups of letters using the feature, and an activity for the child to perform. (Children selected for themselves the activity cards they needed for practice.) An example is provided here.

Tracing Cards A set of large tracing cards, one for each upper- and lower-case letter, was available at the learning center. These cards were made by using wide-ruled paper with a middle line dividing the writing space into halves, so that the formation of the letter was easy to visualize. Each card

---

FILE CARD: *Numeral 3*

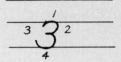

1. Begin below the headline.
2. Curve forward to make a half circle.
3. Make another forward half circle.
4. Rest on the baseline.

Source: Used with permission from *Creative Growth with Handwriting*. Second Edition. Copyright © 1979. Zaner-Bloser, Inc., Columbus, OH.

ACTIVITY CARD: *Connecting Stroke*

The check-stroke ending to an undercurve beginning is a little tricky, especially when connecting with the letters *e, i, u, r,* and *s.* Check stroke is the short, retraced motion before making the ending stroke on *b, o, v,* and *w.*

oil our ore be veal
write brown will

Practice making these letter combinations on your own paper and then use each in one or more words.

---

had the letter written five times on the top line and one time on each of the following lines. (The card was covered with transparent contact paper and drymounted on posterboard.) The cards permitted the children to trace the letter as well as to finish filling in the page with the same letter. Using felt-tip pens, the writing done by the children could be erased after each use.

Manipulative Tools Clay and pencil-sized wooden dowels were provided so that the pupils could trace and form letters in clay and "feel" the letters with their fingers. Wooden blocks about ½ inch thick and 6 inches square were covered with transparent contact paper so that the clay could be pressed on them and then removed.

Tactile Objects One set of upper-case and lower-case letters was cut from sandpaper and then pasted on index cards. One letter, with strokes indicated, was pasted on each card. Pupils could feel the letters with their fingers and listen to the "sounds" of the letter as they traced over them with a wooden dowel pencil. Another set of blank sandpaper cards (sandpaper strips pasted on index cards) was in the activity file so that pupils could write with the dowel pencil and listen to the "sounds" of their letter formations.

Activity File A special file, called "Additional Activities," was provided so that the pupils could have a functional purpose for a handwriting activity; for example, "Use your best cursive handwriting to write the words to your favorite song." These were tasks to be completed in one's best handwriting.

Charts Several charts, like the ones listed below, were posted in the area of the learning center.

A chart naming, illustrating, and showing the uses of each of the different strokes

A chart classifying each of the upper- and lower-case letters according to its strokes and the type of letter

A chart presenting an evaluation scale appropriate for the particular grade level

A chart presenting handwriting errors and ideas on how to correct them

A chart illustrating the correct positions for writing with the right hand, writing with the left hand, and writing on the chalkboard.

Other Equipment Handwriting equipment of various kinds was kept at the center. For example, one dozen ballpoint pens were provided, largely for motivational purposes. These were to be used instead of pencils at times. One dozen felt-tip pens were also placed in a box at the center. Chalk (white and colored) was available for chalkboard writing.

MAINTAINING INTEREST IN HANDWRITING

Beginning pupils are usually eager to learn to write. When the time comes for the addition of cursive writing, interest is high because this form of writing seems more "grown-up" than manuscript. There are times, however, when interest lags and practice seems dull. Extra motivation or a different procedure to give freshness to instruction is needed at these times. Handwriting periods should be varied rather than follow a routine pattern. Some lessons will be functional, others will involve analysis and practice, and some will deal with the historical development of handwriting. The following suggestions may prove useful in adding interest to handwriting lessons.

Study of the historical development of handwriting adds interest and increases appreciation for handwriting as a tool. Below is a list of several excellent books on his topic for children. They are also applicable to spelling since most of them treat the development of the alphabet.

William Cahn and Rhoda Cahn, *The Story of Writing* (Irvington-on-Hudson, NY: Harvey House, 1963).

William Dugan, *How Our Alphabet Grew* (New York: Golden, 1972).

Tom Gourdie, *The Puffin Book of Lettering* (Baltimore: Penguin Books, 1961).

Robert Hofsinde (Gray-Wolf), *Indian Picture Writing* (New York: Morrow, 1959).

Keith Gordon Irwin, *The Romance of Writing* (New York: Viking, 1957).

Murray McCain, *Writing* (New York: Farrar, Straus & Giroux, 1964).

Oscar Ogg, *The Twenty-Six Letters*, rev. ed. (New York: Crowell, 1971).

Solveig P. Russell, *A Is for Apple and Why: The Story of Our Alphabet* (New York: Abingdon Press, 1959).

Joseph Scott and Lenore Scott, *Hieroglyphs for Fun* (New York: Van Nostrand Reinhold, 1974).

Pride in workmanship is often more stimulating than formal practice. Opportunities for such workmanship are found in writing letters, records of work accomplished, announcements for the bulletin board, articles for the school paper, poems, plays, or stories. All these demand neat and legible handwriting.

The opaque projector is a useful aid in motivating the class to analyze handwriting. Samples of handwriting may be projected on the screen for study and discussion of their good and poor qualities. (These samples should not come from class members.) An overhead projector is a good means for giving instruction in the beginning points of letters, the direction of movement, and the shapes of strokes.

Rating handwriting in work done in the other content areas emphasizes the importance of writing. All writing should be purposeful.

Interest in improving writing can be stimulated by asking questions like:

What is your best letter?
What letter is most difficult for you?
How is handwriting useful to you?
What use do you think you will make of handwriting as an adult?

Charts giving suggestions for handwriting can be made. One example is suggested in Chart 9.5.

CHART 9.5: *Reminders for Manuscript Writing*

1. Make all letters with straight line segments and circles.
2. Move from left to right in making letters.
3. Make all capital and tall letters two spaces high and small letters one space high.
4. Space letters close together.
5. Space words one finger apart on ruled paper.

Bulletin boards, displaying pupils' work or other materials related to handwriting, may be prepared. Each child should have an opportunity to display work once or twice during the year.

A study of various handwriting tools (such as pens and pencils) and of various styles of writing and their special uses can be most interesting and provide ideas for some bulletin board displays.

Having pupils' handwriting papers rated by someone outside the classroom—the principal or another teacher—adds interest.

Teacher enthusiasm and respect for good handwriting is of prime importance. Teachers should strive to present good models of handwriting for the pupils. They will find that individual variations in their own writing are likely to be imitated by the children. A positive approach, with praise used more liberally than reproach, is much more likely to produce enthusiasm and good work from boys and girls.

Evaluating handwriting

After reviewing the research on handwriting, Froese concludes, "To date there still appears to be no generally accepted definition of 'legibility.'"[18] He also reports that it is generally conceded that Freeman in 1915 developed the first scale of legibility and based it on five factors: "letter form, uniformity of slant, uniformity of alignment of letters, quality of line, and spacing between letters and words";[19] it must be mentioned, however, that Freeman reduced this scale in 1953 to "general excellence." Froese goes on to distill from various reliable studies what appear to be the best supported (or at least "most-agreed-upon") factors affecting legibility: "letter formation, size, and appropriate rate."[20]

Although the definition of legibility is likely to remain open to discussion, most people "know" what is legible and what is not. Several commercial scales have been developed for measuring the general quality of handwriting. These usually consist of samples of handwriting arranged in order of merit with a letter grade assigned to each. It is important to note that these scales are not absolute guides; they present a general model and are helpful only insofar as the teacher balances the importance of individual style against the social need for common forms of expression. We offer here two of the more popular evaluation scales along with our suggestions for informal evaluations (see Charts 9.6 and 9.7).

Informal Devices

Many informal devices are used to determine quality in handwriting and to locate specific weaknesses.

Letter Form To check letter formation, a card with a hole a little larger than a single letter cut in the center is used. The card is moved along a line of writing so that the letters are exposed one at a time. Illegible or poorly formed letters stand out clearly and may be noted for further practice.

good   poor

18. Froese, "Handwriting," p. 228.
19. Ibid., p. 229.
20. Ibid., p. 236.

Cʜᴀʀᴛ 9.6: *Evaluation Scale, Manuscript (reduced size)*

SATISFACTORY		NEEDS IMPROVEMENT	Example 1 — Excellent for Grade Two
☑	LETTER FORMATION	☐	I asked a tiger
☑	VERTICAL STROKES	☐	to tea.
☑	SPACING	☐	
☑	ALIGNMENT AND PROPORTION	☐	
☑	LINE QUALITY	☐	

SATISFACTORY		NEEDS IMPROVEMENT	Example 2 — Good for Grade Two
☐	LETTER FORMATION	☑	I asked a tiger
☑	VERTICAL STROKES	☐	to tea.
☐	SPACING	☑	
☑	ALIGNMENT AND PROPORTION	☐	
☑	LINE QUALITY	☐	

SATISFACTORY		NEEDS IMPROVEMENT	Example 3 — Average for Grade Two
☐	LETTER FORMATION	☑	I asked a tiger
☐	VERTICAL STROKES	☑	to tea.
☑	SPACING	☐	
☐	ALIGNMENT AND PROPORTION	☑	
☑	LINE QUALITY	☐	

SATISFACTORY		NEEDS IMPROVEMENT	Example 4 — Fair for Grade Two
☐	LETTER FORMATION	☑	I asked a tiger
☐	VERTICAL STROKES	☑	to tea.
☐	SPACING	☑	
☐	ALIGNMENT AND PROPORTION	☑	
☑	LINE QUALITY	☐	

SATISFACTORY		NEEDS IMPROVEMENT	Example 5 — Poor for Grade Two
☐	LETTER FORMATION	☑	Iaskedatiger
☐	VERTICAL STROKES	☑	totea.
☐	SPACING	☑	
☐	ALIGNMENT AND PROPORTION	☑	
☐	LINE QUALITY	☑	

Source: Used with permission from *Creative Growth with Handwriting*, Second Edition. Copyright © 1979. Zaner-Bloser, Inc., Columbus, OH.

CHART 9.7: *Evaluation Scale, Cursive (reduced size)*

Example 1 — Excellent for Grade Five

	SATISFACTORY	NEEDS IMPROVEMENT
LETTER FORMATION	☐	☑
SLANT	☑	☐
SPACING	☑	☐
ALIGNMENT AND PROPORTION	☑	☐
LINE QUALITY	☑	☐

The jellyfish is jellified --
he could not be brave if he tried;
he shakes, he shivers, and he quakes
from the first moment that he wakes
until he's tucked up tight in bed
with seaweed-sheets around his head.

Example 2 — Good for Grade Five

	SATISFACTORY	NEEDS IMPROVEMENT
LETTER FORMATION	☐	☑
SLANT	☑	☐
SPACING	☑	☐
ALIGNMENT AND PROPORTION	☐	☑
LINE QUALITY	☑	☐

The jellyfish is jellified...
he could not be brave if he tried;
he shakes, he shivers and he quakes
from the first moment that he wakes
until he's tucked up tight in bed
with seaweed-sheets around his head.

Example 3 — Average for Grade Five

	SATISFACTORY	NEEDS IMPROVEMENT
LETTER FORMATION	☐	☑
SLANT	☑	☐
SPACING	☑	☐
ALIGNMENT AND PROPORTION	☐	☑
LINE QUALITY	☐	☑

The jellyfish is jellified. --
he could not be brave if he tried;
he shakes, he shivers and he quakes.
from the first moment that he wakes
until he's tucked up tight in bed
with seaweed-sheets around his head.

Example 4 — Fair for Grade Five

	SATISFACTORY	NEEDS IMPROVEMENT
LETTER FORMATION	☐	☑
SLANT	☐	☑
SPACING	☑	☐
ALIGNMENT AND PROPORTION	☐	☑
LINE QUALITY	☐	☑

The jellyfish is jellified -
he could not be brave if he
tried. he shakes, he shivers and he
quakes from the first moment that
he wakes until he's tucked up
tight is bed with seaweed-sheets
around his head.

Example 5 — Poor for Grade Five

	SATISFACTORY	NEEDS IMPROVEMENT
LETTER FORMATION	☐	☑
SLANT	☐	☑
SPACING	☐	☑
ALIGNMENT AND PROPORTION	☐	☑
LINE QUALITY	☐	☑

The jellyfish is jellified - he could not be
brave if he tried he shakes he shivers
and he quakes from the first moment
that he wakes until he's tucked up tight
in bed with seaweed-sheets around his head.

Source: Used with permission from *Creative Growth with Handwriting*, Second Edition. Copyright © 1979. Zaner-Bloser, Inc., Columbus, OH.

CHECKLIST: *Evaluating with a Scale*

Writing

A. The teacher writes on a ruled chalkboard a model of the example.
B. Students practice writing the example on lined paper.
C. Using their best handwriting, students then write the example again.

Evaluation

Compare the students' writing to the examples on the scale, and if no more than one element needs improvement, the writing is rated *excellent* (example 1); if no more than two elements need improvement, the writing is rated *good* (example 2); if no more than three elements need improvement, the writing is rated *average* (example 3); if no more than four elements need improvement, the writing is rated *fair* (example 4); and if five elements need improvement, the writing is rated *poor* (example 5).

Note: The elements to be rated for manuscript include the following:

Satisfactory		Needs Improvement
_____	Letter formation	_____
_____	Vertical strokes	_____
_____	Spacing	_____
_____	Alignment and proportion	_____
_____	Line quality	_____

The elements to be rated for cursive include in the following:

Satisfactory		Needs Improvement
_____	Letter formation	_____
_____	Slant	_____
_____	Spacing	_____
_____	Alignment and proportion	_____
_____	Line quality	_____

For manuscript and cursive writing, lines are drawn along the tops of letters to see if they are of proper height and uniformly written as suggested in the particular handwriting program.

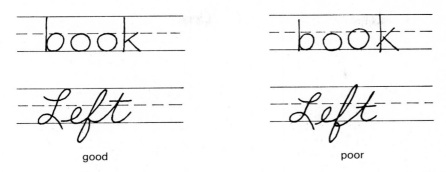

good   poor

Spacing In manuscript, a space of about one letter (small *o*) between letters—with adjustments to the series of letters used—is desirable, with a bit more space between words and sentences. The spacing should be uniform throughout. In cursive writing, there should also be a space of about a small letter between lettters and slightly more space between words and sentences.

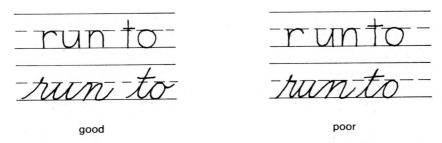

good   poor

Alignment A rule is used to check alignment; a line should be drawn touching the base of as many of the letters as possible.

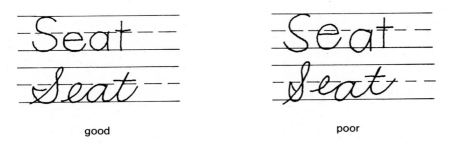

good   poor

Slant Slant applies only to cursive writing. Lines of a straight or uniform slanting nature may be drawn through the letters and the letters marked that are off slant. (Some handwriting experts recommend "slant" as a way of making manuscript writing more individual and attractive, thereby encouraging its continued use.)

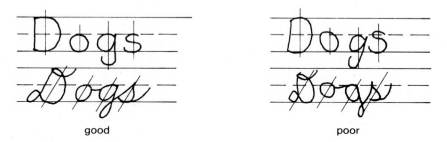

good   poor

Line Quality To check line quality, an examination of the evenness of writing pressure is made. The same consistency is desirable, rather than a mixture of light and heavy, thick and fine writing.

good   poor

Speed of Writing

The major criteria for evaluating handwriting is legibility. Care must be taken to avoid placing too much emphasis on speed. The following is offered as a guide in terms of possible speed attainments by grade levels:[21]

Grade 2	30 letters per minute
Grade 3	40 letters per minute
Grade 4	50 letters per minute
Grade 5	60 letters per minute
Grade 6	67 letters per minute
Grade 7	74 letters per minute
Grade 8	80 letters per minute

A second word of caution. Rates of writing by grade level should not become practice sessions to which all students must conform, since indi-

21. Walter B. Barbe, *Evaluating Handwriting: Cursive* (Columbus, OH: Zaner-Bloser, Inc., © 1977).

vidual differences in developmental rate can be very noticeable in the speed and legibility of handwriting.

TYPEWRITING

Some schools have introduced typewriting after students have achieved a satisfactory degree of success in manuscript and cursive writing, since it is a desirable tool of written communication. At the elementary school level, it is taught to enhance the spelling, reading, and written composition programs. It can be useful as students produce class newspapers, booklets, written reports for the bulletin board, and other such curricular undertakings.

There are typewriting books for younger students, such as D. D. Lessenberry et al., *Introductory Typewriting* (Cincinnati, OH: South-Western Publishing Co., 1975) and Mary Ellen Switzer, *Typing Fun* (Santa Barbara, CA: The Learning Works, 1979). Each presents the touch-typing system in which students become familiar with the keyboard. Often, an aide may be available to provide typing instruction. Some persons recommend the portable electric typewriter as the preferred instrument, but this is not absolutely necessary.

When typewriting is a part of the language arts program, children appear to be highly motivated to write more, and it is thought to support the development of reading ability.

SOME INSTRUCTIONAL CONCERNS

Some teachers may tend to overvalue the skill of handwriting, devoting large periods of time to direct handwriting instruction, and, in the process, increasing the anxiety level of children in striving to become perfectionists. Handwriting must be placed in proper perspective and recognized as a functional skill. It must be related to written composition; the strong desire to communicate becomes the basic motivation for improving discrete aspects of the handwriting process. Handwriting extends into all written work, and attention to it throughout the school day is needed to achieve the best development in the handwriting skills. Handwriting practice should, as often as possible, grow out of the needs of the pupils in practical writing situations. Such an approach helps children accept the importance of good handwriting and develop pride in their own handwriting.

On the other hand, some teachers misuse commercial handwriting materials by simply assigning pages to be done, as if instruction and practice were synonymous. It is the teacher who provides instruction; supplementary materials are only helpful aids.

THOUGHT QUESTIONS

1. Must individual writing styles be lost while teaching handwriting? Which do you consider more important: personal style or uniform style? Can a balance between the two be established?
2. Should left-handed writers be encouraged to become right-handed writers?
3. How may a handwriting learning center be utilized to individualize instruction?
4. How can interest in handwriting be maintained?

LEARNER RESPONSE OPTIONS

1. Recommend a list of activities for a child who lacks handwriting readiness.
2. Prepare a class report on a scope-and-sequence chart of one commercial handwriting program.
3. Utilize features of a perceptual-motor approach to teach a manuscript lesson to a small group of children or peers.
4. Select what might be a major difficulty in manuscript writing and outline procedures to remediate.
5. Utilize features of a perceptual-motor approach to teach a cursive lesson to a small group of children or peers.
6. Demonstrate appropriate positions—seating, paper, and pencil—for right- and left-handed writers at a desk; at a chalkboard.
7. Develop one activity for a handwriting learning center, citing objectives, materials, and procedures.
8. Outline a lesson plan that focuses upon motivational aspects.
9. Score a child's handwriting against a standardized handwriting scale.
10. Collect written papers from an elementary school classroom. Analyze the most common types of handwriting errors and record them in chart form.

PART V: VOCABULARY,

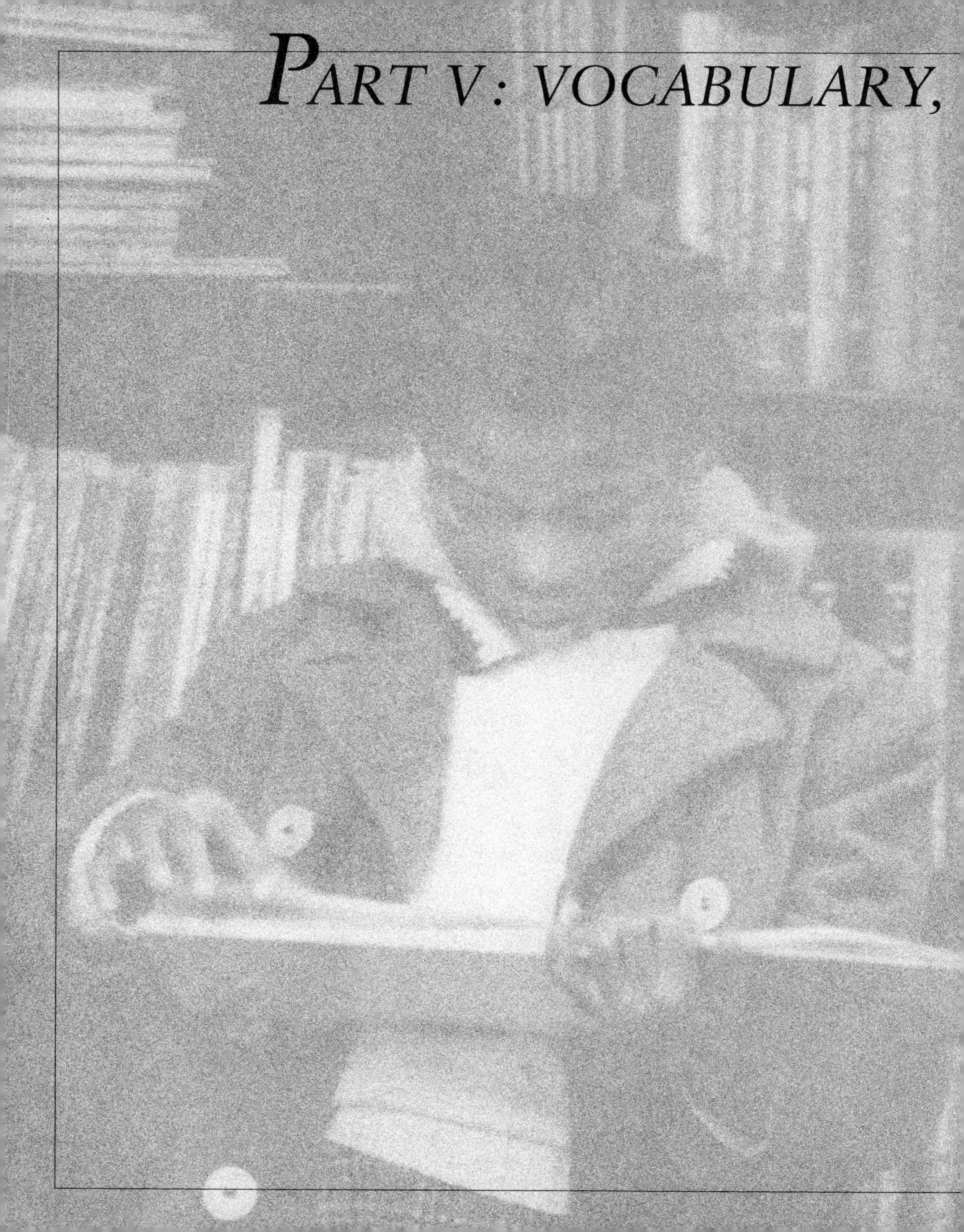

READING, AND LITERATURE

CHAPTER 10: *Vocabulary Development and Research Skills*

OVERVIEW

This chapter treats vocabulary and research skills. Each of these topics is related to both oral and written expression. Various ways through which children may develop vocabulary are explored. Then semantics, the study of meaning in language forms, is discussed with a focus on words and their effects upon people. The chapter concludes with instructional strategies designed to help children develop research skills, particularly those of locating and organizing information.

KEY VOCABULARY

As you read this chapter, check your understanding of these terms.

context clues	semantics
morphology study	referent
homograph	denotative
figurative language	connotative
metaphor	euphemism
simile	functional shift
personification	affective language
inflection	

VOCABULARY DEVELOPMENT

Vocabulary may be defined as the stock of words used by a person, class, or profession. Almost every individual uses several different vocabularies, all having much in common, yet each distinctly different. The most basic of these vocabularies are often designated as hearing, speaking, reading, and writing. Words are symbols of ideas; to express and communicate ideas, one needs facility in the use of words. Teachers must give attention to developing the vocabularies of each child through carefully planned instruction and, to do so, must be aware of what words are (verbal representations of concepts) and how concepts are formed.

A word is not the thing nor the concept nor the experience itself. The word *dog* is not a dog at all—it is a label for the animal we so designate. Many words stand for abstractions, like *beauty* or *justice*, for which there may be no concrete referent in reality.

Since vocabulary development is so closely related to abstract thinking, the teacher is concerned with the number, the breadth, and the depth of concepts with which pupils have some acquaintance. For concept development, the individual should have actual experiences with the concrete object, person, idea, or event—mainly through sense impressions. From a series of experiences, accurate discrimination of essential and nonessential characteristics of the object (person, idea, or event) must be made. Further examples help to ensure adequate learning of the concept.

The teacher's responsibility includes both a *quantitative* approach to vocabulary (particularly for children whose environmental circumstances have not equipped them to conceptualize clearly or to verbalize adequately) and a *qualitative* approach (a broadening and deepening of the children's listening-speaking vocabulary by teaching them ways to make fine discriminations in the use of words in different situations).

Ways to Develop Vocabularies

There are numerous ways of helping children to acquire knowledge of many words and proficiency in their use. As yet, there is insufficient evidence to show which methods of vocabulary instruction work best at different age levels and with pupils of varying degrees of ability. The resourceful teacher will find many opportunities inherent in classroom activities.

Firsthand Experiences A varied background of firsthand experiences, field trips, and excursions is profitable at all grade levels. The nature and quality of the educative experiences that children meet, both inside and outside the classroom, are primary factors that determine speaking, writing, reading, and hearing vocabularies.

Experiences should be followed by oral and written accounts and descriptions. Teachers need to see that the new words derived from these experiences are understood and made vivid and clear. Without follow-up, a child's recollection or understanding is likely to be incomplete or inaccurate. Observation and experience alone will not increase vocabulary. Unless the teacher focuses on words for the object or situation, answers questions, and discusses the experience, the child has no way to acquire the new words that the experience could furnish. Discussion provides an opportunity to correct misunderstanding and wrong concepts.

Teachers should try to discover what experiences the children lack, because children learn early to conceal their inadequacies by silence. Studies have indicated that many pupils, even after several years of schooling, may not know where the farmer gets eggs or that a bank may be something other than a place where they store their money. One teacher reported that many nine-year-old pupils in a class in a depressed urban area had no idea of the meaning of *dandelion*. Children should always be encouraged to ask questions and not be subjected to ridicule if some of the questions seem absurd.

Of course, all direct experiences need not be of a field trip nature, nor can all experiences be direct ones. Vicarious or indirect, secondhand experiences such as films, for example, provide for vocabulary growth. Storytelling and oral reading by the teacher are also valuable ways of imparting experience.

All the experiences of the school day can be used to broaden the child's vocabulary if the teacher is aware of the opportunities: the sharing period, the daily news period, group work period, free conversation, discussion time. The environment and activities of the school will lead the teacher to discover other similar avenues for experiences that will develop new concepts and new vocabulary.

Books Books are another significant source of vocabulary growth, particularly books that provoke questions and discussion. Pupils need a variety of interesting, easy-to-read books so that new words and ideas can be learned from the context. In choosing new vocabulary words, the teacher might ask pupils the following questions:

What words in the selection can be interpreted by examining the context?
What words or phrases encountered in today's reading seem particularly well chosen?
What are some descriptive words in today's reading?

As with direct experiences, it is important to encourage pupils to ask questions about words they do not understand.

Context Clues Children who read extensively can learn many words just through use of context. Wide reading provides the opportunity for context to illuminate word meaning when it is essential to the flow of thought. Through a variety of reading material, the reader can begin to recognize the subtleties and varied meanings of words.

Reading authorities have emphasized the importance of developing effective use of context.[1] Classroom experience suggests that lack of skill in using context is quite prevalent among elementary school pupils, but that instruction in the use of context aids seemed helpful.

Chart 10.1 suggests various types of contextual aids to word meanings.[2]

These contextual clues are the kinds of aids that pupils often encounter. They need to be presented and practiced if contextual analysis is to become an important means of vocabulary growth. Contextual usage can be developed through planned, thoughtful, and intelligent guidance, just as the ability to use other means for vocabulary growth is developed through carefully planned instruction. It is desirable to teach children to read an entire sentence (or the remainder of a paragraph) before attempting to derive the meaning of an unknown word. The practice of immediately stating, "Look it up in a dictionary," is a poor one. It would be better to say, "Try to find a clue to the meaning of the word through the context." Time should then be provided for discussion of how the meaning was arrived at through context.

Pupils do not always derive correct meanings of words from the context. Context invariably *determines* the meaning of a word but does not always reveal its meaning. Context generally reveals only one of the meanings of a word to the reader. Also, context seldom clarifies the whole of any single word meaning. Vocabulary growth through use of context is gradual. Finding one clue here and another there, fitting them together, and making tentative judgments and revising them later are required.

Some representative commercially prepared materials on contextual clues are footnoted.[3]

1. For example, see George D. Sprache, *Reading in the Elementary School*, 4th ed. (Boston: Allyn & Bacon, 1977); pp. 402–406; and P. D. Pearson and A. Studt, "Effects of Word Frequency and Contextual Richness on Children's Word Identification Abilities," *Journal of Educational Psychology* 6, no. 1 (March 1975): 89–95.
2. Lee C. Deighton, *Vocabulary Development in the Classroom* (New York: Teachers College Press, Columbia University, 1959).
3. Richard A. Boning, *Using the Context, Book A* (New York: Barnell Loft, 1973).

CHART 10.1: *Contextual Aids to Word Meanings*

Type	Explanation/Example
Explicit	
1. Grammatical aids	apposition: The *epidermis*, the outer layer of skin, protects from germs.
2. Substitute words	synonyms (or antonyms): What can you do to *mitigate*, or lessen, the miseries of a cold?
3. Pictures, diagrams, charts	
4. Summary clues	John will be here soon for he is usually very *punctual*.
5. Familiar expression	He kept his *cool*.
Implicit	
6. Figures of speech	metaphor: The soldiers, *numerous as the sands in the sea*, march forward.
7. Inference	Because of the mountain ranges and the cold climate, the amount of *arable* land is limited.
8. Experience clues	The crow cawed *raucously*. (Understanding the last word depends on the reader's experience of hearing a crow's harsh voice.)
9. Comparison/contrast words	Is John *clumsy* or is he *agile*?
10. Example	Put an *antiseptic*, such as alcohol, on the skin.
Structure	
11. Typographical aids	parentheses or footnotes
12. Word elements	roots, prefixes, and suffixes

Visual and Other Instructional Aids and Materials Visual aids should be utilized frequently, not only to illustrate words that have been used but to suggest other words. Remember, however, that discussion must accompany seeing.

Programmed materials, either in booklet form or in a machine, can be used to teach vocabulary.[4] Single-concept, language filmloops can be used

---

4. Two volumes, prepared by the Center for Programmed Instruction for the U.S. Office of Education, *Programs '69* and *The Use of Programmed Instruction in U.S. Schools*, survey

for self-study aids.[5] The new filmloops can be operated by any child and viewed individually or projected on the screen for group viewing. There are specially prepared records for vocabulary development. Winick and Wehrenberg have described television's contributions to vocabulary development in children.[6] Of course, films and filmstrips are available for use upon occasion on such topics as *Build Your Vocabulary*[7] or *Increase Your Stock of Words.*[8]

Other instructional aids and materials include the thesaurus and trade books. In addition to many children's dictionaries, beginning thesauri are now available to help children enrich their vocabularies, find substitutes for overused words, and develop an awareness of the flexibility and power of language.[9] The thesaurus may supply such alternatives as *march, stride, stalk, lurch, saunter,* and *clump* for a word to describe how a person walks. Individuals are helped in their word selection by special illustrative sentences, pictures and illustrations, or explanations that dramatize the meaning of a particular word. Special attention may be given to certain word entries: "umbrella words," such as *cute, nice*; slang words, such as *goof-ball, hip*; overworked words such as *love, hate*; and sets of words, such as *pride* of lions, *gaggle* of geese. Some word histories may also be provided. Following is a list of some trade books about words.

Isaac Asimov, *Words from the Myths* (Boston: Houghton Mifflin, 1961).
June Behrens, *What Is a Seal?* (New York: Jay Alden, 1975).
Judy Corwin, *Words, Words, Words, Words* (New York: Platt & Munk, 1977).
Muriel Feelings, *Swahili Counting Book* (New York: Dial, 1973).
Cathleen Fitzgerald, *Let's Find Out About Words* (New York: Watts, 1971).
Charles Funk, *Heavens to Betsy* (New York: Warner, 1972).

---

in detail available programs and their uses in the schools. Both are available from the Superintendent of Documents. U.S. Government Printing Office, Washington, DC 20402. To keep abreast of current developments, the center publishes a bimonthly bulletin, *Programmed Instruction*, 365 West End Ave., New York, NY 10024.
5. "Words and Ideas Series," Sterling Educational Films, 241 East 34th St., New York, NY 10016.
6. Miriam Pezzella Winick and Judith S. Wehrenberg, *Children and TV II: Mediating the Medium* (Washington, DC: Association for Childhood International, 1982). Also see Rosemary L. Potter, *The Positive Use of Commercial Television with Children* (Washington, DC: N.E.A., 1981).
7. Chicago: Coronet Films.
8. Chicago: Society for Visual Education.
9. W. Cabell Greet et al., *In Other Words: A Beginning Thesaurus* (grades K–2) and *Junior Thesaurus: In Other Words* (grades 6 and up) (Chicago: Scott, Foresman, 1969, 1970).

————. *Horsefeathers and Other Curious Words* (New York: Harper & Row, 1958).

Fred Gwynne, *Chocolate Moose for Dinner* (New York: Windmill, 1976).

Joan Hanson, *Homographic Homophones* (New York: Lerner, 1973). (Also see, by the same author, other titles such as *Homographs, Homonyms, Synonyms, Similes,* and others.)

————. *Sound Words* (New York: Lerner, 1976).

Margaret Harmon, *Working with Words* (New York: Westminster, 1977).

Peter Linburg, *What's in the Names of Wild Animals* (New York: Coward, McCann, 1977).

Maxwell Nurnberg, *Fun with Words* (Englewood Cliffs, NJ: Prentice-Hall, 1970).

Colin Pickles and L. Lawrence, *The Beginning of Words: How English Grew* (New York: Putnam, 1970).

Alice Provensen and Martin Provensen, *Play on Words* (New York: Random House, 1972).

Joseph Rosenbloom, *Daffy Dictionary: Funabridged Definitions: From Aardvark to Zuider Zee* (New York: Sterling, 1977).

Alvin Schwartz, *Tom Foolery: Trickery and Foolery with Words* (Philadelphia: Lippincott, 1973).

Elsdon Smith, *The Story of Our Names* (New York: Gale, 1970).

R. Tremain, *Fooling Around with Words* (New York: Greenwillow, 1976).

Richard Wilbur, *Opposites* (New York: Harcourt Brace Jovanovich, 1973).

Content Areas In every subject field, teachers should develop vocabulary carefully. They need to be sure that words met in elementary mathematics, health, science, and social studies have real significance. The importance of this cannot be overemphasized. Children's understanding of concepts is often vague and inaccurate. Note the vocabulary demands made upon the pupil by the following sentences taken from elementary mathematics, science, and social studies textbooks.

Mathematics. The polygon in picture A has four straight sides. Its opposite sides are equal and also parallel. It has four right angles. This polygon is a rectangle.

Science. Between Mars and Jupiter are a great many small planets called *asteroids.* There are more than a thousand of these, and each follows its own path or orbit around the sun. Comets and meteors are also members of the solar system.

Social Studies. On a high plateau of Central Africa live millions of black people. They live four thousand feet above the sea, just at the equator.

The vocabulary problem is more acute in textbooks than it is in general reading material. Selecting textbooks that avoid complicated verbiage and explain new terms clearly when they are introduced is one important way of reducing the vocabulary problem to teachable proportions.

Each of the content areas has a vocabulary of its own that must be learned. One cannot expect a pupil to understand without assistance such technical terms as *commutative, factor,* and *perimeter* in mathematics and similar technical terms in other subjects. Whenever an important new concept is introduced, there is need for a detailed explanation. Content area textbooks and materials can provide a rich source of material to stimulate vocabulary growth.

Oral and Written Expression Teachers should encourage variety in oral and written expression. A conscious effort needs to be made by teachers to encourage use of words that express thought exactly, rather than words that perform omnibus service.

Many children fall victim to the insidious habit of using a small number of stock adjectives and adverbs and fail to develop a command of vocabulary that can express finer shades of meaning. If a party is described as "lousy," it would be profitable to ask the child to describe more exactly the way in which the party was lousy. Was it *boring, dull, dreary, disappointing*? Discussion is one of the better ways of awakening children to the desirability of stating their meanings with precision.

A task card, focusing upon the same idea, may be prepared, like the one here.

TASK CARD: *Descriptive Words*

Directions

Here is a paragraph with some underlined words. See if you can substitute synonyms for the underlined words. A list of substitute words is given to help you.

The children were playing a <u>noisy</u> game and mother smiled as she watched them <u>jump</u> around. She was happy to have her <u>children</u> home with her. Father had been <u>delayed</u> in town that evening and he was late in <u>getting</u> home.

(cavort   family   arriving   detained   rowdy)

Worksheets like the one illustrated here may also be helpful in encouraging use of more descriptive words.

WORKSHEET: *Descriptive Words*

1. For each of the following questions, circle the appropriate word or words. Add a word if needed.
   a. What kind of day is it today?
      (stormy, pleasant, calm, rainy, snowy, bright, dull, clear, brilliant)
   b. What is the sky like today?
      (overcast, cloudless, hazy, somber, darkening, threatening, sunny)
   c. What is the wind like today?
      (gusty, gentle, moderate, howling, whispering, tingling, cold, chilly, biting)
2. Here are some words that can be used to describe a way of walking. Choose ten and use each one in a sentence.
   (hurried, ran, raced, strolled, waddled, limped, stumbled, crawled, leaped, hopped, trudged, trotted, pranced, stamped, stormed, skipped, galloped)
3. Use different words for *said* in ten sentences.
   (whispered, shouted, screamed, laughed, cried, giggled, praised, scolded, bragged, grumbled, argued, answered, announced, agreed, stated, suggested, objected, asked, replied, inquired, remarked, explained)
4. Various words can be used in place of some overworked words. Add as many as you can to the list.

   a. nice: kind, pleasant, helpful, _____
   b. great: enjoyable, amusing, _____
   c. got: collected, found, gathered, _____
   d. bad: awful, _____

Teacher Model The teacher can use new words, sometimes in reading aloud, sometimes in providing explanations. New words used in oral reports may be taught also.

Particularly in the primary years, when most pupils are mainly occupied with developing recognition of words already in their understanding, reading, and speaking vocabulary, the teacher needs to read and tell many stories to the group. In reading to children, it is inadvisable to simplify the vocabulary. After reading a story, new words may be discussed and in later retelling or dramatization, the use of the new words should be encouraged.

Pupils are great imitators and if the teacher employs a good vocabulary, they tend to approach that level of expression. The tendency to talk down to boys and girls is a hindrance, not a help.

Morphology Study Such study includes antonyms, synonyms, homonyms, homographs, root words, figures of speech (metaphor, simile, personification), exaggerations, word associations, and inflectional devices. The slight differences of meaning, especially with synonyms, can be given some attention. For example, "What is the difference between *large, huge,* and *enormous?*" would be an appropriate question for a pupil in the intermediate years.

Following are some games and activities for the study of synonyms, antonyms, and homonyms.

1. Paste words such as *happy, big* and *sad* on several soup cans. Cut out small cards to play the game. Children think of a synonym, write it on a card, and drop it into the appropriate can.
2. "Synonym concentration" for two to four players: First, shuffle synonym cards (with even numbers of synonyms) and spread them out face down. The first player turns up two cards. If they are synonyms, the cards are taken. If not, the cards are turned face down again. Each player, in turn, tries to match two synonyms. The game is played until all cards are paired.
3. A story may be composed, with instructions to use synonyms to replace the underlined words. For example:
   One day a little girl was walking down the street. She saw a coin lying on the sidewalk. She looked all around but no one was there, so she picked up the coin.
4. "Antonym-O" can be played like Bingo. The caller reads words, and the players cover the antonyms on their cards. The first player to complete a row is the winner and the next caller.
5. A series of homonyms, such as *pail* and *pale*, can be listed on a worksheet. The child writes a sentence using each correctly: *The pale boy was carrying a pail of water.*

Homonyms are words with the same oral or written form as another word (as *to, too, two*). *Homographs* are words that are spelled alike but differ in derivation, meaning, or pronunciation (as *bow* of a ship and *bow* and arrow).

A knowledge of the meaning of some of the more common Latin and Greek roots found in many English words is helpful. Pupils can easily learn roots like *port,* meaning "to carry," and *fac* or *fic,* meaning "to make." From one of the roots, it is possible to build up a family of words. Such a family might be *porter, import, export, deport, report, transport, portable*, and so on. Such activities are often a part of the spelling program since spelling and vocabulary development are integrally related.

Children should be helped to identify figurative language, as such language often poses problems for them. Following are some examples of expressions that may not be interpreted correctly by pupils.

The villagers think that the stranger is a wolf in sheep's clothing. (*metaphor*)
She had cheeks like roses. (*simile*)
The sun smiled when Tony's bird escaped from the cat. (*personification*)

Probably the best way to develop a real understanding of figurative or indirect language is through practice in paraphrasing. The attempt to restate another's thoughts in clear, unambiguous language of one's own is a crucial test of whether the thought has really been understood. A sample worksheet appropriate for study of figures of speech is provided on page 324.

Before individual use is made of such figure-of-speech worksheets, several days of whole-class and small-group instruction is appropriate. The following teaching procedure might be followed:

1. The teacher introduces one of the figures of speech—metaphor, simile, personification—for whole-class brainstorming (about ten minutes).
2. A team of about five pupils brainstorms the figure of speech (five to ten minutes).
3. Each child writes a sentence using a figure of speech (five minutes).
4. The children read their sentences to each other in teams (about five minutes).
5. Each team selects one figure of speech to read to the class (about five minutes).
6. The children listen to the teacher read their figures of speech (two to three minutes).

Understanding of *exaggerations*, as in tall tales, colloquial expressions, and regional dialects, is best developed through wide reading and discussion.

Pupils become more aware of word associations as they write compositions. They may find listing words helpful: "happy" words, "sad" words, "beautiful" words, "exciting" words, words describing sounds, and the

WORKSHEET: *Figures of Speech*

Metaphor	**Simile**	**Personification**
His voice was a fog horn.	His feet were as cold as ice cubes.	The stone nestled against the tree.

A. Complete the following:
   (Metaphor)
   1. The fire siren _____.
   2. The high steeple _____.
   3. The diesel engine _____.

   (Simile)
   4. She was as happy as _____.
   5. The cat's fur was like _____.
   6. The bell was as loud as _____.

   (Personification)
   7. The jet plane _____.
   8. The water _____.
   9. The firecracker _____.
B. Find five figures of speech in the story folder on the reading table. Write them on a sheet of paper and give the meaning of each.
C. Try to illustrate three figures of speech.
D. Make up your own figure of speech and illustrate it.

like. The major purpose of this kind of exercise is to clarify the meanings of words through bringing out important relationships between ideas. As the children grasp these relationships, their understanding of the words becomes more accurate.

The study of *inflection* (that is, meaningful changes of form to show certain grammatical relationships) includes such concepts as contractions, possessives, prefixes, and suffixes. The teacher should identify elements with which the class members have difficulty and plan an instructional program on that basis. When studying contractions, ask:

What is a contraction?

Is *don't* a contraction?

Is *do not* a contraction?

Am I using a contraction when I say, "She isn't at home"?

Then read phrases like the following for identification of contractions.

here's Tom
cannot go
toys in boxes
they're playing ball

An instructional bulletin board can also serve for teaching and practicing contractions.

When studying possessives, ask, "What does *possessive* mean? What does *showing ownership* mean? Does *boy's book* show ownership?" Then read phrases like the following for identification of possessives.

children's game
serious people
honest firefighters
dogs' tails

When studying prefixes and suffixes, ask:

What is a prefix?
What is the prefix in *disobey*? How is the prefix spelled?
What is the suffix in *helpful*? How is the suffix spelled?

Then read words like the following, asking the children to write the prefixes or suffixes they hear.

disagree   sillier
submarine   pouches
pretest   ugliest
dwelling   sweetly
murmured   beside

An activity card can serve as a focus for the teaching and practice of prefixes and suffixes, as suggested.

In studying prefixes and suffixes, one researcher found that 24 percent of the words in Thorndike's *Teacher's Word Book* can use prefixes and

ACTIVITY CARD: *Prefix*

Directions

Here are six prefixes, along with their meanings. Use the prefixes to make as many new words as you can from the words at the bottom of the card. Use the words in sentences.

dis—the opposite of; not   *re*—back, again

in—inside or within; not   *super*—over, above

mis—wrong   *un*—the opposite of

- -

action	lay
agree	market
complete	live
correct	place
count	please
highway	take

that fifteen of these prefixes account for 82 percent of the total number of prefixes.[10] Below is a list of these fifteen prefixes.

ab	from	*in*	into
ad	to	*in*	not
be	by	*pre*	before
com	with	*pro*	for, onward
de	from	*re*	back
dis	opposite	*sub*	under
en	in	*un*	not
ex	out		

10. Russell G. Stauffer, "A Study of Prefixes in the Thorndike List to Establish a List of Prefixes That Should Be Taught in the Elementary School," *Journal of Educational Research* 35 (February 1942): 453–458.

The preceding prefixes have fairly constant meanings, and a person who knows the more common prefixes can frequently make a close guess as to the meaning of the word, particularly when it is in a meaningful context. The rarer prefixes are also worth knowing, but probably should be reserved for individual study or for incidental consideration in connection with learning of particular words that contain them.

The problem of teaching the meanings of suffixes is somewhat more complicated. The most common suffixes include *-ing, -ed, -er, -ly, -(e)s, -tion,* and *-y.* This problem has been dealt with in detail by Thorndike, who pointed out that most suffixes in English have several different meanings and that teaching the most common meanings may create confusion.[11]

Dictionary Usage The dictionary is valuable for finding the meanings of unfamiliar words. It is particularly helpful in determining the appropriate meanings of multiple-meaning words or those that have technical meanings. Children should be instructed in choosing the dictionary definition that makes the most sense in the context. For example, children can be given a series of sentences, such as those below, and asked to find the appropriate dictionary definitions.

1. The car fell down the steep *bank.*
2. There was a high *bank* of snow in the yard.
3. He sat on the *bank* and fished.
4. The plane went into a sharp *bank.*
5. The citizens will *bank* earth along the rising river.
6. Bill thought it was time to *bank* the fire.
7. She deposited money in the *bank.*
8. Jean made a visit to the blood *bank.*
9. The new building had a *bank* of elevators.
10. You can *bank* on Tom to do his duty.

Below are other dictionary activities and topics to encourage vocabulary growth.

1. Building lists of synonyms (such as listing as many ways as can be found in which sports writers tell that a team was defeated) or antonyms (contrasting words for winning to words for losing)

---

11. Edward L. Thorndike, *The Teaching of English Suffixes* (New York: Teachers College Press, 1941).

2. Improving colorless paragraphs by using words with more sensory appeal and lively action words
3. Tracing the derivations of words (for example, days of the week, months of the year)
4. Examining the dictionary for new words (especially if there is a "New Words" section)
5. Making a study of how places got their names (*chester, burg, ton, mont, ville, ford, haven, land, port, field, hill*)
6. Studying meanings and origins of proper names
7. Listing slang words and idioms (*rap, hassle, goof off, pealing out, bummer, slick, jiving*)
8. Discussing the fine distinctions between meanings of two words with similar meanings, such as *difficult* and *arduous*
9. Discovering ways our vocabulary grows and changes:
   a. People's names that have become common words (*Colt, Levi*) and names that have been incorporated into our vocabulary (*pasteurize, vulcanize, forsythia, silhouette, iris, voltage, saxophone, macintosh*)
   b. Ways Greek and Roman mythology have influenced English vocabulary (*mercury, volcanoes, herculean, panic*)
   c. Meanings that sports have contributed to words (*baskets, spare, fly, love, crawl, tackle, iron*)
   d. Portmanteau words (*smog, chortle*)
   e. Greek and Latin forms that occur in English words:

	Greek		**Latin**
auto	self	*aqua*	water
bio	life; living things	*audi*	hear
geo	earth; land	*bi*	two; twice
gram	thing written	*inter*	among; between
graph	to write	*multi*	many
logy	kind of speaking or reasoning	*ped*	foot
		post	behind; after
meter	measure	*super*	above; over
peri	around	*visio*	sight; seeing
phon(o)(e)	sound; voice		
phot(o)	light		
tel(e)	far; far off		

Other Recommended Activities The following items may be listed in vocabulary notebooks: new words heard in conversation or discussion, adjectives that are vivid and effective, new words encountered in general reading, descriptive words heard over radio or television, words that can be substituted for overworked or "tired" words, and new uses of old words.

Through activities like the following, special types of vocabulary lists may be encouraged by the teacher.

1. Read a story or poem aloud and ask pupils to pick out the words that "make a noise" (*squeal, purr, growl,* and so on).
2. Let a child, while blindfolded, remove an unknown object from a grab bag and describe its shape, size, and weight.
3. Have individuals feel, then describe, the texture of such materials as sandpaper, cotton batting, sponge, and silk.
4. Bring to class bottles of vanilla and lemon extract, peppermint oil, and other kitchen flavorings. Let several children taste them and then describe the taste.
5. Let pupils smell the bottles mentioned in number 4; then describe the odors.

A learning station is also an appropriate means of providing children with further experience in classifying words into descriptive categories.

LEARNING STATION: *Sensory Words*

Things I Taste	**Things I See**	**Things I Feel**
ice cream	rainbow	fur

Sounds I Hear		**Things I Smell**
whistle		lemon

Directions

1. Write ten words under each of the headings above. One example is provided for each heading.
2. Think of some other titles (categories) and list as many words as you can that fit the categories.
3. When finished, put your papers in the "Words" folder on the table.

A "Learn a New Word Each Day" campaign could be employed. The teacher who is sensitive to word values and enthusiastic about encouraging children to develop their vocabularies may at times put a new word on the bulletin board with directions to answer such questions as:

What does it mean?
How is it pronounced?
How would you use it in a sentence?

Encouraging the children to make use of the new word two or three times during the school day would be an important part of this activity.

Carefully planned instruction can provide the child with many important concepts about words. Six such concepts, and teaching examples, follow.

Words exist in families or clusters. Using the words *ball, house, light,* and *head,* divide the class into four groups so that each is given a family word. Explain that the members of a family look similar and have connected meanings. Examples might be used to motivate the groups: *football, houseboat, lighthouse, headstart.* See how many words each group can find in each of the families.

A bulletin board display can serve as an instructional device to indicate that words come in clusters or groups. A sample bulletin board is illustrated here. The teacher provides words to insert in envelopes at the bottom of the bulletin board. Pupils tack them up in the appropriate boxes. Words (or slips) could include such words as:

Sensory	Emotional	Natural Phenomena	People	Holidays
rattle	glad	sunny	gentle	skeleton
crackle	scared	rainy	honest	reindeer
roar	excited	windy	kind	mistletoe
screech	sad	cloudy		ghost
shrill	kind	overcast		tinsel
splash	depressing			harvest

Words can show a relationship of similarity between two things. Such a relationship is called an analogy. Work with analogies can help build vocabularies, particularly if students are aware of some of the relationships expressed by analogies:

antonyms—*strong* is to *weak* as *hot* is to *cold*
class/member—*canary* is to *bird* as *bass* is to *fish*

BULLETIN BOARD: Fill in the Shelves

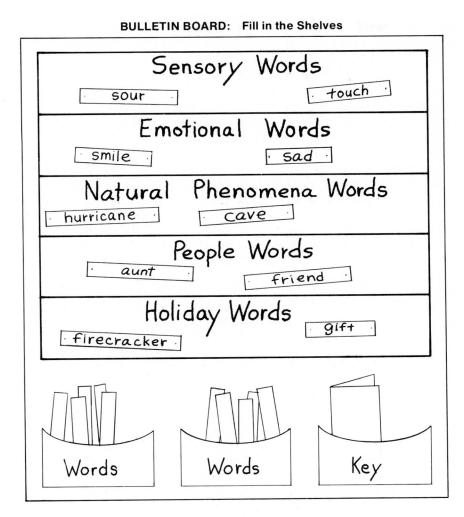

degree—*fast* is to *faster* as *slow* is to *slower*

homonyms—*to* is to *too* as *pain* is to *pane*

object/function—*pen* is to *write* as *knife* is to *cut*

origin/result—*cow* is to *milk* as *chicken* is to *egg*

part/whole—*arm* is to *body* as *handle* is to *cup*

singular/plural—*ox* is to *oxen* as *fox* is to *foxes*

ratio—*one* is to *three* as *two* is to *six*

synonyms—*quick* is to *fast* as *pretty* is to *beautiful*

Words carry feelings. Ask the class a series of questions, such as: Would you rather be *fat* or *plump*? Would you rather be called *unattractive* or *ugly*? Would you rather be *frail* or *puny*? Another idea would be to ask children to act out the feeling of some words, such as *glad, anxious, excited, cuddly, warm, exasperated, grumpy.*

Words stand for things, ideas, and other words. Use a symbol in place of the name of the object. For example: When △ is on the ground we can go sledding. △ stands for _____. Present other words to the class: *happy, nice, friendly, freedom, beautiful, fun.* Ask them if they can find these words and be able to touch, feel, see, or hear them.

And, of course, children like to think of words that can be demonstrated, or the meaning shown, in the way they are written, as in the examples shown here.

Words have origins; they either grow or are coined. Compound words are good examples. Coinage includes such examples as *jalopy, upstage, stickup.* Prepare a list of words that have an interesting history: *bank, candidate, posh.* Or prepare a list of words we use of foreign origin and find their history: *caribou, parfait, mosquitos.*

Words don't always mean what we say. Phrases that can be used include: "That's neat," "I'm starved," "I could just die," and "He kills me."

Finally, there are a number of word games children like to play. One such game is *Password,* adapted from the popular television program. Divide the class into two teams. Have two members from each team go to the front of the room and sit at a table that faces the classroom. Give the same word, printed on a card, to one member of each team at the table. The person with the word card is to give his or her teammate single word clues, and the teammate is to guess the word the partner is holding. Ten points may be earned if the first guess of the word on the card is correctly given. For every clue that must be given, the score is reduced one point. (If the game goes to one point and the word is not guessed, the word is identified and no score is given.) As soon as a word is guessed correctly, the team that did not score replaces its members with two new players. A commercial game that many children like is *Scrabble.* A related game, for which it is possible to make your own letters, is anagrams. Another related game (commercially available) is called *Spill-N-Spell.* Crossword puzzles are always a pleasant way to spend time, and the activity of making as many words as possible using the letters within an original word, such as *Thanksgiving, consideration,* or *leadership,* is enjoyable and educational.

Semantics

Semantics is the study of meaning. What should be taught about semantics and how might it be taught? The following suggestions provide a partial answer to this question.

Understanding symbols. Symbols may be paralinguistic: expressive gestures, traffic lights, road signs, flags, emblems. Language itself is a symbol, along with its derivatives: shorthand, Morse and other codes, Braille alphabets, or the symbols of mathematics.

Understanding referents. A *referent* is something that a word stands for. For communication to occur, there must be an agreed-upon meaning for the referent—an accepted meaning for the sender and receiver. It is at this point that much of the confusion of communication can be traced, particularly of multireferent words. For example, what different meanings might *run* have for a baseball player, a stocking salesman, a playwright? Understanding a referent often involves gleaning meaning from the context— verbal, social, emotional, or historical.

In addition to these problems, some terms are without tangible referential support: *generosity, patriotism, truth, happiness, goodness, democracy, justice, cooperation.* What such a term means will depend on who uses the word, what this person values, the purpose for using the word, and his or her definition of the word. When a writer or speaker uses such terms, it is necessary to pause and think: "Here is a word worth examining. What does this person mean? Is it used to stir emotion or express opinion? Does the word mean to him or her what it seems to mean to me? Do I really understand what the person is saying?"

Understanding the denotative meaning of a word. Denotation refers to the explicit meanings of a word. This appears to be a fairly straightforward concept, but dictionaries are not published frequently enough to keep up with all the new words (or new meanings of words)—particularly technical words—nor do they usually contain slang expressions.

Understanding the connotative meaning of a word. Connotation refers to suggested or implied meaning associated with a word apart from the thing it explicitly names. This is one of the more difficult aspects of understanding words, for many words have multiple or changing connotations. For example, a generation or so ago, the word *square* carried the connotation of true, honest, and forthright when used in describing a person; today, the same word is used to describe a person who is socially inept and out of touch.

Understanding euphemisms. Euphemism is the substitution of an agreeable expression for one that may offend or be unpleasant; for example, *mortician* for *undertaker.* The word *plump* is less offensive than *fat,* and *slender* is more pleasing than *skinny.* Euphemisms require constant updating, as they occur in usage long before they appear in dictionaries.

Understanding functional shift. Functional shift requires an understanding not only of connotative shifts, but also shifts in parts of speech, as a change from a verb to a noun; for example: *They walk to the bus stand each day,* or *Joe went for a walk.* A sample independent activity card dealing with functional shift is illustrated here.

ACTIVITY CARD: *Functional Shift*

Did you know that the same word can be used to mean two different things? Look at these two sentences:

The grocer *ground* the coffee.
The *ground* was too hard to plow.

There are many such words. For example: *leaves, circle, judge, weeds, perch, worry, fall, bruise.* Can you write a pair of sentences using each word as a noun and then as a verb?

Understanding the purposes of slang and various groups who use slang. An activity could be compiling slang words and expressions used by class members and then defining them in standard language. Discussion could include who uses these expressions, when they are appropriate, and how special slang is used by different groups—ethnic, geographical, age, occupational.

Understanding technical language. Technical terms are important, for people are increasingly exposed to technical fields such as space, medicine, and ecology.

Understanding all forms of affective language. Social adjustment and consumer wisdom are absolutely vital to everyone, as they affect every aspect of life. It is important to realize that every form of communication contains a bias because the sender is expressing the concept from one subjective viewpoint and the receiver is accepting it from another subjective viewpoint. When the two viewpoints are not clearly understood, confusion or propagandizing, or both, results. Children should know that catchwords and slogans, such as *justice*, *good citizen*, and *virtue*, can produce stock reactions.

That words can be used to state personal opinion, rather than fact, must be instilled in children at an early age. Children (and adults) must be taught to ask for evidence when hearing a statement such as "That government official is crooked." It must be recognized that there is considerable difference between such statements as "Bill is lazy," and "Bill seems lazy to me."

Appropriate activities for teaching about affective language include scrutiny necessary to distinguish between propaganda or opinions and facts; study of newspapers and magazines to locate examples where writers use opinion or scientific fact; and analysis of propaganda techniques found in writing and speaking, such as name-calling, glittering generality, transfer, testimonial, plain folks, and bandwagon. Listening to a television or a radio commercial provides an opportunity to discuss "sell" words and phrases.

RESEARCH SKILLS

Research skills include locating information in books, reference works, and libraries, and organizing the information. Although research skills, frequently presented as reading/study skills, are needed in all areas of the curriculum, they are given the greatest attention in English textbooks.

Locating Information

Books The preface/introduction can be examined when a textbook is used or studied in the classroom. Similarly, the table of contents of a textbook should be studied to see what topics the book discusses. A brief session can emphasize such points as the topics in the book and their sequence. The index is another important part of a book that should be familiar to students. Most indexes contain both main headings and subheadings to locate the book's information. An activity such as on page 339 gives information about an index and its use.

Glossaries are often found in primary and intermediate textbooks. It should be pointed out to children that glossaries are similar to dictionaries but include only the words presented in the textbook. The skills needed for using a glossary are the same as those needed for using a dictionary (which will be discussed later in this chapter). Elementary school textbooks also contain appendixes which provide supplementary information and sometimes bibliographies or tabular material. Footnotes and bibliographies can help locate further information about a subject. Students can be encouraged to use these sources for clarification of ideas and for additional information.

Reference Books Elementary school children often need to use the dictionary, encyclopedia, almanac, or atlas. Children can be introduced to picture dictionaries as early as the first grade. They can learn how dictionaries are put together and how they function by making their own picture dictionaries. From the picture dictionary, the children can advance to junior dictionaries.

In order to use the dictionary to learn the meaning of unfamiliar words, children must first be able to locate the words in the dictionary and to pronounce them. The dictionary is also helpful in determining the appropriate meaning of words that have multiple meanings or words that have specific technical meanings, as indicated early in this chapter.

There are at least three important skills needed for locating a word in the dictionary. First, the children must learn alphabetical order to gain access to the words they seek. They learn alphabetization by the first letter of the word and then gradually by its first two, three, or more letters. Second, they need to learn that the guide words at the top of the dictionary page tell them the first and last words on that page, so they may know whether or not a word will be found on a particular page. Third, children need to know that more often than not, variants and derivatives are not listed or are listed in conjunction with their root words. If they are not listed, the pronunciation of the root word must be found and the sounds of the added parts combined with that pronunciation.

After they have learned to locate words two important skills are needed to enable the child to pronounce the words correctly. First, the child must be able to interpret the phonetic spellings used in the dictionary. This is done through use of the pronunciation key and knowledge of sounds ordinarily associated with single consonants. There is no need to have pupils memorize the pronunciation (diacritical) marks used in a particular dictionary, since different dictionaries use different markings. Second, the child must be able to interpret the syllabication and accent marks. Some words will have only one accent mark, but others will have marks to show different degrees of accent within a single word. The way of indicating syllabication and accent marks will also vary in different dictionaries.

Other information provided by a dictionary may prove useful to some students. For example, words may be assigned a part of speech, usually by an abbreviation, such as *n* for *noun*, *adj* for *adjective*, and the like. Some dictionaries include etymology of a word, telling what language the word came from and its original meaning. A status label may precede a definition, identifying the nature of the context in which a word ordinarily occurs. Such labels may be *obsolete, archaic, slang, nonstandard, dialect,* and *regional*. Since space is limited, dictionaries use many abbreviations. These are often cited on a separate page, and children may need to refer to the page frequently. Furthermore, many dictionaries provide special features that may be explored, such as a list of abbreviations, arbitrary symbols and proofreaders' marks, biographical names, pronouncing gazetteer, statements about spelling, punctuation, and capitalization, and similar materials.

Dictionary exercises like those suggested in Ideas can be used to provide instruction for the items mentioned above. They are listed roughly in sequential order from the primary to the middle school years.

Certainly, more than one dictionary will enhance the instructional program. If you look up just two words, *cupboard* and *entertainment,* in the newest Webster's and the newest Thorndike-Barnhart, you will note different diacritical marks, syllabic divisions, and phonetic respellings. Although a particular page or copies of the same dictionary may be helpful for a specific lesson, children are denied significant learning about language if only one dictionary is used in the classroom. What often results is talk about "what *the* dictionary says," "*the* meaning of a word," "*the* correct respelling of the word," and the like.

Along with a dictionary, students need a thesaurus. This reference usually differs from the dictionary in format, but newer thesauri have a

Index Search (Intermediate)

Objective: To provide practice with using an index.

Materials: Sample index and a set of questions.

Index

Adjectives
    in complete predicate, 30–34
    in complete subject, 27–29
    definition, 26
    in a series, 25

Adverbs
    definition, 72
    suffix - *ly*, 74–76

Nouns
    common and proper, 8–12
    definition, 7
    noun markers, 10–12
    possessive, 17–19
    proper, 10–12
    singular and plural, 13–15

Pronouns
    definition, 21
    subject, 23–25

Verbs
    definition, 50
    kinds
      action, 56
      linking, 58
(Verbs)
    subject-verb agreement, 60
    tense
      future, 63
      past, 63
      present, 62

Directions: Ask the students to use the index to answer such questions as:

1. On what page would you find the definition of adjective?
2. On what page would you find "linking verbs" mentioned?
3. What pages contain information about noun markers?
4. Where would you look to find information about subject pronouns? What main heading did you look under to find it?
5. Is there information about action verbs on page 52?
6. What page discusses past tense of verbs? What subheading did you look under?
7. Find the meaning of "verb" and write it. Cite the page number.

Source: Burns and Bassett, *Language Arts Activities for Elementary Schools*, pp. 219–220.

IDEAS: *Dictionary Exercises*

1. Ask the pupils to consider the dictionary in three parts: A–G, H–Q, and R–Z. Provide a list of words and have the pupils decide in what part of the dictionary each word may be found, the beginning, middle, or end.
2. Give several word pairs and ask what initial letters are used in each pair (for example, cat-king; circle-soap; jacket-gingerbread)
3. Write several pairs of words on the chalkboard, asking which word in each pair comes first in the dictionary.

   above   hill   race
   across   hunt   rabbit

4. Use a page from a dictionary to explain the purpose of guide words.
5. Supply words (such as *unable, happily, lateness, breaking, tools, sportsmanship, aptness, comfortable, farmer, guiding, regularly*) and ask students to decide the correct entry word for each.
6. Prepare an exercise, asking the pupils to list words they would expect to find between these guide words: flew—food; read—room.
7. Present a sample dictionary entry with pronunciation key, for example, *en-ve-lope (ĕn'-və-lōp)*. Teach the use of the pronunciation key (not memorization of diacritical marks), indicating that in *ĕn*, the *e* has the same sound as in the word *less*; that ə carries the same sound as the *e* you hear in *kitten*; and that ō has the same sound as you hear in *flow*. Point out the accent mark and the marks that suggest syllabication. Provide a list of four to six words, asking for pronunciation.
8. Supply a list of words divided into syllables and ask students to place accent marks where they belong, checking their placement with the dictionary.
9. Ask the children to look up a word with several different meanings, such as play, and write a sentence for each of its meanings.

dictionary format. Whereas a dictionary goes from word to meaning, the thesaurus goes from meaning to word. Words are classified according to their meanings and are indexed and cross-referenced. Practice in using the thesaurus can be provided during its use in writing activities.

FILE CARD: *Thesaurus*

entry word
walk(v)

synonyms
jog—to run or trot slowly (He decided to jog for a while.)
stalk—to walk with an angry stride (The man stalked furiously away.)
strut—to walk proudly (The boy strutted down the street.)
toddle—to walk in short steps (The children toddled toward their father.)
trudge—to walk with effort (The laborer trudged home after work.)

An activity that may be used in helping children make use of the encyclopedia is provided below.

ACTIVITY: *Alphabetical Order in Encyclopedia*

Using the classroom set of encyclopedia, in which volume would you find the following topics?

Abraham Lincoln   Fish
U.S. Constitution   Persian cat
World War II

Check your choices by looking up the terms. Where else might some of the topics appear? Check. Is *Persian cat* found under *P*? Why is *Abraham Lincoln* not found under *A*? Write the page number on which the topic is discussed.

Cities that have been visited by students may be located in atlases. Cities near their own city may be located and information such as the following may be discussed:

Approximate distance in miles
Approximate traveling time
Interstate highways and roads between the two cities
Condition of roads

Even in the primary grades, an atlas may be appropriately studied in terms of land masses and bodies of water, the location of their state, the state flower, and the state bird. Similarly, children may profit from participating in such activities as drawing a map of the classroom, walking routes from home to school, and making a neighborhood map.

Similarly, there is a need in the intermediate years to present the road atlas as a reference tool. The information found in an atlas might include such items as:

Instant map locator
Map symbols
United States mileage chart
U.S. mileage and driving time map
National interstate highways
Individual state maps
Index to counties, cities, and towns
Telephone area code map of the United States
Motor, fish, and game law information

Many children are interested in information provided in such references as almanacs or books of facts. The teacher could prepare sheets of questions for which the children must find the answers. When the worksheets are completed, the answers and the means of finding them should be discussed with the class.

Other Reference Materials Children often need to locate information found in newspapers, magazines, catalogs, schedules, almanacs, and pamphlets of various sorts.

Pupils need guidance in reading newspapers and magazines. Many teachers subscribe to publications written especially for the young. Children need help in scanning headlines, picking out main points in articles, reading with awareness of a newspaper's or a writer's point of view. Children at all grade levels in the elementary schools enjoy reading the comics; at the intermediate grade levels, they enjoy sports articles, local news, national news, foreign news, editorials, and columns.

Activities that may prove helpful for pupils include:

1. Writing a class report on a newspaper
2. Preparing a class newspaper
3. Comparing different newspapers; magazines

4. Learning the reading techniques required by different sections of newspapers and magazines
5. Studying the different parts of newspapers and magazines
6. Evaluating newspapers and magazines, using criteria such as type of information, taste, accuracy, interest
7. Discussing similarities and differences in radio, television, motion pictures, newspapers, magazines

Libraries The librarian and teacher should teach the children the location of books and magazines, card catalogs, and reference materials. Point out that the library contains materials of various types: fiction, nonfiction, biographies, and the like. The arrangement of books under the Dewey Decimal System should be explained, as well as procedures for checking books in and out.

The idea is not to memorize the Dewey Decimal System, but to learn the function of the system and how it is organized. Informal study should begin in the classroom, perhaps by housing books in the reading corner. Nonfiction and fiction books might be separated and then alphabetized by author. Books written by authors whose last name begins with the same letter could be numbered (for example, 1A, 2A, 3A, etc.). More refined classifications and subdivisions—such as fairy tales, reference volumes, and earth sciences—may be introduced when appropriate. Even later, more specific categories can be presented.

The following charts provide the Dewey Decimal Classification System and the Library of Congress Classification System.

CHART 10.2: *Dewey Decimal Classification System*

000	General
100	Philosophy
200	Religion
300	Social Sciences
400	Language
500	Pure Sciences
600	Technology
700	Arts
800	Literature
900	Geography and History

CHART 10.3: *Library of Congress Classification System*

Classes A to Z

A	General Works	L	Education
B	Philosophy, Psychology, Religion	M	Music
C–D	History: General, European, African, Asiatic	N	Fine Arts
		P	Language, Literature
E–F	History: United States, American	Q	Science, Mathematics
G	Geography, Anthropology, etc.	R	Medicine
H	Social Sciences (General), Economics, Sociology, etc.	S	Agriculture
		T	Engineering, Technology, etc.
J	Political Science	U	Military Science
K	Law	V	Naval Science
		Z	Bibliography, Library Science

Sample cards from the card catalog (author, subject, and title cards) should be explained and then given to the children, perhaps before they go to the library. Such advance familiarity would enable them to do their research more effectively and ease their anxiety about using the resources of the library.

FILE CARD: *Card Catalog: Author Card with Dewey Number*

709.02
.G 567 ar
    Glubok, Shirley.
        The Art of the Vikings. designed by Gerard Nook. New York: Macmillan, 1978. 48 pp.; ill; 26 cm
        Summary: A survey of the art and culture of the Norsemen from approximately 800 AD to approximately 1100 AD.
        1   Art, Viking—Juvenile literature
        2   Nook, Gerard
        3   Title

FILE CARD: *Card Catalog: Author Card*

Juv
 F
P296q
    Paterson, Katherine.
        The Great Gilly Hopkins
        New York: Crowell © 1978.
        148pp.; 24 cm.
        Summary: An eleven-year-old foster child tries to cope with her longings and fears as she schemes against everyone who tried to be friendly.

    1 Title

As indicated at the bottom of the author card, there is one other card that refers to this book: the title card. For nonfiction there are two other cards: the subject card and the title card. Both fiction and nonfiction entries may also have a card for the designer or illustrator of the book. Title cards, subject cards and illustrator cards differ little from the author card shown here. A cross-reference card may also be found in elementary school libraries.

Children may enjoy constructing the various types of catalog cards for several books that they have read and then alphabetizing these cards to make a mini–card catalog.

The library should provide many types of specialized reference books for exploration: almanacs, books about authors, books of familiar quotations, and index books to prose and poetry. Many nonbook media are also a part of libraries: audio recordings, films and filmstrips, slides and transparencies, videotapes, and televisions.

Organization of Information

To prepare reports, elementary school children need to organize the ideas they encounter in various sources. Three helpful organization skills are note taking, outlining, and summarizing.

Taking Notes When reading for information on a specific topic in preparation for a written report, the pupil often takes notes to help remember the ideas. As practice for note taking, a short selection (150 to 200 words) could be placed on the overhead projector or chalkboard, with instructions to read it and write notes about the topic. Comparison of notes written by the pupils would be encouraged, the discussion concluding with suggestions for note taking, such as:

Read the whole selection before beginning to take notes
Take notes only on ideas about the subject
Take notes only on ideas that are important and interesting
Write the notes in your own words, but do not change the meaning; if you cannot do this, use the words of the reference
Do not write notes that you do not understand
Number each note.

It is advisable to have the pupils use only one reference source when they begin writing reports; later they can use more than one reference.

Pupils make lists of books as they gather information from many sources. From the beginning, they are taught to note the source of information or quotation and to give credit to an author whose material they use in their writing. This means they need to learn an acceptable form for recording bibliographical data.

A glance at the bibliographies in several books will quickly establish the fact that there is no single, standard form in general use, although most of the forms vary only in small details. Some schools adopt a single form to be used throughout the system. For the primary years, an author-title listing is probably sufficient. Intermediate-grade pupils should also include publisher, place of publication, copyright date, and pages read.

The pupils also need to learn to use bibliographies prepared by others—the ones they find in textbooks, for example. They ought to be able to identify some authors and titles in the lists, to read annotations carefully for clues to the content and usefulness of the books, and to pay particular attention to copyright dates if they are searching for recent information. They should also know how to find out if the books are in the library and where they are located.

Using the suggestions for note taking, children should then be able to prepare a set of notes (first collectively with teacher assistance and then individually) from a reference source. The class members may develop a cooperative list of ideas for organizing information.

1. List the topics contained in the notes.
2. After each topic, write the numbers of the notes that tell about that topic.
3. Plan a separate paragraph for each topic.
4. Put the paragraphs in a logical sequence.

The children are learning to list ideas, group them, order the group, write about the ideas in each group (a paragraph), and organize the paragraphs logically.

Outlining Before writing a report, pupils may be asked to present the report orally. In order to discourage memorizing or reading a report, children should prepare a brief outline to use in their presentation. Two important types of outlines are sentence and topic outlines. Each point in a sentence outline is a complete sentence; the topic outline is composed of key words and phrases that give the main ideas and details.

Outlines are developed with the pupils using the following form:

I. Primary topic (most important point—the paragraph idea)
  A. Subtopic (important fact about the main topic)
    1. Detail (of the subtopic)
    2. Detail
  B. Subtopic 2
II. Secondary topic

An early step in teaching outlining skills is to show children how to use the headings of a well-organized factual passage. The teacher can place an outline of the selection on the chalkboard and discuss the various elements of the selection and how they are related to each other. Together, the class can read another selection for the purpose of cooperatively developing an outline of main points and supporting details. Thus understanding how an outline is organized and the mechanics of grouping ideas in their appropriate relationships with one another, children can begin an outline on their own.

In order to prepare children for outlining, the following activities may be used:

1. Let children categorize a set of items.
   Example: plastic animals like lion, elephant, dog, cat
2. Provide the children with a blank outline of this type:

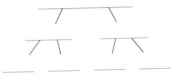

3. Let them fill in the outline, as:

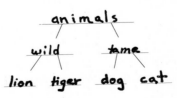

Later the teacher can supply pupils with partially completed outlines of passages in their subject matter textbooks and ask the children to fill in the missing parts. Gradually, more and more details can be left out until the children are doing the complete outline by themselves.

Summarizing When making a summary, a pupil restates what the author has said in a more concise form. The following ideas may be useful in helping children summarize information:

1. Provide copies of news stories without headlines and let the children provide headlines that contain the main ideas of the stories.
2. Give the children a passage to read and three summaries of the passage. Let them choose the best summary, telling why they did not choose the other two.
3. Provide short passages and have the children try to summarize the content of the passage in a single sentence.

SOME INSTRUCTIONAL CONCERNS

One caution should be kept in mind: isolated word study is not the most productive way to promote vocabulary growth. Giving the children a set of words, asking them to look up the definitions in a dictionary, and recording this information does not effectively build vocabularies. Children may be more motivated by some interesting activities involving word play, but there are other considerations. As suggested earlier, basic experiential opportunities within the classroom provide a chance for vocabulary development, not only "hands on" experiences but those involving visualizing and listening. When reading skills are fairly developed, reading should be the principal means of expanding the breadth and depth of vocabularies. When a need exists for specific instructional attention (such as understanding common prefixes), the most effective method would be to utilize a reading lesson in which a number of new words contain prefixes.

In a similar manner, research skills cannot be most effectively taught or learned without relating the particular skill to a functional situation. For example, in doing research on a topic of interest, children will need to use reference books and other reference materials in the library. As they seek to locate information, this is an appropriate time to teach needed locational skills. In order to organize the information gathered, note taking, outlining, and summarizing will be required for preparing a report. Specific instruction may be provided as needed.

Some children meet difficulties in finding appropriate material. Often this is due to researching a topic that is too broad in scope, so that assisting children to narrow a topic will help them determine the type of reference sources they need. To encourage appropriate use of reference sources, children should be taught to include bibliographical data with each note taken, to copy direct quotations exactly, and to indicate carefully which notes are direct quotations and which are reworded.

THOUGHT QUESTIONS

1. How are children's vocabularies developed?
2. How is the development of spelling ability related to vocabulary development?
3. What is the difference between these types of context clues: explicit, implicit, and structure? Supply an example of each.
4. Is the component of semantics an important topic for elementary school language arts? Why or why not?
5. How might the teaching of an encyclopedia skill or use of the card catalog be integrated with content area instruction?
6. How would you relate the teaching of an organization skill (note taking, outlining, or summarizing) to the experience of oral reporting, discussed in Chapter 6?

LEARNER RESPONSE OPTIONS

1. Prepare a list of books that have high potential for enriching the vocabularies of children.
2. Analyze an elementary textbook to note the occurrence and frequency of the contextual aids cited in Chart 10.1.
3. Locate a contextual clue to the meaning of a word that is introduced in an elementary school textbook.
4. Prepare an introduction to a lesson on metaphor for a child or small group.
5. Select one trade book about words for use with a pupil or class. Plan a presentation around it and evaluate your performance.
6. Take the word *man* and help children become aware of its various meanings.
7. Using an elementary school textbook, plan procedures to familiarize children with the parts of the book and the reading aids that the book offers.
8. Visit an elementary school library and listen to the librarian explain the reference materials and library procedures to students. Evaluate the presentation and decide how you might change it if you were responsible for it.

9. Select a passage from a textbook for children. Prepare a plan for helping children (a) outline the material; (b) summarize the material.

REFERENCES AND ADDITIONAL READINGS

Dale, Edgar, and Joseph O'Rourke. *Techniques of Teaching Vocabulary.* Palo Alto, CA: Field Educational Enterprises, 1971.

CHAPTER 11 : Reading

OVERVIEW

This chapter discusses reading in relation to the other language arts. The topics include language concepts that may be enhanced in the reading program, prereading skills that support general language experiences, reading approaches and their components in the other language arts, reading relationships to listening, reading practices that involve speaking, and reading practices that can enhance writing.

KEY VOCABULARY

encoding

decoding

phoneme-grapheme relationships

suprasegmentals

structure or function words

auditory discrimination

letter form discrimination

language-experience approach

individualized reading

basal reader approach

Directed Reading Activity

eye-voice span

audience reading

choral reading

literary skills

LANGUAGE STUDY AND READING

Listening, speaking, and writing involve the processing of language. So, obviously, does reading; it is therefore related to all language experiences. There are two major components in the language process: encoding, that is, expressing meaning in symbols; and decoding, deducing meaning from symbols. Writing and speaking are generally thought of as encoding experience; listening and reading, as receiving and decoding experience expressed in symbols.

Encoding: Expressive	Decoding: Receptive
Speaking	Listening
Writing	Reading

Listening, speaking, reading, and writing assist each other in many ways but remain independent in other ways. Each part of the language arts program ought to capitalize on the strong relationships between and among the areas when appropriate, but instruction that focuses on individual areas will still be needed. This chapter focuses on some relationships between a reading program and other language areas.

Teachers of language arts recognize that the ability to interpret written English is directly related to a child's oral language facility. One way to make use of this relationship and to build on the existing language ability is to have a child dictate a sentence about a drawing he or she has made. While writing the child's sentence, the teacher points out that the talk of the child is being written and shows the child the relationship between speech and writing.

Speech Elements in Printed Form

Phoneme-Grapheme Relationships English is one of many languages for which a written alphabet has been devised. We use twenty-six letters to graphically represent the speech sounds of English; spelling, you may have guessed, is an encoding process. In reading instruction, much effort is made to help children understand the English sound system, since the written language is based in part on letter-sound associations (see Chapter 8, Spelling). Since there are approximately forty speech sounds in English, there is clearly not a one-to-one relationship between letters and sounds; different letters represent different numbers of sounds. This situation helps to account for the large amount of irregular spellings in English; the semantic base of spelling also causes this irregularity.

Specific symbols have been created to represent specific sounds. For clarity, these symbols of phonemes are usually set off in brackets. Thus the sound of the letter *p* in *pet* is shown as /p/; the phoneme for the *e* sound in *pet* is shown as /e/. Diacritical markings are also symbols of sounds. Although most consonants represent a single phoneme, each vowel represents many. See the phoneme-grapheme chart in Chapter 8.

Suprasegmentals This term refers to the three ways pronunciation is varied to give more definite meaning to speech—stress, pitch, and juncture. English writing is an imperfect representation of speech; many nuances are lost in setting down speech. In *oral* reading, the reader's task is to put intonation back into the written thoughts, aided by the useful hints provided by punctuation and other orthographic devices (such as underlining or italicized words.) Intonation, the "melody" of language is a four-tone scale in English. Here is one way to illustrate intonation:

$$\text{I'm going } \overset{2}{\underline{\qquad}}\, \overset{3}{\text{ho}}\text{me.} \downarrow 1$$

Through knowledge and use of intonation, children who are learning to read can recreate the melody of spoken language. The punctuation of writing symbolizes, though imperfectly, the intonation of speech. Children develop intonation in oral reading by listening to recorded tapes of themselves reading or participating in choral reading. Reading aloud to an audience provides yet another opportunity for attention to good phrasing, use of punctuation, and reading with expression.

Stress can be used to differentiate between two words that are spelled the same but have different meanings or functions. In some cases, a related noun and verb are spelled alike but different syllables are stressed. For example, the second syllable is stressed in the following verbs: *con-tráct, com-bát, fore-árm, ex-pórt*. When the same words are used as nouns, the first syllables are stressed.

Pitch is the frequency of sound waves produced when a word is pronounced; this affects how high the voice sounds (acuteness) or how low (gravity). The degree of acuteness or gravity depends on the rapidity (fastness or slowness) of the sound vibrations produced. Children can be taught to use pitch through various ways as illustrated in a later section, "Speaking and Reading." (*Pitch* and *intonation* are sometimes used synonymously.)

Pauses, or junctures, in the flow of speech also affect speaking and, thus, reading. In written language, juncture is usually represented by punctuation marks. Commas, dashes, and periods indicate the pauses of varying lengths that help communicate the meaning of the sentence. In analyzing a sentence for juncture, a single bar (/) indicates phrase divisions (The man/in the car/was laughing); the double bar juncture (//) is a more pronounced interruption and is usually thought of as a comma juncture (My brother // who lives in Boston // came to visit us); the double cross (#) indicates an even more pronounced interruption and is associated with terminal pitch patterns like those that occur at the end of a sentence or thought (I am going home. # Are you going with me? #).

Meaning Units

Meaning as well as sound must be represented by graphemes. The reading instructional program at the elementary school level concentrates on several aspects of morphology and semantics. For example, study of contractions, compound words, syllabication, and accents and inflectional devices is a part of the reading program. Knowledge of the meanings and functions of root words and affixes can improve the ability to discriminate visually among word units (for example: *re-turn-able*). That part of the reading program dealing with such meaning units is often labeled *structural analysis* in the reading program, again supporting the spelling program.

Familiarity with structure, or function, words is also a part of reading instruction. Structure words are those that are essentially meaningless in isolation, have no concrete references, and are primarily used to signal the use of noun or verb phrases, dependent clauses, and questions. There are some three hundred or more frequently used structure words, comprising from 25 to 50 percent of all words used. A few examples are given below:

Noun markers: *a, an, the, their, this, my, some*
Verb markers: *am, are, is, was, have, has been, done, did*
Clause markers: *if, because, although, even, though, that, which*
Question markers: *who, why, how, when, where, what*

Many structure words have irregular spellings. Both their frequent usage and irregular spellings make it mandatory that they be instantly recognized in print (*sight words*) and later learned as such in the spelling program.

Reading activities focusing on meaning units also support the meaning vocabulary program. For example, in context, children meet special types of words such as homonyms, homographs, synonyms, antonyms, and phrases designated as figurative language.

Word Order Children are exposed through the reading program to basic sentence patterns that occur frequently. Similarly, they have opportunities to react to common transformations of basic sentence structures (mentioned in Chapter 3). Children should receive assistance in learning to derive the meaning of various types of sentences. Such help may include attention to subjects and predicates, compound sentences, clauses, and complex sentences.

The common sentence patterns and transformations met in reading situations are likely to be a part of the speaking repertoire of most children. Other language structures may appear in children's reading material that are not a part of their speaking or writing repertoire. For ideas relating sentence structure with the composing program, see the later section entitled "Writing and Reading."

Other Ideas Additional features about language are reinforced in the reading program, such as the concept that the language has been constantly changing and will continue to do so. As children read, they will discover new words coined from parts of old words to represent new meanings: *television*, for example. Folk stories also exhibit old words that are no longer commonly used. In the reading program, the child encounters many words, each of which represents many different meanings; for example, *box* and *ring*. Children also encounter changes in the make-up of words: *beforehand* (compound of *before* and *hand*), *edit* (new word derived from *editor*), *smog* (portmanteau word made from *smoke* and *fog*), *deplane* (derived from *plane*), *LP* (acronym for *long playing*), *Kodak* (coined), and *phone* (shortened from *telephone*). Children in the intermediate years may more formally study the kinds of changes that have occurred in the English language. The reading material also presents an opportunity for study of dialects and usage styles.

PREREADING AND THE YOUNG CHILD

The ideas and activities proposed in Chapter 4 ("Language Arts Experiences for Children Five and Under") encompass those designed to develop readiness for the entire language arts program, emphasizing particularly the many opportunities for oral expression, listening, and writing. A section in Chapter 7 ("Written Composition") further explains "Early Writing Experiences," including the use of experience charts and the language-experience approach.

Some illustrative situations will be cited to indicate prereading skills and their relationship to total language readiness.

1. **Auditory discrimination** (recognizing likenesses and differences of sounds and words). Children must hear differences in sounds before they can begin to associate symbols with sounds. To develop this awareness, simple poems and jingles can be used to draw attention to rhyming and unrhyming words. At times, saying a word that does not begin with the same sound as other words in a group provides an excellent contrast for letter-sound discrimination (*tap, top, bat, toe*).

2. **Instructional words** (understanding instructional words commonly used in the reading program). Prereading activities for following directions use such instructional terms as *on* and *behind*; sharing books with children provide opportunities to introduce such terms as *top* and *bottom*, *left side* and *right side*. Other learning center activities provide an opportunity for other terms, such as *under*, *above*, *in*, and so on. Such terms are also used in handwriting readiness, and later the spatial relationship words are labeled as a particular part of speech.

3. **Oral directions.** Simple directions are often given in the reading program, so children need to develop listening skills that will permit them to perform simple tasks as directed. Instructional strategies for following

directions often include participation in fingerplays, body poems, sound stories, and the like.

4. **Listening comprehension.** Another prereading skill is the ability to listen and recall details from a passage or story read by the teacher. Teacher storytelling and story reading, followed by questions about the main ideas and significant details, is a recommended procedure to promote the skill of listening and remembering.

5. **Sequence.** The concept of sequencing is important as a prereading skill. Opportunities for developing this skill reside in the children's sharing period, storytelling, recognizing a sequence of events in a pictured story, and retelling things in sequential order. Such skills enhance general language facility.

6. **Oral language facility.** Young children develop in oral expression through such experiences as conversing, sharing, storytelling, discussing illustrations, problem solving, dramatic play, and the many other activities that furnish ideas and facts to talk about.

7. **Concept and vocabulary development.** This is an important prereading factor. Children are called upon to name common objects frequently pictured in prereading programs, so the child must have the understanding necessary to interpret the printed word. Sensory experiences are a primary procedure to help the child perceive his or her surroundings of common objects. Also, listening to stories and poems read by the teacher and participating in learning center activities provide names of common objects or things.

8. **Letter form discrimination** (noticing minor differences between letter forms). In terms of prereading skills, ideas like the following may be developed through the handwriting vehicle: teaching letter names, demonstrating that words are composed of letters, introducing the idea that letters represent sounds, and for beginning instruction of some letter-sound associations. Thus, reading and handwriting can be closely associated.

THE LANGUAGE-EXPERIENCE APPROACH

An introduction to experience chart writing and the language-experience approach was presented in Chapter 7, focusing first on its potential for written composition and then relating it to a beginning reading procedure. The language-experience approach has several advantages: it is based on active involvement of the children; it provides for the greatly divergent needs of children; it avoids ability grouping in the classroom; the materials used are relatively inexpensive; and it has strong motivational or remedial applications for many children. Most important, with this approach, learning to read is conceived of as a part of the process of language development, where the close relationship among reading, speaking, writing, and listening is recognized. On the other hand, it has been criticized as promoting an incidental attitude toward teaching and learning the basic reading skills.

In a classroom using the language-experience approach, many devices are used to encourage the children: picture dictionaries, labels on classroom objects, lists of interest or topical words, and charts of all kinds that help pupils extend their reading and writing vocabularies. Various beginning readers, easy-to-read trade books, and other materials are available to the class as resources.

Phonics instruction is developed on a "say it, see it" basis, the children gradually learning how to represent by letters the sounds they wish to record on paper. Small-group or individual help may be provided for various decoding tasks (structural analysis or contextual analysis) as children need it in writing and reading their own and other children's materials. Vocabulary is developed through individual "word banks" maintained by each child. The deposits in the word bank are the words marked in the child's dictated story as known (recognized at sight) words, printed on small cards, and filed in a container. The bank serves as a valuable source for development of many skills.

Many teachers who are not familiar with this approach have found the References and Additional Readings cited at the conclusion of this chapter helpful, particularly for the areas of record keeping, skills development, and evaluation.

OTHER READING APPROACHES INVOLVING VARIOUS COMPONENTS OF LANGUAGE ARTS

Individualized Reading

With the individualized approach, reading is viewed as a personal involvement of pupils. Although there is no universal definition for *individualized reading*, at least seven practices are usually associated with it.

Self-selection Children are allowed to choose material they are interested in reading. Each child in the class may choose a different book. The teacher may offer suggestions or give help if it is requested, but the decision ultimately rests with the child. Thus the individualized reading approach has a built-in motivation for reading: children want to read the material because it is material they have chosen.

Self-pacing The child reads the material at his or her own pace. Slow pupils are not rushed through the reading in order to keep up with the faster ones. Faster children are not held back until others have caught up.

Skills Instruction The teacher helps pupils develop their word recognition and comprehension skills as these are needed. Skills instruction takes place either on an individual basis or in groups.

Record Keeping The teacher records the progress of each child. In order to know which books can be read independently by the child, which are too difficult or frustrating, and which can be read with the teacher's assistance, teachers must know the levels of each child's reading performance and must be aware of the reading strengths and weaknesses of each. Teachers also need a record of the skills help that has been planned and given to each child. Children must keep records of books they have read, new words they have encountered, and effective ways of attacking new words.

Pupil-Teacher Conferences The teacher schedules a conference with each child one or two times a week. The conference will vary from three to fifteen minutes in length, depending on the purpose. Purposes may be to help with book choices, to check comprehension, to check word attack skills and oral reading skills, to give skill assistance, and to plan for sharing.

Sharing Activities The teacher plans some time each week for the children to share with each other books they have read. The children may share with the entire class or with a small group.

Independent Work The children do much independent work at their seats, rather than spending the majority of the assigned reading period in a group with the teacher.

Such an approach necessarily requires a wide variety of materials (trade books, magazines, newspapers, reference books, pamphlet files, reading games, and the like). Between one hundred and three hundred books, representing a variety of interests and readability levels, are suggested for the classroom library.

Teacher guidance is needed along the way. Some of the guidance comes through detecting, broadening, and supporting the child's reading interests. (See Chapter 12, "Literature.")[1] Further guidance is needed in the individ-

1. Informal interest inventories can be particularly helpful. For example, see Chapter 14.

ual conference, where the child discusses a story or book, stimulated by the teacher's thought-provoking questions. The questions usually range from those that probe into the child's interests ("Who is your favorite character?" "Why?") to comprehension ("How does the setting relate to the story?") to audience reading ("Which part would you like to read aloud to me?") to skills ("What is the meaning of *set* as used in this sentence?").

While listening to the child, the teacher notes skills acquired and needed by the individual, later organizing some groups for skills teaching based on the analysis. Many teachers have found checklists helpful for skills analysis, such as the ones provided by Barbe.[2] The teacher using an individualized approach must be familiar with the reading skills, as well as with activities and materials that can develop them.

The individualized reading approach, as described in this section, pro-

2. Walter B. Barbe and Jerry Abbott, *Personalized Reading Instruction* (Englewood Cliffs, NJ: Prentice-Hall, 1975).

vides many opportunities for developing listening and speaking skills (as in pupil-teacher conferences and sharing activities), and writing may be a part of independent work. Where such is the case, the program strengthens each component of the language arts.

Basal Reader Approach

Basal readers are series that provide material to help children develop and practice reading skills in each grade in the elementary school. In addition to readers for students, basal reading series include teacher manuals which provide detailed lesson plans for teaching each story, workbooks, and many other supplementary materials that can be used in conjunction with the basal series. Perhaps the heart of any basal reader series is the teaching plan, often called a Directed Reading Activity (DRA). It incorporates the following parts:

CHART 11.1: *Lesson Plan for DRA*

Preparation for Reading

building on experience background, introducing new concepts and vocabulary, and establishing purposes for reading

First Reading

reading silently to get the sense of the story

Checking Comprehension

answering questions; clearing up confusions through retelling; noting main ideas, details, and inferences; and relating to real experiences

Second Reading

reading orally all or parts of the story as a means of diagnosis, checking on specific skills, developing expression before an audience, and enjoying the story

Related Skills/Abilities

practicing skills: word recognition, comprehension, and vocabulary development

Extension

reading supplementary materials, viewing films/filmstrips, listening to records, participating in activities related to the story

Study of the lesson plan indicates the incorporation of the various language arts components. Certainly, there is considerable speaking and listening involved in the stages of building readiness for a story, introducing the new vocabulary, and setting the purposes for reading. After the children have read the story, there is again time for discussing the content. The second reading (usually orally) provides an opportunity for developing expression before an audience. Much of the related skills/abilities section of the lesson is devoted to word recognition through context, phonic analysis, structural analysis, and reading comprehension skills. Much of the phonic and structural analysis is helpful in the spelling and writing program, as well as the reading program. Comprehension often must focus on many language features, such as vocabulary, multiple-meaning words, synonyms, homonyms, figurative language, and so forth. The idea that it is possible to comprehend material on a number of different levels (literal, interpretive, critical, creative) applies to both reading comprehension and listening comprehension. These ideas suggest activities involving viewing, listening, speaking, and responding to the story or related materials in a number of ways.

Additionally, in order to engage in many study activities, students need to be able to locate necessary reading materials. Thus basal reading materials suggest that the parts of a book be studied as well as the specific skills needed to use reference books. Such instruction supports the research skills utilized in language activities, such as preparing and presenting oral and written reports.

LISTENING AND READING

The importance of listening has been emphasized in an earlier chapter. Indeed, initial learning of language is partly accomplished through children listening to talk by others, and, as noted, the speech patterns exhibited by children are similar to those in their environment. If a student does not listen effectively, he or she may have difficulty in the other areas of the language arts—speaking, reading, and writing.

There are a number of important relationships between listening and reading. In a sense, listening may be termed a foundation for reading. Listening is an important part of the reading instructional program, and the reading program in turn provides many opportunities for enhancing listening ability.

Listening and reading are receptive language arts. Both involve decoding. In listening, one hears and decodes phonemes as they are spoken. In print the graphic representation of language is decoded. In order to be successful in receiving oral messages, the student is required to possess adequate auditory acuity, auditory discrimination, and auditory memory span.

Here are some specific examples of relationships between listening and reading.

1. There is a listening vocabulary as well as a reading vocabulary. The young child is restricted first to a listening vocabulary (words understood when spoken), gradually developing a reading vocabulary (words recognized and understood in print) in the elementary school years. The listening vocabulary is an avenue through which a reading vocabulary is developed. At mature reading levels, reading vocabulary can enlarge listening vocabulary.

2. Listening comprehension is utilized as an indication of reading capacity on some measures, such as the Informal Reading Inventory. On that instrument, after the reading level of frustration has been reached (the point at which the student needs help on more than one word out of ten or responds correctly to less than 50 percent of the questions on the material), it is recommended that the teacher read aloud higher levels of materials to the child until he or she reaches the highest reading level for which the child can correctly answer 75 percent of the comprehension questions. The highest level achieved indicates the child's probable capacity (potential reading level). Some caution must be taken in using listening comprehension as a measure of potential reading ability for two reasons. First, listening ability can be improved through instruction. Second, the difference between listening and reading levels is naturally much greater during the primary school years before children become independent readers. Nonetheless, there is a close relationship between listening comprehension and academic achievement in the other language arts areas, especially between the receptive skills of listening and reading comprehension.[3]

3. There are listening comprehension skills, just as there are reading comprehension skills, and they are probably related. If children cannot comprehend well in listening (when material is read aloud), they often are not performing well in reading comprehension. It has been suggested that listening comprehension must precede reading comprehension. For example, if youngsters have difficulty in reading for details, instructions should focus first on listening for details within orally presented materials. So, if children are having difficulty with general reading comprehension, one recommended procedure is to provide instruction in listening compre-

---

3. Sam Duker, "Listening and Reading," *Listening: Readings, Vol. 2.* (Metuchen, NJ: Scarecrow, 1971), p. 70.

hension. The skills common to both may also be considered at various cognitive levels: literal, interpretive, critical, and creative.

There are several ways to help children develop reading and listening comprehension skills at each level but perhaps one of the most important ways is through questioning by the teacher. As suggested earlier, several major types of questions may be useful in guiding listening to orally read material. If teachers ask only detail questions, then only literal comprehension is tapped. In order to tap the interpretive-thinking level, questions of inference (asking for information implied but not directly stated) should be utilized. To encourage critical thinking, evaluation questions should be asked, calling for judgments about the material. For creative thinking, the children should be asked to create new ideas based on the presented material. Of course, the type of material or situation will dictate, to some extent, the range of questions. Only attentive listening is usually required in a conversation. Listening for main ideas is a major part of listening to a story. Appreciative listening is involved when hearing a drama dialogue, whereas critical listening is recommended when attending to a commercial.

4. Many common factors influence listening comprehension and reading comprehension. Some writers use the term *auding* for listening comprehension to differentiate it from the term *listening*; auding refers to listening with comprehension. In order to emphasize the importance of listening with comprehension, the following comparison may be presented:

Reading	Listening
seeing words	auditory acuity
calling words	listening
reading with meaning	auding

The factor of experiential background is an important part of both listening and reading comprehension. Children with rich background experiences have had more chances to develop understanding of the concepts and vocabulary they hear or encounter in reading than have children with meager experiential backgrounds. For example, a child who has actually seen a helicopter is more likely to attach appropriate meaning to the term *helicopter* when it is heard or encountered in a reading selection than a child who has not seen a helicopter. Moreover, hearing other people tell or read about a subject will also provide vicarious experiences that can build concept and vocabulary development. Therefore, attention to the factor of experiences in the reading program will enhance listening comprehension.

Additionally, thinking skills involved in deriving meanings, such as mentally forming sensory impressions or making comparisons, are common to both listening and reading comprehension.[4]

5. Setting purposes is important for both listening and reading. Children with specific purposes tend to comprehend and retain more than those who have no purpose. In order for children to develop the ability to listen and read for a variety of purposes, various forms of questions need to be a part of classroom instruction. Such practice mutually reinforces reading and listening.

6. As suggested earlier, children speak much like others in their environment. The child who hears "He be sick" is likely to use the same pattern. In listening to the teacher say, "He is sick," the child understands the message. Similarly, when reading the statement, "He is sick," the child may read it as "He be sick." Such differences reflect the dialect more than a reading "error." The chapter on oral composition discusses instructional procedures for promoting standard oral English through oral-aural strategies.

The writers believe that standard English should be taught along with beginning and later reading instruction, since reading activities and language usage may be developed concomitantly. Additionally, two reading programs widely recommended for the nonstandard speaker are the language experience approach, permitting the child to speak and read in his or her natural language, and the individualized reading approach, where dialect materials and ethnic content materials may be provided to create a reading environment consistent with the reader's background.

7. It is important to consider pupil attitudes toward listening and reading since there is a relationship between attitude and achievement; that is, good attitudes or feelings about listening and reading enhance achievement in both and good listening and reading achievement enhances feelings about both. Children who find value in reading generally achieve bettter in reading than those who find no value in the act. A similar statement may be made about listening. Students who value reading exhibit this through such behaviors as making an effort to read, expressing interest in reading, seeking out reading opportunities, reading in their spare time, visiting the library, discussing items that have been read, and so on. What are the children like who have developed a positive attitude toward listening? They understand the difference between hearing and listening, the importance of listening, the responsibilities of a listener, and some of the factors that affect listening, and they try to overcome poor listening habits.

---

4. Sara Lundsteen, *Listening: Its Impact on Reading and the Other Language Arts*, 2d ed. (Urbana, IL: National Council of Teachers of English, 1980).

8. Several of the major approaches to listening and reading instruction can be related. For example, when children are taught reading skills within the content areas, it is analogous to a situation in which listening skills are correlated with the basic instructional areas. The use of the language-experience approach in reading involves all the components of the language arts—a situation similar to that approach labeled as *interrelated* in the chapter on listening. When a specific lesson needs to be taught in some reading skill, the parallel is the directed listening lesson. Furthermore, many classrooms have both reading and listening centers to achieve individualization of instruction.

9. As indicated in the listening chapter, a good listening environment is important for the enhancement of listening abilities. Similarly, a good reading environment is important. Such an environment includes not only physical materials but an emotional and social environment that promotes an enthusiasm for learning. Again, teacher attitude and modeling of behavior with both listening and reading will convey a strong message to the child.

10. Finally, evaluation is an important part for both the listening and reading programs. At the primary levels, much of the evaluation may occur through informal observation; as children mature, more reliance may be placed on self-evaluation. The teacher should evaluate, as well, classroom procedures that enhance or diminish listening or reading achievement.

SPEAKING AND READING

Oral reading requires the basic word identification skills and comprehension skills involved in silent reading. Oral reading also requires the skills of accurate pronunciation, clear enunciation, proper phrasing and intonation, adequate volume, appropriate rate, ability to hold the attention of an audience, and functional eye-voice span (that is, the eye ranging ahead of the voice in oral reading).

Audience Reading

Oral reading is often needed for situations like the following:

1. **To present information:** A student may wish to read orally to prove a point, provide background information, provide instructions for performing some task, make announcements, or give a speech from notes.
2. **To entertain:** A student may wish to share a story or poem, participate in a dramatic reading, or act as a narrator for a play or pantomime.

3. **For personal enjoyment:** A student may read a passage of prose or poetry aloud just to take pleasure in the words.

If the reader is to read for an audience, he or she should have an opportunity to read silently beforehand. During the silent reading preview, the child can become acquainted with the author's style of writing, determine the author's message, and check on the correct pronunciation of unfamiliar words. If the passage is particularly difficult, the reader may need to practice it, or portions of it, aloud in order to ensure proper phrasing and intonation.

Among possible classroom reading activities, some examples of good purposes for audience reading are suggested below:

1. Confirming an answer to a question by reading the portion of the selection in which the answer was found
2. Reading a news story in which other class members should be interested
3. Reading background information for a topic of discussion from a reference book or trade book
4. Sharing a poem or story (published or original)
5. Reading instructions to a person or group so that they can be followed
6. Reading announcements or invitations
7. Reading to demonstrate different expressions/meanings found in a selection
8. Choral reading
9. Reading the narration or parts of characters in a play
10. Reading for a class "radio" or "television" program

Choral reading is an especially useful reading activity. It helps children to develop smooth, fluent reading and to avoid word-by-word reading. It gives them opportunities to interpret good literature orally. And, finally, the most important contribution is that all children can participate without undue anxiety because the mistakes of hesitant oral readers are not as obvious when a group is reading.

Resources

Some sources of material for oral reading instruction include the following:

Basic Reading Skills Program. Bell and Howell, 7100 McCormick Road, Chicago, IL 60645 (Language Master card and read-along stories with cassettes)

Bill Martin's *Instant Readers*. Holt, Rinehart and Winston, 383 Madison
Avenue, New York, NY 10017 (Books and cassettes)
People Profiles. Teaching Resources, 100 Boylston Street, Boston, MA
02116 (Books with read-along records).
Score Reading Improvement Series. Prentice Hall, 150 White Plains Road,
Tarrytown, NY 10591 (Filmstrips, books, and read-along tapes)
Story-Go-Round. Noble and Noble, 1 Dag Hammarskjold Plaza, New
York, NY 10017 (Books and read-along cassettes)

Some sources of material for children to read orally include the following:

Albert Cullum, *Aesop in the Afternoon*. Citation Press, 50 West 44th
Street, New York, NY 10036
Donald D. Durrell and B. Alice Crossley, *Favorite Plays for Classroom
Reading*. Plays, Inc., 8 Arlington Street, Boston, MA 02116
Donald D. Durrell and B. Alice Crossley, *Thirty Plays for Classroom
Reading*. Plays, Inc., 8 Arlington Street, Boston, MA 02116
Mildred Dawson and G. Newman, *Oral Reading and Linguistics*, Book
1–6. Benefic Press, Westchester, IL 60153.
Donald B. Durrell and L. DeMilia, *Plays for Echo Reading*. Harcourt
Brace Jovanovich, 757 Third Avenue, New York, NY 10017
John Deck et al., *Plays for Reading Progress*. Educational Progress Cor-
poration, P.O. Box 45663, Tulsa, OK 74145.
Bill Martin, Jr., *Sounds of Language Readers*. Holt, Rinehart and Winston,
383 Madison Avenue, New York, NY 10017
Plays: The Drama Magazine for Young People. 8 Arlington Street, Boston,
MA 02116
Margaret Rector and Douglas Rector, *Story Plays: Self Directing Materials
for Oral Reading*. Harcourt Brace Jovanovich, 757 Third Avenue, New
York, NY 10017
The Tiger's Bones and Other Plays for Children. Viking Press, 757 Third
Avenue, New York, NY 10017

Two sources of activities for oral reading and drama include the following:

Ruth Kearney Carlsen, *Speaking Aids Through the Grades* (New York:
NY: Teachers College Press, 1975).
Natalie Hutson, *Stage* (Stevensville, MI: Educational Service, 1968).

Activities

1. Provide the children with opportunities to listen to good readers. This may be the teacher, other students, or good models available on records and tape recordings. Do *not* have children watch the text as they are listening. It is not good for developing personal eye movement patterns.

2. Encourage the children to listen to tapes of their own oral reading efforts and analyze their own performances, using such class-developed guidelines, as these:
   a. Be sure you can pronounce each word correctly before you read your selection to an audience.
   b. Say each word clearly and distinctly.
   c. Pause in the right places. Pay attention to punctuation clues.
   d. Emphasize important words.
   e. Speak loudly enough to be easily heard.

3. Share with children the reading clues offered by punctuation marks and provide practice in interpreting punctuation marks in short selections.

4. To provide enjoyment in oral reading and practice precise pronunciation, provide students with copies of several tongue twisters such as the following for practice, and then ask them to read aloud their favorite ones:

   She sells seashells on the seashore.
   The shells she sells are seashells, I'm sure.
   So if she sells seashells on the seashore,
   I'm sure she sells seashore shells.

   A good source of tongue twisters is Alvin Schwartz, *A Twister of Twists, A Tangler of Tongues* (Philadelphia, Pa.: Lippincott, 1972).

5. Provide copies of several verses that contain figures of speech and onomatopoeic words to children. After practice, ask them to read aloud their favorite ones. Some resources include the following:

   Duncan Emrich, *The Nonsense Book* (New York: Four Winds Press, 1970).
   May T. Justus, *The Complete Peddler's Pack: Games, Songs, Rhymes, and Riddles-from-Mountain Folklore* (Knoxville, TN: University of Tennessee Press, 1967).
   Carl A. Withers, *Treasury of Games, Riddles, Stunts, Tricks, Tongue Twisters, Rhymes, Chanting, Singing* (New York: Grosset and Dunlap, 1969).

6. Provide practice in reading sentences to convey particular meanings. This involves stress on key words, use of pitch, and appropriate juncture. Materials needed include sets of sentences like the following one that may be read with different emphases:

Joe is my best friend. (Not Tom)
Joe *is* my best friend. (Not was)
Joe is *my* best friend. (Not someone else's)
Joe is my *best* friend. (Not second or third)
Joe is my best *friend*. (Not enemy)

Give sentences like this to a group of children. As they read them aloud, have others in the group suggest what is *not* meant. Or children may be given a word such as "Oh" and asked to read it as if they were hurt, then as if they were surprised, then as if they were disappointed.

7. Focus attention upon thought phrases or units. A duplicated marked selection is needed. A sample is provided below:

One day/when Susan was playing,/she saw a lost kitten./ The little kitten/ had a sad look in its eyes./ Susan went into the house,/ and found her father/ in the kitchen./ Her father listened/ as Susan asked him,/ "May I have a kitten?"/

This material should be written at the student's independent reading level. After reading it silently and practicing the phrasing, the child is asked to read aloud.

8. Provide practice with choral reading. Choral reading demands the ability to convey meaning and thought, clear enunciation, appropriate rate, proper grouping of words, flexibility of voice, and observation of punctuation as a guide to reading.

Leader

On summer mornings when it's hot
A rider's horse can't even trot,
But pokes along like this—

All

Klip-klop, klip-klop, klip-klop.

Leader

But in the winter brisk
He perks right up and wants to frisk,
And then he goes like this—

All

Klippity-klip, klippity-klip,
Klippity-klip, klop, klip-klip.

The teacher may help groups of five or six children study the speaking of a verse in unison, and may point out the important words that should be given full emphasis in each line, for example, "*Monday's* child is *fair* of *face* . . ." A tape recorder may be helpful for practice before performing for a larger group. A good source for choral readings is *The Arbuthnot Anthology of Children's Literature*, 5th ed. (New York: Lothrop, Lee and Shepard, 1980).
9. Utilize narration/character parts in plays (often presented through class radio, television, or videotape programs). See the listing of resources in the preceding section for prepared materials. Such practice involves interpreting dialogue fluently and meaningfully. The volume and quality of the voice must be used to reflect the feeling and mood of characters.

WRITING AND READING

Various approaches to motivating and helping children better formulate written expression are discussed in detail in Chapter 7. The reading program can support the writing program in a number of ways. We have already suggested some possibilities when we described the language-experience approach and the individualized reading approach. Also the usual opportunities provided for relating writing to reading have been suggested for teachers using basal reading series, particularly in the discussion of the directed reading lesson in which related activities are used. But perhaps it is the literature program that offers the greatest opportunities for enhancing writing development. In addition to the ideas proposed in the literature chapter, where reading and study of prose and poetry and the development of literary skills are explored, we would suggest the many basal readers which have "literary appreciation" as a major component of the reading program.

In many basal reader series, care has been taken to include high quality literature that avoids sex-role, racial, and ethnic stereotypes. Many award-winning works and authors are included, ranging from contemporary works to time-tested favorites. As noted earlier, the individualized reading approach depends heavily on the use of library (trade) book materials.

Through the study of literature, growing writers have the opportunity to become familiar with good writers and can use this information as a model for their own writing. See, for example, the patterned writing ideas suggested in the written composition chapter. Additionally, the reader learns (1) the general framework for a type of writing, (2) ways to handle specific features of writing, and (3) language sensitivity.

In terms of the general framework for a type of writing, the readers learn the characteristics of each type. This means that students must be exposed to many types of literature before being asked to compose on their own. In similar manner, students can analyze the ways authors begin stories, use monologue, and describe events, objects, and characters and then try to use these ideas in their own writing. Language sensitivity suggests becoming aware of descriptive terms, use of figurative expressions, alliteration, and the many literary techniques.

These ideas are explored in detail by Stewig.[5] He shares his views of the relationships between literature and writing, and he suggests that teachers organize composition activities based on literature: (1) sharing literature with children, (2) structuring student interaction with literature, and (3) leading children to create stories and poems based on this sharing and interacting. Stewig devotes attention to the elements of plot, setting, characterization, and use of figurative language. Separate chapters are devoted to poetry. Another author who deals with this topic is Cramer.[6]

Jett-Simpson[7] also has provided a detailed explanation for writing stories using model structures. The models she suggested include the circle story (*Millions of Cats* by Wanda Gag), the cumulative story (*The Gingerbread Boy* by Paul Galdone), and the journal story (*The Fool of the World and the Flying Ship* by Arthur Ransome). The steps presented include:

1. Oral reading of the model story
2. Guidance in comprehension of model story structure
3. Discussion of comprehension activity

5. John W. Stewig, *Read to Write: Using Children's Literature as a Springboard for Teaching Writing*, 2d ed. (New York: Holt, Rinehart and Winston, 1980).
6. Ronald L. Cramer, *Writing, Reading, and Language Growth* (Columbus, OH: Merrill, 1978).
7. Mary Jett-Simpson, "Writing Stories Using Model Structures: The Circle Story," *Language Arts* 58 (March 1981): 293–300.

4. Development of a group model story
5. Children planning their own story based on the model story structure
6. Children writing the story over a period of days, focusing on ideas, and deemphasizing attention to items of form, such as usage, punctuation, spelling, and handwriting
7. Children reshaping stories by deciding on changes, other words to make them more interesting, and the like
8. Children publishing stories, with attention to form
9. Children sharing stories

Using these steps, literature can provide a basis for many activities, such as drama and oral interpretation. These are valuable prewriting activities and may often lead to writing a parallel version of the story or verse or to writing an original or related piece of poetry or prose.

The literature program or literature component of the reading program can also be used to develop more specific writing skills. One area is the sentence pattern. As Pickert[8] points out, sentence repetitions and expansions occur frequently in children's books. *The Three Billy Goats Gruff*[9] is an obvious example, as is *The Judge* by Harve Zemach.[10] Blatt[11] also provides a list of children's books that feature language play, such as patterned language, tongue twisters, homonyms, onomatopoeia, figurative language, plays on meaning, parodies, riddles, and putting words and sentences together. Such word play is a common tool for speaking, reading, and writing. Children who have been exposed to and discuss such language features can be helped to incorporate them into their writing efforts. Noyce and Christie[12] suggest the use of children's literature to promote children's mastery of syntax. Being aware of particular models in stories and poems can help children produce similar syntactic structures (both oral and written). In an integrated reading-writing program, where written sentence-combining exercises are related to reading assignments, there should be gains for both reading and writing. The Noyce-Christie four-step cycle includes (1) having children listen to stories in which the target syntactic structure is repeated many times; (2) talking about the structure in directed oral activities; (3) writing sentences that follow the syntactic pattern and

8. Sarah M. Pickert, "Repetitive Sentence Patterns in Children's Books," *Language Arts* 55 (January 1978): 16–18.
9. Peter Asbjornsen and Jorgen Moe (New York: Harcourt Brace Jovanovich, 1957).
10. New York: Farrar, Straus and Giroux, 1969.
11. Gloria T. Blatt, "Playing with Language," *The Reading Teacher* 31 (February 1978): 487–493.
12. Ruth M. Noyce and James F. Christie, "Using Literature to Develop Children's Grasp of Syntax," *The Reading Teacher* 35 (December 1981): 298–304.

writing stories in which this pattern is repeated; and (4) reading other books that repeat the structure. The authors cite children's books that contain such syntactic patterns as "subordinate sentence, tense shift, if clause" ("If you had an egg, you would scramble it"); "relative clause, without deletion" ("The boy who is playing basketball is my cousin"); and the "subordinate sentence, simultaneous" ("When he rang the bell, the clerk appeared").

Tway[13] proposes another way in which literature encourages writing directly, but subtly. She cites many stories that show the actual processes and satisfactions of writing as participated in by the story's characters. Some children's books cited include *Harriet the Spy*,[14] *Poor Jenny, Bright as a Penny*,[15] *The Real Me*,[16] *Anastasia Krupnik*,[17] *The Limerick Trick*,[18] *I, Trissy*,[19] and others.

SOME INSTRUCTIONAL CONCERNS

Some teachers may not be aware of or utilize certain features of teacher guides for the basal reading instructional program. A number of these features support the total language arts program and should help teachers plan a program that relates the various components of the language without undue duplication of effort and time. For example, listening is used when students are mastering the decoding strategy. When learning to make letter-sound associations, children use their auditory skills. Students also apply listening skills as the teacher reads the listening exercises that are part of comprehension-skill instruction. In addition, planned exercises develop students' abilities to listen for specific purposes, and some lessons help the students understand the connection between reading and listening for specific purposes. Here is a specific example from the Houghton-Mifflin reading program, primary level.

Understanding Cause-Effect Relationships

You have learned that it may help you to understand a story better if you know why something in the story happened. Today I'm going to read something told by a boy named Alfred. Alfred tells what happened to him

13. Eileen Tway, "Come, Write With Me," *Language Arts* 58 (October 1981): 805–810.
14. Louise Fitzhugh (New York: Harper & Row, 1964).
15. Shirley R. Murphy (New York: Viking, 1974).
16. Betty Miles (New York: Knopf, 1974).
17. Lois Lowry (Boston: Houghton Mifflin, 1979).
18. Scott Corbett (Boston: Little, Brown, 1964).
19. Norma Mazer (New York: Delacorte, 1971).

one day when he went exploring in his grandmother's barn. After I finish reading, I will ask you about what happened.

Here is what Alfred said. Listen:

> One summer afternoon, I went exploring in my grandmother's barn. She had a lot of interesting things stored in the barn. There was even an old pair of roller skates with black tops that laced up the front. They were in pretty good shape, and I thought a little oil would make the rusted wheels work like new. So I decided to try them on to see if they would fit. I found the left one and loosened the laces. Then I took off my shoe, and just as I put my foot inside the shoe part of the skate, I felt something warm and fuzzy. Then it moved. I let out a yell and dropped the skate. Across the floor ran a small gray field mouse.

What caused Alfred to drop the shoe-skate and let out a yell? . . . (*There was a small gray field mouse in it.*)[20]

Similarly, the same reading series presents vocabulary development material. Among topics discussed are the importance of unusual words; word origins; why some words are obsolete; and how new words are "invented." Here is a sample from an intermediate level reader:

. . . *Not What They Seem*

In the story about the ship *Neptune's Car*, Marry Patten said of her first journey, "What a *homesick*, *seasick* landlubber I was!" *Homesick* is a compound word made up of *home* and *sick*. You know what each word means on its own, of course. But think about what the words mean when they are used together. *Homesick* means "longing for home; unhappy away from home." In other words, it means "sick *for* home."

Now think for a minute about the word *seasick*. If you changed the word *home* in the definition to the word *sea*, would the definition fit *seasick*? Does *seasick* mean "longing for sea; unhappy away from sea"? It means something quite different. *Seasick* means "made sick by the movement of a boat on the sea." It means "sick *because of* the sea." When you are *homesick*, the only place you want to be is at home. When you are *seasick*, the last place you want to be is at sea!

Have you ever heard of a person being *heartsick*? *Heartsick* doesn't mean that something is wrong with a person's heart. It means "terribly disappointed and sad." People are *heartsick* when they hurt way down deep inside, when they feel as if their hearts are broken. They are "sick *at* heart."

Some people get confused about "sick" words. Read the following conversation between Froop and Boop.

---

20. *Skylights*, Unit 5, Teacher's Guide, Houghton Mifflin Reading Program, Boston: Houghton Mifflin, 1981), p. 55.

Froop: Mary can't take her dog Speck in their old car anymore. Speck
always gets carsick.
Boop: Oh, so that's why Speck was looking at new cars—sick for a car,
eh?
Froop: Boop! *Carsick* doesn't mean sick for a car!
Boop: It doesn't? Oh, will I ever learn about those "sick" words?
Boop will learn someday, we think. *Carsick* is like *seasick*. When you are
carsick, you are "made sick by the movement of a car on the road." You are
sick *because of* the car, not sick *for* it.
You can see, then, that not all compound words are what they seem at first
glance. Think about the words *handshake*, *handstand*, and *handbag*. You
may want to write definitions for them.[21]

Careful analysis of the basic language arts material used (reading, English, spelling, handwriting) will reveal areas of common concern. The spelling chapter indicated certain topics commonly treated in today's spellers—they do not merely provide a list of words for study.

THE COMPUTER AND READING

Computer-assisted instruction provides a programmed instructional sequence. Consideration of the quality of the program that goes into the computer is of primary importance. Computer-assisted instruction has been successfully used to teach various reading skills. One example of a computer-managed reading instruction system is that from Learning Unlimited Corporation in New Canaan, Connecticut. For more information on the role of the computer in reading, see George Mason and Jay Blanchard, *Computer Applications in Reading* (Newark, DE: International Reading Association, 1979), and Jay Blanchard, "Computer-Assisted Instruction in Today's Reading Classrooms," *Journal of Reading* 23 (February 1980): 430–434.

THOUGHT QUESTIONS

1. What general language skills are developed through prereading skills?
2. What are advantages and disadvantages of the language-experience approach? Individualized reading? Basal reader approach?
3. In what ways are listening and reading different?

21. *Gateways*, Houghton Mifflin Reading Program, (Boston: Houghton Mifflin, 1981), pp. 519–520.

4. What aspects of the oral reading program may enhance oral composition?
5. How could using literature as a model work against effective teaching of composition?

Learner response options

1. Study a set of reading materials to see what interrelationships you can locate with other language arts.
2. If possible, visit a school setting where you can observe the following approaches to reading instruction: language experiences, individualized, basal reading. Discuss with the teacher the strategies used for vocabulary development, skills development, and record keeping.
3. Prepare a written critique of a set of commercial reading readiness materials.
4. Compare two basal reading programs. Summarize findings in a short report.
5. Develop a Directed Reading Activity lesson plan for use with a child or group of children.

References and additional readings

Aukerman, Robert C. *The Basal Reader Approach to Reading*. New York: Wiley, 1981.

Barbe, Walter, and Jerry Abbott. *Personalized Reading Instruction*. West Nyack, NY: Parker, 1975.

Durkin, Delores. *Teaching the Young Child to Read*. 3d ed. Boston: Allyn and Bacon, 1980.

Hall, Mary Anne. *Teaching Reading as a Language Experience*. 3d ed. Columbus, OH: Merrill, 1981.

Hennings, Dorothy Grant, and Barbara Moll Grant. *Written Expression in the Language Arts: Ideas and Skills*. 2d ed. New York: Teachers College Press, 1981.

Jones, Margaret, and Denies Nessel. *The Language Experience Approach to Reading*. New York: Teachers College Press, 1981.

Lundsteen, Sara. *Listening: Its Impact on Reading and the Other Language Arts*. 2d ed. Urbana, IL: National Council of Teacher of English, 1980.

Malmstrom, Jean. *Understanding Language: A Primer for the Language Arts Teacher*. New York: St. Martin's, 1977.

Mason, George. *A Primer on Teaching Reading: Basic Concepts and Skills in Early Elementary Years.* Itasca, IL: Peacock Publishers, 1981.

Ollila, Lloyd. *The Kindergarten Child and Reading.* Newark, DE: International Reading Association, 1977.

Page, William, and Gay Pinnell. *Teaching Reading Comprehension: Theory and Practice.* Urbana, IL: National Council of Teachers of English, 1977.

Stauffer, Russell. *The Language-Experience Approach to the Teaching of Reading.* 2d ed. New York: Harper & Row, 1980.

Stewig, John W. *Read to Write: Using Children's Literature as a Springboard for Teaching Writing.* 2d ed. New York: Holt, Rinehart and Winston, 1980.

Veatch, Jeannette. *Reading in the Elementary School.* 2d ed. New York: Wiley, 1978.

CHAPTER 12 : *Literature*

OVERVIEW

Literature, as well as being a subject in itself, unifies and correlates other subjects. This chapter provides facts, activities, materials, and evaluation techniques for the subject matter of literature by:

Describing the purposes, forms, and components of a planned literature program
Suggesting experiences, materials, and strategies for prose and poetry
Identifying inquiry items for close study of literature
Integrating literature with many curricular areas through various media
Analyzing the procedures for setting up a literature response station
Suggesting evaluation measures for a child's reactions to literature.

KEY VOCABULARY

free silent reading	characterization
recreational reading	style
close reading	format
genre	developmental tasks
plot	visual literacy
setting	response stations
theme	literature web

PURPOSES

Literature has a very special place in the language arts program since it provides outlets and challenges for children's reading, speaking, and writing, thus enhancing appreciation of their cultural heritage of fine writing. Experiences with literature can expand vocabulary, stimulate the imagination, provide the sensitivity and stimulus for writing, whet the appetite for further reading, and provoke critical thinking about the world in which we live. As we have seen, literature is an integral part of practically every chapter in this book, demonstrating its potential to enrich the total language arts program in a wide range of ways.

Although literature is a major integrating experience in the elementary school language arts program, it also has value of its own. It provides new perspectives through vicarious experiences, develops insight into human behavior and wisdom, and provides beauty and inspiration.

A good literature program expands students' knowledge of their literary heritage, establishes skills of literary analysis, fosters language skills, enriches content of the curriculum, and stimulates creative activities. The major goal, however, is to promote the experiencing and enjoyment of literature as a means of developing children's reading tastes and lifetime appreciation of the reading materials.

SOME COMPONENTS OF A PLANNED LITERATURE PROGRAM

Many different procedures and activities are used to encourage children to be knowledgeable about and delighted by literature. (Storytelling and drama have been discussed in Chapter 6 and will not be repeated in this chapter.)

Prose

Oral Reading One of the best ways of presenting literature to children is to have the teacher read a story to the class. Primary teachers often have rocking chairs for themselves or for the child who is to read or tell a story to a group or class. The children seat themselves on the floor around the chair. Oral reading may be preceded by some background information or followed by informal discussion; however, neither the background information nor the discussion needs to be analytical. Activities before or after the story should be designed to whet curiosity, catch the pupils' attention, clarify meanings of words vital to interpretation, and give purpose to listening.

Before reading a story aloud, be sure that you are comfortable with the phrasing used in the story; that you can identify the exciting, funny, and sad elements of the story; and that you have selected good stopping points if it is going to take more than one reading period to finish. Primary-age children have difficulty remaining attentive for more than fifteen minutes, and older children usually become restless after thirty minutes.

Teachers should read in natural tones and with expression but not dramatically. Time should be provided for sharing the illustrations with the children, exploring key words and phrases, and evaluating reactions. It is better to read aloud stories that children cannot easily read for themselves, that the teacher personally likes and is thoroughly familiar with, and that possess the qualities characteristic of the best in literature.

At times children may ask to read their favorite story to the class or to a small group of children, and at other times the teacher should encourage children to share stories of general interest orally with the group. Older children reading stories to younger ones can be highly beneficial to both groups. No group should be compelled to listen to a poor reader. The teacher must help the reader be well prepared for presentation of the material. A brief story that is new to the class and presented with visual aids has a good chance of being successful for the reader and for the audience. Following are some suggested read-aloud books.

Bernice G. Anderson, *Trickster Tales from Prairie Lodgefires* (Nashville, TN: Abingdon, 1979).

Byrd Baylor, *Hawk, I'm Your Brother* (New York: Scribner, 1976).

Terry Berger, *The Turtle's Picnic and Other Nonsense Stories* (New York: Crown, 1977).

Joan W. Blos, *A Gathering of Days: A New England Girl's Journal 1830–32* (New York: Scribner, 1979).

Beverly Cleary, *Ramona and Her Father* (New York: Morrow, 1977).

Russell Hoban, *Arthur's New Power* (New York: Crowell, 1978).

Kay Nielson, reteller, *East of the Sun, West of the Moon* (New York: Doubleday, 1977).

Doris Orgel, *Merry, Merry FIBruary* (New York: Parents' Magazine Press, 1977).

Katherine Paterson, *Bridge to Terabithis* (New York: Crowell, 1977).

Marilyn Singer, *Will You Take Me to Town on Strawberry Day?* (New York: Harper & Row Junior Books, 1981).

James Stevenson, *Wilfred the Rat* (New York: Greenwillow, 1977).

Rosemary Sutcliff, *Blood Feud* (New York: Dutton, 1977).

Criteria developed by Whitehead provide an excellent checklist for selecting a story that should be read aloud:[1]

1. Is each book quality literature? Does it contain a meaningful message,
   consistent characterization, a plausible plot, and superlative style? If
   the book is nonfiction, is the content accurate, logical, and well-written?
2. Does the book make a significant contribution to the child's world
   today? Does it offer . . . something for future use: an idea, a value, a
   nugget of knowledge? Does the book give enjoyment to the listener?
   Does it promote appreciation?
3. Does the book spark the imaginations of the children? Does it contain
   genuine emotion?
4. Does the book itself gain from being shared orally because of its humor,
   its thought-provoking qualities, its colorful phrases, or its truths? Is it
   a book that children could or would not be likely to read for themselves?
5. Is the book suitable to the ages and stages of development of the
   students? Are the children psychologically ready for it?
6. What piece of literature is most suitable to the various class groups
   from the standpoint of length? If the book is for preschool or first-
   grade children, can it be completed in one reading? Does the longer
   book for older children have chapters of the proper length so that
   natural stopping-places may be readily identified? Does the book provide natural and stimulating "launching pads" for the next reading
   without necessitating undue review of what has gone before?

Free Silent Reading Frequent opportunities for free silent reading should
be provided. Children need opportunities to browse through books and
magazines in the classroom or library, to find materials that interest them,
and then to read silently. Because this type of reading involves free selection, the materials provided by the school must meet the highest standards
of literary quality.

Some teachers use blocks of time for reading that have been labeled
Sustained Silent Reading (SSR). If a school wishes to participate in SSR
for thirty minutes every day, each person in the school, including the
teachers, read something of his or her own choice during the same thirty-
minute period.

---

1. Robert Whitehead, *Children's Literature: Strategies of Teaching*, © 1968, pp. 93–94.
Reprinted by permission of Prentice-Hall, Inc., Englewood Cliffs, NJ.

Recreational Reading Some teachers have found it helpful to have a definite, regular, and scheduled recreational reading period, separate from the instructional reading time, the free silent reading time, or the literature time. Recreational reading involves introduction of new materials, time for reading, and time for a summary.

During this period of recreation, teachers introduce new books to the class, discuss books that are being read, and provide information about authors or illustrators. During most of the period, the teacher helps slow readers or those who need help with words, but does not interrupt those who are progressing successfully. The final minutes of the class are devoted to sharing interesting ideas and summaries of the books.

Children's preferences are often influenced by the teacher's enthusiasm about a selection of prose or poetry or by other children's likes and dislikes. Enjoyable experiences at school prompt continued reading at home. Since pupils are encouraged to share their at-home reading with the class, parents can play a part by suggesting on occasion that a certain story would be a good one to read or tell to the class; and, of course, the parent's interest in hearing the story read and told is very important. Teachers may further interest parents in at-home reading by sending letters to parents concerning the literature program, encouraging a home library, suggesting reading lists, and recommending specific ways the home can assist with the school's program. Fortunately, there are helpful publications that give parents advice on how to guide children's reading.[2]

Giving Reviews of Books

Too many teachers view book reports simply as checks on whether to give credit for reading a book. Book reports serve to further enjoyment of reading, extend interests, and provide clues toward individual and group evaluation of literature. Reviewing a book reinforces understanding of the setting, characters, and sequence of events; develops skills of analysis; and promotes contrast of the literary experience with real-life experience.

Children often want to share with others the books they have particularly enjoyed. Such sharing should be encouraged but never required. Huck and Kuhn give the following suggestions that the teacher may use in guiding discussion or reviewing for younger children. They are indicative

---

2. Linda Leonard Lamme, Vivian Cox, Jane Metanzo, and Miken Olsen, *Raising Readers: A Guide to Sharing Literature with Young Children* (New York: Walker & Co., 1980); Nancy Larrick, *A Parent's Guide to Children's Reading*, 5th ed. (New York: Doubleday, 1980); Susan Mandel Glazer, *Getting Ready to Read: Creating Readers from Birth Through 6* (Englewood Cliffs, NJ: Prentice-Hall, 1980); Ellen Cromwell, *Feathers in My Cap: Early Reading Through Experience* (Washington, DC: Aeropolis Books, Ltd., 1980).

of the points that may be developed in informal group discussion or in more formal reviews.

Show us your favorite picture.
Tell us about the most exciting part.
What is the setting of this book?
Who is your favorite character?
Tell us about the part you thought was funniest.
What other books has this author written?
Do you think this story could have happened in our town today?
Have you ever had an experience like this?[3]

Older children will be able to make more detailed reports. There should be an indication of what the book is about but not a complete summary of the plot, for this spoils the story for others who may wish to read it later. The report may include an exciting or funny part. A small portion of the book may be read aloud. The book may be compared with others on a similar topic or by the same author. The details included will vary according to the type of book and the individual's particular interests. If a child dislikes a book, he or she should not hesitate to say so, but should give reasons. "This book is no good. I didn't like it," is no more acceptable than "This is a good book. I like it."

We have outlined in the chart on page 388 suggested items for inclusion in oral or written book reports. As suggested in Chapter 6, this guide can be readily adapted to reviews of movies and television programs; items would then include the names of the actors, the date(s), the theatre's name or the station, and whether the show was in color or black and white.

Close Reading and Study of Literature

The primary purpose of the literature program is the enjoyment of prose and poetry; however, to increase the appreciation of literature, some analysis is necessary. Close reading and study does not mean formal (or informal) literary criticism of every story or poem the child reads. It does mean that the teacher should make systematic inquiry into some of the worthy literature read by children. Usually this is best achieved through discussion with small groups of individuals (six to eight) who have read

3. Charlotte S. Huck and Doris Y. Kuhn, *Children's Literature in the Elementary School*, 2d ed. (New York: Holt, Rinehart and Winston, 1968), pp. 680–681.

BOOK REPORTING GUIDES

For Primary Years

Author:
Title:
Characters:
Story (in a few sentences):
Best liked part:

For Intermediate Years

Author:
Title:
Characters (names and descriptions):
Plot:
Setting:
Theme:
Illustrations:
Special features:

a story or poem worthy of analysis. Naturally, the teacher should be thoroughly familiar with the material used for literary study.

Items that lend themselves to study by elementary children are genre, plot, setting, theme, characterization, style, format, comparison of stories or poems, and other study criteria. Each will be discussed briefly in turn.

Genre This term means "a distinctive category of literature." While there are different ways of categorizing types of literature, we will offer a special classification for children's literature. The classification found in most bibliographies for children's books include the following listings.

Picture Book: A book in which the pictures are an integral part of the text. Example: *Anno's Journey* by M. Anno.

Prose Fiction: A narrative using ordinary language. Example: *The Long Winter* by Laura I. Wilder.

Traditional literature:

  Epic: Narrative, combining elements of myth and legend into a story of the working of gods and heroes. Example: *Adventure of the Greek Heroes* by Mollie McLean and Anne Wiseman.

  Folk tale: A narrative, written or oral, that has been handed down through the years. Example: *Clever Gretchen and Other Forgotten Folktales* retold by Alison Lurie.

Fable: A brief tale in which animals or inanimate objects speak as humans. Example: *The Town Mouse and the Country Mouse* by Aesop.
Myth: A story told to explain natural phenomena. Example: *Jason's Search for the Golden Fleece* by Apollonius.
Legend: A story, coming down from the past, of local heroes. Example: *Legends of the North* by Olivia Coolidge.
Realistic Fiction: A story, experienced or imagined by the author, that could have happened to real people living in the natural physical world and social environment. Example: *Trial Valley* by Vera and Bill Cleaver.
Fantasy: An unrealistic story rich in imagination. Example: *Charlotte's Web* by E. B. White.
Poetry: A rhythmic, frequently rhyming composition. Example: *A Book of Animal Poems* ed. William Cole.
Narrative verse: A poem that tells a story or relates a particular event. Example: *The Pied Piper of Hamelin* by Robert Browning.
Lyrical poem: A personal or descriptive poem focusing on emotions. Example: *The Swing* by Robert Louis Stevenson.
Science Fiction: Fantasy, using scientific or futuristic developments as part of the plot or background. Example: *A Wind in the Door* by M. L'Engle.
Historical fiction: Story with historical setting. Example: *Four Days in Philadelphia—1776* by Mary Kay Phelan.
Informational book: A book written to give facts. Example: *Where in the World* by Philip Egan.
Biography: A true story about the life of a person. Example: *An Eye on the World: Margaret Bourke-White* by Beatrice Siegel.

Children profit from knowing some classification pattern, for knowledge of the types of literature will help them in two ways. It will enable them to pursue a particular preference and to apply the appropriate criteria for evaluation. This suggests that books lend themselves to various analyses.

To bring out the desired information as to genre, ask questions such as the following:

What kind of book was this?
Would you read the opening paragraphs of the book aloud to me to show that this story is of a fantasy type?

Plot Plot refers to the plan of a story. It should be well constructed and credible. If the plot is original and fresh—not trite or predictable—interest will be high. For historical fiction, the story must be historically accurate; and for biographies, authenticity (a true and accurate picture) is essential.

Questions like the following help the teacher to evaluate the child's understanding of the plot:

What did you discover about this book?
How do events build to a climax?

Even for most historical fiction, the question "Did it tell a good story?" may be asked.

Setting Setting involves placing the story in the past, present, or future. A specific locale is often described or can be implied by dialect and activities. The setting answers the questions of when and where. In a well-written book, the setting affects the actions, characters, and theme of the story.
    Questions of the following type are used to direct attention to the setting:

Where and when did the story take place?
Did the story capture the spirit and feeling of the place or the age?
How did the author reveal the setting?

Theme The theme of a book reveals the author's purpose in writing the story. A good book or story will have a significant, worthy theme and may have a deeper theme—a theme of several layers, so to speak. For example, an obvious theme for *Where the Wild Things Are* might be a story of a boy's dream, but there is also a deeper theme; that is, a mother's way to symbolize love and forgiveness. Even historical fiction usually has a theme. Here the questions to be asked might include:

What is the "big idea" of this story?
What do you think the author is trying to tell the reader?

Characterization A good story will convincingly portray real and lifelike characters who display strengths and weaknesses. Characters come to life by the writer's telling about the person, reporting the person's conversations, giving the thoughts of the character, providing the thoughts of others about the character, and showing the character through specific actions. Not all these devices may occur in any one story, but such techniques of characterization enliven children's literature. Too, an author may indicate character development or change through events and reasons. In biographies, a worthy subject is chosen to be the main character. In children's literature, some liberties may be taken with the character, such as the omission of unsavory aspects. At the same time, suitable shortcomings and virtues are recognized.

Questions such as the following help stimulate awareness and attention to characters and events:

How did the author reveal the characters in the story?
If a character changed, what was the change? What caused it?
When did it happen?
Are the characters real?

Style This term refers to the author's mode of expressing thoughts in words. Of course, the style should be appropriate to plot, theme, and characters. Usually the writer strives for a variety of sentence patterns. Children prefer action and conversation; they do not like too much description or figurative and symbolic meanings. Style includes the author's point of view when telling the story; one may use one's own (first person), the main character's (first person), or the omniscient narrator's (third person) who can reveal the inner thoughts and emotions of the characters.

The following questions are useful for directing attention to the author's style:

What would you say about the way the author wrote?
Did the author tell the story from his or her own personal point of view or from the viewpoint of the omniscient narrator?

Format Format refers to the size, shape, design of pages, illustrations, typography, paper, and binding of a publication. Particularly with picture books, pictures are an integral part of the text; they help create the mood of the story and show character delineation.

Questions such as the following develop sensitivity to these items:

What are the sizes of the pictures? Why?
What colors are used in the illustrations? Why?
How is the format related to the story?
Do any pictures help to explain the characters?

Comparison of Stories or Poems Frequently it is helpful to ask questions relating two or more stories or poems:

How are they alike?
How are they different?

What is the theme of each?
What are some other stories or poems with the same theme?

In addition to stories or poems with the same or different themes, comparisons are achieved through classical models or through previous works or other works in a series by the same author.

Other Study Criteria Different study criteria are applied to different types of literature. For example, questions such as the following might be most applicable for a modern fantasy tale:

What are the fantastic elements?
How does the author make the story believable?
Is the story logical and consistent within its framework?
Is the plot original and ingenious?

For informational books, questions such as the following may be asked:

What are the qualifications of the author?
Are the facts accurate?
Is the book up-to-date?
Are differing viewpoints presented?
Is this a general survey book or one of specific interest?
Is there an appropriate amount of detail?
Did it encourage further study and reading on the topic?
Did the illustrations help explain the text?
Did the table of contents, index, headings and subheadings, appendix, and bibliography provide help for you in locating information?

For poetry, items such as the following are important for literary study: sensitivity to an idea or mood; rhythm; rhyme and sound (alliteration, assonance, onomatopoeia); imagery (sense, simile, metaphor, allusion, personification); and form (narrative, lyric, limerick, free verse, sonnet).
Here is an example of a sheet that may be maintained in a notebook of books to receive close study and analysis.

NOTEBOOK: *Folk Tale*

It Could Always Be Worse
Margot Zemach
New York: Farrar, Straus & Giroux
1976

Lower Elementary
Folk tale

Difficult words

unfortunate, quarreling, feathers, misfortune, nightmare, trampled

Summary

This Yiddish folk tale tells of a man, his mother, his wife, and the six children who live in a little one-room hut. He goes to the Rabbi about the crowdedness and noise in the hut. The Rabbi advises him to take into the hut various animals he owns. He takes in the animals, returns again and again to the Rabbi who continues to offer the same advice until life is so bad, he can stand it no longer. The Rabbi's final advice solves the problem.

Questions

1. To whom did the man turn for advice? (F) (Rabbi)
2. What do you think the Rabbi was trying to teach the man? (I) (Things could always be worse.)
3. What caused the man to be surprised at the Rabbi's advice to take the animals into his hut? (I) (Life in the little hut was getting worse each time he brought in an animal.)
4. Was it important for the man to follow the Rabbi's advice? Why or why not? (E) (Yes, it was a way of learning to appreciate things as they are.)
5. How would you have felt about the Rabbi's advice if you had been the man? (A) (Answers will vary: surprised; unbelieving; that the Rabbi was crazy.)

(F = Factual; I = Inferential; E = Evaluative; A = Appreciative)

Other Possible Items for Attention

1. Discuss meaning of folk tales.
2. What is the "big idea" of this story?
3. How would you describe the main character?
4. How do the pictures help tell the story?
5. What other stories like this one do you know?

Continued

Activities
1. Have the children role play the story of the man and the Rabbi.
2. Have the children compose a story telling what they would have done if they were advising the man.

Other books by Zemach: *To Hilda for Helping* (New York: Farrar, 1977. (She has also illustrated books written by Harve Zemach.)

On page 395 is an example of questions that might be used in upper elementary classes for close study and analysis of the poem "Ozymandias" by Percy B. Shelley.

Book Clubs, Paperbacks, Magazines, and Newspapers

To encourage further learning and reading in the home, when children become independent readers, membership in a book club may stimulate recreational reading at home. Reading for enjoyment is one of the most important activities that teachers can provide for all elementary school children. The pleasure of owning their own books plus the advantage of having the books come through the mail to their home can create an added stimulus for children to try out their skills on new material. Below is a selected list of book clubs:

Arrow Book Club: Scholastic Book Service
Beginning Reader's Program: Grolier Enterprises, Inc.
Buddy Books Paperback Book Club: Xerox Educational Publishers
Campus Book Club: Scholastic Book Service
Discovering Books Paperback Book Club: Xerox Educational Publishers
Disney's Wonderful World of Reading: Grolier Enterprises, Inc.
Goodtime Books Paperback Club: Xerox Educational Publishers
I Can Read Book Club: Xerox Educational Publishers
Junior Literary Guild: Literary Guild
Lucky Book Club: Scholastic Book Service
Parents' Magazine Read Aloud & Easy Reading Program: Parents' Magazine Press
Read Paperback Book Club: Xerox Educational Publishers
See-Saw Book Program: Scholastic Book Service
Weekly Readers Children's Book Club: Xerox Educational Publishers

NOTEBOOK: *Poetry*

Ozymandias

I met a traveler from an antique land
Who said: Two vast and trunkless legs of stone
Stand in the desert . . . . Near them, on the sand,
Half sunk, a shattered visage lies, whose frown,
And wrinkled lip, and sneer of cold command,
Tell that its sculptor well those passions read
Which yet survive, stamped on these lifeless things,
The hand that mocked them, and the heart that fed:
And on the pedestal these words appear:
"My name is Ozymandias, King of Kings:
Look on my works, ye Mighty, and despair!"
Nothing beside remains. Round the decay
Of that colossal wreck, boundless and bare
The lone and level sands stretch far away.

Questions

1. Does the poem tell a story?
2. Describe what the traveler saw in the desert.
3. What words appear on the pedestal? What do they mean?
4. What is the "big idea" of the poem?
5. Can you make an expression on your face like that on the king's face?
6. What opinion did the king have of himself?
7. What feelings do you think you would have had if you had been one of the king's subjects?
8. What "lesson" could be gained from the poem's story?
9. What is the meaning of each of these words: *antique, visage, vast, trunkless, colossal, boundless*?
10. What is the meaning of "The hand that mocked them, and the heart that fed"?
11. What is the rhyme pattern for the first eight lines? The last six lines?
12. What is the special name for this type of poem?

Activities

1. Do research to find if Ozymandias was a real king.
2. Find some information about the poet. What other poems has he written?
3. Write a paper (in the first person), pretending you were a traveler in an old land and came across a sight you want to tell others about.

The paperback is now an essential supplement for elementary school classrooms. Paperbacks can be made accessible to children in the classroom and in the central school library; they are appealing, easily portable, and less formidable and less expensive than hardback books. The available selection is wide: classics, modern fiction favorites, poetry, series on science and social studies, and the like. Two reference sources most appropriate for those who are interested in the use of paperbacks are *Paperback Books for Children*[4] and *Excellent Paperbacks for Children.*[5]

Magazines and periodicals for elementary school children have been available for several years. Some favorites include:

American Girl	*Jack & Jill*
Badger History	*Mad*
Boing	*Model Airplane News*
Boys' Life	*National Geographic World*
Child Life	*Odyssey*
Children's Digest	*Penny Power*
Children's Playmate Magazine	*Plays, The Drama Magazine*
Cricket: The Magazine for Children	*for Young People*
	Ranger Rick's Nature Magazine
Daisy	*Read*
Dynamite	*Science World*
Ebony Jr.	*Scienceland*
The Electric Company Magazine	*Sports Illustrated*
The Friend	*Tiger Beat*
Highlights for Children	*Wee Wisdom*
Hot Rod	*World Over*
Humpty Dumpty	*Young World*

Many teachers subscribe to newspapers written specifically for the young. Moreover, children often begin at an early age to read all kinds of articles from the daily local newspapers, such as comics, sports, society, local news, national news, foreign news, editorials, and columns. Consequently, pupils should know something about newspapers as a medium of information and entertainment and how to read and judge them. Pupils certainly need to be told that just because an item is in print, it is not

4. New York: Citation Press.
5. Washington, DC: Association for Childhood Education International, 1979.

necessarily correct. Children need help in scanning headlines, picking out main points in articles, and reading with an awareness of a newspaper's or a writer's point of view.

As an introductory activity in the study of newspapers, some teachers give a newspaper-reading survey questionnaire to their class. Developmental activities might include locating examples of the types of materials to be found in a newspaper, comparing neighborhood papers, finding illustrations of stories with accurate or misleading captions, identifying the five Ws and an H in the leading paragraphs, studying how news agencies operate, learning about what a reporter does, finding out about some famous cartoonists, discussing the types of illustrations used, and studying the advertisements. A visit to a newspaper plant may be made or the local editor invited to speak to the class.

Pupils may wish to publish a class newspaper. Activities required in this effort involve pupils in many aspects of the language arts. They plan, discuss, write, and proofread their newspapers, thereby strengthening skills in listening, speaking, writing, spelling, and reading. The collection of news may not always appear on paper. Note the "chalkboard" newspaper sketch here.

Weather	Interesting Events	Jokes, Riddles	Lost/Found
Story/Poem		Favorite Books	Safety Tips

Poetry

Long ago, Goethe wrote, "One ought, every day at least, to hear a little song, read a good poem, see a fine picture, and if it were possible, speak a few reasonable words." If teachers would read a good poem to children every day, the essential elements of rich language use (form, rhythm, words, and subject matter) might be more quickly acquired by the children. The teacher who shares the enjoyment of poetry with children experiences the rewarding satisfaction of seeing young faces light up in response to the beauty of rhythmic words.

Poetry is likely to be neglected because many adults (including teachers) experienced negative teaching of poetry during their school years. For too long, children have been required to memorize inappropriate poems. The required memorization of the same poem by the entire class developed a resistance on the part of many children to further poetry reading and study. The child's response to poetry will be influenced strongly by the teacher's response to poetry.

One of the problems in teaching poetry is selecting a suitable poem. A suitable poem should amuse, inspire, move emotionally, or interest intellectually those who are going to hear it or read it. The poem should not only be understandable and enjoyable but should extend the interest of the child to discovering still other poems. When children begin reading poems rather than being read to, the teacher must remember to provide them with poems having familiar content and words. Children are more willing to read more difficult and longer poems if their first attempts have been successful and enjoyable.

The kinds of poetry children prefer is another important factor to consider when teaching poetry.

A clue to young children's likes and dislikes is presented in a 1979 study by Carol Fisher and Margaret Natarella.[6] Their study was divided into three categories—poetic forms, poetic elements, and poetry content. This study revealed that young children liked the narrative form of poetry and disliked free verse, lyric poetry, and haiku. They enjoyed rhymed and metered poetry and disliked poems depending on metaphorical language. Young children enjoyed poetry that had children or animals in the content, and they also enjoyed humorous poems.

Older children also had definite likes and dislikes in poetry. Ann Terry undertook a national study of the upper elementary grades.[7] She divided the study into the same three categories—poetic form, poetic elements, and poetry content. In poetic form, older children enjoyed limericks and narratives and disliked free verse, haiku, and lyric poems. In the poetic elements, the children like rhyme, rhythm, and powerful sounds. They disliked poems using figurative language and imagery. In the category of poetry content, older children liked poems of familiar experiences, animals, and humor. They did not like unknown content poems.

Teachers of older children often have to overcome a prejudice against poetry. One procedure is to request children to bring to class humorous

6. Carol J. Fisher and Margaret A. Natarella, "Of Cabbages and Kings: Or What Kinds of Poetry Young Children Like," *Language Arts* 56 (April 1979): 380–385.
7. Ann Terry, *Children's Poetry Preferences: A National Survey of Upper Elementary Grades* (Urbana, IL: National Council of Teachers of English, 1974).

poems found in periodicals or newspapers. Some children will wish to read their poems aloud to the class, and others may prefer that the teacher or another child share them with the group. After the poem is read, the central idea of the poem can be discussed. Often, older children will compare and contrast the poem with other poems they know. Another promising approach involves introduction of pupils to such poetry anthologies as the following:

Quentin Blake, *Custard and Company: Poems by Ogden Nash* (Boston: Little, Brown, 1980).
N. M. Bodecker, *Let's Marry Said the Cherry, and Other Nonsense Poems* (New York: Atheneum, 1974).
Sara Westbrook Brewton, *Shrieks at Midnight* (New York: Crowell, 1969).
John Ciardi, *The Monster Den* (Philadelphia: Lippincott, 1966).
William Cole, *Beastly Boys and Ghastly Girls* (New York: World, 1964).
———. *Oh, That's Ridiculous* (New York: Viking Press, 1972).
Edgar Lear, *Whizz!* (New York: Macmillan, 1973).
Myra Cohn Livingston, *A Lollygag of Limericks* (New York: Atheneum, 1978).
David McCord, *Take Sky* (Boston: Little, Brown, 1962).
Lillian Morrison, *Remember Me When This You See* (New York: Crowell, 1961).
Jack Prelutsky, *Rolling Harvey Down the Hill* (New York: Greenwillow, 1980).
William Jay Smith, *Mr. Smith and Other Nonsense* (New York: Dial Press, 1968).

In 1977, the National Council of Teachers of English established an award for poetry for children, given to a living poet for the entire body of work produced. The first recipient of the award was David McCord; recipients in 1978, 1979, 1980, and 1981 were Aileen Fisher, Karla Kuskin, Myra Cohn Livingston, and Eve Merriam, respectively. Collections like the following from these poets are worthy of study and consideration by teachers:

Aileen Fisher, *Animal House* (Los Angeles: Bowmar, 1973).
Karla Kuskin, *Dogs and Dragons, Trees and Dreams* (New York: Harper & Row, 1980).
Myra Cohn Livingston, *No Way of Knowing: Dallas Poems* (New York: Atheneum, 1980).
Eve Merriam, *Out Loud* (New York: Atheneum, 1973).

Poetry Reading The reading of poetry by a teacher should be a pleasant experience for both the listeners and the speaker. Often, an overly dramatic interpretation of a poem will cause the listener to pay more attention to the manner in which it is being read than to what the poem itself portrays in its own rhythmic pattern. When presenting a poem to the class, a teacher should:

Select a poem that will interest the listening audience
Practice reading the poem before presenting it to the class
Speak in a clear, vital, moderate voice, preserving the poem's rhythm
Avoid overdramatization
Provide time for reading the poem more than once to the audience

A few excellent read-aloud poems include: "Who Has Seen the Wind?" by Christina G. Rossetti, "Mice," by Rose Fyleman, "Eletelephony" and "The Monkeys and the Crocodile" by Laura E. Richards, "The Owl and the Pussycat" by Edward Lear, "Every Time I Climb a Tree" by David McCord, "Godfrey Gordon Gustavus Gore" by William B. Rands, and "Father William" by Lewis Carroll.

When children start to read poetry orally to other members of their class, the purpose should be to share an enjoyable poetic experience. Each child will read a poem in his or her own style if the child understands the content and knows the vocabulary. Only in the upper elementary school should rhythm and critical interpretation of the content of a poem be stressed.

Often teachers teach poetry that they themselves have heard or read and that they have enjoyed. Because of past emphasis on traditional types of poetry, the new poets and the new content of poetry might not be taught. To expand a teacher's knowledge of what is available for instruction in today's classrooms, teachers need to be aware of newer poetry anthologies.

The following poetry collections have been chosen to keep the teacher aware of the varieties of poetry.

Brian Alderson, comp., *Cakes and Custard: Children's Rhymes* (New York: Morrow, 1975).
Edna Barth, comp., *A Christmas Feast* (New York: Clarion, 1979).
Sara Brewton and John E. Brewton, comps., *My Tang's Tungled and Other Ridiculous Situations* (New York: Crowell, 1973).
Eloise Greenfield, *Honey, I Love, and Other Love Poems* (New York: Crowell, 1978).

Helen Hill, Agnes Perkins, and Alethea Hellig, sels., *Straight on Till Morning: Poems of the Imaginary World* (New York: Harper, 1977).

Myra Cohn Livingston, ed., *Callook! Callay! Holiday Poems for Young Readers* (New York: Atheneum, 1978).

―――. *Ofralyious Day: Poetry for Holidays and Special Occasions* (New York: Atheneum, 1977).

David McCord, *Away and Ago: Rhymes of the Never Was and Always Will Be* (Boston: Little, Brown, 1975).

―――. *One at a Time* (Boston: Little, Brown, 1977).

Edna St. Vincent Millay, *Poems, Selected for Young People* (New York: Harper & Row, 1979).

Kazue Mizumura, *Flower Moon Snow: A Book of Haiku* (New York: Crowell, 1977).

Lilian Moore, comp., *Go with the Poem* (New York: McGraw-Hill, 1979).

Lillian Morrison, *The Sidewalk Racer, and Other Poems of Sports and Motion* (New York: Lothrop, Lee & Shepard Books, 1977).

Helen Plotz, comp., *As I Walked Out One Evening: A Book of Ballads* (New York: Greenwillow, 1976).

―――. *The Gift Outright: America to Her Poets* (New York: Greenwillow, 1977).

Daisy Wallace, ed., *Fairy Poems* (New York: Holiday, 1980).

Isabel Wilner, comp., *The Poetry Trouple: Poems to Read Aloud* (New York: Scribners, 1977).

Valarie Worth, *Still More Small Poems* (New York: Farrar, Straus & Giroux, 1978).

Films and filmstrips can be used effectively in presenting poetry. Two major educational film companies are Coronet Films, Chicago, Ill., and Weston Woods, Weston, Conn. Recordings and tapes of poetry for the elementary school may be obtained from Caedmon Records, New York, NY; Folkways Records, New York, NY; and Spoken Arts, Inc., New Rochelle, NY. Teachers unsure of themselves can learn from poetry records and will find recordings extremely helpful in presenting a quality poetry program. Virginia Haviland and William Jay Smith's *Children and Poetry: A Selective Annotated Bibliography* (Washington, DC: U.S. Printing Office, 1979) is a good source for selecting poems to fit various instructional needs.

Instructional Suggestions All children need to be familiar with many different kinds of poetry: poems about experiences familiar to them; poems of today; poems grasped at first hearing; poems within their reading vocabulary; short poems; poems written to and for children, but not condescending to them. Poetry should be used to enrich music, science, and social studies activities.

A planned poetry program would include a balance of poems of various characteristics as suggested by the following illustrative titles. (For each set, the first poem is more appropriate for the primary school years; the second for the intermediate school years.)

Action: "Indian" by Rosemary and Stephen Vincent Benét; "Dunkirk" by Robert Nathan

Fantasy: "Stocking Fairy" by Winifred Welles; "Day Dreams" by Harry Behn

Humor: "Eletelephony" by Laura E. Richards; "The Panther" by Ogden Nash

Imagery: "Snow" by Dorothy Aldis; "Far and Near" by Harry Behn

Mood: "Tired Tim" by Walter De La Mare; "Otto" by Gwendolyn Brooks

Rhythm: "Hello and Goodbye" by Mary Ann Hoberman; "The Swing" by Robert Louis Stevenson

Story: "The King's Breakfast" by A. A. Milne; "The Mountain Whip-poorwill" by Stephen Vincent Benét

In addition to a balance of types of poems, children enjoy poems about various content topics: everyday happenings ("Bedtime" by Elizabeth Farjeon and "City" by Langston Hughes); the family ("Me Myself and I" and "Thumbprint" by Eve Merriam); interesting people ("My Friend, Leona" by Mary O'Neill and "Portrait by a Neighbor" by Edna St. Vincent Millay); weather and the seasons ("Morning and Afternoon" by Elizabeth Coatsworth and "Something Told the Wild Geese" by Rachel Field); and poems about animals.

Children should also experience various forms of poetry: *ballads* ("Beth Gelert" by William Spencer and "The Ballad of the Harp Weaver" by Edna St. Vincent Millay); *free verse* ("Mouse" by Hilda Conkling and "Fog" by Carl Sandburg); *narrative verse* ("A Visit from St. Nicholas" by Clement Moore and "Pied Piper of Hamelin" by Robert Browning); *lyric* ("Where Go the Boats?" by Robert Louis Stevenson and "The Lone Day" by Irene McCleod).

Poetry reading should be introduced at the beginning of the school year by reading three or four humorous poems, followed by a discussion of

"Which did you like best?" Gradually during the school year, some of the elements of poetry may be brought to the pupils' attention: alliteration, comparisons (similes and metaphors), condensation, contrasts, imagery, mood, repetition, rhythm, suggestion, and symbolism. By the time they understand such elements, the children should be able to respond to poetry with an enthusiastic awareness that will delight both them and the teacher.

As a means of correlating music and poetry, the teacher may select two or three musical records and ask pupils to choose the most appropriate background music for the poem or poems. Later on, the children may be encouraged to undertake the selection of the music for the poem.

When a child finds a poem that he or she intensely enjoys, memorizing it may enrich the experience, foster a deeper appreciation of the language, and extend the enjoyment. Having the whole class memorize the same selection is not generally recommended, but there may be some favorites that the whole class will want to memorize. The amount of memorization will vary with the individual, but in a good poetry program a child will likely memorize a few poems.

LITERATURE AND LIFE VALUES

There are numerous books and poems that can be associated with principles of child development and can be matched with the characteristics and needs of children at different ages and stages of growth patterns.

Arbuthnot has stated that books should relate to appropriate developmental tasks or values of childhood.[8] Not only do books satisfy needs of children as they grow through the normal developmental stages, but they also provide examples, illustrations, and explanations of life events or experiences. Behavior problems, death, divorce, illness, family problems, and handicaps are all presented in today's literature. Children do not need to feel alone or that no one else ever had such a problem. Teachers can select books to help children cope and have a better understanding of the "why" of the unpleasant emotional problems they may face. Children should be able to find in the literature they hear and read some vicarious satisfaction of their basic needs. Among the needs that literature can help children meet are security, reassurance, compassion, loving and being loved, esthetic beauty, achievement, insight into life, reverence for life, and a zest for living.

The Summer of the Swans by Betsy Byars (New York: Viking Press, 1971) provides several good examples of values a child may gain through the hearing or reading of good literature. Briefly, the story is about Sara, a teen-ager who found her summer dull and miserable. Her moods were as unaccountable as the sudden appearance of the swans on the lake. The swans fascinated her mentally retarded brother, Charlie. Charlie disappeared in the middle of one night and Sara had to leave her own small miseries behind during a frantic search for him. The search added new dimensions to Sara's horizons and at the end of that long day, Sara knew she would never again be quite the same person. Specifically, the values are presented in the following ways.

Security and Reassurance: Charlie, the mentally retarded boy, needed security and reassurance and Sara did her share in providing this for him. She cared for him, held his hand, and talked to him although he couldn't talk back. Charlie also had a watch and the ticking of the watch helped make him feel secure.

Compassion: Sara was very sensitive in her feelings toward Charlie. She understood the situation and nearly always showed concern for him and his feelings. She was also concerned about how others felt about Charlie.

8. May Hill Arbuthnot, "Developing Life Values Through Reading," *Elementary English* 43 (January 1966): 10–16.

Loving and Being Loved: One of the beautiful aspects of *The Summer of the Swans* is the love shown between Sara and Charlie. Sara is in no way ashamed of her brother and openly defends him and expresses her love for him. The feeling of love that Sara has for her aunt, sister, father, and friend can also be detected although Sara is often at conflict with these people.

Esthetic Beauty: The author's descriptions of the swans on the lake and the peaceful surroundings should help children see and appreciate things of beauty.

Achievement: Sara experiences achievement when she finds Charlie, when she gets invited to a party, and when she finally understands and overcomes her problems.

Insight into Life: Following the search for Charlie, Sara finally begins to see things more clearly than ever before. She comes to grips with her attitudes, she makes friends with Joe, her former enemy, and she realizes the position of her father, whom she had previously resented.

Reverence for Life: Sara's attitude toward Charlie is one of love, respect, and understanding. She sees in the swans at the lake something painfully beautiful and she thoroughly enjoys them.

Zest for Living: Throughout much of the story, Sara maintained a poor self-concept. Her life had become dull and miserable and she didn't understand why. When the search for Charlie made her forget her personal problems, her zest for living was renewed. Children can learn that seemingly insurmountable situations can be overcome and life can become more meaningful.

Some stories worth exploring on such a basis with children include those in the following brief list. The reader is encouraged to explore the realm of children's literature for other examples.

Primary

Beatrice S. deReginers, *Everyone Is Good for Something* (New York: Houghton/Clarion, 1980).

Judith Vigna, *She's Not My Real Mother* (Chicago: Whitman, 1980).

Charlotte Zolotow, *If You Listen* (New York: Harper, 1980).

Intermediate

Bruce Clements, *Anywhere Else but Here* (New York: Farrar, 1980).

Belinda Hurmence, *Tough Tiffany* (New York: Doubleday, 1980).

Jan Slepian, *The Alfred Summer* (New York: Macmillan, 1980).

LITERATURE AND THE VISUAL ARTS

The content of films, like the content of books, can awaken the child to the world of human experiences and values. One way to begin using films is to choose those based on books read in the language arts program (such as *Black Beauty, Johnny Tremain,* or *The Yearling*). Another way is to plan a film program based on a topic that is being studied in the language arts class—such as animal stories like *Lassie Come Home.* Some introductory activities may help to prepare the pupils for a film and also to stimulate their interest in seeing it. Discussion of a film should center about questions relating to:

Setting, characters, plot
Special or striking effects in the film (music and other background sounds)
Performance of the actors
Other related films or television programs
Recent events that relate to the film
Topics of special interest to the children

Follow-up activities are also valuable: written answers to specific questions, acting out scenes, research projects, illustrations, and prose or poetry writing. The possibilities for activities are limited only by the imagination of the teacher and the children.

Films are one aspect of visual literacy. *Visual literacy* refers to the ability to interpret various symbols, pictures, and other items that send messages in our environment, including color, dance, music, and space. Visual literacy includes reading graphic symbols (signs, maps, charts, graphs, diagrams); interpreting pictures, paintings, photographs, and sculptures; and explaining films and television. One aspect of visual literacy includes action, such as interpreting body language in drama, especially pantomime (see Chapter 6 for a discussion of television).[9]

Classroom activities used to help children achieve visual literacy include:

Recognizing ways in which symbols are a form of communication
Interpreting a message in a picture (through a sequence, such as telling what is missing in a picture, following picture panels in stories or poems, identifying incongruities in pictures, putting pictures in correct order, explaining a sequence of pictures, and describing sensory qualities in a picture)

9. See also Jill P. May, *Films and Filmstrips for Language Arts* (Urbana, IL: National Council of Teachers of English, 1980).

Interpreting paintings, photographs, and sculptures
Interpreting color, dance, music, and space
Recognizing effects of print and electronic media

Many authorities feel that poetry, in particular, and the visual arts
belong together. One idea would be the production of color slides to
accompany the reading of poetry by children. To produce your own slides,
using commercially available materials, follow the procedure shown in the
card.[10]

FILE CARD: *Color Slides*

1. Cut a piece of adhesive transparent vinyl (such as ConTact) to a size
   slightly larger than the image to be transferred. It should be big enough
   to be mounted in an Easymount and handled without leaving finger-
   prints on the image.
2. Peel paper backing from the vinyl.
3. Place vinyl on the image (picture), sticky side down.
4. Press vinyl firmly onto image. Use a hard object such as a spoon to rub
   the vinyl down smooth and eliminate air bubbles. Image will appear
   darker when fully pressed down.
5. Soak in a dishpan of water until the paper can be peeled from the vinyl.
   Soaking time varies, depending on the paper stock.
6. The ink from the picture will transfer to the vinyl exactly as the image
   appeared in print. (The original picture will be ruined.)
7. The whitish clay base should be washed gently from the slides by
   rubbing with a moist thumb and rinsing the slide clear.
8. Air dry the completed slide.
9. Place another piece of like-sized vinyl, sticky side to sticky side, and
   rub to bond them together.
10. Cut to fit and mount in 35 mm. double-frame Easymount.

LITERATURE RESPONSE STATIONS

The role of the literature receiver (reader or listener) is very important
within the literature program. The teacher can provide many opportunities
for receiver response. An area within the classroom (called a response

10. Myra Weiger. "Getting Together with Poetry," *Elementary English* 52 (January 1975):
105–107. Copyright © 1975 by the National Council of Teachers of English. Reprinted
with permission.

station or center) may be established where children may plan for various modes of response.

For example, working stations were initiated in one classroom after the teacher read *Pinocchio* to the class. Group discussion led to the organization of teams of three to five pupils to share episodes from the book (or to prepare an original Pinocchio episode) with the other class members. Total class planning included three factors: a review of various ways of sharing, the need to practice with the tape recorder prior to class presentation, and reference to storytelling criteria discussed earlier in the year.

Initial planning periods were scheduled for group work sessions, and copies of *Pinocchio*, both complete and simplified, were available for each team. On succeeding days, time was scheduled for groups to get together. The teacher rotated among the groups as plans evolved and scripts were being prepared. The following work stations were developed:

1. One team decided upon a slide or slide-tape presentation, prepared by the ecktograph (visual recorder) and instamatic camera. The children drew some of their own pictures and also photographed pictures from the book.
2. Another team decided to make a silhouette presentation. Pictures were drawn or traced from the book and then cut out. They told the chosen episode while manipulating the pictures on the overhead projector.
3. A third team drew pictures and taped them together in a sequence. Then the strip was pulled through the opaque projector while the episode was being told.
4. Another group prepared flannelgraph characters—made from construction paper—to be used in their presentation.
5. Another group made puppets of various types: stick, sack, sock, finger. One group made string puppets. The work station contained the following materials: cardboard rolls from wax paper or paper towels, crayons, strings, paste, scissors, paint, boxes for making a stage, and so on. They told chosen episodes while manipulating the puppets.

For children who did not choose to participate in any of these classroom presentations, alternate activities were provided, such as the following task card on *Pinocchio* and the book report activity. Other such activities may, of course, be developed so as to provide a variety of learning opportunities.

TASK CARD: *Pinocchio*

To do this exercise, you may use your thesaurus or dictionary and work
alone or with a friend.
Think of words that tell how Pinocchio walked when he
a. ran around old Gepetto's work bench.
b. went to school.
c. went away from the island.
d. looked for old Gepetto.
e. became a real boy.

BOOK REPORT: *Literature*

Go to the nook for bookworms. Select a book to read for fun. Fill out a slip
when you have finished and place it in your folder.

Name _____   Date _____
Title of book _____
Author _____
I read the whole book. Yes _____ No _____
I read from page _____ to page _____
Comments:

On various days, the "final" presentations to the class by the groups
were videotaped during the actual performance. Later, the children viewed
the videotape, evaluating their presentations against previously established
criteria for storytelling.

Children's literature provides an excellent springboard for response stations related to art—mural painting, diorama construction, peep boxes,
clay modeling, bulletin board displays, mobiles, and wall hangings.

Literature response stations provide opportunities for enrichment items,
such as:

1. Art objects (book-related items): available from F. A. O. Schwarz, 745
   Fifth Ave., New York, NY 10022
2. Calendars (such as *Winnie the Pooh's Calendar Book*): available from
   E. P. Dutton, 201 Park Ave. South, New York, NY 10003 or at local
   bookstores

ACTIVITY CARD: *Literature*

Go to the literature center. Select a tape, record, filmstrip, videotape, or film for listening or viewing. You may choose someone to share this with you. When you have finished, fill out a slip and put it it in your folder.

Name _____   Date _____
Title of story _____
Author _____
(Check one)   Tape _____ Record _____ Filmstrip _____ Other _____
I saw/listened alone. Yes _____ No _____
I shared this with _____
I (we) enjoyed this. Yes _____ No _____
Other comments:

3. Facsimile editions (for example, *Kate Greenaway's Alphabet*): available from G. P. Putnam's Sons, 200 Madison Ave., New York, NY 10016
4. Note cards, bookmarks: available from Children's Book Council, Inc., 175 Fifth Ave., New York, NY 10010
5. Pictures and poster sets: available for certain authors—for example, Joan Walsh Anglund, Harcourt Brace Jovanovich, 757 Third Ave., New York, NY 10017; Ezra Jack Keats, Macmillan Publishing Co., Inc., 866 Third Ave., New York, NY 10022; or Brian Wildsmith, Franklin Watts, Inc., 845 Third Ave., New York, NY 10022
6. Nonprint media such as:

   American Folk Heroes from Society for Visual Education, 1345 Diversey Parkway, Chicago, IL 60614 (multimedia kit of 6 sound color filmstrips, teacher guides, records or cassettes)
   Chinese Tales from Warren Schloat Productions, Inc., 150 White Plains Road, Tarrytown, NY 10591 (multimedia kit of four sound color filmstrips, teacher's guide, cassettes)
   Meet the Newbery Author from Miller-Brody Productions, Inc., 342 Madison Ave., New York, NY 10017 (Each set includes one sound color filmstrip, with record or with cassette)
   A Pocketful of Poetry from Guidance Associates, 757 Third Ave., New York, NY 10017 (two sound color filmstrips, teacher's guidebook)
   Scribner/Miller-Brody Filmstrip and Listening Cassette Library from Miller-Brody Productions, Inc., 342 Madison Ave., New York,

NY 10017 (Complete set consists of fifteen sound color filmstrips, fourteen listening cassettes, multiple copies of paperback books, teacher's guide)

Show Me a Poem from Doubleday Multimedia, Box 11607, 1371 Reynolds Ave., Santa Ana, CA 92705 (multimedia kit of six sound color filmstrips, teacher's manual)

What Is a Folktale? from Guidance Associates, 757 Third Ave., New York, NY 10017 (multimedia kit of three sound color filmstrips, thirty activity cards, map, teacher's guide, with records or cassettes)

Another way to respond to literature is through what has been termed "a literature web." A web provides a pattern for looking at literature not only as an esthetic experience, or as entertainment, but in all its ramifications—as a source of values, concepts, and insights into ourselves and others, as a way of acquiring information and learning about the world, and as a source of vicarious experience. A web offers a framework for organizing old learnings and new ones so that they form a coherent whole, and for synthesizing the many facets of human experience that make up what we call culture. See page 412 for an example of a literature web.

LITERATURE FOR ALL CURRICULAR AREAS

The scope of children's literature is constantly expanding as educators become aware of the value of trade books. The library corner is the literature learning center and can take a greater role in the literature program if it is no longer used only for "free reading." Reading, the other language arts, social studies, mathematics, and science can be more fully developed when each is enriched with good literature.

One approach to reading instruction, called *individualized*, or *personalized*, has stressed the importance of the reading of library books. Trade books cover a wider range of personality, emotion, and action than basal readers. Perhaps one of the advantages of the individualized reading approach is the impact on the reader of encountering varied sentence patterns; basal readers are usually more restrictive than trade books in their choice of sentence patterns for beginning readers. (See Chapter 11 for a discussion of individualized reading.)

The use of the individualized approach has accelerated the production of commercially packaged literature programs.

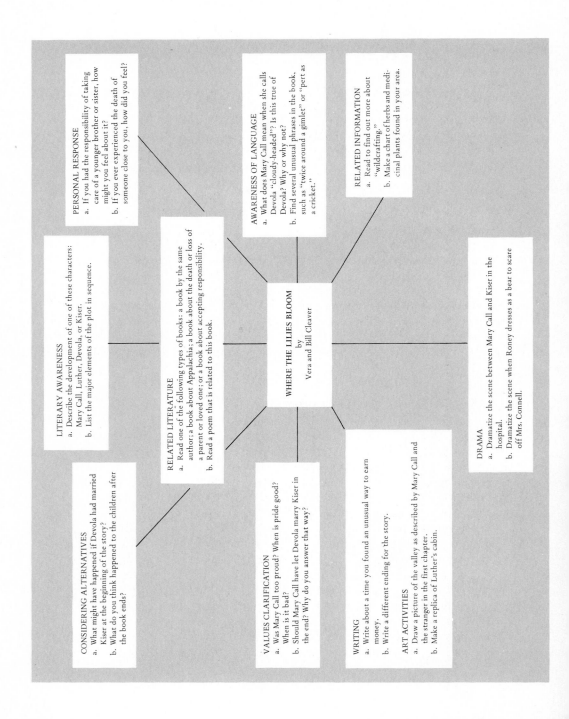

PERSONAL RESPONSE
a. If you had the responsibility of taking care of a younger brother or sister, how might you feel about it?
b. If you ever experienced the death of someone close to you, how did you feel?

LITERARY AWARENESS
a. Describe the development of one of these characters: Mary Call, Luther, Devola, or Kiser.
b. List the major elements of the plot in sequence.

RELATED LITERATURE
a. Read one of the following types of books: a book by the same author; a book about Appalachia; a book about the death or loss of a parent or loved one; or a book about accepting responsibility.
b. Read a poem that is related to this book.

CONSIDERING ALTERNATIVES
a. What might have happened if Devola had married Kiser at the beginning of the story?
b. What do you think happened to the children after the book ends?

AWARENESS OF LANGUAGE
a. What does Mary Call mean when she calls Devola "cloudy-headed"? Is this true of Devola? Why or why not?
b. Find several unusual phrases in the book, such as "twice around a gimlet" or "pert as a cricket."

RELATED INFORMATION
a. Read to find out more about "wildcrafting."
b. Make a chart of herbs and medicinal plants found in your area.

WHERE THE LILIES BLOOM
by
Vera and Bill Cleaver

VALUES CLARIFICATION
a. Was Mary Call too proud? When is pride good? When is it bad?
b. Should Mary Call have let Devola marry Kiser in the end? Why do you answer that way?

WRITING
a. Write about a time you found an unusual way to earn money.
b. Write a different ending for the story.

ART ACTIVITIES
a. Draw a picture of the valley as described by Mary Call and the stranger in the first chapter.
b. Make a replica of Luther's cabin.

DRAMA
a. Dramatize the scene between Mary Call and Kiser in the hospital.
b. Dramatize the scene when Roney dresses as a bear to scare off Mrs. Connell.

Thus literature is not only a basis for teaching reading but can be used for enriching math, art, and music as well.[11] The ability of the story to teach, demonstrate, illustrate, and integrate one subject with another is one of the most important aspects of a good literature program. Literature as the oral reading of a story to a group of children is only one part of a complex network of literature involvement in a curriculum plan.

By utilizing children's literature in all curricular areas, teachers will consolidate their teaching efforts. However, children do not profit from the interrelationship of various subject areas when teachers conduct a literature period and then consistently develop an entirely separate program for each subject.

ISSUES IN LITERATURE INSTRUCTION

The Role of Interests, Preferences, and Habits

Elementary school children are influenced by two factors in their selection of reading material: accessibility of material and subject matter of the book. Children cannot learn to read worthwhile literature if they are not exposed to an abundance of good books and magazines at home and in the classroom.

The literature program should be planned to broaden and deepen the children's existing interests, develop new interests, and direct undesirable tendencies to more acceptable lines. The most important fact to remember about reading interests is that interests are *learned*! One maxim teachers might find useful is: "The interests that children bring to school are our opportunity; the interests they take from school are our responsibility." Children's interests do not develop out of a vacuum. They become interested in things because they have been exposed to them.

An analysis of studies of children's interests seems to suggest that primary children like stories about animals, home and family, and make-believe; they also show some interest in history and science information materials. At about age nine, both boys and girls like mystery, animals, adventure, comics, and humor. Additionally, boys like sports, science, cars and racing, history, and other informational subjects. Girls like make-believe, people and problems, social themes, and hobbies. Although sex

11. *An Annotated Bibliography of Children's Literature Related to the Elementary School Mathematics Curriculum* (Indiana State Department of Public Instruction, 1980), and *The Interdisciplinary Use of Art, Music and Literature in Habilitation of the Young Handicapped Child* (Wisconsin State Department of Public Instruction, 1980).

differences are apparent, these may actually be due to factors like our culture's definition of sex roles rather than to innate sex differences. Most of these findings are not surprising to those who work with children, but it may appear striking to some that children's basic interests have remained about the same for the past twenty-five years.

A recent summary of a review of children's interests suggests that the following factors affect interests:

1. **Sex:** Boys and girls differ in their reading interests, beginning about age nine or ten. This is younger than found in previous studies, which noted age twelve as the time when interests diverge.
2. **Age:** Interests are usually influenced by age, although some researchers found interests rather consistent over age.
3. **Social class:** Conflicting evidence is shown regarding the effect of social class. Some researchers have found socioeconomic level of little importance, whereas others have found social class of influence at lower grade levels.
4. **Race:** Race does not appear to be a determining factor in reading interests.
5. **Location:** Location (inner city, suburban, rural) is not a significant determiner of differences in reading interests.
6. **Grade:** Children's interests peak at grade five and reading tastes are crystallized.
7. **Literary quality:** Aspects of literary quality, like plot and characterization, influence children's book preferences.
8. **Authors:** Children tend to read books by known authors.
9. **Favorites:** Children still read favorite books remembered by elementary school teachers as well as contemporary titles.
10. **Reading program:** The type of instructional program influences children's interest in books.[12]

A 1979 publication, *Children's Choices for 1979,*[13] can be useful to teachers and librarians in selecting books to meet the children's interests as suggested above.

12. Helen Huus, "A New Look at Children's Interests," in *Using Literature and Poetry Affectively,* ed. John E. Shapiro (Newark, DE: International Reading Association, 1979), pp. 37–45; reprinted with permission of Helen Huus and the International Reading Association. Also see Betty S. Heathington, "Reading Interests of Students in Middle Grades," *The Educational Catalyst* 11 (Fall 1981): 37–39.
13. International Reading Association/Children's Book Council Joint Committee, *Children's Choices for 1979* (New York: The Children's Book Council, 1979).

Current Concerns in Children's Literature

In the past, children's literature focused on Caucasian children and their heritage. The children of minority groups in the United States—blacks, Indians, Asians, Jews, and Spanish-Americans—found few books and poems that related to the background of their own culture. Current programs in children's literature must strive to incorporate literature by and about minority groups into the regular curriculum. Selections must fulfill the following three purposes: to establish an awareness of the minority groups' role in our literary heritage; to engender respect for and pride in the contributions made by all regardless of race, color, or creed; and to promote understanding and brotherhood through the study of literature.

A first step in selecting stories or poems is to identify the minority group you want to include in your literature program. The second step is to check your library reference material for lists of books that may satisfy the need. Sometimes a teacher wishes to continue to use children's favorites, augmenting them with new selections. The third step is to be sensitive to character portrayals and to watch for the inclusion of minority culture groups.

Particular attention should be given to poetry by and about special groups. To expand a teacher's knowledge of what is available for instruction in today's classrooms, teachers need to be aware of the culturally diverse materials available. The teacher should first analyze the children's environmental and cultural backgrounds. This information is then used (1) to establish an awareness of the different ways of life and (2) to select appropriate material that will enhance cultural heritages and individual differences and interests.

The following books help the teacher begin an annotated card file for children or situations:

Arnold Adoff, ed., *Black Out Loud: An Anthology of Modern Poems by Black Americans* (New York: Macmillan, 1970).

Association for Childhood Education International, *Sung Under the Silver Umbrella* (New York: Macmillan, 1972).

Virginia O. Baron, ed., *Sunset in a Spider Web* (New York: Holt, 1974).

Barbara Baskin and Karen Harris, *Books for the Gifted Child* (New York: Bowker, 1979).

John Bierhorst, ed., *In the Trail of the Wind: American Indian Poems and Ritual Orations* (New York: Farrar, 1971).

Norma Farber, *How Does It Feel to Be Old?* (New York: Dutton, 1979).

Jeanette Hotchkiss, *African-Asian Reading Guide for Children and Young Adults* (New York: Scarecrow, 1976).

Lillian Morrison, *The Sidewalk Racer, and Other Poems of Sports and Motions* (New York: Lothrop, 1977).

New York Public Library, *Libros En Espanol: An Annotated List of Children's Books in Spanish* (New York: Office of Children's Services, 1977).

George D. Spache, *Good Reading for the Disadvantaged Reader: Multi-Ethnic Resources*, rev. ed. (New York: Garrard, 1975).

Another issue in literature is the role of women. The model of women presented in some books has been characterized by passive acceptance, gentleness, and resignation to domesticity. The characterization of the girl as a watcher, the "I'll-get-it-for-you" type, cleaning and picking up after the boys, is coming under increasing criticism. A good list of old and new favorites is given in *Little Miss Muffet Fights Back: Recommended Non-Sexist Books About Girls for Young Readers.*[14]

Teachers, when selecting books for the literature program, should be sensitive to the character portrayals of males and females, as well as watching for sexism manifested through personal pronouns, names, clothing, and physical characteristics.

Literature sometimes treats such topics as drugs, the many facets of sexuality, and mental illness. Realistic themes can include those that are important to maturing young adults, but harsh realities in and of themselves are not necessarily more "realistic" or better literature. The issue is not so much a matter of what is portrayed as how it is portrayed.

Rewritten classics often destroy the language that made the book a classic in the first place; for example, comic books often adapt a story of acknowledged worth. Perhaps the best solution is to help children judge the difference between the original version and the adaptation.

In the matter of censorship, the Council of the American Library Association has drawn up a "Library Bill of Rights," which sets forth a six-point policy that it feels should govern the service of all libraries.

The amount and importance of television was discussed in the chapter on listening. Teachers can utilize some of children's televiewing to promote reading. Further, some television scripts can be used effectively to build interest in reading.

Literature about children with special needs (see Chapter 13 for types of exceptional children) can be useful. If the story is a good one, children can learn to understand others and those with special needs may be helped

---

14. Feminists on Children's Media, P.O. Box 4315, Grand Central Station, New York, NY 10017.

to identify with others in similar circumstances. For recommended titles, see Barbara H. Baskin and Karen H. Harris, *Notes from a Different Drummer: A Guide to Juvenile Fiction Portraying the Handicapped* (New York: Bowker, 1977).

EVALUATION OF THE LITERATURE PROGRAM

The quality of a child's reaction to literature can possibly best be judged by an observant teacher who takes time to be a sensitive and yet critical evaluator of the child's progress.

The following questions will help the teacher in the evaluating process.

1. Is the pupil growing in appreciation of good literature? How do you know?
2. Does he or she make good use of time spent in the library and in free reading of books and periodicals?
3. Does he or she enjoy storytelling, reading aloud, choral reading, and creative drama?
4. Is he or she gaining self-knowledge through literature experiences?
5. Is the pupil increasing in the understanding of his or her own culture and the culture of others through knowledge of the contributions of his or her own people and those of other lands?
6. How sensitive is the pupil to sounds, rhythms, moods, and feelings as displayed in prose and poetry?
7. How mature is the awareness of the structure and forms of literature?
8. Does he or she like to dictate stories, read aloud to others, exchange books with friends?

Answers to these questions may be gained through the child's spontaneous remarks to the teacher (for example, "Do you know any other good books about space travel?"); through directed conversation with the class ("What books would you like to add to our classroom library?"); and during individual conferences when the child has an opportunity to describe books he or she likes and does not like.

Within every school day, countless opportunities for obtaining information present themselves: conversation between children, observation of their creative activities, studying library circulation records for children, conferring with parents, and the like. Time spent with a child looking through and discussing various books in the library will provide the teacher with great insight into the child's reactions.

Some instructional concerns

In the area of literature study, there are some points to note. First, all teachers need to continue to increase their knowledge of children's literature. There are several ways this can be accomplished. Professional books and journals provide up-to-date information concerning children's literature, and everyone who teaches language arts to children should read *Language Arts*, which regularly gives attention to children's literature. The National Council of Teachers of English presents a number of conferences each year in addition to holding an annual meeting. These conferences feature speakers and workshops by authorities in children's literature and displays of professional materials. Local councils of the NCTE also provide stimulating programs. Colleges and universities, as well as school districts, serve as an opportunity for continuing one's study of children's literature. Cultivating a children's librarian will also provide an avenue for continuing to learn about children's literature.

As was suggested earlier in the poetry section, there is a need for presenting a balanced literature program to children. Although teacher favorites will certainly determine certain selections for use with children, an overemphasis on one or a few literary forms, characteristics, or content results in the neglect of many other valuable experiences. A card file or notebook for various literary forms with ideas for their use can be updated each year, new ideas being added and older or less successful ones discarded. A good anthology, such as *The Arbuthnot Anthology of Children's Literature*, 5th ed. (New York: Lothrop, Lee & Shepard, 1980), is an invaluable aid in planning and implementing a balanced program.

Literature should not be restricted to a set period. With the wide range of literature available, it can pervade the elementary school curriculum. As a start, read Ruth M. Noyce, "Team Up and Teach with Trade Books," *The Reading Teacher* 32 (January 1979): 442–448. Noyce recommends trade books and teacher resources for ten different curricular areas.

Sharing of literature by students is too often a rather boring experience for the listeners. This need not be if teachers will help children prepare properly, as suggested in the oral composition chapter and in this one. Greater information on sharing is provided in children's literature textbooks, such as those cited in References and Additional Readings at the conclusion of this chapter.

Thought questions

1. What ideas should be kept in mind in reading aloud to children?
2. What is meant by close reading/study of a piece of literature?
3. How may poetry be shared with children?

4. How are values related to literature study?
5. Do the studies of children's poetry preferences (cited in this chapter) agree with your experiences with children?
6. What ideas would you propose for evaluating a literature program?

LEARNER RESPONSE OPTIONS

1. Select a read-aloud story for an age level of your choice. Share it with a small group of children or peers. Tape your reading and then evaluate it.
2. Write a critical analysis of one example from each of the various genre: fairy tales, folk tales, picture stories, informational books, and poetry.
3. Select a picture book, a fiction story, or a poem. Develop a set of questions to be used for close study of it by a group of children.
4. After examining several children's magazines and newspapers, report their features to the class.
5. Select a read-aloud poem for an age level of your interest. Share it with a small group of children or peers. Tape your reading and then evaluate it.
6. Select an age level and list stories and poems, focusing on minority groups, that might be recommended for them.
7. List five poems and explain possible uses with children in developing these skills: a sense of rhythm, awareness of euphonious sounds, feelings, and imagery.
8. Videotape a teaching demonstration of one of these three literary forms: fairy tale, fable, folk story.
9. Select a book and provide examples of values a child may gain through the hearing or reading of it.
10. If feasible, preview one film appropriate for literature study. Prepare a list of literary concepts associated with it.
11. Produce a set of color slides to accompany the reading of a poem to children.
12. Outline a response station plan for a literature project. Utilize your media knowledge.
13. Prepare a literature web for use with one book or story.
14. Select one subject area, such as social studies, mathematics, or science. Annotate five books and a couple of poems that could be used to develop concepts of the subject area.
15. Make a class survey of books the children have read or would like to read. Give an oral report on your findings.
16. Discuss with a teacher and a librarian some ways to determine children's literary interests.

17. Study a review of children's books in *Language Arts* and *The Reading Teacher*.
18. Write and present a review of a newly published children's book.

REFERENCES AND ADDITIONAL READINGS

Arbuthnot, May Hill, Zena Sutherland, and Dianne Monson. *Children and Books*. 6th ed. Chicago: Scott, Foresman, 1981.

Association for Childhood Education International. *Bibliography of Books for Children*. Washington, DC: Association for Childhood Education International, 1980.

————. *Excellent Paperbacks for Children*. Washington, DC: Association for Childhood Education International, 1979.

Baker, Donald. *Functions of Folk and Fairy Tales*. Washington, DC: Association for Childhood Education International, 1981.

Boyd, Gertrude. *Teaching Poetry in the Elementary Schools*, Columbus, OH: Merrill, 1973.

Butler, Francelia. *Sharing Literature with Children*. New York: McKay, 1977.

Coody, Betty. *Using Literature with Young Children*. Dubuque, IA: Brown, 1973.

Cullinan, Bernice E. *Literature and the Child*. New York: Harcourt Brace Jovanovich, 1981.

Cullinan, Bernice E. *Literature and Young Children*. Urbana, IL: National Council of Teachers of English, 1977.

Fisher, Margery. *Who's Who in Children's Books: A Treasury of the Familiar Characters of Childhood*. New York: Holt, Rinehart and Winston, 1975.

Gillespie, John T., and Christine B. Gilbert. *Best Books for Children: Preschool through the Middle Grades*. New York: Bowker, 1978.

Gillespie, Margaret, and John Conner. *Creative Growth Through Literature for Children and Adolescents*. Columbus, OH: Merrill, 1975.

Glazer, Joan I., and Gurney Williams II. *Introduction to Children's Literature*. New York: McGraw-Hill, 1979.

Glazer, Joan I. *Literature for Young Children*, Columbus, OH: Merrill, 1981.

Hearne, B. *Choosing for Children: A Common Sense Guide*. New York: Delacorte, 1981.

Hopkins, Lee Bennett. *Pass the Poetry Please*. New York: Scholastic Book Services, 1972.

Huck, Charlotte S. *Children's Literature in the Elementary School*. 3d ed. New York: Holt, Rinehart and Winston, 1975.

International Reading Association/Children's Book Council Joint Committee, *Children's Choices for 1979.* New York: Children's Book Council, 1980.

Larrick, Nancy. *A Parent's Guide to Children's Reading.* 5th ed. Garden City, NY: Doubleday, 1980.

Lonsdale, Bernard, and Helen K. Mackintosh. *Children Experience Literature.* New York: Random House, 1972.

Lukens, Rebecca. *A Critical Handbook of Children's Literature.* 2d ed. Chicago: Scott, Foresman, 1981.

Mabkmann, Lewis, and David Cadwalader Jones. *Folktales for Puppets.* Boston: Plays, Inc., 1980.

Nelson, Mary Ann. *A Comparative Anthology of Children's Literature.* New York: Holt, Rinehart and Winston, 1972.

Root, Shelton, et al., eds. *Adventuring with Books.* Urbana, IL: National Council of Teachers of English, 1973.

Rudman, Marsha K. *Children's Literature.* Lexington, MA: Heath, 1976.

Sadker, Myra Pollack, and David M. Sadker. *Now upon a Time: A Contemporary View of Children's Literature.* New York: Harper & Row, 1977.

Sebesta, Sam, and William J. Iverson. *Literature for Thursday's Children.* Chicago: Science Research Associates, 1975.

Smith, James A., and Dorothy M. Park. *Word Music and Word Magic: Children's Literature Methods.* Boston: Allyn & Bacon, 1977.

Stewig, John. *Children and Literature.* Boston: Houghton Mifflin, 1982.

Sutherland, Zena, and May Hill Arbuthnot. *Children and Books.* Glenview, IL: Scott, Foresman, 1977.

Sutherland, Zena, ed. *The Best in Children's Books: The University of Chicago Guide to Children's Literature, 1966–1972.* Chicago: University of Chicago Press, 1973.

Terry, C. Ann. *Children's Poetry Preferences: A National Survey of Upper Elementary Grades.* Urbana, IL: National Council of Teachers of English, 1974.

Tiedt, Iris M. *Exploring Books with Children.* Boston: Houghton Mifflin Co., 1980.

Tucker, Nicholas, ed. *Controversies in Children's Literature.* Berkeley, CA: University of California Press, 1976.

Tway, Eileen, ed. *Reading Ladders for Human Relations.* 6th ed. Washington, DC: American Council of Education, 1981.

White, Mary Lou. *Children's Literature: Criticism and Response.* Columbus, OH: Merrill, 1976.

Wilner, Isabel. *The Poetry Troupe: An Anthology of Poems to Read Aloud.* New York: Scribner's, 1977.

PART VI: ISSUES

AND TEACHING

CHAPTER 13: Language Arts for Exceptional Children

OVERVIEW

This chapter discusses youngsters who are somewhat different from those for whom most instructional sequences are designed. It proposes ways to deal with the child with mild to moderate difficulties. The suggestions focus on what the classroom teacher—not the specialist—can do.

The chapter begins with a set of general guidelines for working with children who need additional or different instruction. Specific types of pupil differences are then discussed, including language variations, mental deviations, sensory handicaps, and health impairments.

A distinction should be noted here, however. Language diversity and bilingualism should not be considered in the same context with language arts problems arising from mental or physical handicaps. Linguistically different children are not deficient in linguistic skills. Their dialectal patterns diverge from the language of instruction, so they must learn English as a second language. Thus, though they may need special modes of instruction, their "exceptionality," unlike that of the physically and mentally handicapped, has environmental origins.

KEY VOCABULARY

exceptional	slow learners
language disadvantaged	sensory handicaps
ESOL	kinesthetic
bilingual	VAK
bidialectal	Gillingham method
articulation	mainstream
stuttering	IEP
gifted children	

GENERAL GUIDELINES

Most of the procedures and materials already recommended in this book can be effectively used with exceptional children when reasonable adjustments are made for particular difficulties. Individualizing instruction and de-emphasizing arbitrary age and grade standards will enable teachers to focus on each child's educational needs. The exceptional child's basic needs and goals are not very different from those of the "ordinary" child; however, the means of achieving those goals and fulfilling those needs are different. The following general guidelines apply to all learners, but they are crucial in teaching exceptional children.

1. The teacher's attitude toward a child is of paramount importance. Special children require much encouragement and understanding. Show that you are interested in these learners; talk with them about their interests; note what they have done; be friendly and encouraging. Each child's personal worth and mental health must be given primary consideration; in every way possible, assist the child to develop personally and socially, as well as academically.

2. Special children need to realize success in their undertakings. Progress charts are one visible way of making growth apparent. Compliment the child on gains made; indicate that each is competing with his or her own achievements rather than with others. Make every effort to build self-confidence and avoid frustrating situations that may aggravate learning problems.

3. Provide materials the child is capable of using as well as ones that are of interest to each individual. Carefully select what to use in initial instruction—usually concrete and firsthand experiences are safe beginning activities. Audiovisual materials can be very helpful. Do not use materials with which the child has previously failed. Become familiar with various instructional strategies and learn how to adapt them to each child's individual learning style. And don't overlook the power and usefulness of such things as television commercials, games, comic books, and other contemporary materials.

4. An extended readiness period is needed for each task. For the slow learner, many readiness activities are needed in preparation for manuscript writing. Activities that help to develop eye-hand coordination, such as construction with tools, drawing and painting, clay modeling, and coloring, are helpful.

5. One instructional item should be presented at a time. Instead of teaching "oral expression experiences" in a combined or unified manner, provide instruction about making introductions, then later about giving directions, and so on. For some exceptional children, instruction should

probably be more direct and more systematic than for the average child. Much instruction should be conducted with small groups or individuals. Proceed from the easy to the more difficult. For example, when teaching manuscript, the letters *o* and *c* might be presented first, followed by *l*, *i*, and *v*; then *b* and *f*; then *g* and *j*; and so on.

6. Expectations should be consistent with what children can realistically produce; for example, assign only five new spelling words per week for some children.

7. Frequent provision must be made for practice, review, and evaluation.

8. Attention should be given to seating (in terms of the chalkboard, the teacher's position, and lighting); special tables, desks, and other work areas may be required for some physically impaired children.

9. Thoughtful consideration must be given to the learning problems of each child. For example, if poor motor coordination is affecting a child's handwriting ability, he or she should be encouraged to produce large handwriting; in severe cases, it may be well for the child to use manuscript only. Due to the distinctness of the separate letter forms, manuscript style may also be most advantageous for the pupil with defective vision. For the brain-injured child, however, cursive writing is generally recommended by authorities.[1]

10. Sound teaching procedures should be utilized with all learners. Skills should be emphasized through actual application, not through artificial drills. Help the child see a reason for learning the skills. Moreover, use a variety of instructional procedures, corrective techniques, and materials rather than searching for one magic elixir.

LANGUAGE VARIATIONS

Language acquisition and development of the so-called typical child was outlined in Chapter 2. The variations that can occur among speech patterns have been discussed also (see the section on dialectal differences in Chapter 6). The term *linguistically different* is often used to label the child whose language varies from standard English.

---

1. Articles of the following nature are extremely valuable to teachers of special children: Virginia Cieslicki, "Working with Children with Handwriting Problems," *Academic Therapy* 15 (May 1980): 591–596; I. W. Hanson, "Teaching Remedial Handwriting," *Language Arts* 52 (April 1976): 428–431: L. K. Westbrooks, "More Prescriptions for Ailing Penmanship," *Teacher* 94 (March 1977): 59–62.

Linguistically Different Children

During the early years, a child may have had a lack of vocal stimulation, few experiences in conversation with verbally mature adults, and limited experiential contacts. Such a child will likely learn how to speak using different—not necessarily deficient—vocabulary and sentence structures: simple, monosyllabic words; infrequent descriptive or qualifying terms; simple sentences; and regionalisms, slang, and cant.[2] Such a child may deviate from standard English by speaking with nonagreement of subject and verb, sentence fragments, omission of some auxiliaries, and poor articulation of sounds.

This child should not be labeled as nonverbal, or verbally destitute, unless he or she truly has less language ability than other children. Sometimes children have an underdeveloped language ability because they do not have a fund of conceptualized experiences with which to verbalize certain meanings valued by schools. They usually express themselves well in unstructured, spontaneous situations and verbalize freely around actions and things they can taste, touch, smell, manipulate, see, and feel. (This is the way all children learn—by active encounter with things that make a difference to them.)

First, concern for such children must be focused on the child's self-concept. This is important in all teaching and learning situations, but it is crucial in the case of a child who may have acquired a poor self-image. Study of heroes' lives has been shown to help pupils gain a sense of their own worth. Thus the lives and works of heroes who interest children might well serve as subjects for oral and written compositions. Whenever possible, the interests of the child—sports, adventure, science fiction, or whatever—should be utilized.

Second, a listening climate should be established. It is most important that the teacher be a good listener to the child. Teachers frequently are guilty of half listening or ignoring what the child is trying to tell them, and this undoubtedly has an impact on the child's view of the importance of listening. (Read *Nobody Listens to Andrew* by Elizabeth Guilfoile.)[3] Listening attitudes and experiences must be put to use in the classroom through conversations among pupils, activities at the listening center, and teacher-pupil conferences.

Third, oral expression should be encouraged. Rich, concrete experiences, in which there is an explicit aim to name and to discuss, should be a major

2. Frederick Williams, ed., *Language and Poverty: Perspectives on a Theme* (Chicago: Markham, 1970); also see Judy I. Schwartz, ed., *Teaching the Linguistically Diverse* (Urbana, IL: National Council of Teachers of English, 1980).
3. Chicago: Follett, 1957.

factor in the language arts program. Particular provisions should be made for many speaking activities following each new experience. Role playing can be utilized in numerous ways. (For example, see Chapter 6 for the acting out of ideas.) Role playing is a good stimulus for discussion and appeals to children's love of action. They will enjoy talking about the scenes they have acted out or have seen other children dramatize. They find this exciting and are often keenly articulate in the discussion period that follows role playing. Later, the teacher may be able to arouse considerable discussion merely by reminding the children of the incident acted out on a previous occasion.

The school library can offer valuable services for the child. A library with a large collection of books representing a variety of subjects can satisfy the interests of every child. A good picture book collection is particularly valuable. Books with appealing illustrations and a brief, simple text can be introduced to children not yet able to read; this can encourage them to select books in the library to take to their classrooms for the teacher to read to the class or to small groups. The librarian can supplement books with filmstrips and films, storytelling, and recordings.

Bilingual Children

Some linguists use the term *bilingualism* to refer to a child who speaks two languages equally well. Others, however, consider the term more broadly to include bidialectal learners—those who speak two dialects of a language; in this view, the difference in proficiency between the two languages or systems is *not* considered. Using the broader definition, bilinguals in the classroom would include some children who speak very little English and others who speak English almost as well as their native tongue. In other instances, the child may actually be a monolingual, understanding and speaking only a native language (such as Spanish) upon entry into school. Bilingualism is especially prevalent in the large metropolitan areas, in rural areas of the Midwest and South, in five southwestern states, and in Hawaii. In some areas, bilinguals constitute nearly all the school population: the Puerto Rican districts in New York City; the Chicano sections in cities in the Southwest; and the Chinatown areas of New York City, San Francisco, and Los Angeles.

In 1968 Congress enacted the Bilingual Education Act (Title VII, ESEA—Elementary and Secondary Education Act). *Bilingual education*, as defined in the act, referred to education in two languages, one of which is English. The United States Supreme Court decision of *Lau Nichols* (1974) stated that any school district enrolling a minimum of ten students of limited English-speaking ability must consider offering a bilingual program. An integral part of bilingual education is *English for Speakers of Other Languages* (ESOL). Such a program seeks first to try to help students understand and speak oral English, then to read materials in English with comprehension, and finally to write in English.

Teachers must recall that their purpose is to introduce the children to a new language and culture, not to erase the old. This is expressed through encouraging the children to share their home and daily experiences as well as their personal interests and aspirations; providing books and other artifacts relating to the cultural heritage of the children; and involving parents and siblings in class activities.

All teachers ought to provide a good model in their own speech, encourage free expression, and demonstrate an appreciation of positive results. Much should be done to develop the child's ego strength through encouragement and praise, accepting the child's language and helping each see the importance of learning to use English in certain situations. The native language may remain the preferred language in many social situations.

English as a second language should be taught orally, informally, and in an atmosphere of play. The person responsible for such instruction may be the classroom teacher, a specialized teacher who works in different classes within the school, or a language specialist who travels throughout a school district. The spoken language is given primary attention, developed through the dialog, or conversation, approach and the story, or narrative, approach. In the dialog approach, the teacher explains a topic, models several times in conversation, and calls for the student to imitate, repeat, and memorize a correct line of the dialog, and then to apply the dialog utterance through role playing, improvisations, or questioning. The narrative, or story, approach involves telling a story, usually a traditional folk tale, in both first language and English; questioning the student about it; working intensively on parts of the story for the child to imitate and memorize; and then reviewing the entire story.

The child learns the language through specific techniques like telling stories; dramatizing stories; telephoning; playing sound and word games; using picture books, puppets, and toys; singing songs and saying rhymes; choral speaking; and conversing about classroom activities, news of the day, and personal experiences. In brief, language is taught to the child through many situations; it would be best to choose lifelike experiences. Many experiences (firsthand and vicarious) must be introduced prior to the child's reading and writing of English. In helping children become familiar with common words and their meanings, teachers may prepare lists of foods, animals, parts of the body, types of clothing, and words relating to the home, school, and neighborhood. The object and word should be associated wherever possible. Active words (*in, on, under, run, sleep*) may be dramatized, illustrated, and discussed. After the understanding of a stock of words has been developed, children should be given opportunities to read them in various contexts and situations. Field trips may also be used to enrich the children's concepts and vocabularies and to provide material for talking, reading, and writing. Experience stories and original stories may then be used to develop the other literary skills of reading and writing English.

Ideally, the teacher should know the native language of the children in the class in order to recognize possible trouble spots; at the least, they should be familiar with structural and pronunciation patterns of the first language. Activities to develop auditory discrimination would be based on awareness of the points of linguistic interferences and conflicts in sound and structure between the child's native language and English. (See, for example, the items about the Spanish language cited in Chapter 6.[4])

Some of the following ESOL series include workbooks and other related teaching materials for use with elementary school pupils.

Lawrence S. Finkel and Ruth Krawitz, *Learning English as a Second Language*, 3 levels, Grades 1–4 (Dobbs Ferry, NY: Oceana Publications, 1971).

Doris Kernan, *Steps to English*, 6 books, Grades K–6 (New York: Webster/McGraw Hill, 1975).

Thomas Lismore, *Welcome to English Series*, 5 books, Grades 3–8 (New York: Regents, 1973).

W. F. Marquardt et al., *English Around the World*, 6 levels, Grades 1–6 (Glenview, IL: Scott, Foresman, 1977).

Lars Mellgren and Michael Walker, *Yes! English for Children*, 3 levels, Grades K–4 (Reading, MA: Addison-Wesley, 1977).

Lois Morton, *Learning English as a Second Language*, 2 levels, Grades 4–8 (Dobbs Ferry, NY: Oceana Publications, 1976).

Ralph Robinett et al., *Miami Linguistic Readers*, 2 levels, 15 books, Grades 1–2 (Lexington, MA: D. C. Heath, 1974).

W. R. Slager et al., *Core English*, 4 levels, 4 kits, Grades K–3 (Lexington, MA: Ginn, 1972).

W. R. Slager et al., *English for Today*, 2nd ed., 6 books, Grades 2–8 (New York: Webster/McGraw-Hill, 1973).

4. Also see Raymond J. Rodrigues and Robert H. White, *Mainstreaming the Non-English Speaking Student* (Urbana, IL: National Council of Teachers of English, 1981).

Speech Impairments

Speech is considered deviant, according to one authority, "when it calls attention to itself, interferes with communication, or causes its possessor to be maladjusted."[5] Speech problems are considered to be a part of the more extensive category of communication disorders. Understanding the label, however, is significantly less important than understanding how speech difficulties may affect the development of language arts skills.

Basically, seven kinds of speech difficulties have been identified:

Articulation disorders
Stuttering disorders
Delayed speech disorders
Voice disorders
Cleft palate disorders
Cerebral palsy disorders
Impaired hearing and deafness disorders

In this chapter we shall highlight two of the most common speech disorders with which the classroom teacher must deal: articulation problems and stuttering problems.

Articulation Articulatory disorders are by far the most common type of speech disorder among schoolchildren and the type with which a classroom teacher can accomplish the most. Such a disorder is indicated when a child persists in one or more of the following practices:

Substitutes one sound for another ("wittle" for "little")
Omits a sound ("pane" for "plane")
Distorts a sound (the sounds of *s, z,* and *r* are the most commonly distorted ones)

Without being pedantic and without making the child self-conscious about speaking, the teacher should try to encourage distinct enunciation and pronunciation from the very start. Many of the deviant speech characteristics of five-year-olds have no organic or physical basis. Many are due to nothing more serious than immaturity and will disappear in time.

5. Charles Van Riper, *Speech Correction* 6th ed. (Englewood Cliffs, NJ: Prentice-Hall, 1978), p. 29.

The value of group instruction in providing speech practice and opportunities to hear accurate articulation has long been established.[6] The teacher of young children can make considerable use of rhymes, stories, and songs in group situations. More formal lessons, organized around the speech sounds that are most likely to cause difficulties, may be planned where observation indicates a need. Some of the most common error patterns can be readily identified by teachers who have trained themselves to listen; a teacher should listen for a child substituting *w* for *r* and *l* (as in *wed* and *wamp*), voiceless *th* for *s* (as in *thun*), voiced *th* for *z* (as in *thebra*), *f* for the voiceless *th* (as in *fumb*), *d* for the voiced *th* and *g* (as in *dis* and *det*), *b* for *v* (as in *balentine*), *s* or *ch* for *sh* (as in *soe* or *choe*), and *t* for *k* (as in *tandy*).[7] Every language experience may become an opportunity for informal speech development and improvement. For many children, a social situation where they are encouraged to talk freely can result in increased self-confidence and independence, reflected in rapidly increasing control of speech.

When a child continues to use substitutions, omissions, or distortions, the teacher must create exercises to sensitize the child's ear to the mispronunciation and provide a variety of opportunities to help the child practice the correct sound. For children who often misarticulate, the teacher should emphasize ear training—recognizing a sound and distinguishing it from other sounds. The teacher should explain how a sound is correctly produced, and the child should be encouraged to produce the sound correctly in isolation or in short simple words before being called upon to produce it in a consonant blend situation. The child should work on only one sound at a time and only at specific times. The child who is corrected constantly may begin to resent correction and become indifferent to sound.

Perhaps one of the most constructive steps the teacher can take is to help the child and parents develop healthy attitudes toward a speech handicap, relieving anxieties and tensions and enhancing the child's environment at school by improving the attitudes of peers. This may be more important than more formalized speech assistance.

Some articulation disorders are the result of neuromuscular or structural deviations, such as cleft palate, cleft lip, cerebral palsy, or extreme malocclusion of the teeth. Although children with these disorders may go to

6. A. T. Sommer, "The Effect of Group Training upon the Correction of Articulatory Defects in Preschool Children." *Child Development* 3 (June 1932): 91–107.
7. Margaret C. Byrne, *The Child Speaks: A Speech Improvement Program for Kindergarten and First Grade* (New York: Harper & Row, 1965).

a specialist for help, the classroom teacher still has the responsibility of working with the child during the major part of the school day. The teacher has an opportunity to assist the child in carrying over newly learned speech habits, that is, in integrating speech into normal and everyday activities. Classroom teachers who hope to be successful in helping these children must attend with special awareness to each child's particular speech needs.

Stuttering Stuttering is one of the most complicated and difficult of the speech problems. The stuttering child may have silent periods during which he or she is unable to produce any sound, or may repeat a sound, a word, or a phrase. He or she may prolong the initial sound of a word. Along with this, the child may show signs of excessive muscular strain, such as blinking the eyes.

It is normal for the child between the ages of two and six to repeat a sound, a word, or a phrase forty to fifty times in every one hundred words spoken. If no undue attention is focused on the child's speech during this period of nonfluency, maturation will usually make it possible to overcome repetition.

It is probably wise for the classroom teacher to face the problem of stuttering—when it appears in the classroom—in a rather indirect way. Help from parents in eliminating sources of tension is important. It is equally important for the classroom teacher to realize that there is no such thing as "perfect speech." In adult speech, many nonfluencies are accepted as normal speech.

The safest suggestion to the classroom teacher with regard to helping children who stutter is a general "don't." Do not ask them to stop and start over, to slow down, to speed up, to take a breath; this may only make them more concerned about the way they talk and may cause even more stuttering. Do not deny the right to read and recite in class as they choose—speaking should be made a rewarding experience for the pupil as often as possible. In fact, these pupils should be encouraged to talk and keep on talking even if they stutter. Help them to develop confidence in their speaking ability. As far as possible, treat these children as if they had no stuttering problem. Accept and react to stuttering as you would to normal speech; help the other members of the class develop this same attitude of acceptance.

Language Materials

Some frequently used materials for language and speech development are described here.

FIGURE 13.1: *Sample Distar Exercise*

Some, All, None

The children are introduced to the concept *some* incidentally before it is formally taught in the Distar Language I Program. They probably have an idea (but perhaps not a precise one) of what *some* means. Most of them probably know what *none* means. The teaching involved in clarifying the meanings of *some, all,* and *none* is not extensive. However, it is important.

The concept *some* is treated as an extension of what the children have already learned about *only.* First the children are taught the meaning of *all.* The statement "All of the candles are burning" means that every candle presented is burning. *Some* is a limitation of *all:* "Are all of the candles burning? No, *only some* of the candles are burning."

Presentations. The concepts *some, all,* and *none* are presented simultaneously. Presentation 168, Task 2, illustrates this type of presentation.

168   SOME, ALL, NONE
Praise the children for correct responses.
Correct mistakes immediately.

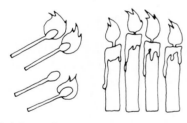

Task 2   Teaching Some, All, and None
Group Activity

a. Point. Are all the matches burning in this picture? *No.* Not all of the matches are burning. Only some of the matches are burning. Let's all say it. *Only some of the matches are burning.* Ask the children to repeat the statement.

b. Point. Are all of the candles burning in this picture? *Yes.* All of the candles are burning. Let's all say it. *All of the candles are burning.* Ask the children to repeat the statement.

Individual Activity
C. Call on individual children to do one of the following.
   Find the picture that shows none of the candles burning.
   Find the picture that shows only some of the matches burning.

Point. Are all of the matches burning in this picture? *Yes.* All of the matches are burning. Let's all say it. *All of the matches are burning.* Ask the children to repeat the statement.

Point. Are all of the candles burning in this picture? *No.* None of the candles is burning. Point to each candle and ask: Is this candle burning? *No.* None of the candles is burning. Let's all say it. *None of the candles is burning.* Ask the children to repeat the statement.

Find the picture that shows all of the candles burning.
Find the picture that shows all of the matches burning.
Find the picture that shows only some of the candles burning.

Source: Siegfried Englemann, Jean Osborn, and Therese Engelmann, *Distar TM Language I*, Book C—Part II (Chicago: Science Research Associates, 1971). Reprinted with permission of the publisher.

The *New Peabody Language Development Kits*, by L. Dunn and others. Circle Pines, Minn.: American Guidance Services, 1981. Four kits that emphasize sensation, expression, and conceptualization. Sensory experiences are provided that stimulate sight, hearing, and touch. Vocal and motor (writing) expression are encouraged. Exercises concentrate on intellectual development. The kits stress an overall oral program. No reading or writing is required.

New Distar Language Program, by Siegfried Engelmann and J. Osborn. Chicago: Science Research Associates, 1976. This instructional system is designed to teach basic language concepts. The program provides remedial work on language and communication skills through drill presentation in a logical sequence. The instructions for each lesson are outlined in detail. The teacher presents the task of the day, the children respond, and the answers are evaluated. The children who have performed well are rewarded with reinforcing take-home material. A representative exercise is presented in Figure 13.1. There is considerable controversy surrounding this program and similar compensatory educational materials. *Distar* is based on a deficit model of language development, a point of view not accepted by all educators. These same educators would also argue that the emphasis of these materials on rote drill and memorization is an unnatural approach to language instruction.

English Now, by Irvin Fiegenbaum. New York: New Century, 1970. Fiegenbaum's materials include workbooks, manuals, and cassette tapes. An oral approach is used in teaching standard English as a second dialect the same way English is taught as a second language. Sound discrimination drills are employed, as are identification drills and translation drills. The final drills deal with pronunciation of standard English.

MENTAL DEVIATIONS

Two extremes of mental deviation are considered in this section: the gifted child and the slow learner.

The Gifted Child

One of the ways in which brightness first becomes evident is through precociously early reading. Frequently, extremely bright children teach themselves to read without any formal instruction and often are able to read easily and independently those materials designed for beginning reading before they enter school. Studies show that approximately half of the children classified as gifted by intelligence tests could read at the kindergarten level, and nearly all of them at the beginning of first grade.

The gifted child usually is advanced in linguistic development. He or she is accelerated in use of and understanding of vocabulary, in maturity of sentence structure, and in originality of expression. Two studies have confirmed the fact that bright children tend to be ahead of others in the use of oral language.[8] In Loban's analysis of all forms of language used by a wide cross section of elementary school children, the highest correlation was between results of the Kuhlmann-Anderson intelligence test and an oral vocabulary test. Bright children, according to Strickland, use longer, more complex sentences and more mature expressions than do other children their age. Although all normal young children learn the language of their environment without formal instruction, the bright child learns the language faster.

Within the school setting, gifted children are likely to progress mentally at a rate of 1¼ (or more) years within one calendar year as compared to the average child who has one year of mental growth for each year of life. However, there are both "normal" achievers and underachievers among the gifted; they do not always demonstrate their potential. The following factors may interfere with the recognition of the abilities of the gifted— physical defects, emotional instability, and poor study habits.

Although each mentally advanced child is, of course, different, some characteristics common to most include:

Interest in books and reading

Large vocabulary, with an interest in words and their meanings

Ability to express themselves verbally in a mature style

Enjoyment of activities usually liked best by older children

Curiosity to know more, shown by using the dictionary, encyclopedia, and other reference sources

Long attention span combined with initiative and the abilities to plan and set goals

High level of abstract thinking

Creative talent with a wide range of interests

8. Walter D. Loban, *Language of Elementary School Children* (Urbana, IL: National Council of Teachers of English, 1963), p. 79; Ruth G. Strickland, "The Language of Elementary School Children," *Bulletin of the School of Education* no. 38 (Bloomington: Indiana University Press, 1960), p. 4. Also see R. C. Shepherd, "Oral Language Performance and Reading Instruction," *Elementary English* 51 (April 1974): 544–546, 560.

These advanced pupils have the same basic needs as all others in terms of acceptance, achievement, and affection. They need the same basic language tools as others but to a different degree and at different times. Gifted children need to work at their own levels regardless of other members of the class. Some teacher direction is needed, though advanced pupils are capable of directing many of their own activities. They are ready for long-term projects and should have the opportunity to pursue and broaden their interests and hobbies. They need to be encouraged to think critically. In attending to the special needs of a gifted child, the teacher must not overlook the overall development of the child, which includes being accepted by others and being able to interact effectively with others.

Within the language arts program, many opportunities can be found at every age level to provide for the gifted. One general approach would be to supply the classroom with a variety of books and allow the pupils to read widely.[9] Four follow-up techniques from this type of environmental setting might arise. First, storytelling to classmates and other classes, perhaps with suitable background music and sound effects, would be encouraged. Dramatization (perhaps puppet or shadow-play) of stories read would be utilized. Art and construction activities could also be utilized, such as making dioramas, illustrating favorite books, or making murals and posters about books. A literature club could be established in which pupils set their own goals and rules.

Special long-term enrichment projects may be developed throughout the school year. One example of such a project might be an in-depth study of the newspaper, the radio, television, or other communication media.

Special language arts bulletin boards (anecdotes, cartoons, news, reports, or word trees) and language arts displays (children's own poetry, creative writing) may be developed by the children themselves.

Other opportunities for the language-gifted may be categorized more specifically under oral and written composition, spelling, and handwriting. Each will be discussed briefly in turn.

Oral and Written Composition These expressive phases of the language arts, supported by a strong literature program, can provide many opportunities for the gifted child. Since output depends upon input, a stimulating environment of books in the classroom should aid immeasurably in providing the best possible learning situation. Library or trade books, encyclopedias, and general references dealing with mathematics, language arts, social studies, science, fiction, and poetry should be specifically selected

9. Michael Labuda, *Creative Reading for Gifted Learners* (Newark, DE: International Reading Association, 1974).

and maintained in the classroom library. Additional books should be provided in the centralized school library. Although the emphasis may be upon challenging the talented to do research for language arts assignments during the "language arts period," there is no need for study to be restricted solely in that direction. (Topics for supplemental research could include "What is the Newbery Prize?" "What are the names and uses of diacritical marks, and how did they come into usage?" What is the history of the word *shibboleth*?" and "What is Roget's *Thesaurus* and how is it used?") Pupils can be encouraged to maintain a notebook to hold the reports on these topics and to use the information should they be called upon for it.

In terms of listening, language-advanced children can be helped to refine listening comprehension skills, particularly those of the critical and creative levels. Additionally, their responses to listening experiences may be in a creative vein, such as drawing a cartoon to represent a story or writing a story or poem to accompany a piece of music.

As an outgrowth of a strong literature background, creative writing of prose and poetry deserves special consideration as a suitable activity for the language-gifted child. Capable of developing more comprehensive thought and expression than the average child, these children should be encouraged to note how other writers create word pictures and express their ideas effectively. A wide range of choice in vocabulary and variety in sentence structure should also be emphasized in original written composition. Some of their writing may relate to hypothetical situations, problems related to the natural or social sciences, or issues represented in children's literature. Formats may vary widely—from biographies to plays or scripts for radio or television presentation.

In word study, advanced exercises using a dictionary may be developed, covering topics such as synonyms and antonyms, derivation of words, "new" words, slang words, and etymology. Language games should be available for pupil use: Scrabble, anagrams, crossword puzzles, and the like. These children profit from experimenting with puns, playing charades with familiar clichés, and engaging in similar interest-cultivating word activities.

Spelling A number of specific suggestions may be offered to those interested in challenging the gifted pupil in the area of spelling: bonus words, maintenance of personal spelling lists, study of the history of words, listing rare or newly coined words, and spelling games.

Handwriting Books, films, filmstrips, and similar sources are valuable references for children who are interested in the study of handwriting.

Topics that can be introduced through these media include: history of handwriting; study of writing surfaces; production of newspapers, magazines, and books; history of handwriting instruments; writing letters to foreign correspondents; and comparing handwriting.

Additional Ideas Following are examples of the types of materials teachers may develop for enrichment purposes. Occasionally, there should be a discussion of the material prepared by children in response to the ideas. The discussion may be carried on with an individual or a small group.

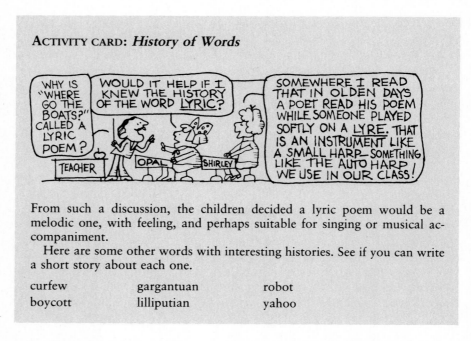

ACTIVITY CARD: *History of Words*

From such a discussion, the children decided a lyric poem would be a melodic one, with feeling, and perhaps suitable for singing or musical accompaniment.

   Here are some other words with interesting histories. See if you can write a short story about each one.

curfew	gargantuan	robot
boycott	lilliputian	yahoo

Pupil participation in the preparation of instructional materials often creates interest and understanding. It is desirable for children to select an idea that is best suited to their ability. Following are some topics for bulletin board displays:

Listening Games

Variations in Speech (lists of words associated with different dialects)

Anecdotes (for telling aloud)

Guess Who (riddles or illustrations about book characters)

WORKSHEET: *Language in Literature*

A. Do the following
   1. Go to the listening center.
   2. Read "The Pied Piper of Hamelin" by Robert Browning.
   3. Listen carefully to the record of "The Pied Piper of Hamelin."
B. Answer these questions and do these exercises
   1. What does *pied* mean?
   2. Who do you think the Pied Piper was?
   3. Why did the mayor "quake with consternation"?
   4. What do you think the Pied Piper looked like? The city of Hamelin?
   5. Choose four or five other children who have heard this record. Prepare a round-table discussion to present to the class on the topic, "Do you think the ending is happy or sad? Why?"
   6. Write a story about what you think the children of Hamelin found on the other side of the door in the mountain.

News
How to Give a Good Report
Creative Writing
Announcements and Reports
A New Word for Today (or a crossword puzzle)
My Best Handwriting

The teacher can use the language arts table to assist in differentiation of instruction by placing items like the following on it: poetry books, a daily journal maintained by the class, a story box for children's contributions, language games, and trade books about the study of language.

The Slow Learner

The primary characteristic of slow-learning children is that they do not learn as readily as others of the same chronological age. Slow learners are unable to make complicated generalizations and are usually unable to learn material incidentally without instruction. The slow learner needs systematically presented instruction.

Slow learners form 15 to 17 percent of the school population that cannot quite "keep up" and are usually doing the poorest work in the regular classroom. Slow learners are essentially normal in their emotional, social, physical, and motor development. In intellectual development, the slow learners are the lower range of the normal group.[10]

Children of low-normal ability (at the bottom range of normal performance) should be offered an extended readiness program, one that may last for as long as two years. Formal instruction per se should be introduced later, progress more slowly, and develop more gradually than is usually the case. Instruction should be planned with the understanding that the slow learner will stay in each stage of learning development longer than the average pupil. The slow learner will profit from using materials that do not have demanding vocabularies, and from repetition in the instructional program. A variety of teaching methods should be used to produce the best results.

Some pupils in almost every classroom (slow learners and others) are in need of special corrective or remedial instruction in the language arts; this need becomes particularly apparent during the intermediate school years.

The first major step would be the administration of a survey-of-language-arts test to all pupils in the class. The survey test should probably not be given until the third or fourth week of school in the fall. The results of the survey test should be examined in detail by the children. In individual conferences with the teacher, an effort should be made to determine why the overall score is low and why individual items on the test have caused difficulty.

After this analysis, the teacher could say, "Perhaps the results were not so good for several reasons. For example, you might have missed something in your earlier study. I have some other tests that may help in locating your difficulties more specifically." The teacher would have a number of tests dealing with specific skills, like listening, capitalization, punctuation, usage, vocabulary, spelling, and handwriting. A sample set of questions from a test dealing with punctuation is provided on the file card here. It can be seen that the items being tested involve four instances of use of the period: at the end of a sentence, after an abbreviation of the title of a person, after an abbreviation of the name of a business organization, and after the initials in a proper name.

Then, the teacher might say, "There are a number of these tests. You may start with any one, but as it is likely that you will want to take all or most of them, I suggest that you begin with the one on punctuation. Remember, you are taking these tests to find out what is causing your difficulty, so do your best, follow the instructions, and try each item, but do not spend too much time on any one item." At a later time, items

10. William C. Cruickshank and G. Orville Johnson, eds., *Education of Exceptional Children and Youth*, 3d ed. (Englewood Cliffs, NJ: Prentice-Hall, 1975), p. 202.

FILE CARD: *Punctuation Exercises*

These are exercises dealing with the period. Each sentence illustrates one usage of the period. Insert the needed period(s) for each sentence.

1. Bill is at his desk
2. Dr Jones is out of his office.
3. The Baker Co is located in Columbus, Ohio.
4. B F Brown is absent today.

missed on any test would be discussed with the pupil until he or she is aware of the difficulty.

For each test, there would be a package of follow-up materials and exercises. In introducing them to the children, the teacher might say, "These special worksheets may help you to get a better start in punctuation. Look them over and see whether you wish to work on some of them instead of the regular work." (These worksheets may come from workbooks, other textbooks, programmed materials, or teacher-made materials.) Samples of the types of exercise used on these corrective worksheets, for handwriting and punctuation, are presented here.

CORRECTIVE WORKSHEET: *Punctuation (Period)*

Doing this exercise may give you a new look at the uses of the period. Read each item carefully and think about what is called for before you mark or write.

1. Study each sentence below. Notice each circled period and try to figure out why it is used in each case.
   a. John is not at home.
   b. Mr. Brown is a very busy person.
   c. The Book Supply Co. is located in a large city.
   d. His name is R. T. Jones.
2. Is the period used in 1a at the end of a sentence? Place periods correctly in each of the following sentences.
   a. The skaters danced gracefully
   b. Cats like fish
   c. Bill is a good football player

Continued

3. Read aloud the sentences in 2. Did your voice drop at the end? Is that where you put a period?
4. Is the period used in 1b after an abbreviation of a person's title? Place periods correctly in each of the following sentences.
   a. Dr Jones is out of town.
   b. Mrs Brooks lives next door to us.
   c. The parade was led by Mr Davis.
5. Is the period used in 1c after an abbreviation of the name of a business organization? Place periods correctly in each of the following sentences.
   a. The Randolph Co makes many toys.
   b. Le Grand, Inc is the name of a large firm.
   c. Jim wrote a letter to Baxter Co for some materials.
6. Is the period used in 1d after initials in a proper name? Place periods correctly in each of these.
   a. G L Meers is our class president.
   b. Billy C Stone took a trip to Chicago.
   c. The book was written by T Robert Smith.
7. Place periods correctly in each sentence below.
   a. We saw some squirrels in the park
   b. The squirrels were eating nuts It was fun to watch them
8. Write four sentences to show the four uses of period studied on this worksheet.
9. Find examples of these four uses of periods in your reading material.
10. If you would like more work with using the period, see your language arts textbook, page _____.

The teacher must give frequent attention to pupils using corrective materials, get them started, discuss the materials, and encourage them as much as possible by showing an interest in what they are doing. Sometimes, the more able class members can successfully assist those engaged in corrective work. The pupils are encouraged to use special worksheets and to redo some worksheets several times. Some workbooks contain parts, though not specifically designed for corrective work, they may serve quite well for some deficiencies. Some programmed materials are also suitable.

Review procedures are utilized after intensive study of a particular topic in such a way that they can be of benefit to the slower learner. Sets of thought-provoking questions over the major topics of the year should greatly enhance a program of differentiation.

Corrective worksheet: *Cursive a*

1. Write this word and see how well you can make the *a*.

road

   a. Where does *a* begin?
   b. Is *a* closed or open?
   c. Is the upstroke retraced or looped?
   d. Does the concluding stroke sit on the baseline?
2. Make a row of *a*'s. Make each one look like the one at the beginning.

a

3. Look at the letters below.

a d o

   a. Are *a* and *d* the same width?
   b. What is the only difference between *a* and *d*?
   c. Write *a*, *d*, and *o* on the next line.

4. Write the words below, making good *a*'s.

draw gave

5. Write the sentence below, making your *a*'s correctly.

I had to read it again

6. Are you now making better *a*'s?
   a. Are you closing all your *a*'s?
   b. Are you retracing, not looping, the upstroke?
   c. Does the connecting stroke sit on the baseline?
   d. Do any of your *a*'s look like *o*'s, *u*'s, or *i*'s? (They should not.)

SENSORY HANDICAPS

Hearing-Impaired Children

The terms *hard of hearing* or *hearing impaired* applies to those whose sense of hearing is defective but functions for ordinary purposes, with or without a hearing aid. The older a child is when hearing becomes impaired and the more advanced the child's speech, the easier language learning will be. Of course, the extent of hearing impairment is also an important consideration.

Special arrangements within a classroom can often help hard-of-hearing youngsters. Such children should be seated near the teacher so that they have adequate opportunities to hear explanations and directions. Children who are hard of hearing should also be seated so they can see the teacher's face, thus increasing opportunities for lip-reading.

When new words are being presented, the teacher should stand so that the hard-of-hearing child can easily see his or her lips when a word is pronounced. Light should fall on the teacher's face; bright light behind the teacher can cause a glare in the child's eyes and shadow the teacher's face. After the child has watched the teacher pronounce a word, he or she should be shown the printed form of the word on the chalkboard.

Some children with impaired hearing may have trouble with spelling instruction. They will need to be shown how a sound "looks" on a person's mouth. A sight approach may be more effective than an auditory approach.

A teacher who has children with auditory difficulties should follow these five directions:

1. Speak slowly, clearly, and with adequate volume.
2. Seat the child as far as possible from distracting sounds.
3. Minimize the use of auditory channels in instruction.
4. Provide practice materials that have clearly written instructions.
5. Assign a "listening buddy."

Visually Handicapped Children

A *partially sighted child* is one whose visual acuity is better than 20/200 but not better than 20/70 in the better eye with the best correction available. Educationally, the partially sighted, or *visually impaired*, child is hindered, but is able to learn to read print, as opposed to the blind child, who must learn to read braille.

In general, the language of visually handicapped children is not deficient. The visually handicapped child's ability to listen and relate and remember

must be developed to the fullest. Several instructional ideas are proposed below for the visually handicapped child.

Manipulatives Children with limited vision gain knowledge primarily through touch and hearing, and should be presented with many concrete objects to touch and manipulate. Verbal explanations should often accompany tactile experiences, describing shape, size, weight, hardness, texture, pliability, and temperature. Many teacher-made boxes could abound in the classroom: a cloth box containing fabrics to develop concepts of soft, stiff, smooth, rough, silky, sticky, furry, thick, thin, hairy, or bumpy; a rock box; a shell box; a wood box; a sandpaper box; and a box of building materials such as brick, foam, plastic, sheet rock, rubber, metal pipes, and wiring. Other objects that could be used are tools of various trades—carpentry, automechanics, gardening, electrical, architecture, baking, and the like. Conversations based on shape, size, texture, and usage will help expand basic concepts and vocabulary. A great deal of verbal input is desirable; tape recorders are good for presenting information.

Additional Stimulation To expand the child's horizons, to develop imagery, and to orient the child to a wide and varied environment, stimulation must be provided. Mapping the classroom, the school, and, later, the community can help fulfill these needs. Trips and experiences about the school and the community are a natural base for writing experiences. The child should be permitted to dictate many of the stories, with the teacher or aide serving as transcribers; or the youngster can dictate into a tape recorder.

Reading Aloud This activity is one of the most rewarding ways to build listening skills in children. This is doubly true with the visually impaired child. Commercially prepared records are available in which well-known actors read aloud children's classics. Carol Channing reading the "Madeline" stories (Caedmon), Hans Conried reading highlights from *Treasure Island* (Literary Records), and Danny Kaye reading *Grimm's Fairy Tales* (Golden Records) and the *Winnie the Pooh* series by Sterling Holloway (Disneyland Records) are but a few of those available. Many children's picture books have been recorded by Columbia Records.

Tape Recordings Utilize sets of cassette tapes on listening skills (such as the ones developed by Dorothy Bracken and available from Science Research Associates). Other records of sounds are available: *Authentic Sound Effects* (Electra Records); *Sound Effects* (Audio-Fidelity); and *Sounds of My City* (Folkways Records).

Seating Location Children with impaired vision should be seated close to the chalkboard or wherever there is material to be studied. Many schools have large-type books (duplicated from original text or trade materials) for the visually impaired. Utilize manuscript writing.

Aids Encourage the child to use properly fitted glasses when reading.

Work Span and Variety Plan several short periods of close work (such as writing) rather than one extended period of continuous work. Provide active assignments of some kind after close work. Adjust length of assignment, if needed, and modify test situations (recorded, enlarged, orally given, and so on).

Lighting Adjust shades so there will be no glare on the chalkboard. Minimize the use of machines that utilize a lighted screen.

HEALTH IMPAIRMENTS

The physically handicapped child should be grouped with nonhandicapped children. Education of physically handicapped children (excluding those with cerebral palsy) is not as "special," from the teacher's point of view, as is the education of other types of exceptional children. The learning process is the same for the child who has been crippled by muscular dystrophy as for the child who is not crippled (although there may be extra psychological and emotional hurdles in the former case). Since each problem is different, only more general types of teacher modifications and aids can be suggested here. Ramps, elevators, sturdy equipment, hand rails, wide hallways, spacious classrooms, readily available lavatories, special chairs, cutout tables, book racks for those who cannot hold books, ceiling projectors for children in bed, cots for special rest periods, and so on can all be used to make the handicapped child as independent as possible.

ADDITIONAL METHODS AND MATERIALS

This section discusses special methods and materials for teaching exceptional children. The materials and methods apply mainly to reading and spelling.

Kinesthetic Method

The Fernald kinesthetic method[11] of teaching disabled learners a procedure based on tracing the shapes of letters in words, involves four developmental stages:

1. **Tracing:** As the child requests a word, it is written or printed with black crayon in large script on a piece of heavy paper. The child traces the word firmly with two fingers and says the word aloud in syllables as he or she traces. The process is repeated until the child can write the word correctly twice without looking at the sample. (After the lesson, the words are filed alphabetically, to provide a bank of the words learned.)

---

11. Grace Fernald, *Remedial Techniques in Basic School Subjects* (New York: McGraw-Hill, 1943): Also see Larry A. Gentry, "A Clinical Method in Classroom Success—Kinesthetic Teaching," *The Reading Teacher* 28 (December 1974): 298–300.

2. **Writing without tracing:** The child learns a new word by following the looking, saying, and writing steps of the first phase above, but the tactile step is discontinued.
3. **Recognition of printed words:** The child learns a new word merely by looking at the sample and saying it.
4. **Word analysis:** In the fourth phase, the child is able to recognize new words by their similarity to words or parts of words that he or she has already learned.

VAK (Visual-Auditory-Kinesthetic)

This method by Gillingham and Stillman[12] is based on the theoretical work of Orton.[13] In this program, the children learn both the names of the letters and the sounds of the letters. Sounding is used for reading, but letter names are used for spelling. The student moves from learning the names of letters to learning the sounds of letters, to reading words, sentences, stories, and finally to reading books. Teachers are urged by Gillingham and Stillman to follow the teacher's manual provided in the program. This system stresses auditory discrimination with supplementary emphasis on kinesthetic or tactile experiences. Visual perception is used minimally.

Other Sensory Methods

Montessori The sensory approach has been advocated by Montessori[14] and many other educators. The basic procedure involves some system of color cueing for vowels, consonants, and sight words which must be memorized. Words may be traced over, used orally in a sentence, visually studied, traced, and sounded out, until the word can be spelled and written independently.

Phonovisual This phonetic system provides direct training in visual and auditory discrimination.[15] Wall charts are used to introduce consonants

---

12. A. Gillingham and B. Stillman, *Remedial Training for Children with Specific Disability in Reading, Spelling, and Penmanship* (Cambridge, MA: Educators Publishing Service, 1970).
13. Samuel Orton, *Reading, Writing and Speech Problems in Children* (New York: Norton, 1961).
14. Maria Montessori, *Spontaneous Activity in Education* (New York: Schocken Books, 1965).
15. Lucille D. Schoolfield and Josephine B. Timerlake, *Phonovisual Method* (Rockville, MD: Phonovisual Products Co., 1960).

and vowels orally. The introduction of consonant and vowel sounds is well organized and pictures on the charts provide the pupil with familiar visual images to associate with the letter sounds.

Visual A method based on Getman's theory of spelling as visualization trains for visual memory.[16] The pupil repeatedly traces over a word on the chalkboard, saying the name of each letter while tracing it. Tracing in the air with eyes closed continues until the child thinks that he or she can "see" the word in the mind.

THE MAINSTREAMED EXCEPTIONAL CHILD

Mainstreaming—integrating handicapped with nonhandicapped children —is "the law of the land" now. We will summarize the implications of the legal mandate for mainstreaming and then show how mainstreaming can work in language arts programs.[17]

Education of All Handicapped Children

Public Law 94–142 (Education for All Handicapped Children Act of 1975) involves the following rules or regulations:[18]

1. All handicapped children (ages three to twenty-one) will be provided a free and appropriate public education in the "least restrictive environment." This means that handicapped children should be educated with nonhandicapped children "to the maximum extent appropriate." Mainstreaming will depend on the type and severity of the child's handicaps.
2. Testing and evaluation materials used for the purposes of evaluation and placement will be selected and administered so as not to be racially or culturally discriminatory. Such materials or procedures shall be provided and administered in the child's native language or manner of communication. The tests and other evaluation material shall have been validated and will be administered by trained personnel. The tests shall be tailored to assess specific areas of educational needs and must

16. G. N. Getman, *Developing Learning Readiness* (New York: McGraw-Hill-Webster Div., 1968).
17. Appreciation is extended to Dr. W. Jean Schindler, College of Education, The University of Tennessee, Knoxville, for preparation of this section.
18. Information summarized from *Federal Register*, November 21, 1975; and *Federal Register*, August 23, 1977.

not reflect the child's impairment except when those particular skills are the factors being measured by a test. No single test or evaluation materials shall be used as the sole criterion for determining the appropriate educational program. The child is to be assessed in all areas related to the suspected disability. The evaluation is made by a multidisciplinary team (M-team), including at least one teacher or other specialist with knowledge in the area of the suspected disability, along with, possibly, administrators, school psychologists, counselors, health agents, medical personnel, and so on.

3. Placement of children in the least restrictive environment must be based on the student's Individual Educational Plan (IEP). The IEP—written by members of the IEP committee, usually including a regular classroom teacher and a special education teacher—follows a format such as the following:

   a. The child's present levels of educational performance, including academic achievement, social adaptation, prevocational and vocational skills, psychomotor skills, and self-help skills

   b. Annual goals, which describe the educational performance to be achieved by the end of the school year under the child's individualized education program

   c. Short-term instructional objectives, which must be measurable intermediate steps between the present level of educational performance and the annual goals

   d. Specific educational services needed by the child, including a description of all special education and related services that are needed to meet the unique needs of the child, including the type of physical education program in which the child will participate, plus any special instructional media and materials that are needed

   e. The date when the services will begin and length of time the services will be given

   f. The extent to which the child will participate in regular education programs

   g. The type of educational placement the child will have

   h. The individuals who are responsible for implementation of the individual education program

   i. Objective criteria, evaluation procedures, and schedules for determining, on at least an annual basis, whether the short-term instructional objectives are being achieved

4. Due process procedures are clearly stated, and pertain to identification, evaluation, and placement. Parental consent must be obtained prior to formal evaluation and parents must be informed of their rights to be informed of results of their child's evaluation and how they will be

involved in developing their child's IEP. These procedures include the parent's or guardian's right to examine all relevant records and to present complaints with respect to any matter related to the identification, evaluation, or educational placement of the child. Parents must "fully understand" all releases that they agree to sign.

In addition, the Buckley Admendment (Educational Aid 464, 1974) prohibits "the release of a student's records without parental consent" and provides that all information obtained in a parent interview for background information about a child must be kept confidential. Parental permission must be secured to record the interview through audio- or videotaping or to have others present at the interview.

Examples of case studies and IEPs for several students are provided in Sandra B. Cohen and Stephen P. Plaskon's *Language Arts for the Mildly Handicapped* (Columbus, OH: Merrill, 1980).

Mainstreaming in Language Arts Programs

Language arts education is possibly the most important area of academic skill learning for the exceptional pupil. In this area many professionals prefer the term *communication arts* and usually include reading as one of the skills to be learned. Oral language, writing, spelling, and listening skills are prerequisites for many basic life functions and are, therefore, necessary for exceptional children as well as "typical" students.

Teachers who are involved in working with a handicapped child in the mainstreamed setting face a very difficult task. They must work with a large number of average learners.

Often they wish to individualize instruction, but find it difficult because of the limited amount of time and large number of children involved. Often they feel they must finish all books and curriculum guides in the system for their grade level; in fact, this is often expected by supervisory personnel. The added weight of working with exceptional students can sometimes prove to be an overwhelming burden.

What can the general educator do to alleviate this problem and still maintain reasonable standards for instruction? In resolving this problem, a number of more specific questions need to be asked.

1. *Does this child need this skill at this time?* Why? Is there something else more basic to his or her life that is needed? For instance, children need to dress themselves, feed themselves, ask questions, and so on, before they need to spell.

2. *Am I the person who should teach or reinforce the skill?* If I don't teach the skill, who will?
3. *How is this skill best taught to this child?*
4. *What will I need to know, what equipment will I need, and what prerequisite skills must the child have in order to obtain the skill I've chosen to teach?* For instance, a child who is mentally handicapped or learning disabled can only tolerate the presentation of about 2 to 5 percent of unknown items at a time. This suggests that typical spelling lessons will not work. Also, words we expect the child to spell must be in the child's vocabulary for a considerable period of time. We don't spell words we don't use.
5. *Where is the best place to teach this skill?* This question can be asked about the curriculum and the actual physical location.
6. *When* is another important question to ask. Some handicapped children work best in the afternoon. When can also refer to later in the school year. Even if the child needs a skill, but lacks the prerequisites, now is not the time to teach that skill.

To answer all these questions, there must be communication between the general educator and the special educator. These two individuals should work closely together to maximize the child's potential without duplication of efforts. It is important for the generalist to understand the projected learning potential of the handicapped child. Most people expect too much. For instance, an educable mentally retarded child with an IQ of 70 cannot be expected to have two- and three-year academic growth spurts. Academically, it is very doubtful that the child will ever work close to chronological age level. The child may, however, with good instruction, be able to work up to 70 percent of that expectation.

Achievement test scores in and of themselves do little to aid the teacher in preparing for the handicapped in the classroom. Individual items on such a test may be valuable in helping the teacher identify exact skills needed.

Good listening skills should have the highest priority for most handicapped youngsters. Most normal adults appear to have difficulty when required to listen closely and to comprehend what is heard. Auditory stimulation programs are available and resource room special educators should make them available to the generalists. Use of pre-made cassettes, head sets, and records can help to develop auditory skills and can do much to provide for individual needs.

A second priority is that of developing and extending oral language. Children must make their wants and needs known. Many handicapped children have difficulty expressing themselves, and general educators may hesitate to make oral language demands of them. They *should* be asked to explain, describe, infer, and question, and to make value judgments. Being able to ask for help, to use a telephone, and to listen to and answer questions are important basic life skills that need to be fostered.

As the child develops the ability to answer questions and to ask them orally, he or she usually becomes ready to respond to written questions and answers. The third priority, therefore, is writing. Creative writing is not as important, however, as utilitarian writing skills. The filling out of forms needs to be stressed very early.

The child needs to be able to write simple letters of inquiry or business. These become another priority area, as does interviewing. The generalist can interview children for classroom jobs, thus training them in listening to questions and categorizing their own information, and providing them experience with a basic life skill. Identifying basic life skills or needs of the handicapped is important for all the teachers responsible for their education.

The following ideas are proposed as a start in considering this topic:

1. The interests of exceptional children need to be fully utilized. If a child is interested in a particular topic (animals, pets, hobbies, games/sports, or the like), then he or she will make the effort to master the language arts skills in order to learn about the topic.
2. Instruction must be tailored to meet the needs of the individual child. Some criterion-referenced tests with accompanying guides to sets of material for follow-up instruction include:
   a. General: *The Brigance Diagnostic Inventory of Basic Skills* (K–6) (Woburn, MA: Curriculum Associates, Inc., 1976).
   b. Handwriting: *Barbe-Lucas Handwriting Skill Guide Check List* (Readiness through Grade 8) (Columbus, OH: Zaner-Blozer, Inc., 1978).
3. Skills to be taught must be related to the learning characteristic and potential of the child. Use of learning center materials (such as "Special Needs Learning Centers" available from Curriculum Associates) and special language arts kits or packaged materials that are multileveled may be helpful. Different approaches and materials will be successful with different pupils.
4. The language arts activities should be as highly motivational as possible. Activities, games, audiovisual materials, and the like may assist.
5. The help of parents of children in corrective/remedial situations should be sought. Parents can be of most assistance through helping the child maintain an optimal state of physical health; attending to the child's emotional health by providing an atmosphere of security and support;

surrounding the child with conversation, listening, reading, and writing opportunities; becoming familiar with the child's language arts program; and discussing the child's language arts program with the teacher or teachers.

6. Teachers in many states are required to take an introductory course in the education of exceptional children. Although it usually is very general in nature, it does help one to know and understand the terminology and kinds of questions to ask. Additional courses may be available that deal with diagnosis and correction of classroom language arts problems.

As teachers gain skills in working with special children, they will learn how to make the language arts special for all children.

THOUGHT QUESTIONS

1. What are some important instructional ideas that should be kept in mind in terms of the language-different child? the bilingual child? the speech-handicapped child?
2. How may the instructional program be adjusted for (a) gifted pupils and (b) slower learners?
3. What are some desirable instructional modifications for children of impaired hearing or limited vision?
4. How do you, personally, feel about mainstreaming? Do you react to the legal mandate reluctantly or as a challenge to your teaching abilities?

LEARNER RESPONSE OPTIONS

1. List the ten general guidelines given in this chapter in order of importance in your opinion. Be prepared to justify your reasoning.
2. Visit a classroom. Which specific types of exceptional children are in evidence? Compare your judgments with those of the teacher.
3. Examine an elementary school language arts textbook. What provisions are made for different instruction for the gifted and the slower learning child?
4. Find a book you think would appeal to an exceptional child. Plan how you would present it to the child, along with several activities for sharing the book with others. See George D. Spache, *Good Reading for the Disadvantaged* (Champaign, IL: Garrard, 1974).

5. Talk with a speech correction teacher about the role of the regular classroom teacher in assisting children who need special speech help.
6. Prepare a language arts activity for a gifted child or group of children.
7. Sketch a bulletin board plan for a group of language-gifted children.
8. Design a corrective worksheet for a child needing special help with numeral formation.
9. Prepare an analytical test and some follow-up exercises for a technical language skill.
10. If feasible, examine some of the materials cited in the section on materials. Report to the class on possible uses.

REFERENCES AND ADDITIONAL READINGS

Anastasiow, Nicholas J. et al. *Language and Reading Strategies for Poverty Children*. Baltimore: University Park Press, 1982.

Birch, Jack W. *Mainstreaming: Educable Retarded Children in Regular Classes*. Reston, VA: Council for Exceptional Children, 1974.

Cheney, Arnold. *Teaching Children of Different Cultures in the Classroom: A Language Approach*. Columbus, OH: Merrill, 1979.

Coble, Charles R., et al., *Mainstreaming Language Arts and Social Studies*. Santa Monica, CA: Goodyear, 1976.

Cohen, Sandra, and Stephen Plaskon. *Language Arts for the Mildly Handicapped*. Columbus, OH: Merrill, 1980.

Geyer, James R., and Joseph Matanzo. *Programmed Diagnosis and Prescription for Teachers*. Columbus, OH: Merrill, 1977.

Hammill, Donald D., and Nettie R. Bartell. *Teaching Children with Learning and Behavior Problems*. 2d ed. Boston: Allyn & Bacon, 1978.

Hansen-Krening, Nancy. *Competency and Creativity in Language Arts: A Multiethnic Focus*. Reading, MA: Addison-Wesley, 1979.

Joyce, William W., and James A. Banks. *Teaching the Language Arts to Culturally Different Children*. Reading, MA: Addison-Wesley, 1971.

Kirk, Samuel A. and James J. Gallagher. *Educating Exceptional Children*. 3d ed. Boston: Houghton Mifflin, 1979.

Knight, Lester N. *Language Arts for the Exceptional: The Gifted and Linguistically Different*. Itasca, IL: Peacock, 1974.

Laffey, James, and Roger Shuy. *Language Differences: Do They Interfere?* Newark, DE: International Reading Association, 1973.

Marcus, Marie. *Diagnostic Teaching of the Language Arts*. New York: Wiley, 1977.

Markhoff, Annabelle Most. *Teaching Low-Achieving Children Reading, Spelling, and Handwriting*. Springfield, IL: Thomas, 1977.

Otto, Wayne, and Richard A. McMenemy. *Corrective and Remedial Teaching*. 3d ed. Boston: Houghton Mifflin, 1980.

Thomas, Janet K. *Teaching Language Arts to Mentally Retarded Children*. Minneapolis: Denison, 1971.

Turnbull, Ann P., and Jane B. Schultz. *Mainstreaming Handicapped Students: Guide for Classroom Teachers*. Boston: Allyn & Bacon, 1979.

PROFESSIONAL ORGANIZATIONS FOR THE EXCEPTIONAL

Alexander Graham Bell Association for the Deaf, Inc.
3417 Volta Place
Washington, DC 20007

American Association on Mental Deficiency
5201 Connecticut Ave. N.W.
Washington, DC 20015

American Foundation for the Blind
15 West 16th Street
New York, NY 10011

American Speech and Hearing Association
9030 Old Georgetown Road
Washington, DC 20014

National Association for Creative Children and Adults
8080 Springvalley Drive
Cincinnati, OH 45236

National Association for Retarded Citizens
2709 Avenue East
Arlington, TX 76010

National Center on Educational Media and Materials for the Handicapped
Ohio State University
220 West Twelfth Ave.
Columbus, OH 43210

CHAPTER 14: Classroom Organization and Management

OVERVIEW

Classroom organization and management is the factor that makes good teaching and the use of materials and equipment productive in providing appropriate learning opportunities for children. This chapter discusses patterns for organization and management, factors affecting organization and management, and the role of parents and paraprofessionals in the school. The goal is to provide information and activities that will enhance children's learning.

KEY VOCABULARY

self-contained

intraclass

interclass

achievement grouping

special skills or needs grouping

interest grouping

pairs or partners

individualized instruction

departmentalization

team teaching

open curriculum

observational rating scales

paraprofessionals

Organizational and management patterns

There are several reasons for considering alternative organizational and management plans. First, modern technology makes it possible for teachers to serve in new roles. Second, numerous self-directing materials are available that allow children to move at their own rates and in their own styles. Third, diagnostic and prescriptive instruction based on objectives and individual needs is now possible because of the first two changes. A fourth reason for using alternative patterns is based on research findings that children learn best when the size and description of the group changes according to the subject to be taught and the children's individual needs.

Before discussing specific patterns, some general guidelines for organization of the classroom should be considered.

1. No single classroom pattern or structure is better than another; the local situation, the strengths of individual teachers, and the abilities of the children involved will help dictate the best system for a particular school.
2. Many criteria should be considered in deciding on a particular organizational plan; results of informal and formal tests, children's interests, and specific goals of instruction are but a few.
3. Patterns should be flexible and should be altered as better ways are discovered.
4. There is no absolute criterion that states the proper size for groups within a class. Corrective or remedial work usually requires small groups; the number involved may be greater when children can assume considerable responsibility for independent work.
5. Children learn from one another; opportunities to share within a group are basic to good instruction.
6. Organization and management provide only a framework or a system, not a "method of instruction." They can only facilitate or hinder effective instruction.

In this section, we will discuss two major patterns.

Self-contained classroom patterns

In many schools, teachers and principals have chosen to use a self-contained organizational pattern. This means at the beginning of the school year a principal (perhaps with grade-level teachers) organizes the children

by grade level and divides them into teachable groups either by achievement and individual personal needs or by random selection.

Because of the vast differences in ability and achievement among pupils, teachers need to group and regroup their children during the school year. There are two basic plans in general use: intraclass (within the class) and interclass (between classes).

Intraclass Grouping

Criteria for grouping children may be achievement, skills, interests, or any combination of the three.

Achievement Grouping Placing children in reading groups based on ability (high, average, and low) is an almost universal practice, but the same grouping for the other language arts is far less common. Subgroups of this nature (*achievement grouping*) have not met the different needs of children; most often pupils remain rigidly in their assigned groups and the same material is used with each member of the group, even though there is undoubtedly a diversity of abilities within any one group. Table 14.1 suggests an achievement grouping.

Total class activities may include participating in dictionary activities, reviewing skills taught to each group earlier, reading aloud to the class by the teacher or children, sharing newspaper reports, choral reading, dramatization, participating in library activities, and the like. Independent work may include doing practice exercises and playing language arts skills games; library reading provides time for recreational reading or research activities.

If there has been a mistake in an original placement, if a child has a sudden spurt of growth, or if a child's growth pattern slows down, the teacher should promptly place the child in another, more appropriate group. Grouping should always be flexible. A single grouping pattern is often misused; instead of forming a flexible schedule, rigid groups will be maintained for as long as an academic year. This can cause damaging stigmas to be attached to children in the lower groups. By using flexible grouping for other subjects during the day, the low-group stigma can be avoided because usually a child will excel in one or two other areas. Also, once the children have been grouped for instruction, the teacher must remember that within each group are many differences that need special attention.

TABLE 14.1: *A General Plan for Grouping Within the Classroom*

	Group A	Group B	Group C
10 min.		Total Class Language Arts Activities	
30 min.	Teacher-directed activity	Independent work	Library reading/ research
30 min.	Independent work	Library reading/ research	Teacher-directed activity
30 min.	Library reading/ research	Teacher-directed activity	Independent work
10 min.		Total Class Language Arts Activities	

Note: The table suggests that all groups possess the same ability to work independently. In actual classroom situations, there may be a need for more teacher-directed activities for the slower learning group(s).

The following is a variation of an ability, or achievement, organizational plan. It is designed for a seventy-five-minute language arts session in the fifth grade where four groups and several individuals are at work at the same time.

Group 1 (Low-ability group): A group of six children will meet with the teacher for help with using commas. The teacher will use compositions that have been saved to help the children identify mistakes and will reteach a lesson on the use of commas.

Group 2 (Average-ability group): Five children will write business letters, the form for which was taught previously. They are choosing from a list of companies provided by the school librarian and are writing for free materials for a unit of work.

Group 3 (High-ability group): Three children will be organizing the material collected in a class literary box for use in the publication of the monthly class newspaper. As soon as the material has been arranged by category (stories, cartoons, sports, editorials, and so on), they will begin to read and edit the material. Two other children in this group are working together on writing a script for a play to be presented at a program for the third grade.

Group 4 (All-ability-level group): Eight children will work on corrective exercises provided by the teacher on punctuation. Each of these is different from others and comes from a file of skills which is arranged sequentially from easy to difficult and is prepared in such a fashion that the children can do the exercises independently.

Individual work: One average-ability child is preparing a book report to be presented to the entire class on the following day. Another above-average-ability child is writing a poem for the monthly calendar. Three low-ability children are practicing handwriting skills by copying some letters from a corrective sheet prepared by the teacher. One low-ability child is taking a diagnostic test prepared by the teacher to identify capitalization skills.

One teacher's initiation of achievement-level grouping illustrates certain features considered desirable. Initially, the pupils work together on the same or common topic, eventually selecting their own work; this reduces the stigma and feelings of resentment of being with a particular group. The materials used avoid those designed for use in much earlier or later years of schooling. It is necessary for the teacher to produce considerable supplementary materials appropriate to the abilities of the children. The possibilities for using this plan are evident in every facet of the language arts field: oral composition, literature, written composition, usage, and spelling.

After a few days of studying oral composition, a sixth-grade teacher of a small group of gifted children said, "We had such a great time listening to the Halloween stories told by the storyteller at assembly last Friday, I thought that perhaps you'd like to learn how to tell stories yourself. You should work on such items as speech patterns, outlining a story, organizing events in sequence, making a good beginning, and using interesting words. Here is a special worksheet that suggests some advanced, independent exercises and activities. Look at it to see if you want to do the exercises now or whether you first want to become more familiar with the ideas suggested in our textbook about storytelling." After examination of the worksheet and the book exercises, the teacher said, "I'm going to work the first part of the period with those interested in the textbook exercises. If you wish to work with me, put the worksheet in your folder. You may want to try it later. Those wishing to work with the worksheet may proceed." An example of one of these worksheets is provided here.

For a part of the period, the teacher may discuss these projects and ideas with interested children. It may be suggested that although they are not required to attempt all the items on the worksheet, it is desirable to do so. Children should be complimented on good work and their efforts often shared with the entire class. After two levels of work (average and advanced) have been fairly well established, the third or fourth level should be added for particular phases of the topic under consideration for the slower achieving children.

Special Skills or Needs Grouping This arrangement involves putting together children who need work on the same skill. After introductory study of a new language arts concept or idea, additional follow-up will likely be needed. At this point, instructional strategies may involve the use of small skills groups or needs groups. For example, an intermediate grade teacher has received a set of written compositions. The teacher bases the next day's lesson on these corrections, making a list of the following items:

1. Weaknesses in ideas, organization of thoughts, use of descriptive words or phrases, revision, and proofreading
2. Errors in capitalization, punctuation, sentence sense, or paragraph sense
3. Spelling difficulties
4. Usage problems
5. Handwriting deficiencies

To this list would be added the names of class members, indicating who

WORKSHEET: *Becoming a First-Rate Storyteller*

1. You and a friend record your pronunciation of these words with a tape recorder. Then listen to the tape, noting differences in pronunciation.

again	depths	governor	poetry
arctic	dictionary	height	probably
attached	drowned	hollow	pumpkin
burst	elm	lion	rinse
creek	evening	memory	such
crept	every	numerator	tune
deaf	family	partner	vanilla

2. List five words you have read or heard that are rarely used today. How many picturesque words have you encountered recently? List five.

Old Words	Picturesque Words
Example: fetch	bookworm
_____	_____
_____	_____
_____	_____
_____	_____

3. Listen to the record story of *The Hundred Dresses* by Eleanor Estes. Note the voice patterns. Then tell the portion of the story you liked best to a friend, trying to keep your voice flexible.
4. Work with a partner and develop a pantomime of Robert Browning's "The Pied Piper of Hamelin."
5. Prepare a short speech on different ways of "talking."
6. Prepare a favorite fairy tale (for example, "The Princess on the Glass Hill") to tell to a small group.
7. Prepare a story (for example, one of Aesop's Fables or one of the *Just So Stories*) to tell to another class member.
8. Give an oral review of a movie or TV program to a partner. Ask your partner to use the checklist on the language arts table for evaluation. Then listen to his or her performance and evaluate it.

had difficulty in the above items and which items were general for the class.

Interest Grouping This arrangement is formed on the basis of friendship or common interests and is recommended for certain language arts activities. The degree to which a group develops the ability to work together determines its learning of the tasks assigned. Teachers need to be cautious when using interest groups because some individuals might be interested in the topic but lack the basic knowledge to be a contributing individual to the task development. One solution may be to have groups within interest groups, which allows for individual differences. Interest groupings are recommended for such language arts activities as creative writing, producing a class newspaper, or completing study exercises. Skills instruction for children of similar abilities can still be presented at other times.

From temporary interest groupings, more formal and longer term groups often evolve (for example, library groups, choral groups, dramatic clubs, readers' theatres, and book fair groups).

Pairs or Partners This grouping permits students to work cooperatively on such activities as spelling, dictionary practice (location of words, location of definition that fits the context, and the like), solving crossword puzzles, and language arts games. Partners may work better on skill tasks if they have about the same degree of language ability and if they are congenial. The directions for a paired task must be clear, the task specific, and the time limited to that needed for the task just as with the other types of grouping.

Such intraclass groupings have several advantages. They capitalize on the kind of plan that provides opportunities to correlate language arts instruction with other content areas and to use the interrelationships that exist among the language arts. Also the children have the opportunity of choosing or being placed in a variety of group situations, and recognition is given the fact that some things are best learned in groups and others on an individual basis.

Interclass Grouping

An integrative arrangement, this type involves parallel scheduling of language arts lessons among several sections of a grade or grades. Groups divided according to general language arts level go to different rooms (or spaces within an open classroom). Different teachers provide instruction for each ability group. This kind of grouping is based on the assumption that the range of skills that need attention will be limited by the needs of a particular group and will be reduced for each teacher. Evidence indicates, however, that the range of skills in such situations is not appreciably lessened.

For such grouping to be homogeneous, knowledge of many criteria is needed. Each student's achievement levels, intelligence, interests, preferred learning modality, and academic motivation should be discovered. Interclass grouping tends to ignore age and maturity differences, sometimes combining pupils from several grade levels. Often it tends to separate language activities from instruction in content areas.

Individualized Instruction

An individualized classroom would be represented by all pupils working on individual assignments, much like the Individually Prescribed Instruction (IPI) program for spelling.[1] IPI was begun in Pittsburgh in the midsixties in an attempt to prepare an individualized program of instruction for each child. This is an expensive approach, involving preliminary evaluation of performance and diagnosis of specific needs of pupils in terms of abilities and skills. The steps in the continuous program involve: placement ⟶ unit pretest ⟶ prescription ⟶ instructional activities ⟶ scoring of work ⟶ unit posttest ⟶ demonstration of mastery ⟶ next unit pretest.

The instructional units are arranged in convenient skills boxes. These boxes contain student skill booklets, answer keys, and teacher packages containing testing materials and a guide. This individualized program relies on self-help and self-corrective instructional materials. Programmed materials provide avenues for individualization.

Even though the idea of totally individualized instruction (all children working alone at their own rate and ability) is appealing, the reality of providing such instruction is generally overwhelming to many teachers, so they utilize a partially individualized plan.

Two frequently used plans implemented within the language arts classroom to aid individualization include the use of learning centers and the language arts contracts. Each will be explained in turn.

Learning Center It is often necessary to supplement the language arts program with additional skill development activities. The teacher can identify skill needs of children, then prescribe activities for additional practice to be done in a learning center. These types of centers can also be used conveniently to provide the resources and motivation for extensive reading for information and enjoyment. A successful learning center contains these four components:

1. Philadelphia: Research for Better Schools, Inc., in cooperation with the Learning and Development Center, University of Pittsburgh.

Self-direction for the child

Provision for different ability levels

Stated objectives for each specific skill with a sequence of tasks from easiest to most difficult

Clearly defined means of evaluation

A brief list of the types of language arts stations applicable in the classroom include:

Library corner for reading

Center for creative drama or puppet shows

Listen and read centers

Oral reading with partners or on tape

Language experience (writing) centers

Language arts game centers

Centers for skill development using worksheets, tapes, activity cards, or folders

Project centers for research purposes

To assign children to stations, you might consider some of the techniques others have found successful: listing assignments on the chalkboard or a chart, listing assignments on duplicating paper, discussing assignments orally, giving tickets for the various stations. Teachers have found many ways of establishing learning centers. Screens, bookcases, corrugated cardboard boxes, portable chalkboards, and filing cabinets are but a few of the possibilities for dividers and center walls. One example of recording a child's work at the center is shown here.

ACTIVITY: *Learning Center Record*

Name _____

I worked at the _____ center or station.

Time in _____ Time out _____

How did you like the work? _____ (Good, Fair, Poor)

Continued

Activity

I read _____
I worked on _____
I listened to _____
I read aloud with _____
I wrote _____
I played a language arts game _____
I also _____

There are many references that deal with learning centers. Among them are:

Frances Bennie, *Learning Centers: Development & Operation* (Englewood Cliffs, NJ: Educational Technology Publications, Inc., 1977).

Howard E. Blake, *Creating a Learning-Centered Classroom* (New York: Hart, 1976).

June Crabtree, *Learning Center Ideas* (Cincinnati, OH: Standard, 1977).

Tom Davidson, *Learning Center Book* (Salt Lake City, UT: Goodyear, 1976).

Kasper N. Greff and Eunice N. Askov, *Learning Centers: An Idea-book for Reading and Language Arts* (Dubuque, IA: Kendall/Hunt, 1974).

Hiram Johnson et al., *Learning Center Ideabook: Activities for the Elementary and Middle Grades* (Boston: Allyn & Bacon, 1978).

Sandra Kaplin et al., *Change for Children* (Pacific Palisades, CA: Goodyear, 1980).

George W. Maxim, *Learning Centers for Young Children* (New York: Hart, 1976).

John E. Morlan, *Classroom Learning Centers* (Belmont, CA: Fearon, 1974).

Jimmy E. Nations, ed., *Learning Centers in the Classroom* (Washington, DC: National Education Association, 1975).

Gary T. Peterson, *Learning Center: A Sphere for Non-Traditional Approaches to Education* (Hamden, CT: Shoestring, 1975).

Susan S. Ptreshene, *A Complete Guide to Learning Centers* (Palo Alto, CA: Pendragon House, 1977).

John I. Thomas, *Learning Centers: Opening up the Classroom* (Boston: Holbrook, 1975).

Language Arts Contract Some teachers find that they are able to provide assignments and tasks by negotiating them with individual pupils. The agreement may be formalized through the use of a contract that is signed by the teacher and the child, as shown in Chart 14.1. The contract simply states what the pupil is to do and when the task is to be completed. Once agreed upon, the contract should be completed as specified.

CHART 14.1: *A Sample Pupil Contract Form*

Primary level

1. In magazines find 5 pictures of things that move or "go" (such as a car).
2. Draw 5 pictures of things that "go."
3. Write 5 words that tell the name of things that "go."
4. Find 5 things in the classroom that "go." Put a tag on each.

I will do _____ and _____ for my contract.
My name _____ Today's date _____
Teacher's name _____ Due date _____

Intermediate Level

After reading about Paul Bunyan:
To learn more about tall tales, read about one of the following:

A. 1. Pecos Bill
   2. John Henry
   3. Tony Beaver
   4. Old Stormalong
   5. Mike Fink or John Darling

Share your research one of these ways:

B. 1. Compare the character with "The Bionic Woman" or "Grizzly Adams."
   2. Make a drawing or a model of the hero.
   3. Illustrate an incident in the story.
   4. Make up your own tall tale character and write a brief story of his or her feats.
   5. Write a play or a poem dramatizing one incident.

Choose one topic from A and one method from B for your contract.
I plan to do A _____ and B _____. I will have this contract completed by _____.
Student's signature _____
Teacher's signature _____

A teacher can prepare and have available contracts calling for a variety of assignments and tasks. From these, pupils can select those most appropriate to their needs, or a pupil can propose a new contract and negotiate it with the teacher.

A modification of the contract plan is sometimes called the "assignment" or "job sheet." In making such a sheet, the teacher first identifies a definite instructional goal—for example, the mastery of a specific skill or subskill—and then organizes available material (textbooks, workbooks, and so on) so that the learner is guided toward that goal. Each child can proceed as fast as mastery permits. At times, children can work in pairs or teams of three to complete the assignment, which may take from three to five class periods.

SCHOOLWIDE ORGANIZATIONAL AND MANAGEMENT PATTERNS

Elementary schools often have patterns of organization that cross grade levels and/or also combine several classes at one grade level. There are two major reasons for such organizational patterns. One, teacher strengths can be utilized, making planning easier and more concentrated. Two, children can have more individual help because small groups or individualized instruction can be given to those who need it, whereas those children who can work independently can be placed in larger groups or work on their own. The following discussion of schoolwide organizational and management patterns will provide you with basic ways for developing them.

Nongraded

A nongraded class incorporates pupils of a wider than usual age span with a wide range of academic performances. For example, if there are ninety children of the ages six, seven, and eight years (traditionally first, second, and third graders), ten from each age level might be randomly selected to form a class of thirty pupils; thus, three nongraded classrooms can be produced instead of one first grade, one second grade, and one third grade. The children may continue with the same teacher for as long as three years. Sometimes this pattern is called a multiple-graded or leveled or continuous-progress pattern. Individual differences within a nongraded class may be no greater than those in a single grade situation. In such a situation, again it is possible to group by specific skills and according to maturity and needs. Nongraded classes can provide for differing pupil

rates of growth by directing the teacher's attention toward the need for individualization of instruction.

Departmentalization

This has seemed to be on the increase in the past few years, particularly in the middle schools. Departmentalization suggests a separate teacher for each subject, such as one teacher for the language arts program, one for the social studies program, one for the science program, and so on. Under a departmentalized plan of teaching, a teacher may teach the same subject for five to six classes a day, with one period free or devoted to giving individual help. Some correlation between language arts and other subjects is possible when one teacher works as part of a team with another, such as the social studies teacher. In such a case, the two subjects can be scheduled to be taught back to back, and the two teachers can make use of a large block of time. Within the allotted time, many types of teaching and grouping can take place. The skills of one subject can be used to complement or develop the content of another subject; for example, since the children in social studies will need to know how to do research, the language arts teacher can focus on how to use reference materials. The major advantage of departmentalization is that the greater the teacher's understanding of a subject the greater the possibility for excellent instruction. The greatest disadvantage is probably that departmentalization tends to make the curriculum subject-centered rather than process- or child-centered.

Team Arrangement

This involves combining two or three classes in one large area with a staff of several teachers. Team teaching has developed from the belief that all teachers are not equally skilled or enthusiastic in all curriculum areas. One teacher may instruct the entire class or a group in a language arts area of his or her particular competence while others work with other groups or individuals on other subjects. The team situation can offer a variety of activities in the best possible circumstances. For example, it enables diagnosis of the language deficiencies of a child and grouping of the child with other children who have the same problem. It allows one teacher to give undivided attention to that group with no interference from the rest of the class, while another teacher works with a group on a poetry unit, an activity he or she likes very much. Still another teacher might work with a group planning a book fair, while another teacher helps some children with a particular language arts difficulty. On other days, the teachers can work with the same children but on different problems or on the same problems with different children.

Open Curriculum

With this approach, modeled on the British infant and primary schools, classrooms are usually divided into separate areas, often called interest or learning centers.[2] These areas, such as science, art, and language arts learning centers, are filled with related learning materials. For example, the language arts center might have word games and books designed for a variety of reading levels. Children actively engage in planning their activities and usually work independently or in small groups. A basic tenet of open classroom philosophy is that children learn language arts skills in a "natural" way, as they learn about other subjects, and at their own

2. See Evelyn B. Rothstein and Barbara K. Gold, "Reading in an Open Classroom—Extending the Gifted," *The Reading Teacher* 27 (February 1974): 443–445; and Roberta Wiener, "A Look at Reading Practices in the Open Classroom," *The Reading Teacher* 27 (February 1974): 438–442.

pace. Therefore, skills are not programmed according to a predetermined sequence. The language-experience approach is often used in an open curriculum during the primary years. Children's compositions are also used as instructional reading material. Temporary groups are often formed around common interests, and individual and small-group conferences are part of the instructional plan. Dewey's concept of exploration,[3] Montessori's focus on extensive use of objects and games and instructional materials,[4] Rousseau's faith in the child's natural curiosity and growth,[5] and Piaget's idea that children learn in varying stages through direct experience[6] are all roots of the program.

The following example illustrates one way of grouping in an open curriculum in terms of language arts skill development.

A teacher gives diagnostic tests to check language arts skills of all the children in one section of the classroom. Diagnostic testing is this teacher's particular job, while other teachers in the unit are taking the responsibility for different assignments. As part of this diagnostic job, this teacher also groups the children according to skills difficulties and then divides these groups into subgroups according to general ability. When a group of children have difficulty in handwriting, the whole multi-aged group is provided with appropriate instruction. As some tasks require subgroupings because of the nature and difficulty of the task, the teacher subdivides a group that has special problems with spelling. Thus, the teacher sets up two (or more) groups divided as to achievement level because the task is affected by the difficulty of the material.

As soon as the groupings have been determined, the teacher reports his or her plans to the other teachers in the unit, and a schedule is set up for meeting with various groups in quiet places to work on their specific problems. The schedule for special help is posted on a common announcement board or given to each person concerned on a dittoed schedule. Children plan their day's work and are responsible for being in the right place at the right time.

Too often, an open environment exists only in the physical arrangement of the classroom rather than in the operation of a flexible educational program.

---

3. See John Dewey, *Experiences and Education* (New York: Macmillan, 1938).
4. See John McVey Hunt, *Revisiting Montessori: Introduction to the Montessori Method* (New York: Schocken Books, 1964).
5. See Jean Jacques Rousseau, *Emile, Julie, and Other Writings*, ed. S. E. Frost, Jr., and trans. R. Archer (Woodbury, NY: Barron's Educational Series, 1964).
6. See Jean Piaget, *The Language and Thought of the Child* (Cleveland, OH: World, 1955).

AFFECTIVE DIMENSIONS

Three affective dimensions or emotional aspects of learning are discussed in this section: interests, attitudes, and self-concept.

Interests

The teacher must know the specific interest of each pupil and how these interests can be used to encourage full participation in the language arts activity. From such data, the teachers may direct the learner within the various areas of the language arts, particularly in speaking and writing opportunities. Interest is often the key that unlocks effort.

One of the ways of studying children's interests is through observation in daily class contacts. The teacher notes the books the students choose to read, their eagerness to talk about certain topics, their desire to write about topics.

More detailed information may be obtained from an interest inventory. An inventory should include both general interests and language arts interests. A sample inventory is shown on page 477.

As suggested throughout the preceding chapters, the list of ways to promote interest in the language arts include:

Oral reading of stories, books, and poems by the teacher and by the pupils. (See the literature chapter for some excellent collections of children's stories and verses.)

Audiovisual materials to supplement instruction

Special resources to supplement the basic language arts program (books about special groups, such as Eileen Tway's *Reading Ladders for Human Relations*, 6th ed.,[7] and children's paperbacks and paperback book clubs, as cited in the literature chapter)

Children's trade books that focus on language arts topics (as suggested in Chapter 2)

Attitudes

Classroom teachers should be sensitive to the probable causes of likes and dislikes of language arts. It is important to consider attitudes toward language arts since there is a relationship between attitude and achieve-

7. Urbana, IL: National Council of Teachers of English, 1980.

GENERAL AND LANGUAGE ARTS INTEREST INVENTORY

Name: _____   Grade: _____
Age: _____   Sex: _____

General Interests

1. What do you like to do in your free time?
2. What are your favorite TV shows?
3. What are your favorite hobbies?
4. What games or sports do you like best?
5. What clubs or other groups do you belong to?
6. Do you have any pets? If yes, what?
7. What are your favorite types of movies?
8. What is your favorite school subject?
9. What is your most disliked school subject?
10. What kind of work do you want to do when you grow up?

Language Arts Interests

1. What things do you like to read about?
2. Which comic books, magazines, newspapers do you read?
3. Do you like to read books about language (history, printing, alphabet, word origins, dictionary, word play, etc.)?
4. What topics do you like for oral expression activities?
5. What topics do you like for written expression activities?
6. What types of language arts games do you enjoy (listening, vocabulary, spelling, etc.)?

ment; that is, good attitudes or feelings about language arts enhance achievement, and, in turn, good achievement enhances better feelings about language arts. David Krathwohl and others classify attitudes,[8] or the affective domain, into several main levels, and describe how to recognize each stage. Note that the first three levels listed here are most appropriate for the elementary school years.

1. **Receiving (attending):** The student is at least willing to hear or study the information.
   a. Can perceive the language concepts.
   b. Will read on occasion, particularly on a topic of interest

---

8. David Krathwohl et al., *Taxonomy of Educational Objectives, Handbook 2: The Affective Domain* (New York: McKay, 1964), Appendix A, pp. 176–185.

  c. Wishes to identify what he or she does not understand in language arts
2. **Responding:** The student will respond about the material being studied.
  a. Completes language arts assignments
  b. Makes an effort to figure out words and to understand what he or she reads
  c. Seeks out opportunities to read about word origins, or solves a word puzzle
3. **Valuing:** The student has a commitment to what is being learned and believes it has worth.
  a. Will voluntarily work to improve language arts skills
  b. Chooses language arts activities when other activities are available
  c. Uses spare time on language arts activities

Behavior can be measured by observational rating scales scored by the teacher. The preceding levels of attitudes can be developed into a chart by listing the levels and then grading each by categories of attainment, such as A for Always, B for Often, C for Occasionally, D for Seldom, and E for Never. A chart for each child will be needed; it can be designed for use throughout the year by providing enough blanks for four evaluations.

Attitudes can be measured by other methods also. These include a self-evaluation inventory for children to use, essay questions, multiple-choice and standard-scaling-type items.

Of these methods, probably a simple oral or written self-evaluation inventory will be the most satisfactory. Elementary age children are very honest, and if they are allowed to express their true feelings, they can provide a good basis for understanding how and what they are learning. The other methods do well with advanced or older children. Chart 14.2 is an example of a self-inventory that can be presented orally or can be answered in written form.

The inventory in Chart 14.2 can be presented orally to primary age children and in printed form to intermediate age children. The results should be tabulated for the group as a whole as well as individually. Teachers will learn how well they are teaching spelling at the same time children are learning how well they are learning to spell. The results need to be analyzed individually with children to help them understand their strengths and weaknesses.

In addition, teachers might try a multiple-choice questionnaire with items like this: I like spelling because (1) it is fun, (2) I can use it to write, (3) it is easy, (4) I do not like spelling. Or give a completion test, using this statement: Spelling is _____ because _____. An adjective checklist could be developed using the words *fun, hard, easy,*

CHART 14.2: *Self-evaluation Inventory*

Directions:
Make a mark in the column that identifies your feelings about spelling.

Always   Sometimes   Never

Always	Sometimes	Never	
___	___	___	1. I enjoy learning to spell new words.
___	___	___	2. Spelling lessons help me understand how a word is spelled.
___	___	___	3. I need to practice learning to spell words everyday.
___	___	___	4. Copying the spelling words five times each helps me remember the word.
___	___	___	5. I enjoy dictation of spelling words.
___	___	___	6. Learning to spell words is hard work.
___	___	___	7. I learn to spell more words when words that are alike are taught.
___	___	___	8. I use my spelling skills when I write creatively.
___	___	___	9. I learn how to spell words in reading class.
___	___	___	10. If I don't know how a word is spelled, I can think about it and spell it.

boring, and *worthless.* The child would describe the different aspects of spelling by circling the appropriate word, and could write a paragraph telling of his or her feelings about the subject.

Although the authors recognize the possible limitations of these examples of attitude probes, it is nevertheless necessary for teachers to learn children's attitudes toward the topics, materials, learning activities, and teaching strategies involved in the study of language arts.

The various uses that may be made of the results of informal probes include identification of major topics and procedures of interest to children, utilization of highly stimulating learning experiences and teaching strategies with areas of study where negative feelings are evident, and determination of topics or teaching and learning procedures where attitudes and interests may need expansion.

Self-Concept

The teacher should become a careful observer of students' behaviors. The following questions can serve as a checklist during language arts activities. (A substantial number of "Yes" responses should be considered a matter of concern.)

Does the student:

1. Frequently make negative comments about himself or herself?
2. Frequently avoid working with peers?
3. Usually avoid working with peers and vice versa?
4. Often ridicule peers and vice versa?
5. Constantly seek attention?
6. Seldom volunteer?
7. Compulsively seek information concerning progress?
8. Rarely seek information concerning progress?
9. Frequently manifest negative nonverbal behavior (nail-biting, facial expressions, and the like)?
10. Often set goals that are not within his or her ability to attain?

Additional information concerning the child's self-esteem can be obtained from conferences with parents or with former teachers. At the intermediate level, the teacher may consider administering a self-concept scale, such as "How I See Myself" by Ira Gordon, reproduced in C. M. Charles, *Individualizing Instruction* (St. Louis: C. V. Mosby Co., 1976).

After evaluating self-concept, the teacher should use activities that will build self-esteem. Here are a few suggestions:

1. In every possible way, help the child to feel accepted by the teacher. A definite relationship exists between the teacher's attitude toward a child, as perceived by the child, and the child's self-concept. One of the best ways to make a child feel accepted is to share his or her interests, utilizing them in planning for language arts instruction. Accept the child's contribution to an activity even if it is a faltering contribution.
2. Provide the child with feelings of success by providing activities that are simple enough virtually to guarantee their satisfactory completion. Providing children with assignments geared to their level and directing them toward obtainable goals will give opportunities to achieve success.

3. Avoid comparing a child with other pupils. Rather, compare progress with his or her own previous work. Private records of books read, skills mastered, or words learned are much preferred over public records when one child consistently compares unfavorably with others.
4. Minimize the differences between language arts groups to avoid giving the child the idea that unless one is a member of the top group one is a less worthy human being. Avoid comparisons and competition among groups and vary the bases on which groups are formed.
5. Give opportunities to hold individual conferences with the learner. These one-to-one experiences can be used to diagnose strengths and weaknesses, to teach needed skills, and to engage in conversation. They are also a time to ask specific questions about the child's favorite hobbies, sports, television programs, movies, magazines, and comic books.
6. Utilize *Reading Ladders* (see footnote 7) to improve human relations in areas such as creating a positive self-image, living with others, appreciating different cultures, and coping with change.
7. Utilize parents and properly trained paraprofessionals to stimulate positive growth. The next section of this chapter is devoted to these important people.

PARENTS AND PARAPROFESSIONALS

Parents

Among the traditional methods of communication between teachers and parents are newsletters (carefully written letters and bulletins to keep the parents informed about happenings at school); school booklets (including rules and regulations and helpful information that parents need to know before and after sending their child to school); Parent-Teacher Association meetings; written reports in the form of a personal letter or checklist; telephone calls; social or covered-dish suppers; home visits (which give the parents and teacher a chance to discuss a particular problem and acquaint the teacher with the home environment of the child); and open house (a day when the parents visit in the classroom—with or without the presence of the children—to familiarize themselves with the materials, schedules, and routines of the school day). For years, schools have utilized these methods to foster communication between school and home.

Many avenues are open to the language arts teacher who wishes to communicate with parents. For example, one can suggest general and specific activities for the children to do at home; hold conferences about reporting devices, tests, and homework; or send out letters or bulletins to keep parents informed of what is going on at school.

Home Activities As noted in an earlier chapter, oral language has been initiated long before children come to school. Much of this development is due to parental language stimulation. Parents have provided for their children many experiences that develop concepts and words, and they have encouraged verbal interaction. Parents who read a lot, have plenty of reading materials around the home, and talk about materials read provide a role model that is important to language acquisition and development. Parents who share experiences with children, listen to them, and talk with them are providing a good background for language arts instruction. When parents need information about providing desirable experiences for children, the following suggestions may be offered:

1. Provide and share experiences with younger children through short visits to nearby stores, recreation centers, and public services like a fire station or water plant. Answer children's questions and explain the meanings of words used to talk about the experiences. As children become older, trips might involve visits to the museum, zoo, or art gallery. Longer trips provide opportunities to broaden the child's knowledge about roads, mountains, rivers, and surrounding cities.
2. Read to the children. Stories and poems help to provide experiences that contribute to language arts learning. Concepts are formed, information is provided, and the listening vocabulary is increased. As children talk about the stories and poems, ask questions, and dramatize or retell them, oral language is strengthened. Trips to the public library would be a natural part of these experiences, and children should be encouraged to make use of the library facilities.
3. Listen and speak with the children in meaningful ways. Through hearing parents speak, children can gain much information and learn many words and grammatical structures. Conversational skills, as noted in an earlier chapter, are developed when practiced in this natural way. Parents and children may converse throughout the day about food, clothing, games, pets, or the weather. As children help about the kitchen, parents and children have many opportunities to discuss items related to the kitchen. By working with parents in a vegetable garden, the children can share an enjoyable experience while many questions are answered and the meaning of new words are explained.

The foundation for all learning experiences must rest within a home environment wherein the children feel secure, are given encouragement, and are provided wholesome food and adequate rest.

The teacher and school could sponsor workshops, give demonstrations or in other ways assist parents to guide their children in such ways as to promote language arts growth. Some topics for consideration might include:

1. What we know about how children learn language (emphasizing individual differences and levels of development)
2. The importance of self-concept in language arts learning
3. The use of games in the language arts and making homemade games for children
4. Using the mass media for enhancing language arts learning—the library, television, radio, newspaper, movies.

Reports, Tests, and Homework The report card is a report to parents and children about the child's performance in school. There are additional facts, however, that teachers want parents to know about their children and the school program that are not included on a report card.

To prepare an individual report or to hold a parent-teacher conference, the teacher needs a folder of work samples. In addition to the child's work samples, classroom charts giving information on weekly test scores or other achievement records should be kept.

With regard to parent-teacher conferences, many schools schedule three conferences per year—around the last week of November, the first week of February, and the second week of May. Frequently, a standard form is utilized at this conference, on which comments about the child's personal and social growth and progress in the various academic subjects are entered. A record may be maintained of main points discussed with parents, conclusions reached, and recommendations by the teacher and the parents.

At the November conference, the language arts materials used in school may be presented to the parents, as well as an explanation of the language arts experiences, abilities, and skills to be emphasized that particular year. Some explanation may be given about how the language arts program is organized and the general approaches the teacher uses. At this time, some idea of what (if anything) will be required of the child in terms of homework may be suggested, as well as what to do when the child requests help.

In an early parent meeting, the teacher also might suggest supporting materials, such as language arts games (homemade or commercially produced) and trade books that present language arts concepts.

The February conference may consist of sharing children's work and test results (textbook, teacher, standardized). When a standardized language arts test has been administered, it is usually a good idea to report the results to parents. The range, the median score of the class, and the individual pupil's score are considered to be essential information to give to the parents. In parent-teacher conferences, test results provide some tangible information for discussion. Furthermore, this type of information is relatively free of teacher bias and therefore lends itself well to discussion of problems. In these parent-teacher conferences, teachers should attempt, just as in discussion with pupils, to give parents a true picture of the test results and their implications.

The teacher should explain why and how he or she is attempting to help when particular difficulties of the child are brought up in discussion. Interested parents may request additional ideas to use with their child for reinforcement purposes.

The final conference is often more of an evaluation session. Again, the child's progress since the last conference is reported, along with possible ideas and suggestions for summer activities. Parents should have the opportunity to ask questions and to find ways they can be of help.

Homework certainly involves the entire family. When homework assignments are made, they should be carefully planned, with the pupils motivated to complete the assignment. Most homework should be of an informal nature, supplementing formal preparation in the classroom, and should only be made after children understand the concepts and ideas sufficiently to do the homework unaided. Most homework assignments should be personalized—with little or no regularly assigned, drill-type homework for the entire class.

Letters and Bulletins Teachers should recognize that the report card or the teacher-parent conference are still only two means of interpreting the child's interaction with the school language arts program. Another means is a simple progress report, containing news the children bring home in their own handwriting. For example: "Everyone in the first grade can write the numerals to 10." A school or districtwide pamphlet on "Our Language Arts Program" may meet a common need and be more efficient than a teacher's individual efforts. Some teachers provide a letter with each report. Topics suitable for bulletins or letters include:

How parents can help in building language arts concepts prior to school entrance

How new language arts experiences are introduced in the classroom

An illustrative lesson taught in the classroom

Explanation of various modern procedures

How fast and slow learners are managed in the language arts classroom

Paraprofessionals

There is a growing use of adults as paid or volunteer assistants to the teacher. Programs involving adult assistance take many forms: working with an individual or small groups while the teacher conducts a lesson for the rest of the class; tutoring after school hours; and helping with clerical work, marking workbooks, making displays or other audiovisual materials, and performing many other tasks inherent in the operation of the classroom.

Many teachers have reacted positively to this new source of assistance. When aides are used to assist in instruction, it is apparent that they need some professional training in how to relate to children positively, how to teach a simple skill, and how to judge pupil progress. Under the best conditions, the role of the paraprofessional in the language arts classroom can be that of an instructional aide as well as a clerical aide. Basically, the classroom teacher is responsible for the activities the aide performs; the teacher is also responsible for preparing the aide to carry out these activities. Supervision of the aide is mandatory, and the teacher assumes the major responsibility of this supervision. Assuming the paraprofessional is a capable and responsible person, the following items suggest some areas where he or she may be of assistance within the classroom.

Score teacher-made tests or worksheets
Work with small groups or individuals on particular language arts skills
Read to large or small groups
Set up and use audiovisual materials (transparencies, charts, posters, tape recorders, projectors)
Prepare instructional materials, such as word files, skills boxes, and so forth
Arrange for guests to speak to the class
Assist in planning and supervising field trips
Work with small groups in instructional games
Assist children in the use of reference materials
Set up displays and bulletin boards
Develop and set up learning center activities
Assist in maintaining records that evaluate pupil progress

In addition, student aides or tutors (older students helping younger students) have been used during the past decade with varying degrees of success. Where most successful, extensive preplanning has been involved and special attention has been given to attitude and approach, orientation to the program and materials, a clear-cut plan of organizational structure and supervision, and record-keeping procedures.

SOME INSTRUCTIONAL CONCERNS

One problem that frequently occurs is that organization rather than individual needs determines the type of instructional program provided children. In selecting an organization, whether for a whole school or for a classroom, the first step is to analyze the needs of the children to be taught. The second step is to analyze the strengths and weaknesses of the faculty, and the third is to analyze the attributes of the building. After all these factors are analyzed, an organization may be selected to provide the means by which the children will learn best.

Classroom management techniques may also cause the same type of problem. Before establishing what type of classroom management is to be used, determine how children are to participate in the program both physically and verbally. When you have determined the children's involvement in their learning, reward them for their success.

THOUGHT QUESTIONS

1. What are some advantages of interclass grouping?
2. How may language arts instruction differ in organizational plans, such as nongraded, departmentalization, team teaching, and open curriculum?
3. Why should interests, attitudes, and self-concepts be considered within the language arts program? How may these affective dimensions be assessed?
4. How may the language arts be interpreted to parents?

LEARNER RESPONSE OPTIONS

1. Talk to at least two teachers at different levels to determine how they organize their classes during formal language arts instruction. If possible, find out why they use the plan.
2. In small groups, discuss the advantages and disadvantages of the proposed organizational plans. Try to sketch the physical layout of a classroom of your choice.

3. Interview a child of the age level of your interest. Seek to determine his or her general and language arts interests.
4. If feasible, use one of the affective domain devices with a child, small group, or class.
5. Prepare a letter or bulletin to parents on one of the suggested topics.
6. Talk with a paraprofessional about his or her role in the language arts program. Share your findings with members of the class.

REFERENCES AND ADDITIONAL READINGS

Blitz, Barbara. *Open Classroom: Making It Work*. Boston: Allyn & Bacon, 1973.

Johnson, David, and Roger Johnson. *Learning Together and Alone*. Englewood Cliffs, NJ: Prentice-Hall, 1975.

Smith, James A. *Classroom Organization for the Language Arts*. Itasca, IL: Peacock, 1977.

APPENDIX A: CHECKLIST: Qualifications Needed by Language Arts Teachers

| | Degree of development | | | |
| | *Not developed* | | | *Highly developed* |
Qualification	1	2	3	4

KNOWLEDGE Teachers of English need to know, and how to draw on for their teaching, according to the needs and interests of their students:

1. Processes by which children develop in their ability to acquire, understand, and use language, both oral and written, from early childhood onward

2. The relationship between students' learning of language and the social, cultural, and economic conditions within which they are reared

3. The workings (phonological, grammatical, semantic) and uses of the language in general and of the English language in particular; and the processes of development and change in language

4. Linguistic, rhetorical, and stylistic concepts that furnish useful ways of understanding and talking about the substance, structure, development, and manner of expression in written and oral discourse

5. The activities that make up the process of oral and written composing (these activities may differ among different students)

6. Processes by which one learns to read, from initial exposure to language in early childhood through the first stages of readiness-to-read to the more advanced stages by which the reader comes increasingly to understand and respond to details of meaning and nuances of expression

Qualification	Degree of development			
	Not developed 1	2	3	*Highly developed* 4

7. An extensive body of literature in English (including literature for children and adolescents, popular literature, oral literature, non-Western literature, and literature by women and minority groups)

8. Varied ways of responding to, discussing, and understanding works of literature in all forms

9. Ways in which nonprint and nonverbal media differ from print and verbal media, and ways of discussing works in nonprint and nonverbal media

10. Ways in which nonprint and nonverbal media can supplement and extend the experiences of print and verbal media

11. Instructional resources (including educational technology) and varied sources of information (books, magazines, newspapers, tapes, recordings, films, pictures, and other nonverbal materials) that will help students understand—through intellect and imagination—the subjects and issues they are studying

12. The uses and abuses of language in our society, particularly the ways in which language is manipulated by various interests for varied purposes

13. Problems faced and procedures used by teachers and educational leaders in designing curricula in English for students of different ages, abilities, and linguistic backgrounds

14. The uses and abuses of testing procedures and other evaluative tech-

Qualification	Degree of development			
	Not developed 1	2	3	*Highly developed* 4

niques for describing students' progress in the handling and understanding of language

15. Major research studies on acquisition and growth of language in children and adults, on reading, on response to literature, on the processes of composing, and on the building of curricula for different kinds of students in different settings

ABILITIES   Teachers of English must be able:

16. To identify, assess, and interpret student progress in listening, reading, speaking, and writing
17. To take appropriate steps to help students improve their skill in responding to and using language
18. To work effectively with students of different ethnic groups, including those who do not speak English as their native language
19. To organize groups of learners for a variety of purposes appropriate to the English classroom; for example, discussion, creative problem solving, composing, and commenting on compositions
20. To engage both the intellect and the imagination of students in their listening, reading, speaking, and writing
21. To ask questions (at varying levels of abstraction) that elicit facts, opinions,

	Degree of development			
Qualification	*Not developed* 1	2	3	*Highly developed* 4

    and judgments appropriate to the subject and occasion

22. To respond specifically and constructively to student discourse

23. To communicate to students, parents, administrators, and officials the conclusions that can be legitimately inferred from results of tests purporting to measure progress in using and understanding language

24. To set professional goals for themselves and evaluate their progress toward them

25. To guide students in producing discourse that satisfies their own distinctive needs

26. To help students distinguish between effective and ineffective discourse

27. To help students experience the connection between the experience of reading and the experience of writing

28. To help students learn to observe and report accurately

29. To help students distinguish among the language options (such as registers and levels of usage) open to them in various social and cultural settings

30. To help students respond appropriately to the differing demands made on speech and writing by different contexts, audiences, and purposes

31. To help both beginning and maturing readers apply varied techniques to improve reading comprehension

32. To help students learn to listen effectively for information, for understanding, and for pleasure

	Degree of development			
Qualification	Not developed 1	2	3	Highly developed 4

33. To help students develop satisfying ways of responding to, and productive ways of talking about, works of literature
34. To help students identify and weigh facts, implications, inferences, and judgments in both spoken and written discourse
35. To help students develop the ability to respond appropriately to and create nonprint and nonverbal forms of communication, including both symbolic forms and other visual and aural forms (including film, videotape, photography, dramatic performance, song, and other art forms)

ATTITUDES   Teachers of English at all levels need to reveal in their classes and in their work with individual students:

36. A conviction that by helping students increase their power to use and respond to language both creatively and responsibly, they are helping those students to grow as human beings
37. A respect for the individual language and dialect of each student
38. A willingness to respond and help students respond to work in different media of communication
39. A desire to help students become familiar with the diverse cultures and their art

| | Degree of development | | | |
| | Not developed | | | Highly developed |
Qualification	1	2	3	4

40. A recognition that, whatever their rate of growth and progress, all children are worthy of a teacher's sympathetic attention

41. A sensitivity to the impact that events and developments in the world outside the school may have on themselves and their students

42. A flexibility in teaching strategies and a willingness to seek a match between students' needs and the teacher's objectives, methods, and materials

43. A commitment to continued professional growth

Source: From National Council of Teachers of English, *A Statement on the Preparation of Teachers of English and the Language Arts* (Urbana, IL: National Council of Teachers of English, 1976).

APPENDIX B: Glossary of Language Arts Terms

The following terms are presented throughout the text; the definitions here will help you recall key concepts and vocabulary in the language arts. The numeral refers to the chapter in which the term appears.[1]

Achievement grouping placing pupils in various groups on the basis of the results of standardized tests (14)

Acronym word formed from initial letters of words (10)

Activity (game) way to develop or reinforce important instructional objectives (1)

Affective dimensions appreciations, feelings, values, and attitudes (14)

Affective language language producing personal reactions (10)

Alignment feature of handwriting referring to evenness of letters along the baseline and along tops (9)

Analogical substitution utterances, such as *digged*, that a child uses before becoming familiar with exceptions to a generalization (in this case, past tense) (2)

Anecdote brief story of an interesting, usually biographical, incident (6)

Antiphonal form of choral presentation performed by two alternating groups (6)

Appositives words or phrases placed beside another word or phrase as an added explanation (3)

Articulation producing comprehensible speech (13)

Ask-tell relationship sentence components that differentiate "who" and "what" is asking and telling (2)

Aspect term which designates or describes verb action with reference to time; tense (3)

Audience reading reading aloud for others who are listening (11)

Auding listening with comprehension (11)

Auditory discrimination ability to differentiate among sounds (11)

Basal reader approach use of a coordinate, graded set of textbooks, teacher guides, and supplementary materials to provide reading instruction (11)

Baseline line serving as a base for manuscript or cursive handwriting (9)

Basic sentence pattern sentence arrangement, such as S-V-O (subject-verb-object), as "Bill hit the ball" (3)

Basic words (spelling) core of words deemed most important to study and learn (8)

Bilingual one who speaks two languages or two dialects of a language (13)

---

1. For a more complete and comprehensive listing of language arts terms, see *The Dictionary of Reading and Related Terms*, ed. Theodore L. Harris and Richard E. Hodges (Newark, DE: International Reading Association, 1981); though the terms listed here appear as defined in our text, we have borrowed several ideas from the *Dictionary of Reading*.

Body poem poem that lends itself to movements of the body (4)

Brainstorming way of getting ideas from a group on a particular problem through accepting all suggestions as an initial procedure (6)

Buzz group discussion group considering a specific problem within a set amount of time (6)

Characterization portrayal of real and lifelike characters by a writer (6)

Check stroke in cursive writing, the short, retraced motion before making the ending stroke on *b, o, v,* and *w;* the stroke that makes the point on *r* and *s* (9)

Choral reading group reading aloud (11)

Cinquain poetry pattern: first line, one word giving the title; second line, two words describing the title; third line, three words expressing an action; fourth line, four words expressing a feeling; fifth line, another word for the title (7)

Close reading and study analysis of literature in terms of genre, plot, setting, theme, characterization, style, format, and other criteria (12)

Cloze procedure method of estimating reading difficulty by omitting selected words (usually every fifth) in a reading passage and observing the number of correct words a reader can supply (8)

Competence individual, intuitive knowledge of grammar (3)

Connotative suggested meaning in addition to the explicit meaning; *compare* Denotative (10)

Context clues meanings provided for unknown word, either through semantic relationship or syntax (10)

Contract (language arts) arrangement between pupil and teacher that states what the pupil is to do and when the task will be completed (1)

Coordinator word used to join words or word groups of the same rank (3)

Corrected test technique procedure of teacher spelling aloud slowly, letter by letter, each word administered on a spelling pretest (8)

Couplet simple, two-line, rhymed pattern (7)

Creative listening listening which involves inference or "reading" beyond the lines (5)

Critical listening listening for evaluation (5)

Cursive writing form with the strokes of the letters joined together and the angles rounded; *compare* Manuscript (9)

Decoding changing communication signals into message (11)

Deep structure underlying set of semantic relations (meaning) expressed in a sentence (3)

Denotative explicit meaning; dictionary definition (10)

Departmentalization instructional systems in which there is one teacher for each major subject area (14)

Dialect regional or social modifications of a language; features may include pronunciation, vocabulary, and syntax (2)

Dictation exercise orally dictated sentences or paragraphs, under studied or unstudied conditions (8)

Directed Listening Activity step-by-step process of dealing with a listening lesson by the teacher (5)

Directed Reading Activity strategy in which detailed lesson plans are followed to teach the reading of stories in basal readers (11)

Directed Writing Activity step-by-step process of dealing with a writing lesson by the teacher (7)

Double-function word word describing a psychological characteristic of persons and a physical characteristic of objects (example: *sweet*) (2)

Echoic verse reader says a line which is then repeated by audience (6)

Encoding changing a message into symbols, as oral language into writing (11)

ESOL English for speakers of other languages (13)

Euphemism substitution of a less offensive word or phrase for an unpleasant term or expression (10)

Exceptional (child) one who deviates from the norm to such an extent that he or she cannot derive maximum benefit from regular classroom instruction; additional or different curriculum instruction or setting is required (13)

Expansion (sentence) elaboration by modification, subordination, and co-ordination (2)

Experience chart writing written record of an interesting experience; developed cooperatively by teacher and pupils; through the discussion, writing down, and reading of the story, the pupils are exposed to a reading experience based on their own language and interests (7)

Exploratory approach guided discovery pattern of instruction involving a problem situation, conclusion from pupils, and mastery of skills through multiple methods (1)

Eye-voice span distance by which the eye is ahead of the voice in oral reading (11)

Facilitated conversing teacher aided and organized conversation; *compare* Spontaneous conversing (4)

Figurative language nonliteral language (10)

Fingerplay "acting out" of a poem with the fingers and hands (4)

Flannel board board covered with flannel, often used with cutouts for storytelling (6)

Form class in structural grammar, categories for the major parts of speech (that is, Class I words, nouns; Class II, verbs; Class III, adjectives, and Class IV, adverbs) (3)

Format size, shape, and design of pages, illustrations, typography, paper, and binding of a publication (12)

Free silent reading opportunity to browse and read through books or magazines of one's own choice (12)

Free verse verse whose meter is irregular or whose rhythm is not metrical (7)

Function (structure) word noun markers or determiners, prepositions, auxiliary verbs, modals, intensifiers, and conjunctions (all words in a sentence not classified as major parts of speech) (3)

Functional shift shift in meaning or part of speech of a word, or both (example: *ground* as noun or verb) (10)

Genre distinctive type or category of literary composition (12)

Gifted possessing high intellectual development and a mental age that is above the norm, consequently, a high IQ (13)

Gillingham method synthetic phonics system reinforced by writing and speaking practice (13)

Grammar systematic description and analysis of the structure of a language—its sound structure, word structure, phrase and sentence structure (3)

Haiku verse of seventeen syllables over three lines; the first and third lines have five syllables, the second, seven; there is no metrical pattern and lines do not rhyme; refers to nature, particular event, and the present (7)

Hand dominance consistent preference in use of left or right hand (9)

Holophrase single-word utterance expressing a complex of ideas (examples: "milk" for "I want some milk to drink") (2)

Homograph words that have identical spellings but have different meanings (example: *pen*); in some cases the words, though spelled identically are pronounced differently (examples: *bow* and *read*) (10)

Idiolect language characteristics of particular individual (2)

Idiom group of words with meaning different from the literal meaning of the phrase (10)

IEP Individual Educational Plan (13)

Improvisation to compose, recite, make, or arrange on the spur of the moment (6)

Individualized reading reading instruction characterized by pupils' selection of reading materials, self-pacing, and pupil-teacher conferences (11)

Inflection change of form that words undergo to make case, gender, number, tense, person, mood, or voice (10)

Intensifier (qualifier) words like *very* or *considerable* that strengthen or limit (3)

Interclass forming groups from a number of classrooms (14)

Interest grouping placing pupils into various groups on the basis of common interests or friendships (14)

Interest inventory device used to assess pupil's preferences (14)

Intermediate years grades 4 through 6 or 8 (1)

Interpretive comprehension listening and/or reading in evaluative and critical manner (5)

Interrelated listening activity language tasks that involve listening with speaking, reading, and writing (5)

Intonation variations in the pitch of spoken language (2)

Intraclass grouping within a classroom (14)

IPI Individually Prescribed Instruction (14)

Irregular adjective or adverb adjective or adverb forming the comparative or superlative other than by adding -er or -est, or by using the words *more* or *most* (3)

Irregular verb verb which indicates past and perfect aspects (tenses) by other means than adding -ed (example: *go, went, gone*) (3)

Juncture pauses in speech (2)

Kernel sentence simple, declarative sentence (3)

Kinesthetic physical movements (8)

Language-experience approach approach in which reading and the other language arts are interrelated in the instructional program, and the experiences of children are used as the basis for reading materials (7)

Language functions various uses of language (2)

Lanterne verse pattern containing five lines with the following number of syllables: 1, 2, 3, 4, 1 (7)

Learning center designated area in classroom for materials, supplies, equipment, and suggested activities related to particular skills or knowledge (1)

Lesson plan systematic guide for teaching (1)

Letter form refers to size and proportion of letters in manuscript and cursive (9)

Letter form discrimination ability to differentiate shapes of letters (11)

Limerick light or humorous poem of five lines with a rhyme scheme of *aabba*; the first, second, and fifth lines have three beats, and the third and fourth lines have two beats (7)

Line-a-child form of choral reading or speaking in which each child reads one or two lines individually (6)

Line quality evenness of pressure (heavy or light) in handwriting (9)

Listening hearing with comprehension (5)

Listening comprehension understanding through the oral-aural avenue at the literal, interpretive, or critical level (5)

Listening learning center designated area in classroom for materials, equipment, and suggested activities related to listening skills or knowledge (5)

Literal listening understanding ideas that are directly stated (5)

Literary skills knowledge designed to enhance study and appreciation of works of literature (12)

Literature web plan for discussion and activities for exploring a book in depth (12)

Looped stroke stroke whereby a line crosses itself in a cursive letter, as in *e* and *l* (9)

Lower-loop letter in cursive writing, a letter whose loop extends below the baseline, as *g, p, y,* and *q* (9)

Mainstreaming practice of placing handicapped students in regular classrooms with nonhandicapped students (13)

Manuscript writing in which the letters are not joined and the pencil is lifted after most strokes; printing; *compare* Cursive (9)

Manuscript form neatness, appropriate spacing, even margins, and attractive arrangement of items on a page of written work (7)

Metaphor direct comparison without using *like* or *as* (10)

Modals auxiliary verbs like *can, may, will, shall, must, could, might, would, should* (3)

Morpheme minimal meaning unit of a language; it may be free (as *car*) or bound (as *pre* in prefix) (2)

Morphology study study of word formations (10)

Movement story story to accompany body movements (6)

Nongraded system in which grade labels are not applied and instruction is given according to individual needs (14)

Nonlooped stroke in a cursive letter, a line that does not cross itself, as in *i* (9)

Nonslant cursive writing in which the letters are joined together but written in a vertical manner (9)

Nonverbal language communication through means other than oral expression (2)

Open curriculum major elements include individualized teaching, pupil choices, integration of learning, democratic procedures, communication, and concern for the entire child (14)

Overcurve in cursive writing, upward clockwise oval motion, as in *n* (9)

Panel discussion similar to a round-table discussion but somewhat more formal and more audience oriented (6)

Pantomime dramatizing through movement; nonverbal (6)

Paraprofessional teacher's aide or other adult with some professional training who works in the classroom to assist the teacher (14)

Parse to give a grammatical description of a word or group of words (3)

Parts of speech grammatical categories of words (as noun, pronoun, verb, preposition) (3)

Patterned writing composition based on illustrative model or pattern (7)

Perceptual-motor interpreting through visual and tactile stimuli (9)

Performance signifies the use a person can make of language knowledge at a particular stage of development; *compare* Competence (3)

Personification giving the attributes of a person to an inanimate object or abstract idea (10)

Phoneme smallest linguistic unit in speech (2)

Phoneme-grapheme correspondence sound-to-letter relationship (8)

Phonologically irregular word word not spelled the way it sounds (example: *guess*) (8)

Phrase structure rule instruction for rewriting a phrase structure (3)

Picture file collection of pictures used for instructional purposes (1)

Pitch rise and fall of the voice (2)

Pivot-open class language construction in which same word serves as pivot (as *more*) followed by a wide selection of words (as *cake, milk, soup,* and so on) (2)

Plot overall plan of the action of the story (12)

Poetry file systematically organized collection of poems for instructional use (1)

Primary years grades K–3 (1)

Proofreading checking written material for sentence structure, punctuation, word choice, capitalization, spelling, and the like (7)

Propaganda techniques techniques of writing and speaking used to influence people's thinking and actions, including bandwagon techniques, card stacking, glittering generalities, name calling, plain folks talk, testimonial techniques, and transfer techniques (5)

Pupil pair or partners groups of pupils placed in pairs or partners (14)

Quatrain unit of four lines of verse, with *abab* rhyming pattern (7)

Reader's theater simply staged performance of literature (6)

Recreational reading voluntary reading for interest and appreciation (12)

Reduction speech without function words (example: "Baby sleep") (2)

Referent thing or idea a word stands for (10)

Refrain phrase or verse recurring regularly in a poem (6)

Response station (literature) area within the classroom where children may plan for various modes of responding to literature (12)

Retrace backtracking on same line for a short distance (9)

Reversals changing the position or orientation of letters, parts of a word, or words (9)

Revision checking a written paper for interest, development of the topic, paragraph organization, and the like (7)

Role playing form of drama, sometimes called sociodrama, in which problems in the area of interpersonal relations are acted out (6)

Round-table discussion sharing of ideas by a small group (three to eight people), including a moderator (6)

Secondary phonemes phonemes of stress, pitch, and juncture (3)

Self-evaluation inventory assessment list to be responded to by the individual (14)

Semantics study of meaning in language (2)

Sensory handicap hearing or visual impairment or both (13)

Sentence-combining combining two or more related sentences into one sentence (3)

Sentence expansion elaboration by modification, coordination, subordination (2)

Sentence function categorization of sentences according to function: declarative, interrogative, imperative, exclamatory (3)

Sentence structure categorization of sentences in terms of structure (simple, compound, complex) (3)

Sentence type categorization of sentences by function or structure (7)

Septolet seven-line verse with the following number of syllables in each line: 1, 2, 3, 4, 3, 2, 1 (7)

Setting location (geographic, historic, and social) of a story (12)

Simile comparison using *like* or *as* (10)

Size height of letters (9)

Skill file collection of graded-level material, grouped according to skill (1)

Slant degree of tilt of the downstrokes of letters (9)

Slow learner one whose intellectual development is in the lower range of normal group (IQ of 80 to 90); general level of reading is below grade and age level but commensurate with limited learning potential (13)

Social utility theory selection of content on the basis of its importance in various everyday activities (8)

Sound story story that lends itself to accompanying sounds (4)

Spacing distance between letters, between sentences, and between lines (9)

Special skills or needs grouping placing pupils into various groups on the basis of skills deficiencies (14)

Spelling consciousness pride in spelling achievement (8)

Spelling notebook individual word list maintained by pupil (8)

Spelling pattern generalization about a major spelling form (example: C-V-C (short vowel)—*cat*) (8)

Spelling rule generalization that applies to a large number of words and has few exceptions (8)

Spontaneous conversing casual conversation; *compare* Facilitated conversing (4)

Standard American English socially accepted language (6)

Story file collection of stories kept on index cards or in a notebook to be used for instructional purposes (1)

Storytelling versus reading aloud telling a story from memory as opposed to reading from a book (4)

Stress emphasis from force of breath in speech (2)

Structural grammar description of the grammar of speech (3)

Stuttering disorder of speech production in which one sound is blocked or repeated (13)

Style author's mode of expressing thoughts in words (12)

Subordination relationship between dependent and independent clauses in a sentence (7)

Subordinator word that introduces a dependent clause, such as *after, as if, because, before, if, since, so, that, than, unless, until, when, whether, while* (3)

Suprasegmentals phonological features of juncture, stress, intonation (11)

Surface structure form of a sentence as read or heard (3)

Sustained Silent Reading period of time during school when pupils read books of their own choosing (11 and 12)

Sustained Silent Writing period of time when pupils write on topics of their choosing (7)

Syntax the rules for combining words to form grammatical sentences (2)

Systematic approach identifying a specific skill, pretesting, providing direct instruction, posttesting, and reteaching if necessary (1)

Tanka five-line verse in which lines are arranged in 5, 7, 5, 7, 7 poetic pattern of thirty-one syllables (7)

Task card exercise or assignment written on card (7)

Team arrangement two or more classes combined with a staff of several teachers (14)

Telegraphic speech reduced speech that omits function words (example: "Baby sleep") (2)

Test-study-test plan procedure of first pretesting, then studying and testing again (8)

Text (story) grammar grammar designed to specify relations among episodes of a story (7)

Theme main idea that the writer wishes to convey to the reader (12)

Thesaurus dictionary of synonyms (10)

Trade book book written and marketed for the general public through bookstores and libraries; not a textbook (2)

Transformational-generative grammar grammar that provides principles for generating sentences (3)

Tree diagram model for representing grammatical relationships within a sentence; feature of transformational-generative grammar (3)

Triplet unit of three lines of verse (7)

Undercurve in cursive writing, an upward counterclockwise oval motion as in *u* (9)

Unison group of voices in choral reading and speaking (6)

Upper-loop letter a cursive letter with a loop that extends above the midline, as *l, b, f, h,* and *k* (9)

Usage common speech, particularly choice of words (6)

VAK program that incorporates visual, auditory, and kinesthetic experiences (13)

Verb, nontransitive either an intransitive verb or a verb with linking and complement; verb, intransitive needs nothing else to make a verb phrase, as *walk.* Verb, linking is followed by an adjective, as *feel* (3)

Visual literacy ability to interpret various symbols, pictures, and other items that send messages in our environment, including color, dance, music, and space (12)

Word file collection of words related to a topic and grouped together with instructional purposes (1)

Wordless (textless) book told by a series of pictures alone (6)

Writing center designated area in classroom for materials, equipment, and suggested activities related to written composition skills or knowledge (7)

Writing readiness level of preparedness for formal writing instruction (9)

INDEX

YOUR OPINION OF THIS BOOK

The authors and editors of *The Language Arts in Childhood Education* would like your opinion of the book after you have read it. Your comments will help us not only in improving the next edition of the text but also in developing other books. We would appreciate it if you would take a few minutes to respond to the following questions and return the form to: College Marketing, Houghton Mifflin Company, One Beacon Street, Boston, MA 02108.

1. We would like to know your reaction to the following features of the text:

	Excellent	Good	Adequate	Poor
a. General interest level of the book compared to other educational texts.	_____	_____	_____	_____
b. Writing style and readability.	_____	_____	_____	_____
c. Clarity of presentation of ideas.	_____	_____	_____	_____
d. Value of specific teaching ideas in each chapter.	_____	_____	_____	_____
e. Value of the Thought Questions.	_____	_____	_____	_____
f. Usefulness of the sections that indicate instructional concerns.	_____	_____	_____	_____
g. Helpfulness of the vocabulary lists at the beginning of chapters.	_____	_____	_____	_____
h. Your overall evaluation of the book.	_____	_____	_____	_____

2. Check one or more of the responses and complete the information requested. I read this text as part of

_____ an undergraduate course called _____

_____ a graduate course called _____

_____ a workshop called _____

_____ other. Explain: _____

3. Check one or more of the responses. I am currently

_____ a teacher of preschoolers.   _____ a teacher of primary chil-
                                                             dren.

_____ a teacher of intermediate-   _____ a supervisor.
         school children.

_____ an undergraduate in a four-   _____ an administrator.
         year college.

_____ an undergraduate in a two-   _____ a librarian.
         year college.

_____ other. Explain _____

_____

_____

4. Do you intend to keep the book as part of your professional library?
Yes   No   Maybe

Please tell us why. _____

_____

5. Please indicate the numbers of the chapters you found most helpful to you as

an educator or educator-to-be. _____

Why did you find these chapters most helpful? _____

_____

6. Please indicate the numbers of the chapters you found least helpful to you.

_____

Why did you find these chapters least helpful? _____

_____

_____

7. What did you like best about this book? _____

_____

_____

8. What did you like least about this book? _____

_____

_____